ALSO BY ELIA KAZAN

Beyond the Aegean

An American Odyssey

A Life

The Anatolian

Acts of Love

The Understudy

The Assassins

The Arrangement

America America

KAZAN ON DIRECTING

Elia Kazan

KAZAN
ON DIRECTING

ALFRED A. KNOPF *New York* 2009

Grateful acknowledgment is made to the following for
permission to reprint previously published material:

Michel Ciment, who edited his 1971 and 1972 interviews with Elia Kazan for the revelatory Kazan on Kazan, *published by Viking in 1974, and who selected the pieces in Kazan's collection* An American Odyssey, *published by Bloomsbury in 1988.*

Grove/Atlantic, Inc.: Excerpts from Memo from Darryl F. Zanuck *by Ruth Behlmer, copyright © 1993 by the Estate of Darryl F. Zanuck. Reprinted by permission of Grove/Atlantic, Inc.*

Grove/Atlantic, Inc., and The Wylie Agency (UK) Ltd.: Excerpts from Timebends: A Life *by Arthur Miller, copyright © 1987, 1995 by Arthur Miller. All rights reserved. Reprinted by permission of Grove/Atlantic, Inc. and The Wylie Agency (UK) Ltd.*

Houghton Mifflin Harcourt Publishing Company: Excerpt from "From a Letter to Elia" by Archibald MacLeish (Esquire, April 1959), copyright © 1959 by Archibald MacLeish. Reprinted by permission of Houghton Mifflin Harcourt Publishing Company.

New Directions Publishing Corp.: Excerpts from Selected Letters, Volume II: 1946–1957 *by Tennessee Williams, copyright © 2002 by The University of the South; and excerpts from* A Streetcar Named Desire *by Tennessee Williams, copyright © 1947 by The University of the South. Reprinted by permission of New Directions Publishing Corp.*

The New York Times: Excerpts from "In Quest of the Dream: Filmmaker Reflects on His Heritage and the Inspiration for New Drama" by Elia Kazan (The New York Times, December 15, 1963), copyright © 1963 by The New York Times. All rights reserved. Reprinted by permission of The New York Times and protected by the Copyright Laws of the United States. The printing, copyright, redistribution, or retransmission of the material without express written permission is prohibited.

Newmarket Press: Excerpt from Kazan: The Master Director Discusses His Films *by Jeff Young, copyright © 1999 by Jeff Young. Reprinted by permission of Newmarket Press.*

SLL/Sterling Lord Literistic, Inc.: Excerpts from "Gadg" by Frederic Morton (Esquire, February 1957), copyright © 1957 by Frederic Morton. Reprinted by permission of SLL/Sterling Lord Literistic, Inc.

Stella Adler Studio of Acting: Excerpts from Lies Like Truth *by Harold Clurman (Macmillan, 1958). Reprinted by permission of Stella Adler Studio of Acting.*

Library of Congress Cataloging-in-Publication Data
Kazan, Elia.
Kazan on directing / Elia Kazan. — 1st ed.
p. cm.
ISBN 978-0-307-26477-0
1. Motion pictures — Production and direction.
2. Theater — Production and direction. 3. Kazan, Elia. I. Title.
PN1995.9.P7K39 2009
791.4302'33 — dc22   2008048345

Manufactured in the United States of America
First Edition

Robert Cornfield selected the contents, with the exception of the section "The Pleasures of Directing," and provided commentary, notes, and chronology for this volume.

Contents

FILMS

THE PLEASURES OF DIRECTING

Foreword
John Lahr

Elia Kazan was the first auteur of the American theatre: the first director to insist on having control of the entire production, the first to be billed above the title, the first to succeed both on Broadway and in Hollywood. A good director is part visionary, part showman, part critic, part father: Kazan was all these things, and more. In 1959, after the first rehearsal of *Sweet Bird of Youth*, Tennessee Williams wrote to Kazan, "Some day you will know how much I value the great things you did with my work, how you lifted it above its measure by your great gift. I have been disloyal to nearly all lovers and friends but not to the one or two who brought my work to life. Believe me. I think I admire and value you more than anyone I have known in this profession." "Kazan was the best actor's director I've worked for," Marlon Brando, himself the greatest actor of his era, said. He added, "[He] got into a part with me and virtually acted it with me. . . . He was an arch manipulator of actors' feelings, and he was extraordinarily talented: perhaps we will never see his like again."

We will certainly never again see so unique a career. Kazan seemed to be part of most of the major theatrical turning points of his time. In 1932, as a stage manager and aspiring actor, he began his theatrical life with the Group Theatre; as a sidekick of both Harold Clurman and Clifford Odets, he was part of the ruling elite who reconstituted the Group Theatre during its most influential years, between 1937 and 1940. For a while, along with some other unemployed Group Theatre folk, he lived in the director Lee Strasberg's railroad flat—nicknamed the "Groupstroi"—where Odets, working in a closet kitchen so small that he had to rest his typewriter on his lap, wrote his groundbreaking play *Awake and Sing!* (1935). (Kazan stage-managed the play, which was Clurman's directing debut.) In *Waiting for Lefty*, Odets's polemical agitprop salvo, which defined the voice of protest among thirties' youth, it was Kazan, a middle-class cum laude graduate of Williams College and Yale Drama School, who shouted the play's rousing final lines: "Strike! Strike!! Strike!!!" The press dubbed him "the Proletariat Thunderbolt," and he took to wearing a working-class cloth cap with a rabbit's foot pinned under the brim. Luck was certainly with him.

In his eight years as a professional actor, Kazan appeared in Odets's biggest Group Theatre hit, *Golden Boy,* and his biggest flop, *Night Music,* the last production before the Group Theatre disbanded, in 1940. As a stage director, he made Broadway hits of the three most influential midcentury American plays: Thornton Wilder's *The Skin of Our Teeth,* Tennessee Williams's *A Streetcar Named Desire,* and Arthur Miller's *Death of a Salesman.* As a film director, he brought the Group Theatre's emphasis on psychological realism to the screen, playing midwife to many iconic performances, including James Dean's in *East of Eden,* Andy Griffith's in *A Face in the Crowd,* and Brando's in *A Streetcar Named Desire* and *On the Waterfront.* In 1948, Kazan conceived the idea of the Actors Studio—he was also part of the triumvirate who ran it—a Stanislavsky-inspired school whose techniques brought new, far-reaching depth and nuance to performance. For his films, Kazan drew from a pool of Actors Studio alumni: Brando, Lee Remick, Jo Van Fleet, Geraldine Page, Karl Malden, Julie Harris, Eli Wallach, Eva Marie Saint, Carroll Baker, and Robert De Niro. Later, in 1963, when the idea of a national repertory theatre was mooted at Lincoln Center, Kazan was chosen, along with the producer Robert Whitehead, to be its first artistic director. The theatre's debut production was Arthur Miller's *After the Fall* (1964), a play that explored the debacle of Miller's marriage to Marilyn Monroe. Kazan was not only the play's director, he was also the man who, in 1951, had introduced Monroe to Miller.

Kazan's rise to directorial preeminence coincided with a crucial psychic shift in American culture. Between 1945 and 1955, the per capita American income nearly tripled, the greatest increase in individual wealth in the history of Western civilization. Having endured a decade of Depression, then a world war, Americans, who had postponed their desires, were now in a hurry to fulfill them. The hegemony of America's political and economic power was also played out on an individual level. The kingdom of self, not society, became the nation's obsession. Public discourse shifted from the external to the internal: from social realism to abstract expressionism; from stage naturalism to Williams's personal lyricism, from Marxism to Freudianism. This mutation in the collective imagination suited Kazan's particular directorial skill set, which understood about the subconscious and the power of the sub-text. For Kazan, the greatest show on earth was the show of human emotions. In his actors and in the stories he told, Kazan's particular gift was to highlight and to release the interior drama of conflicting desires. Kazan's great contribution was to discover a theatrical vocabulary that turned psychology into behavior. "My work would be to turn the inner events of the psyche into a choreography of external life," he said. He brought a new dynamism to the winded, baggy American theatre.

What books and photographs don't convey about Kazan is the force of his presence. Even in old age, he had a thrust and a focus that were pal-pable. He was small, compact, virile; it was easy to understand his tal-ent for insinuation. He looked at you with avid eyes; he made a powerful connection. Although he spent his last years more or less housebound on the top floor of his Manhattan townhouse—he died in 2003, at the age of ninety-four—Kazan lived most of his life with "the devil's energy," as Miller called it.

Kazan, who walked on the balls of his feet, projected himself through the world with the outcast's desire for revenge. From 1926, when he entered the WASP enclave of Williams College, his own posi-tion in American society was clear to him. "I remember thinking, what the hell is wrong with me, anyway?" Kazan said, who referred to him-self then as "a nigger." "I knew what I was. An outsider. An Anatolian, not an American. . . . Every time I saw privilege from then on, I wanted to tear it down or to possess it." For his entire life, Kazan was a creature of envy; fame was the only defense against his sense of humil-iation. As an actor, he carried his chippie swagger onstage. " 'Fuck you all, big and small!' I used to mutter onstage during those years—to myself, of course, secretly," he wrote in his autobiography.

Kazan's particular appetite for vindictive triumph—his compulsive ambition and his habitual, unrepentant womanizing, which was another aspect of it—stems, in part, from one inescapable childhood wound: he was not handsome. "Don't you look in the mirror?" his father, George, a first-generation Anatolian Greek carpet salesman, said when Kazan announced that he was going to acting school. Kazan's gnarly mug, with its large jagged nose, telegraphed both his foreignness and his ferocity. It made Kazan credible in the edgy tough-guy roles, such as Kewpie (in *Paradise Lost*) and Fuseli (in *Golden Boy*), that he played for the Group Theatre; it also made his Hollywood film career a nonstarter. As a director, however, Kazan was always on everyone's mind. "I was where I wanted to be, the source of everything," he wrote.

As a child Kazan had been the "undisputed darling" of his mother, Athena, the "special child" she adopted as confidant and husbandly stand-in. "We entered a secret life together, which Father never breached," Kazan wrote of his relationship to Athena, who was betrothed at the age of eighteen in an arranged marriage. He added: "That is where the conspiracy began." Directing allowed Kazan to re-create the triumphant feeling of the original maternal conspiracy. His rehearsals had "the hushed air of conspiracy," according to Miller, "not only against the existing theatre but society, capitalism—in fact everybody who was not part of the production." Miller went on, "People were always coming up to whisper in his ear." In time, Kazan's plays and films put him at the center of the nation's consciousness.

Of Kazan's many gifts as a director, perhaps the most crucial was the ability to cast with intuitive brilliance by decoding his actors' core. "Their life experience is the director's material," Kazan said. "They can have all the training, all the techniques their teachers have taught them—private moments, improvisations, substitutions, associative memories—but if the precious material is not in them, the director cannot get it out. That is why it's so important for the director to have an intimate acquaintance with the people." In this area of investigation, Kazan was forensic. "Kazan's capacity to objectify actors' personalities was really an exercise in clinical psychology," Miller wrote in *Timebends.* For Miller's *All My Sons* (1947), for instance, Kazan cast Ed Begley as the father "not only because Begley was a good actor but because he was a reformed alcoholic and still carried the alcoholic's guilt." He insisted on casting Barbara Bel Geddes as Maggie in *Cat on a Hot Tin Roof,* over Williams's objections, because, Kazan said, "I'd known her when she was a plump young girl, and I had a theory . . . that when a girl is fat in her early and middle teens and slims down later, she is left with an uncertainty about her appeal to boys, and what often results is a strong sexual appetite, intensified by the continuing anxiety of believing herself undesirable." He added, "In every basic she resembled Maggie the Cat. I trusted my knowledge of her own nature." Kazan was not above exploiting the unpleasantness of an actor's personality—the surliness of James Dean, for instance—in service of his story. Raymond Massey, who played Dean's father in *East of Eden,* was scornful of the sullen young star. "This was an antagonism I didn't try to heal; I aggravated it," Kazan wrote, adding, "The screen was alive with precisely what I wanted: they detested each other."

In addition to his technical virtuosity, Kazan was able to pay proper attention to his collaborators. He worked by insinuation not command; he understood that to force an interpretation on an actor was an exercise in futility; the idea that was easily imposed could just as easily be forgotten. Stimulation and dissimulation were his twin talents. "He would send one actor to listen to a particular piece of jazz, another to read a certain novel, another to see a psychiatrist, and another he would simply kiss," Miller recalled. During rehearsals, according to Miller, Kazan "grinned a lot but said as little as possible." "Instinctively, when he had something important to tell an actor, he would huddle with him privately rather than instruct before the others, sensing that anything that really penetrates is always to some degree an embarrassment. . . . A mystery grew up around what he might be thinking, and this threw the actor back upon himself." Kazan's trick was to make his own ideas seem like the actors' discoveries. "He let the actors talk themselves into a performance," Miller said. "He allowed the actors to excite themselves with their own discoveries, which they would carry back to him like children offering some found object back to a parent."

And, like any good parent, when things were going in the right direction, Kazan knew how to stay out of the way. A case in point is the famous scene in *On the Waterfront,* in which the two brothers played by Brando and Rod Steiger—one longshoreman determined to do good by informing, the other determined to stop him—face off against each other in the backseat of a car. ("I coulda been a contenda, Charlie.") "Brando and Steiger knew who they were and what the scene was about—they knew all that better than I did—so I didn't say anything," Kazan wrote. "Sometimes it's important for a director to withdraw a little. If the characters are going right, to begin to talk about who they are and motivation and so forth may result in the actors' becoming concerned with satisfying you instead of playing the scene. You can spoil a scene by being too much of a genuine director—call it showing off."

The weird alchemy of Kazan's interpretive genius comes down to a highly developed understanding of structure and of psychology. (He was much analyzed.) Like a ghost in the fun machine, Kazan's distinctiveness is hard to pin down and even harder to see. For a new generation, he may not be a household name, but he is present in the stories and in the performances that, for fifty years, showed the nation its Gorgon's head. He is there in Willy Loman's exhaustion, in Stanley Kowal-ski's recklessness, in Big Daddy's ruthlessness, in Baby Doll Meighan's hungering heart, in Terry Malloy's divided loyalties. In the panorama of twentieth-century popular culture, Kazan's contribution must be judged the most far-ranging and the most influential of all the modern theatricals; he alone among his peers could lay claim to Walt Whit-man's boast in *Leaves of Grass*: "I am the man, I suffer'd, I was there."

Preface
Martin Scorsese

Elia Kazan, a great American artist, born one hundred years ago this year.

He is one of the most important figures in the history of movies. It's that simple. His documentary eye, his ability to home in on the subtlest behaviors and interactions, his sense of surprise and beauty within the frame, his remarkable ear for sound, his astonishing sensitivity to atmosphere . . . these were just a few of his gifts as a filmmaker.

For me, Kazan is beyond "important," "central," or "influential." I grew up watching his pictures, and they were instrumental in forming my ideas of cinema, what it was and what it could be. They were equally instrumental in helping me to understand myself, I think. And as I watched and rewatched them over the years, my experience of them evolved. It still does—every viewing of *On the Waterfront* or *East of Eden* or *Wild River* or *America America* yields something new.

This volume of notes and memories offers us an invaluable look at Kazan's working methods and personal approach to his craft—his thorough analyses of character and plot, his relentless judgments of his own finished work, his meticulous attention to every aspect of filmmaking. And it gives the reader a wonderful sense of his development as an artist, the way his understanding of theatre and his experience as an actor affecting his fimmaking, his growing confidence as a director, his growing dissatisfaction with the studio system followed by his "arrival" as an independent filmmaker with *America America*.

And, of course, there is the man himself. I got to know Kazan in the last twenty years or so of his life, and I recognize him within these pages, as I do in *A Life*, his extraordinary autobiography. The sense of humor, the brutal honesty (about himself most of all), the complete lack of sentimentality, and most of all the immersion in the work itself . . . they're all vividly present.

For students of Kazan, this book is invaluable. But it's just as invaluable to anyone interested in the creation of movies. Because, after all, these are selections from the notebooks of a master. A master named Elia Kazan.

Introduction
Robert Cornfield

In soft-covered composition notebooks, master stage and film director Elia Kazan studiously penned and penciled preliminary notes for his productions. He capitalized sentences, triple-underlined key words, sketched the sets, and sought resemblances in the characters to people he knew. But his most searching quest was to uncover the work's particular relevance to his own life.

What impelled him to do his best work was his need to find in the play clues to his existence; working on a script engaged him in the most trenchant matters of life and death. He ferreted out in Arthur Miller's or Tennessee Williams's or John Steinbeck's works—whether it be a play about Blanche DuBois or Willy Loman, or a film telling the story of Cal Trask or Emiliano Zapata—the drama of self-revelation, taking via the script a perilous and demanding trek in discovery and intimate revelation. To an important extent, this accounts for the power of his work; in Kazan's productions there are no irrelevant moments, all is dynamic, all surges with vitality. Most times, there was a match of the director's and author's conceptions; yet sometimes Kazan, well, went his own way. Playwrights were (mostly) grateful for Kazan's clarifications—"So this is what I was meaning!"—for the best American playwrights of the twentieth century trusted Kazan to give the performance of their plays vivid reality, to expose their poetry, to better their work.

In the late 1940s, Kazan directed virtually back to back the first major American dramas (*A Streetcar Named Desire* and *Death of a Salesman*) since the works of Eugene O'Neill. And he was the American theatre's most sought-after director of actors. As Stanley Kowalski in Kazan's production of *Streetcar*, Marlon Brando signaled the triumph of the long-prepared-for revolution in American acting. And two years later Lee J. Cobb's performance of Willy Loman in *Death of a Salesman* was heralded as a pinnacle of American theatre. Brando and

Cobb set the terms for all subsequent interpretations of these roles, just as Elia Kazan's mark is on all subsequent stagings of these plays. Without having contributed a word (though some suspect that he contributed quite a few), Kazan is in the weave of Tennessee Williams's and Arthur Miller's best work.

As director and teacher, Kazan was the most renowned American exponent of the American adaptation of "The Method" (though Lee Strasberg garnered the publicity), an acting discipline based on the innovative ideas of the early-twentieth-century Russian director Konstantin Stanislavsky, whose early goal was naturalistic acting through a psychological identification of role and performer. Stanislavsky's overarching belief was in Theatre as an art equal to painting or literature or music, a Total Theatre that would encompass all arts (an aspiration derived from Richard Wagner's concept of music-drama); by example he encouraged other theatre theorists, including Gordon Craig, Yevgeny Vakhtangov, and Vsevolod Meyerhold. It was theatre conceived of as a joining of play, performers, designer, music, environment—and the chief manipulator, the master choreographer, the dictating shaper of all the elements was The Director. It was a role, in all its diverse responsibilities, that Kazan relished.

After graduating from Williams College in 1930, Elia Kazan attended Yale's School of Drama for two years, working his way through productions with hammer and nail. His backstage adeptness at set construction and lighting, at all aspects of stagecraft, caused him to be dubbed "Gadg," for someone handy with gadgets. But he found the significance and purpose of drama in his apprentice years with the Group Theatre, a collective organized in 1931 by Harold Clurman, Lee Strasberg, and Cheryl Crawford; in the mid-1920s Clurman and Strasberg had studied with Maria Ouspenskaya and Richard Boleslavsky, former members of Stanislavsky's Moscow Art Theatre, at the American Laboratory Theatre. The Group based its teachings on Stanislavsky's principles, but its aspirations were to reform acting by the application of rigorous discipline and methodology; to create a theatre of excellence that was relevant and of consequence to an American audience; and to produce the work of American playwrights only. It was a nationalistic enterprise, shaped by and steeped in the social tensions of the 1920s and 1930s. With only one exception, for the whole of his career Kazan devoted himself in theatre and film to the work of contemporary American writers (including himself) and themes.

Kazan's staging techniques—how he elicited a performance, his conception of drama—were developed under Clurman and Strasberg's tutelage. In achievement and celebrity and power, he would outstrip his teachers, having a better intuitive grasp of movement, a stronger ability to motivate actors, and a rigor in working to a play's strength. The acerbic Clurman was never ungrudgingly pleased with his student's productions (lecturing and hectoring Kazan in his theatrical reviews), and the bitter Strasberg later regarded him as an upstart, ingrate, and traitor; but throughout Kazan's career they remained his artistic consciences. Like fraternal rivals, they were competitive, jealous, and contemptuous of each other, yet were bound by enduring affection and the deepest reverence for their common artistic aspirations. In the 1940s Kazan formed a producing partnership with Clurman that lasted only three years, but Clurman's critical opinion was the one Kazan most valued throughout his life. In the early 1950s Kazan delegated the training arm of the Actors Studio to Lee Strasberg, but ten years later denied him participation in the training and artistic program in the first incarnation of the Repertory Theatre of Lincoln Center.

Though allied with the radical theatre movement, the Group's prime purpose was theatrical, not social, revolution. Some of the Group's members, including Kazan, joined the Communist Party, but when the party demanded a stronger voice in the Group's policies, Kazan was reprimanded for noncooperation, and in 1936 he quit. Kazan's two-year membership would have a contentious and transforming effect on his personal and professional life when in 1952 he volunteered the names of former fellow party members to the House Un-American Activities Committee. Paradoxically, though all of his work was motivated by his interest in social issues and though he thought of himself as a liberal, Kazan was at heart apolitical, an artistic loner determined to actualize his artistic vision. In his autobiography he ruefully reconsidered his HUAC testimony: "How is the world better for what I did? It had just been a game of power and influence, and I'd been taken in and twisted from my true self. I'd fallen for something I shouldn't have, no matter how hard the pressure and no matter how sound my reasons. The simple fact was that I wasn't political—not then, not now."

His early Broadway successes, Thornton Wilder's *The Skin of Our Teeth* and a Helen Hayes vehicle, *Harriet,* brought him Hollywood offers, and in 1944 he accepted the proposal of producer Louis Lighton to direct for Twentieth Century–Fox the film version of Betty Smith's best-seller *A Tree Grows in Brooklyn.* But Kazan wasn't a total novice to moviemaking. In the 1930s he had contributed to documentaries, usually in the cause of unionization; served as an assistant to Hollywood director Lewis Milestone; and in 1940–41 acted in two Warner Bros. movies, as a gangster in *City for Conquest* and a jazz musician in *Blues in the Night*, both directed by Anatole Litvak.

From then on his Broadway and Hollywood successes were concurrent. In the mid- to late 1940s he directed *A Tree Grows in Brooklyn* (movie), *All My Sons* (stage), *Boomerang!* (movie), *A Streetcar Named Desire* (stage), *Gentleman's Agreement* (movie), and *Death of a Salesman* (stage). And in a spare moment he established the premier workshop for theatre professionals, the Actors Studio. In the 1950s and 1960s he gave us, among other works, *Cat on a Hot Tin Roof* (stage), the classic film of *A Streetcar Named Desire*, *Viva Zapata!* (film), *Tea and Sympathy* (stage), *On the Waterfront* (film), *The Dark at the Top of the Stairs* (stage), *East of Eden* (film), the films *Baby Doll*, *A Face in the Crowd*, *Wild River*, and *Splendor in the Grass;* onstage, *Sweet Bird of Youth;* and then his film masterpiece, *America America*. There is no directorial achievement in America to equal his.

By the 1940s, the best young American actors had been trained in the method-derived discipline by such teachers as Harold Clurman, Phoebe Brand, Joe Bromberg, Morris Carnovsky, Mary Morris, Lee Strasberg, Robert Lewis, Stella Adler, and Sanford Meisner, all former members of the Group Theatre. The Group had been dissolved in 1941 after years of financial brinkmanship and internal division; its true successor was the Actors Studio, formed by Kazan and producer Cheryl Crawford in 1948, whose approach to character analysis was primarily Stanislavskyan. For his stage and film work, Kazan employed a virtual repertory company of ex–Group Theatre and Studio actors, including Eli Wallach, Karl Malden, Julie Harris, Jo Van Fleet, Marlon Brando, James Dean, Lee J. Cobb, Eva Marie Saint, Geraldine Page, Paul Newman, and Robert De Niro. He cast "to type"—requiring that the role be within the emotional and imaginative range of the performer: "You have to start from the actor, and you have to find out where the part is alive for him. Somewhere within them the part must exist. You've got to find out before you cast them that the element that you need in the performance is there." He thrashed his actors and writers with the same rigor of self-excoriation to which he subjected himself. His program for Studio members, which he designed originally with Robert Lewis, was to expand on the Stanislavsky method, "developing the senses, developing imagination, developing spontaneity, developing the force of the actor and, above all, arousing his emotional resources."

The play and the actors were the starting points, but Kazan was after Total Theatre—the maximal effect from all elements, a sense of expansive grandeur. A form more congenial to that ambition was the movies, and from the early 1930s he aspired to be a filmmaker. The first movies that sparked his ambition were the agitprop and quasi-poetic Soviet docudramas of the 1920s and 1930s, films like Eisenstein's *Battleship Potemkin,* a reenactment of the brutal suppression of a 1905 navy revolt in Odessa, and Dovzhenko's *Arsenal* and *Aerograd,* the latter set on the Far Eastern borders of the Soviet Union. These were epic-scaled movies, typically propagandistic, yet using a mix of amateur and professional actors for both trenchantly real and archetypical performances, filmed on location, stressing the impact of city and natural landscape. He later remembered an episode in *Aerograd* that was transformative: "There's a conversation in the woods between two old men. They are many hundreds of yards apart. They have to yell at each other. I never forgot that. It's one of the great moments in film for me." Man's fate shaped by his environment is the grand subject of Kazan's movies: the mountains and villages of Mexico in *Viva Zapata!;* the waterfront in *On the Waterfront;* the South in *Baby Doll* and *Wild River;* the terrain of Turkey in *America America* (filmed in both Turkey and Greece); Salinas, California, in *East of Eden.*

His working methods remained the same throughout his career. Once he discovered what a play meant for himself, once he found the clue to self-identification with the theme and the characters, or determined their resemblance to people he knew, he decided upon the style of presentation, how to cast and to direct, and what instructions he would give the set designer and costumer. He studied the stage and filmscript to find the single encompassing motive that powers the work, its core sentiment, what he terms its "spine." Next, he sought the "spine" of the character. He imagines a backstory to the characters that would provide a base for improvisations for the actors before they turned to the actual text. In *Streetcar* Blanche DuBois has to find a safe haven—that is the spine of her character. She glances at Stanley with either terror or lust—her "beat," the telling response. Stanley Kowalski's anal-compulsive habits are indicated by his chewing on a cigar, his constant eating or drinking. All these traits are general guides for the actors, meant to stir their imagination, and they are points of reference for the mise-en-scène, the positioning, movement, and arrangement of the performers. Kazan's mastery of placement and choreographic movement he regarded as instinctive, which is why he writes about it so infrequently. Arthur Miller said that Kazan "does not direct," he creates "a center point and then goes to each actor and creates the desire to move toward it." "All my actors come on strong, they're alive, they're all dynamic—no matter how quiet," Kazan said.

Kazan's first notes are not his ultimate interpretations, but they exhibit his early and most consequential struggle with the material. At times, these notes are unsparing self-examinations, evidencing the same ruthless and exculpatory candor that dismayed many when his autobiography was published. His understandings here underpin not only the staging but the demands he would place on the actors—pushing them in private sessions to similar recognitions. During the rehearsals he constantly reread his initial formulations, adding to, underlining, and rewording his insights.

A compulsive teacher and didact, he worked sporadically throughout his life on a book on acting and directing, sometimes in the form of lectures (given at the New School for Social Research and for fellow Group members), and he developed with Strasberg and Joe Bromberg an acting course for the New School. He attempted a textbook in 1940 and 1945 (probably in collaboration with Clurman), and in 1947 he prepared a syllabus for the Actors Studio. In the late 1980s he began serious work on what was to be his final book, mostly, in its general section, on film directing. He made a selection of his writings over the course of his career, and the first chapters of this book, dealing with his Group Theatre years and his early commercial productions, consist of writings that are substantially his own choice.

The remainder is drawn from his notebooks, journals, and scraps of manuscript; from interviews; from his autobiography, *A Life;* from letters and criticism; and from reminiscences of the actors and playwrights he worked with. His notebooks for his film work are slighter than those for his theatre work, because conception and revisions were worked into preliminary treatments and script revisions. Because this book is drawn from material composed over six decades, there are immense contradictions and reconsiderations, providing only proof of Kazan's compulsive vitality.

The format of this book is modeled on Harold Clurman's *On Directing,* a work that Kazan greatly admired. The plays and films represented have been chosen for continuing interest and to exemplify Kazan's approaches and involvements.

"The Pleasures of Directing" includes material from his unfinished book on directing, which had been commissioned by Katherine Hourigan, who was his last editor at Knopf. Kazan's manuscript is informal, conversational, provocative, and combative—a wise old pro telling the kid what to watch out for. But he instructs best by his manner, passion, dedication, and conviction that art is essential to existence. For Kazan, bringing life to a play or film was as risky, painful, and rewarding as giving birth. Some of his productions disappoint him, some are favorites, but all are embraced.

THE DIRECTOR'S NOTES

PLAYS

For the Group Theatre

: With an impassioned determination to create an American theatre that would emulate the commitment and artistic conscience of Stanislavsky's Moscow Art Theatre and that would foster new drama responsive to American life, Cheryl Crawford, a manager at Broadway's most prestigious producing organization, the Theatre Guild, and two brazen and self-assured intellects, Harold Clurman and Lee Strasberg, formed a collective of actors called the Group Theatre in 1931. For a decade the Group Theatre members argued and fought among themselves, broke into factions that hated and admired, despised and adored each other, but their approach was at base steadily coherent enough to revolutionize American theatre and consequently American film. The most notable acting teachers of the 1940s had been associated with the Group Theatre: Sanford Meisner, Stella Adler, Robert Lewis, and Lee Strasberg. And almost all significant new American drama of the 1940s through the 1950s was directed either by Harold Clurman or Elia Kazan; the succeeding generation of preeminent directors—Sidney Lumet, Martin Ritt, Arthur Penn, Daniel Mann, Joseph Anthony—were trained under the auspices of the Group Theatre or its successor, the Actors Studio.

In 1932, after two years at Yale Drama School, Elia Kazan came to New York and was taken on, with some hesitation, as an apprentice for the Group's second summer boot camp. But he was extraordinarily ambitious, adept, and enthusiastic, so quick to understand and often even challenge the Group's goals, that within three years he was lecturing at the New School and at the New York Drama League on drama and acting and theory. After Cheryl Crawford and Lee Strasberg resigned in 1935, Harold Clurman re-formed the Group with a governing advisory committee, chief among whose members was Kazan.

Kazan acted in the Group's most notable productions, making a personal splash in Clifford Odets's *Waiting for Lefty* and *Golden Boy*. In 1938 he made his Broadway directorial debut with the Group Theatre's production

Kazan, with his arms raised, as Agate Keller in *Waiting for Lefty*

of Robert Ardrey's *Casey Jones,* and the next year he prepared two work-shop performances of Irwin Shaw's *Quiet City.*

What follows are two excerpts from his lectures, which Kazan intended to include in a textbook on acting that he worked on intermittently from the late 1930s through the 1940s, a confidential memo to Clurman assessing the actors, and an assessment of his problems directing Shaw's *Quiet City.*

Style and Spine (1938)

Directing is fundamentally the central effective agency in a produc-tion. The direction is the core of the production, and all decisions, choices, and discriminations come from what we call "the direction."

The first problem of the director then is to determine what his direction is to be. And as this direction is to give organic unity to the whole production, his first job is to find a "center" or "core" for the work and for the production. The more integrated this center is, the more integrated will be the production. Once it is established, the base decision has been made. All else devolves from this.

The director has to restate succinctly the play, its meaning and form, in his own terms; he has to reconceive it as if he had created it. What does it mean to him? What does it arouse in him? How does the manuscript affect his soul? In short, what is his relationship as an artist to this document, this manuscript?

It is not necessary that the director's reaction match the author's intention. Different periods have different values and meanings. And a director might want to produce a work for reasons other than the writer's. Examples abound; the clearest is Shakespearean productions from Shakespeare's time to ours.

Therefore, the director's first question in approaching a script is not what the author intended, but what is his own response as an independent artist. A script might give a director simply nothing more than a feeling, an impression, as *Casey Jones* meant to me primarily "the loneliness of American life." Here is where the director's work starts: he examines all the resources of his personality, reading and rereading the script to find out just what in the subject has significance for him.

As his study of the script intensifies, the director explores the meaning of the theme for the author. This becomes more active, as he supervises the author's rewrite, guiding the author to best express his intent. But the focus of the director as he prepares his direction (as opposed to working on the script) must be his own feeling and thoughts on the theme, subject, the story and characters.

The study of the script should result in a simple formulation that sums up the play in one phrase, a phrase that will be a guide for everything the director does. He begins with the simple words: "For me, this play is about . . ." The phrase should delineate the essence of the action that transpires on stage; it should reflect what is happening, what the characters are doing. It must imply effort, progression, transition, MOVEMENT. The concept must suggest not only the events, but the play's mood and color, its emotional landscape and form. It is to serve as the key to the production, what will give it unity.

For example, the spine of Harold Clurman's production of Clifford Odets's *Awake and Sing!* gives in its succinct formula, "Search for hap-

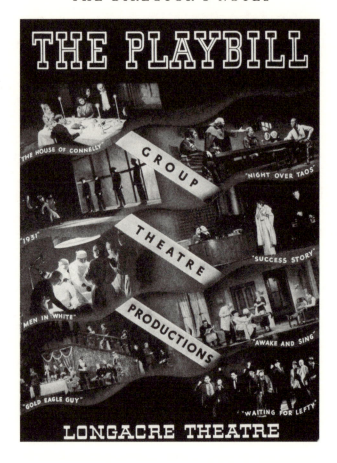

piness among petty objects," the opposing elements of the play, the spiritual striving for happiness amidst the banalities of daily existence. For Clurman, the play gave the impression of a confused world. He asked Boris Aronson to create a set that included both the mundane and the realm of the soul. Aronson divided the stage into two rooms between which the characters moved constantly; they were juxtaposed spaces: one in shades of red and one in shades of green, so that there was at times a blend and at others, a contrast. The actors too were directed to play in alternating moods, sometimes comic, and sometimes with the anguish of spiritual striving; in fact, its playing was not naturalistic. Clurman depended heavily on offstage music both for transitions and for emotional highlighting. You could almost understand the action without the dialogue, as if it were a pantomime. The truest and most individually poignant moments of the play were where laughter and tears alternated in quick succession, deriving from the same incident.

Harold Clurman

Clurman's spine for Odets's *Golden Boy:* "Fight for achievement." Mordecai Gorelik's inspiration for his set was the fight ring. And he lit the show with sometimes blinding white light, giving sharp edges to the outlines of actors and playing space. The acting too was stripped to the essential; the emphasis was not on depth characterization but on basic character. The villain was a certain kind of villain, but always a villain who functioned as a villain. The play was not deep; it did its work—just as the fighters do in a ring: they get down to the essential reason for being in the ring.

The "achievement" part in the spine has to do with the ego. The play deals with hurt egos and how the hurt has to be healed. There is no implied value judgment in the word "achievement," although there is in Odets's play. The production did not stop to moralize. It simply told its story, which was like an allegory, and any judgment came from thinking about the whole story.

Style in the Theatre (1938)

"Style" is considered an arty term in the theatre, yet when an agent advises a playwright that the only director for his play is George Abbott (for farce or a musical) or Jed Harris (for drama), they are talking about "style," the style of production. Even safe directors have a style. Any sensible agent would be only too happy to entrust his client's play to Guthrie McClintic, for McClintic gives a play "tone." He's definitely the modern expression of the old school who believes that show business was show business and that the theatre had to sell glamorous, mysterious, and legendary beautiful personalities, and surround them with sterling actors, and beautiful decor—featuring flowers and the latest chapeaux. Thus Mr. McClintic takes an energetic, wholesome, intelligent woman with considerable beauty but with about as much mystery as a bar of soup and creates out of her a theatrical personality.*

There are some of the younger geniuses—everybody who has done one successful production on Broadway is a genius—who are aware of the rewards that a conscious attitude brings. And chief among them is Orson Welles. Mr. Welles admits that his chief preoccupation is STYLE in his productions. He stars in an "Orson Welles Production." George Buckner or William Shakespeare can't say what they feel about what Welles has done to their plays, but if you ask any of the actors who appeared in these works they tell you that all Welles is interested in is production.[†] Mr. Welles hasn't been able to hold a single important actor; witness, Hiram Sherman, Martin Gabel, Burgess Meredith, George Coulouris, all of them quit Mr. Welles in disgust because they refused to be swamped in production or used as working parts in an affair of style, where nothing was suggested except Mr. Welles's style.

Mr. Welles is only interested in HOW he does a production. He is a little vague as to what Caesar meant [in Welles's fascist-themed production of Shakespeare's *Julius Caesar*], or whether Danton was "revolutionary" or "counter revolutionary," but he knew what he wanted from the lights in each case. He has never consistently told an actor what he wanted from a performance in a way to make an actor know himself to be an artist, conscious and working toward a real performance, but he has without fail been able to tell an actor where to stand, where to run into the darkness, when to emerge from nowhere. In short, Mr. Welles has for two seasons done STUNTS with old plays. He has focused attention on the production, upon production as an art,

---

* Kazan is referring to McClintic's wife, Katharine Cornell, an eminent and admired Broadway actress from the 1920s through the 1950s.
† Welles produced Georg Büchner's classic drama *Danton's Death* for his Mercury Theatre company. Later Welles adapted Shakespeare's history cycles into a one-evening event called *Five Kings* that was among the most celebrated theatrical disasters of the 1930s. The Group Theatre regarded Welles's Mercury Theatre and the government-sponsored Federal Theatre Project as rival institutions.

and taken it off the play and the star—where it has been for the entire history of the American Theatre. But Mr. Welles, being merely interested in showing off, in stunting, in shocking, surprising, and upsetting a staid Broadway theatre, has nothing more to say than the theatre he is revolting against. In Mr. Welles's productions there is a certain vitality and energy, but no total meaning, no sense of the thick fabric of life, of its real BODY. Welles reduced theatre to the level of theatricalism, and this is anemic fare.

Quiet City (1939)
by Irwin Shaw

EDITOR: Two workshop performances were given of Irwin Shaw's play *Quiet City* on consecutive Sunday nights, April 16 and April 23, 1939, at the Belasco Theatre in front of the sets for the Group Theatre's production of Shaw's *The Gentle People*. Mordecai Gorelik provided a work setting, and Aaron Copland wrote a background score. It is a memory play in which a department store mogul examines the betrayals of his life, of his religion, class, and family. Wendy Smith claims in her history of the Group Theatre, *Real Life Drama*, that Kazan "was inwardly uncertain and worried about getting his vision across to the company. . . . To make matters more difficult, Kazan had a discipline problem with Morris Carnovsky, who was chronically late for rehearsals. Carnovsky always apologized, but Kazan didn't believe he meant it; he interpreted the tardiness as a challenge to his authority." Because of the lack of audience enthusiasm Clurman halted further work on the production. Cast members Luther Adler, Morris Carnovsky, and Frances Farmer appeared later that year in Robert Ardrey's *Thunder Rock*, again under Kazan's direction.

A Postmortem

You didn't actually and really and LITERALLY accomplish what you set out to do. Always orientate yourself to your original intention.

Improvisation sometimes became an end in itself. You did not describe to the actors fully and completely the characters they were playing; not only in respect to essence and spine, but especially in respect to certain "obvious" or eternal elements: IMAGE, BEHAVIOR, SIMPLE TYPE. It is most important to do this because the tendency will otherwise be to get trapped in worthless "subtleties" that are not related to the solid base of fundamentals of each character.

Above all, describe the image you have to the actor with particulars, especially with particulars of typical behavior, the kind of things he is habitually doing. A quietly discussed series of self questions on this will clarify and particularize a lot of things for the actor. All art is particular. The particular is evocative in a way nothing else can be. The images that your notion of the character bring to mind are also very evocative. You, the director, must search with the actor for that one image, or that one particularization, that makes the character clear. That will start fruitful processes of unconscious as well as conscious thought. The secret to finding these images is in your knowledge of the personality of the actor. His AFFECTIVE MEMORY! The one thing that stirs the actor and makes him DO!

A spine is meaningless except where and when it operates for the actor. In a certain sense, the actor must always find his own spine. It is most certainly true that he must find his equivalent of the spine that the director has given him.

Once the actor really has found the spine, it may be profitable for him to search for his visualization of the character, THROUGH THE SPINE. What does a physicalization of the verb of the spine bring to his mind? What, rather, does it make him DO in the way of external movement? What typical and habitual BEHAVIOR does the spine call for or suggest? Is there an image for this behavior? The visualization must be related to the spine, and is best when it is a physicalization of the spine.

The actor must never lose the sense of himself in the part. He himself, the actor, must do the doing. Later, if there is a fusion of the actor and the part that results in a new character, well and good.

Certain actors never found (and usually do not find) that strain in their true personality which is the part and which is the equal to the spine of the character. One way for the actor to arrive at an understanding of HIMSELF is through examining the most intense moment of the part.

Are actors creative artists? "Yes, when they're creative." Positively not at other times. As a director, I know that the biggest job is casting them correctly. Then you give them a hint or two and wait. Like a cook with a cake, you mustn't open the oven door until the cake is all done—if you do, the cake is spoiled. There are some valuable members of the Group who are not creative artists. The best they can do is give you exactly what is written in a part, and no more. Frances Farmer is a beginner. (A big fault of mine was trying to make Frances like and respect me.) That is essential; after that you can say she is very lazy; also, being a very good girl, she strives to overcome her spiritual inertia by will power. But will power doesn't touch one certain spot. She needs to be shaped a little. There's something in her soul that is hibernating, and maybe spring will never come from her.

Morris [Carnovsky] is the finest craftsman so far. He is also a very fine man, though a creep and really not my type. He is very weak, has a terrific inferiority complex and the deanish righteousness we know. He is the most cliquish person in the Group and his clique consists of charter members of Carnovsky lovers. He should never direct, never coach. He could lead a Carnovsky studio of five or six young people who love him. But the trouble with him is that his loves don't last long. The best actor in the Group is Luther Adler. An intuitive actor who either strikes or misses, has no technique worthy of the name. And with him the job of the director is to be patient and wait till the cake is done before peeking in the oven. You give him the part and then tolerate more shit than ever one man should take from another, and as your reward, he may give you a great performance and make your show. His contribution is ninety-five percent through natural equipment. At the same time he has no eyes to see, is incredibly naïve, is completely insensitive to the effect of his actions on other people. Add to this his conceit, his passion for mothering and babying and coddling, his profound laziness. Luther is not an artist—he is a mechanism—he is there to be used. He and Morris are two sides of one coin.

My complaint is not that the Group actors have egos. We all have overgrown egos. The trouble is that too many of theirs operate on a low level. A creative actor must be a creative artist. He must have a sense of destiny, a sense of his character, a sense of his materials, a sense of his development and progress, a sense of self-criticism, a terrible inner drive, and therefore a sense of accomplishment and with it a sense of defeat.

We should gather around us all the young actors we can, choosing those we believe can be Group members. We must train them from the beginning. We must train their voices, train their bodies, we must train them so they can become our kind of actors. Harold is fundamentally a director, not at all a teacher. He has no patience to train people day by day as craftsmen. Neither has Stella [Adler]. Bobby [Lewis] and I are the best bets, and we should each be given charge of a group.

The Group. Art Smith is on the floor, *center.* Cheryl Crawford is seated second from left, and Phoebe Brand fourth from left. *Standing, from left:* Stella Adler, Morris Carnovsky, Tony Kraber in back of Luther Adler, Ruth Nelson. Kazan is at right with his arms on Sanford Meisner *(left)* and Clifford Odets.

Art is created through commitment—every production should be a matter of life and death. The experience out of which art is created—and acting is an art—must be an intense one, and the result of an intense involvement in something may be elation or depression, victory or defeat. For myself, I know no other way.

Hot Nocturne (1940)
by Edwin Gilbert

EDITOR: Kazan worked on developing *Hot Nocturne*, a melodrama about a jazz group that becomes involved, professionally and romantically, with a bunch of criminals, for a Broadway production, but it ended up as a 1941 film, *Blues in the Night,* directed by Anatole Litvak, with a screenplay by Robert Rossen. Originally, Kazan was to receive a screenwriting credit but agreed to withdraw his name. He appeared in the movie as Nickie Haroyen, his second and final movie performance. Others in the cast included Priscilla Lane, Jack Carson, Richard Whorf, and Betty Field. Kazan came away from the experience with the knowledge that "I sure as hell can direct better than Anatole Litvak." In a journal entry, before the sale of *Hot Nocturne* to Warner Bros., Kazan reconsidered his original involvement.

FROM THE JOURNAL

DECEMBER 25, 1940

I have made a number of very serious mistakes in connection with *Hot Nocturne.*

I must never embark on the production of a play (example, offering it to backers, other theatre workers, etc.) unless I am convinced it is in the best possible shape. Also, unless I am really sold on it. If I am not sold on the play, something is wrong. And I should keep after it until I have it fixed. This is what is known as Professional Integrity. This play was not in shape for production three months ago when I first started peddling it.

I even avoided thinking of certain embarrassing elements. You simply must never again sponsor a play that embarrasses you in any way whatever. You should fix the places that are patently wrong. It can be done. It is being done now with *Hot Nocturne.* Ask yourself why something affects you poorly. Analyze! Trace it down! In this way you will learn. Insist on complete credibility for yourself. This must be there, even though the vision of the playwright is of a low order, limited and superficial; nevertheless, what he does see and set down must be true to you.

You are now doing work on *Hot Nocturne* that you should have done months ago. It is inexcusable. You have reasons and so forth; they are not valid here. You can never really work creatively until you make the play you are going to direct completely yourself! Insist on this. Be conceited, insist on it. Sell it completely to yourself before you begin to sell it to others. Never apologize for anything you do.

The other serious mistake is of a more technical nature. It is a cardinal mistake of mine today that any producer or director who hopes to work successfully in the theatre today must understand and be able to work in playwriting. You made one serious mistake in working with Gilbert on his play. You outlined for him a plot, which was not a plot. You laid out in the Brad Kay story, for example, a series of scenes revelatory of the state of his relationship, which were presented as progressive stages. In other words, instead of showing one person trying to do something to another, we saw two people clashing generally on a difference in point of view. You revealed them in one relationship in Act One and then in a different relationship in Act Two. This progression (static progression, each scene is fundamentally static) you mistook for the story. It may be one way (the worst) of telling a story (the worst because the action is not shown, it is inferred), but it is certainly not PLOT.

You should make it an artistic task of yours to study twenty plays for their story, their fundamental plot, as it could be told in one sentence, one paragraph, and in one page; the kernel which is the essence of a play. Then you will train yourself to know what a story is, how it may be dramatically unfolded (you see things taking place—versus revealing the resultant condition). Also, you will learn what is enough story for three acts and what is not enough.

The Skin of Our Teeth (1942)
by Thornton Wilder

"This was the first play I directed that I found challenging beyond my talent and technique. I didn't immediately, as I had done with other plays, try to figure out how to cover its faults, but rather how to extend my own capabilities; I admired its theatrical imagination. There was a curious contrast here: The form of the play was novel and constantly surprising, but the author's values, on which it was built, were conventional and finally stuffy."

FROM THE PROGRAM NOTE: *The Skin of Our Teeth* is a comedy about George Antrobus, his wife and two children, and their general utility maid, Lily Sabina, all of Excelsior, New Jersey. George Antrobus is John Doe or George Spevin or you—the average American at grips with a destiny, sometimes sour, sometimes sweet.

The Antrobuses have survived fire, flood, pestilence, the seven-year locusts, the ice age, the black pox, the double feature, a dozen wars, and as many Depressions. They have run many a gamut, are as durable as radiators, and look upon the future with a disarming optimism. Ultimately, bewitched, befuddled, and becalmed, they are the stuff of which heroes are made—heroes and buffoons. They are true offspring of Adam and Eve, victims of all the ills that flesh is heir to. They have survived a thousand calamities by the skin of their teeth, and Mr. Wilder's play is a tribute to their indestructibility.

FROM SCRIPT NOTES

A Portrait of Thornton Wilder

New England. Energetic. Mental, straight, clear. Mentally agile, an acrobat of the mind, of the imagination. Unsentimental. No mush, no milking of sentiment. Also skittish, an awkward bug, grotesque, admires humor. Humor is a function of thought.

A voracious learner. A tireless teacher, in his mind all things are related. For him, all knowledge has pertinence and glamour, in its interrelatedness, overtones, associations. With him one fact evokes a related fact, and in this leap of the mind, there is pleasure and JOY. His facts are evocative, they are meaningful and alive, not cold. Thus, essentially playful in his writing. And this is healthy. It is essentially deeply optimistic.

That doesn't mean the thinking is trivial. It is not abstruse, or profound, but it is always fundamental AND CLEAR.

He plays in and about an idea like a dolphin in the sea. They are home to him. He enjoys it, the past, the future, metaphysics, the psychology of beautiful women, the Greeks, modern types.

Thus his play is lively, allusive, playful. It seems to enjoy its own leaps and bounds and makes them effortlessly.

There should be nothing vague or gauze-like. Everything is itself, simple and clear and crisp as celery.

Wilder is not sensual, is not sensuous. Sex here is a kind of play, not a basic urge.

He is always generous. No harm is ever intended, but real criticism is made.

He has feeling, but it is always controlled, tempered. It is never mushy. On the other hand, feeling is always there.

Spine: Show with pride the lasting power of the human race. To celebrate its durability. Note: The play is a comedy. The race will endure! (In the past, you have often not actually effected the spine.)

Theme: Despite the fact that we are all as wicked as we can be, the human cell, the human animal can't be licked—it will go on and go forward.

And I don't mean any strong rude Superman of a bygone era. I mean people just like you and me, and Uncle Joe and Aunt Clara. When the chips are down, they'll do you proud.

But always by the skin of our teeth because we're pretty wicked.

WHAT I WANT THE AUDIENCE TO FEEL:

This group of awkward, thick-headed, occasionally evil, fundamentally good, dumb monkeys are unbeatable. They do funny, silly, ridiculous things, but then in the end, they turn up with something pretty grand. They are vain, funny, silly, pompous, ridiculous, dopey, like the clown that keeps getting up, like the palooka that keeps leading with his chin. Well, you just can't kill them off, and then hell there's something there that just keeps trying—like Mr. A, who will, by God, turn up with the solution to it all. He'll probably arrive upon it accidentally, ass backward, but he will. Meantime, let's have some fun watching what he goes through, the slaphappy dope. Thank God he's too dumb to notice how silly he is, or he'd quit. The point is that the grandeur comes through this fool. He writes the masterpiece, just when his pants are down. I want the audience to feel "Gee, we're silly and funny and ridiculous, but by God we're pretty grand!"

Direction: There are no real situations, only theatrical events. There are some conflicts, but they appear on short notice, mostly completely uncomplicated, completely unexpected, and endure for only a few pages. One situation does not anticipate another, and that is the essence of theatre situations.

So in directing, the situations must be posed, clear, forceful. But they must not be milked or stretched. If they are dwelt on too heavily, their essential thinness will be too evident. They cannot be relied on to sustain interest. The play must be interesting at every moment. It must be full of surprise. It must have the unrelenting energy of Wilder's reading. You will be secure as a director on this show only if you have

Tallulah Bankhead in the center; Florence Eldridge (March) to her right; Florence Reed to her extreme right; Fredric March and Montgomery Clift to her left

every bit of external life and business worked out very precisely. Only when things are precise—can they be comically observed.

The acting should be presentational, nonpsychological. It must stress ease, clarity of point, simple optimism, zest, Wilder's vigor and precision.

[1988] *The Skin of Our Teeth* made my reputation as a Broadway director. It was the work of Thornton Wilder, a man influenced by James Joyce but quite unlike him. It was a rather bookish jape, and provided excellent roles for four Broadway stars, Freddie March, Tallulah Bankhead, Florence March and Florence Reed; it was my business to keep them in order. The play was timely, coming when the United States had just entered the war and everyone was concerned about the race surviving. It did—at least that war—and so did the play, which was an enormous success. I'm not sure how much I contributed to this, but to be "associated"—that's the word—with a success makes a reputation in our theatre.

Dunnigan's Daughter (1945)
by S. N. Behrman

EDITOR: In 1944 Kazan had directed a hit production of S. N. Behrman's adaptation of Franz Werfel's *Jacobowsky and the Colonel* and would later direct Behrman's *But for Whom Charlie* for the 1963 opening season of the Lincoln Center Repertory Theatre. Because of *Jacobowsky's* success, Behrman for a time thought Kazan a miracle worker, the director best able to realize his intentions. *Dunnigan's Daughter*, a "high comedy," dealt with "an American businessman who possessed his wives without either enjoying them or helping them realize whatever human capabilities they had." Kazan confessed that "I'd cast the play uncertainly. . . . The woman at the core of the play had to be a model of feminine sensitivity—and humor. The businessman had to be something besides a villain." The play got dismal reviews out of town, and Kazan was pressured by the producers and Behrman's agent to recast the play and stress the comedy. Kazan felt he caved in to their demands: "What followed shamed me." He resolved that with his next production he would secure his power and control. It would be billed "An Elia Kazan Production"; he was "giving notice to the backers, the agents, and everyone else not responsible for the creative work that the production power was in my hands."

The night before *Dunnigan's Daughter* closed, he recorded in his journal more personal reasons for his disappointment, not so much with the play as with his involvement—or lack of it.

FROM THE JOURNAL

JANUARY 25, 1946

Tonight I went to see *Dunnigan's Daughter*. It closes tomorrow and I wanted to get one more look at it before it disappears completely. I was shocked at what I saw. It's bad. And the worst thing about it is that nowhere in it, nowhere, is there one drop of human feeling. You care about no one, you aren't moved by anything. And I'd say that the worst thing about my work (my work, my basic work on the script and on Behrman) is that initially I didn't work through my feelings. I gave a damn about no one. Theoretically, I did. With my mind, in my thinking I did, or felt that I should. But truly, actually no one, absolutely no one. In my heart, nothing. In fact, I never used my feelings in working on this. Perhaps that is Behrman: mental, cerebral, witty, concealing. But then it simply doesn't fit the subject matter, which is serious, passionate, and involves the fates of people. Perhaps Behrman should be kicked around by Stars like the Lunts [Alfred Lunt and Lynn Fontanne] only. The only person that had a breath of life in him was, of course, the heavy, KING [Dennis King]. But how did I come to fool myself in saying: "It's the story of a woman." Baloney! Perhaps, abstractly, it is. Perhaps in theory. But as measured by the heart: Not at all!!! And that's the only measure in the theatre, the only one. The rest is "poetry." The rest is plus or minus a little, but there is only one question, and that one must be put to the heart, and answered through the feelings. And that is it. That is Theatre. And that's all.

I remembered a note I had given myself, in which I wrote that I didn't care one whit about Ferne D. That an audience wouldn't, that she had neither capability, nor aspiration, that she had no use in the world, no human worth, that she amounted to a kept woman, and why the hell should anyone be expected to give a damn about her. Later, I answered this question in many ways, but I never could say to myself that I myself gave a damn about her. I didn't. Your brain can lie to you. Your heart not. If you leave it alone and just be kind of simple about it, it will tell you the Basic Theatre fact.

Second essential criticism; and that is the old, old one: <u>NO STORY</u>.

A set of developing human relationships is delineated. Or rather, we are shown various stages of a series of character relationships, but that is still not really story.

Story has to do with cause and effect, a chain of cause and effects linked together in such a way that the end is inevitable in the beginning.

You have a little of this, you tried to get a little of this, thus: A woman who is unhappy with her marriage is further shaken by the criticism, or rather, alienation of a very close and very good old friend. Her state of feeling is further clarified for her by the questioning of a Mexican artist who happened to be on the spot. She is prompted by these events to begin asking her husband a series of questions—the final one being; How about a divorce? Then the Mexican, fortuitously happening on the scene again, pulls her out of a state of fear and depression by telling her "you are yourself." What this means, or what it might lead to, is not known. Then in Act Two we see her make an effort to win her husband back and to make a solid marriage, cementing it with a child. He refuses to have a child. She is then embarrassed by the clumsy attempt of the Mexican to frighten her husband into paying her more mind.

Then she starts asking a State Department fellow questions about her husband. He won't answer them, but in effect suggests that she is not in love with her husband. In angrily replying to this, she breaks down and cries.

In the first place, just as a story this is terribly dull. It is terribly constipated. It is haphazard. It is not inevitable. It is not enough, big enough, moving enough, interesting enough.

Furthermore, it is not even as clear as I am putting it. It is beclouded with other issues. It starts, for instance, in a conflict between a State Department fellow and the stepdaughter, which makes a point about the father, if it makes any; and leads nowhere—as far as our main story is concerned.

Actually there is no inevitability. The author pulls out of the bag of the Past whatever he chooses, whenever he chooses to reveal it.

Finally, when you combine the two faults, the two major faults—well, it's simply fatal! For the ideal job of storytelling is to involve the audience emotionally with someone right off the bat, then get the chain of inevitable cause and effect rolling so that before the audience knows it, they are going through exactly what the character is going through. They feel <u>with!!</u> They are involved. They suffer and sigh with relief. They are actively and emotionally interested.

This Fault Number Two is an old, old fault of yours. You substitute for story the step-by-step revelation of a series of relationships, each step being a step in deterioration or improvement, but not really in the inevitable cause and effect link which makes it roll and seem to be unstoppable. Like the second act of *Deep Are the Roots*, once it starts you feel you can't stop it. That's really plotting, That's really storytelling. And that's real work, and it takes real time.

Truckline Café (1946)
by Maxwell Anderson

EDITOR: In 1946 Kazan formed a producing partnership with Harold Clurman, his mentor and colleague from the Group Theatre. Their first venture, though a flop, became legendary for the impact Marlon Brando made in a small part. The play was directed by Harold Clurman, though Kazan seems to have attended all rehearsals.

FROM THE JOURNAL

FEBRUARY 22, 1946

This play that we've just produced, *Truckline Café*, is going to be a flop. A complete flop. And you will have made the same mistake you have made scores of times in the past. You have allowed yourself to be beguiled by the "quality" of the incidentals of a piece and saddled yourself with a central story which you yourself did not believe. As a show takes life on the stage, the incidentals always become less and less important and certainly never take on a crucial importance, while the central story becomes more and more important. Because it is the function of the central story to carry emotion. If it comes off, the audience is moved and goes home moved. If it doesn't, then the audience will go home empty and dissatisfied, no matter how charming the incidentals of the earlier part of the play have been.

Time and time again, when you have read a play, you have allowed yourself to be beguiled by a charming mood or atmosphere or trappings of a dialogue. But you have not yet developed a certain toughness of mind, a real penetration of thought, a doggedness of analysis, that will serve to carry you past these thickets and into the heart of the problem: Will the central story grip and move the audience? Will they believe it in the first place? This done, will it make them wish for something, will it involve them? Will it satisfy this wish some way, etc.? These are the basic questions, and you have to dig down past the dead leaves, the pretty dead leaves, the twigs, the gay green grass, the sod itself—down to the heart of the drama and TEST THAT.

What disheartens me is that you seem to have a desire to NOT penetrate too deeply, because that will upset something simple and secure

Marlon Brando and Ann Shepherd in *Truckline Café*.

in your attitude, namely: I'm going to do this play. Stop it. Grow up. Force yourself to really look at the meat, the lean meat. Ask yourself: Do I believe it? You did not believe the central story of *Truckline Café*. What a foolish, absurd position you find yourself in as you expect the audience to believe it! Of course, they don't.

EDITOR: On the day of its opening, Kazan was certain of its failure and analyzed what went wrong.

FEBRUARY 27, 1946

The Dying Scene. What a man does when he dies (usually) is not to try to die but to try to keep on living. This should be noticed by actors. For what they should act in a "dying scene" is the effort of the person to keep on living, and what they should feel is not the lassitude but the desire to keep going. That is most certainly what characterizes the last desperate tossings of an animal that has been hit in a vital spot, to keep going, not the opposite.

    Casting. Speaking of Virginia Gilmore, don't cast for a negative quality.* (Virginia looks right for the part of Anne Carruth, we had said, because she looks wounded, as though something had been deeply and irrevocably hurt in her.) Don't cast for the negative quality that an actor needs at the beginning of a part, but for the positive quality that the actor needs at the end. And—as in this case—where the lines and the situations are full of sentiments, emotions, and circumstances that

---

* Virginia Gilmore (1919–1986) was a notable Broadway ingénue who appeared in leading roles in *Those Endearing Young Charms* (1943) and *Dear Ruth* (1944). She was married to Yul Brynner from 1944 to 1960.

serve to keep the actors apart, what the actor's quality, his personality, should contribute is the yearning to get together, the thirst for health and happiness which wars with the situation which is leading her toward unhappiness. Don't cast for the "dead" quality. An actor can be made to play that. But you can't feign much life, much desire, much yearning, where none exists. You can't act life. You have to be alive. You can act dead.

The failure of *Truckline Café* (opens tonight) is due to a number of things:

One of the most important is that we lead the audience to expect (with the light and humorous part of the first act, especially the Karl Malden scene) something much lighter and much funnier, more collo-quial, more active. The melodrama of Marlon Brando and Anne Shep-herd fits in fine—it is terse, curt, active in the same inner tempo. The last scene of Act One is the first place where the audience really becomes restless and this "talky" stuff is not of the same order. In the second act the same thing happens. The first half is funny, folksy, light, young, swift, not lingering, not deep, and then in comes Mort, and the audience resents him immediately. They don't want to hear. The styles are mixed. The audience has not been conditioned by the first part of the play to sit and listen with sensitivity to the poetry. They've been conditioned to leap from one highly and brightly colored fragment to another. The very fact of slowing down seems difficult.

Just as it's hard to take an enjoyable stroll over the same stretch of country that one has just before whizzed over in a car at seventy mph, the audience has been led to expect a different experience. This is sim-ply a stylistic point. True, in ten minutes or so [Richard] Waring and Gilmore have won the audience back to some extent. But it's not so much the scene that loses the play, it's the going into the scene. What goes flat is the portion of the scene before they've had a chance to find out what the hell it's all about. They just don't want that kind of a story at that point; they feel disturbed or cheated, since they've been led to expect something quite, quite different.

What Harold [Clurman] might have done about this is to ring out a little more of the tenderness of [Karl] Malden and try to blend the comedy into the coming poetic-prose, Mort-Anne story that is coming. Malden is too broad, too funny. If you want to go that far, then the Mort-Anne story should have been more and more humanized. We both made a mistake in the casting. We cast to emphasize the breach where we should have cast to the bridge. Kirk Douglas was a much better type [than Karl Malden]. And any plain, regular, nonpoetic, non-wistful little girl with a thirst for life and a very active nature would have been much better than Virginia. Her passivity, her whining, emphasizes every goddamn fault of the piece. I don't honestly know whether this all might have made the play "work," but it's quite possible.

All this that I now feel so strongly, I vaguely felt when I started work on the script. The trick, the merit, is to have really thought it through. That's what I don't do: really think things through. I get misled by the surface values, the humor, the characters and color, and don't really look as long and hard and persistently as I should at the major problem; THE CORE. For the other values tend to recede in production. They are nice and help, but what is crucial is the *core,* and it is in relation to the core that you don't do enough thinking, enough analysis and enough preparation, rewriting.

All My Sons (1947)*
by Arthur Miller

"But this boy was the only one without a solution. He had a SINGLE VIOLENT EMOTION like yours. He said the hell with it. Fuck it, for chrissake. But he went a step further. Not only did he say it stank, but he stood up against it."

EDITOR: The setting is a small midwestern town, shortly after the end of World War II. Kate Keller refuses to accept the death of her son Larry, a pilot missing in action. Her husband, Joe, does little to counter her delusion, but her other son Chris wants to compel her to admit Larry's death so he can receive her blessing to marry his dead brother's fiancée, Ann Deever.

Some three years before, Joe Keller and his partner Steve Deever, Ann's father, were charged with supplying defective airplane parts to the Air Force. Joe was exonerated because he was not at the factory the day the parts were shipped; however, Deever claims that he received phone instructions from Joe to make the shipment. The jury had accepted Joe's false alibi, and Deever, found guilty, is still serving prison time. Ann has not forgiven her father for his presumed complicity in causing the death of American fliers.

When the news of this war-profiteering scandal reached the battle zone, Larry Keller, from shame at his father's presumed involvement with pilots' deaths, committed suicide by intentionally crashing his plane. He had written his fiancée of his intention in a last letter, which Ann reveals when her brother George, who has visited their father in prison, has become convinced of their father's innocence.

When Chris is compelled to accept the evidence of his father's guilt, he asks his father to turn himself over to the police. Forced to confront the truth of his involvement in his son's death, and the loss of Chris's respect, Joe shoots himself.

FROM THE NOTEBOOK

WILLIAMSTOWN, NOVEMBER 1946

The major conflict in the play comes from the contrast between the comradeship of men in arms, their mutual dependence, and the every-man-out-for-himself capitalist world that soldiers return to—the con-

* Credits for the plays and movies are given in the Chronology, starting on page 302.

tradiction of the world of men in war and the social mores of American society. This is worked out in a father/son plot where the mother is also conceived of as a villain. It is the young versus the old.

In preparing the play I must consider: 1. What it should all mean. 2. Each character's intent. 3. How each character reacts, how they work to achieve their goal. 4. How this is externalized.

The greatest and most devastatingly encompassing crisis that our civilization can experience is war. Each man's life depends upon the courage, integrity, and even philosophy of his neighbor in arms. Take young Gene Murphy [unidentified]. His code of ethics and his standard of values are still those of the battlefield—the first battlefield of all: the skies over Europe. What does he prize? Honesty, courage, guts, truth, strength, trustworthiness, etc., etc., integrity. Every man's life depended upon the trustworthiness of his fighting neighbor. The essential difference to Chris Keller was that every man is against his neighbor in the mad scramble for money. Basically, no man could be trusted because he was fighting you for your job, conning you for your money, deceiving you for your trust. The climax for Chris comes when he finds that he can't even trust his own father. Chris automatically contrasts his father's behavior with that of his crew chief. For one burning moment in the third act, he feels and acts upon an obligation to something bigger than his comfort, his gain, his reputation, his pocketbook. For a moment, in Act Three, he is a hero! He feels an obligation not to his ego but to the race—to all men, to justice! But incarnating as he does this burning force, for an instant, in this instant, he kills his father.

The Big Conflict is between the forces of Honor, of Responsibility to your neighbor, of equality and democracy, of Christlikeness, of One World–ism. Versus this, the Capitalist System, the competitive system, the jungle where one man exists only by the death (yes, sooner or later, the death) of his neighbor. The competitive system, which basically says, "Beat up the next guy. Say anything you want, think anything you want, but one thing don't risk: that the other guy might get ahead of you, that is your death."

FROM SCRIPT NOTES

DECEMBER 6–7, 1946

The spine of the play has something to do with how to live in this age and in this civilization. All the people seem to be shrinking back, rejecting, or combating this civilization.

George feels shut out and robbed, exploited, and unrewarded (like Karl Malden). Now goddammit, he's going to get his due. (There is a degree of self-pity in this.)

Chris despises what he sees all around him. He despises the commercial activities he has allowed his father to drag him into. He doesn't know what to do about it because that seems to be in the nature of things today. That's the way people live today. But he is determined to create one decent thing. He is determined to create one community, one place of harmony, one place where he can trust and believe and love and be needed and feel safe and honorable. (The theme of this spine is, in its simplest, most normal "regular-guy" terms: "Chris is a great guy.") He thinks he can find it in a love nest with Ann. He is determined to achieve this, though he gives in on every other particular. What he discovers is that honor is indivisible, that the irresponsibility of his neighbor affects him. That as soon as he accepts his neighbor's irresponsibility, then he's soiled himself. That in order to put himself in the right, he's got to make others live in a just world. Finally, he has to put his father in jail . . . or else he can't live with an easy conscience. He wants only one thing: to live with other people in honor and trust. Though it of course starts with Ann, it ends with ALL!

Jim, his best friend, also despises what he sees. But he has an easy solution for a way to live. He lives within himself. He turns inward. He wants nothing to do with other people. He wants to live alone with his craft and his self. (This can be physicalized.) *FLOATS.*

Joe has given in to the corruption that Miller sees everywhere; he has in effect turned against his fellow man. Now, he's trying desperately to correct his relationships with people, to gain forgiveness and to be with them. (This can be physicalized.) *FRIENDLY.* He likes people.

Kate excludes it all, denies there is any life except the life of her instinct and experiences. She is the most integrated person in the play. She wants to hold on to her children. She uses any and all tricks and means to achieve this—all is fair in love and war, and this is both. She even mothers other people. But she is ruthless; she would rather see the world dissolve in flames than see a scratch on her children's flesh. *As long as they are true to her.* She is jealous as a cunt in this respect. Mother, *FIERCE.*

Lydia, having never had a chance, is trying to live through the lives of other people. She has no hope for herself. She lives in movies, magazines, etc. There is something longing and wistful and pleading about her. *WINSOME.*

Arthur Kennedy, Karl Malden, Beth Merrill, Ed Begley,
and Lois Wheeler.

Sue, caught and trapped, with a hopeless man in a hopeless situation, is trying to do as well as she can. <u>*DESPERATE.*</u> Bert lives in games. Frank lives by the rules. He believes in them. They've put him where he is today. He is the perfect product. The <u>OPTIMIST.</u>

One thing is basic. The people are all good people, but they are in difficulty with this particular society, USA 1946.

Secondly, also basic, these people all love each other. That's why there is pain.

Style. This is a poetic play dealing with the basic ethical question of our times, the basic responsibility of every individual to every other individual.

There was a time when man was responsible to God. Then there was a time when every man was responsible to his own soul. *Today* every man is responsible to every other man. If you do something, no matter how distant from home, it comes home to roost. That is what the allegory of the play says. The play, therefore, in its feeling and production style, has to be supranaturalistic. The play is poetic in *the size of its feelings.*

It is important that the play start simply and winningly, and that the people are very likable.

But the play must not stay on that level. It must reach in its production the same size and stature as the theme. Just as *Oedipus* dealt with a basic huge moral issue, so does this play. At the end it must be naked souls in the terrible darkness of this civilization. Today, man must have a mutual religion; the religion of every other man is me and I am him. This is about man's soul . . . the third act must be luminous souls in the dark purgatory of this world, this steaming world . . . this misty ineluctable world.

The spine of the play is the spine of Chris. The line of the play is the line of Chris. This play is about an effort of Chris to live with honor, to live like a man, in love and together with other people, rather than against them.

At the beginning of the play he is ready to settle for very little. He is gradually becoming adjusted to civilian life. In this case that doesn't mean anything good. It means accepting the inevitability of evil. He has given up hope of doing anything about his public existence, about the work part of his days. He only wants his private life, his intimate life to be decent. He'll settle for that. He can't hope to do anything about the way things are socially. That's too big for him. But he can do something about himself. His personal life will be clean. His private life, *that* he can control. That will be good. He won't take no for an answer there. He'd rather go back to the war. He'd rather die. Nothing will stop him. His resolution has built and built, and built into a swollen river of nearly hysterical feeling.

It is this boy's resolve that creates the play. He's going to make a livable life for himself. He knows there are some obstacles, even to this. But it will happen. He doesn't know how deep he'll have to go. But on the other hand, he doesn't realize how powerful his resolve is.

The play depends on two hooks. The propulsive force is Chris's drive toward a decent life for himself. It's as simple as that. It is the story of how this drive through its very force roots up the obstacles in its course (like a plow digs up huge hidden boulders and thick powerful roots), how the drive overcomes these obstacles one by one, at the price of much pain, and how finally even the last obstacle, the very considerable bond this boy has with his father, is encountered and overcome. At the end, the boy has cleared a path to this decent life. By the side of the road lies the dead body of his father. That's how deeply interrelated everything is, how final the cost, how painful the struggle.

Anatomizing Act One. Find the stage action and behavior from these basic interpretations.

All the people we meet here are the people among whom Chris has to live. They are all nice people. But at the same time, all of them have long given up hope of living with honor. Jim is disappointed. He is comically presented, but he is really tragic—a man who has given up his talent, or hope of the future, and who lives by running away from his wife and what she represents, namely the demands of the world. His wife, Sue, is disappointed not only in her husband but in the role she has to play in the world because of him, namely a nag. Lydia too is disappointed. She never knew love. She is married to a man who gives her everything you are supposed to want in this world: security, toasters, a paid-off mortgage, faithfulness, except for the one thing she wants more than anything else—romantic love. One woman then nags her husband, the other dreams all day, is absent-minded, not there, given up. Both have been defeated by society.

Frank is one of those men that do everything exactly right. He is precise and exact and mechanically proficient (like Hume Cronyn) but oh, oh so dull. Both couples are hopeless.

At the same time, the father lives with a smothered guilt, for which he is trying to gain forgiveness. This drives his anxiety to be liked, to be a host, to be the life of the block. And he is a nice guy too and he has succeeded in creating an air of jolly hospitality. At the same time there is a barely discernable air of "overdoing" it.

And the mother is nuts. There should be a suggestion that the neighborhood doesn't think she's quite right about the way she's reacted to Larry's death. In fact, she's a legend in the immediate neighborhood.

So, this is the world of Chris: disappointment and escape from a life without love. Hidden guilt, coming out in amusing anxiety. A person on the road to insanity. BUT ALL THIS SHOULD ONLY BE HINTED AT COMICALLY.

This beat is the revelation of the strength of Chris's drive. The father discovers it. He discovers it is stronger and stronger. He finally realizes that the boy would turn against him completely and would abandon the business.

There is a simple triangle here. The boy wants the father to help him fight the mother. The mother has a hold on the father. She knows his guilt. And in a way his guilt created her obsession. The father is scared of her and scared of the son. In this scene the father is driven into a desperate position. He has his back against the wall.

The scene all comes from Chris's action. The scene could be called

"Zero Hour for Chris." There is an element of pinning the old man down. At the end of the scene he's cornered the old man. Mother's call saves the old man.

The father cowers against the side arbor bench. When the mother calls, the boy walks into the arbor, leaving the father alone. Another way and probably a better way to do this last beat is to have Chris walk away from the old man and go sit down by himself. The old man comes and stands over the kid. The kid doesn't move.

EDITOR: The following is appended at the end of the play script:

I have made a mistake in laying out Chris's spine, and his course of action. The way I finally realized that was that his spine doesn't inspire any stage action. It is a description and an analysis. A "spine" should be a motor.

This is another way of saying that it is not human. It hasn't got the breath of life. It doesn't sweat, pee, and procreate.

Also, it hasn't got the breath of my life. I don't understand it. I understand Joe K's seeking forgiveness because it springs from a sense of guilt and other anxieties that you have too. I understand Kate's: to mother, or to keep her children alive, because I know Evanthia [Kazan's paternal grandmother] and love her, and my mother and love her, because I am a father, and have a feeling for mothers.

I understand Ann's very simple simple spine: looking for someone she can give herself to, or getting Chris, especially the sexual aspects of this last. Her search for a man is frantic. She is starved for love, sex, and connection. She needs help. I know this in Molly [Kazan's wife], and I know it in myself too.

But what I put down for Chris is worthless.

The above three give you stage business ideas. Kate's looking to make everyone a slave to her motherly solicitude and mother feeding and mother endurance and mother understanding, while her main edge is to keep her children alive. It's outwardly social: She'd like to mother the whole world, it appears. But inwardly she's tough and self-ish as hell. She tries to get these people in her power. She makes them need, look forward to, her ministrations.

Chris must not be gloomy, lofty, ideal, abstract, mentally cold, theo-retical, or self-righteous. He's a normal, simple, naïve, slow-witted, sweet, good-natured American kid, slow to anger, tough when he needs to be, and all the other bromidic things true of the typical American boy. Put flesh and blood on him. He wants to enjoy life.

He doesn't want to be in conflict with other people. He wants to be close to them so his friendliness is constantly being taken advantage of, especially and above all by his mother. His mother is ruthless—while Chris pities and feels for her, she uses her feeling and her power over his feelings as a kind of weapon. She takes advantage of the fact that he loves her.

In this respect he is just like me. He wants above all to be liked. Of course, this isn't entirely healthy. It means that he smothers resentments. This brings him close to you. He sloughs off fights, etc. He is not comfortable fighting. Some people are.

Up until a fundamental belief in a person is undermined. Then it all breaks down. Then he can turn completely against someone. He can still have a sense of pity. But then everything has changed. You are this way too.

I know Chris resented his father once. Once, he concealed this resentment. He still does to an extent. Chris never quite gets tough in Act One. He wishes, he asks for help, he asks for understanding, he tries to laugh away real issues, he tries to love everybody and to hurt no one. Nothing is ever accomplished that way. In Act Two he is tough; in Act Three he is desperate. These are TONES not actions, but still they help.

Your emotion in the piece. Work with your feelings.

<u>The piece should transmit above all one piece of violent feeling from you.</u>

It says that our society stinks. That it must be changed. That it submerges the good and elevates the bad. That it places no prize on the ennobling qualities of man and that it pays off double to all the mean ones. It rewards the jungle qualities of craftiness, cunning, hate, ruthlessness.

I don't want a soft civilization, Mr. Lighton [Hollywood producer Louis D. "Bud" Lighton]. I want a violent one, a tough one, and the first piece of violence I want is to clean out the shits and the thieves who hold our country in bondage. The money shits, the bankers.

I don't want to live in a gamblers' civilization, the paradise that belongs to Jack Wildberg, Lee Shubert, Jules Leventhal (a nice guy but a loan guy), Jack Warner, Louis Mayer, Harry Ginsberg, the Schenk boys, Charlie Feldman, and all the goddamn crummy predatory reptiles [a litany of Broadway and Hollywood executives, producers, and agents].

It's about time someone should speak out. Someone's got to be the first to speak, to say he won't stand for it anymore. To say that that's it, that's all, brother.

No more. It's leading us right back to another war.

No more. Our civilization is fired with only one ideal: make money.

No more. Our civilization is corrupting the faces of all our people.

No more. It's ruining what's wonderful in our land, in its tradition.

It is already eating away at our clean fresh children.

No more.

Someone's got to be the first one to speak up. *To say the hell with it.* I'll get ruined. I'll be outlawed. I'll be out of step, too. I won't belong. It will be painful. But I'll be the first. I'll say no.

This play is about a boy who says no. He stood up against it.

Chris stands against everyone else in the play. The mother says: To hell with everyone else on earth; look out for yourself. The father says: Everyone else is doing it. You can't blame me for doing it too. What else could I do? I did it for you. The girl says: I just want you. (But in order to have him complete and strong and sound, she has to see to it that he said no.) The brother-in-law said: I'm going to get my due. I've been cut out long enough.

Jim the neighbor said: Live like me, live by yourself. Shut out the corruption of the world. Don't notice it. But he left his WIFE to do the job of dealing with it. He shirked it and left it to her, and she did what she could.

The other neighbor lived by the rules and they ironed him out so the rules flowered in him, but his wife suffered. His wife got no nourishment. And his wife, giving up ever trying to get anything from her life, tried to get into the life of everyone, especially those not there, those dream figures in the movies, the mags, the radio.

But this boy was the only one without a solution. He had a SINGLE VIOLENT EMOTION like yours. He said the hell with it. Fuck it, for chrissake. But he went a step further. Not only did he say it stank, but he stood up against it.

HE WAS THE ONLY ONE
AND THE FIRST ONE WHO
DID SOMETHING ABOUT IT.

He just said he wouldn't stand for it. He wouldn't acquiesce, nor would he run away, nor shrink (though he thought of this at first). He said he wouldn't live with it. He wouldn't go on living with it. Don't think this was an easy decision to make.

Because the boy wanted above all to be with people, to live with them in happiness.

And at the beginning of the piece he is willing to settle for much LESS.

HE HAD TO BE FORCED TO BE A HERO.

For at the beginning he despised the world he found himself in, but he thought to build a little clean corner with his girl. He was very determined to do this. But he didn't mean to say NO to the rest. That he had no hopes to do anything about.

He just had that marked lousy.

But one thing led to another. The way things do today. It's an indivisible world, one world. And peace is indivisible. And so is honor. And no one can do bad without hurting you, so you might as well face it.

But this boy doesn't want to fight with people. So that tempered his violence. And he loved his parents very much, one man that did. And he certainly didn't want to fight with them, so that tempered his violence.

BUT this time (and that is what the play does: create this crisis) it is necessary to do something or give up himself completely. He's forced to say no by the incidence of his nature and the circumstances of the play.

And he finally does, though it means his father's death. So he becomes a moral hero, though all he wanted to do is live alone with his girl and be happy at night and surrender his days to a corrupt world.

This play must speak one piece of your violence.

The world is wrong. Make no mistake about that. Our civilization, our dollar civilization, is foul. And it's consuming your life.

Rather than giving it soil to flower . . .

YOU too live in the hothouse, for chrissake.

And in this play you stand up and say NO! NO! NO!!!

The hell with it.

ALL THE CONFLICTS ARE AGGRAVATED BY THE FACT THAT THESE PEOPLE LIKE EACH OTHER.

EDITOR

In 1946 Kazan formed a production company with Harold Clurman and Walter Fried, and the next play after *Truckline Café* they chose for their venture was Arthur Miller's *All My Sons,* first entitled *The Sign of the Archer.* Miller and Kazan quickly became intimate friends. "We were both out of the Depression, both left-wingers, both had had problems with our fathers, considered their business worlds antihuman." Though Clurman had selected the play, Miller preferred that Kazan direct, adding another item to the complex of devotion, admiration, and distrust that marked the Kazan-Clurman relationship throughout their lives. "Clurman kept saying that it didn't matter, he wasn't upset, he went his cheery way, saying that I did indeed have certain useful qualifications for the job, among them the ones he always mentioned: energy, clarity, and mechanical dexterity. He, the implication remained, was the artist, with the extra-fine sensibilities and broad cultural outlook. Although there was some truth in this, it annoyed me." One way Kazan wooed Miller from Clurman was to invite Miller to the set of *Boomerang!,* which Kazan was filming in Connecticut, and give Miller a stint as an extra in a police lineup scene. With Miller's blessing, three members of the *Boomerang!* cast were given lead roles in *All My Sons:* Ed Begley, Arthur Kennedy, and Karl Malden.

The play had both personal and social resonance for Kazan, but its most consequent effect was that it clarified for him his most compelling artistic intentions. Staging it allowed him to utilize all his theatrical expertise and to explore and to shape an idiosyncratic directorial method. What he had done before was based on his smarts, his intelligence, the stagecraft he had honed while a member of the Group Theatre, the assurance and authority that came with his first Broadway successes. But Miller's play demanded relentless self-exposure, a ruthless examination of his own motives of ambition and competition, and as a consequence the stage came alive with exuberance and energy. He strove to make every moment count—what his critics called his attraction to the violent and overwrought.

Like many other Kazan projects, this play internalized a social issue. "Like other plays being written then, it concerned guilt, but not that of a person being falsely accused; the guilt in Art's play was real. By not setting up an accusation that was to be disproved in three acts, the play dramatized a true moral confrontation. . . . The guilt uncovered was that of the hero's father, whom he loved. The fact—a strong emotional attachment on hazard—deepened the theme. Since the guilt was that of a businessman, ergo that of our business community, the play made a social statement."

With the Second World War ended, the country went through an interrupted self-analysis, confronting the inescapable social issues that had destabilized the nation during the Depression (which was brought to an end by the military economy of the war): inequality, political injustice, bigotry, the economic risks of uncontrolled capitalism, and loosened sexual mores. The social criticism that had been the *raison* of the plays and movies of the 1930s was reactivated. And the fresh mode for this scrutiny was psychologi-

All My Sons (the Chicago company), set design by Mordecai Gorelik

cal analysis on a grand scale. It is not merely the social order that was corrupt; it was the soul of the country. Something wasn't working, something was wrong. Seemingly, prosperity and military triumph brought with it disillusionment and an insidious guilt, and the only solution would be an anxious scourging of an inherent national malaise. Poverty (Hollywood style) was the reality of Kazan's first movie, *A Tree Grows in Brooklyn;* miscegenation, of his Broadway production *Deep Are the Roots;* legal injustice, of the film *Boomerang!;* anti-Semitism, of *Gentleman's Agreement;* and the entire ground of American values in *Death of a Salesman.* Other "socially worthy" Hollywood projects of the late 1940s include *The Best Years of Our Lives* (returning vets), *Lost Boundaries* ("passing for white"), *Home of the Brave* (prejudice in the military), and *Crossfire* (anti-Semitism): anxiety, anger, failure. *All My Sons* linked the filicidal war profiteer Joe Keller and American business ethics. The father fails, and the country fails. Joe Keller is a run-through for *Death of a Salesman*'s Willy Loman, just as *Salesman* expands upon *All My Sons*' theme of the heritage passed from father to son. The fathers of these plays are no abstractions; they are the fathers of Arthur Miller and Elia Kazan.

The dynamism and invention of Kazan's directorial manner, and his obsessive devotion to searching out the fullest implications of the play, thrilled Arthur Miller. He recalled how Kazan kept reworking the staging up to the moment of its Broadway premiere:

> He had cast Ed Begley to play the father, Keller, in *All My Sons* not only because Begley was a good actor (although not as yet of great distinction) but because he was a reformed alcoholic and still carried the alcoholic's guilt. Keller is of course a guilty man, although not an alcoholic; this trait could be matched while their causes were completely unrelated. The play had already run in New Haven and had shown its impact, but Elia Kazan continued rehearsing sections of it every day even now, driving it to ever more intensified climaxes, working it like a piece of music that had to be sustained here and hushed there. To keep the cast from routinizing their characters' conflicts, he would stimulate arguments among them by seeming to favor one over the other, seeding little fungi of jealousy that made them compete all over again for his affection. A small, compact man who walked on the balls of his feet, he had the devil's energy and knew how to pay attention to what the writer or his actors were trying to tell him; he could make each actor think he was his closest friend. I think his method, if it can be given so self-conscious a name, was to let the actors talk themselves into a performance. Far more by insinuation than by command, he allowed the actors to excite themselves with their own discoveries, which they would carry back to him like children offering some found object to a parent. And he respected rather than scoffed at actors' childishness, knowing that it was not a grown-up occupation and that the sources of their best intentions were in their earliest years. Instinctively, when he has something important to tell an actor, he would huddle with him privately rather than instruct before the others, sensing that anything that really penetrates is always to some degree an embarrassment. . . . His most reassuring side, for me, was a natural tendency to seek out the organic, and hew to its demands.

Later in *Timebends* Miller expands upon Kazan's directorial acumen:

> Life in a Kazan production had that hushed air of conspiracy I've described before, a conspiracy not only against the existing theatre but society, capitalism—in fact, everybody who was not part of the production. . . . The path to victory was opened up by a clarity about the play's mission, its reason for existing, as well as about the

actor's motives and the shape of his personality and talent . . . But Kazan's was no mere technical virtuosity; from the Group and its Russian and European antecedents, he had learned that a theatrical production is, or should be, a slice through the thickness of the culture from which it emerges, and that it is speaking not only to its audience but to other plays, to painting and dance, to music and to all forms of human expression by which at any moment we read our time. And so he would send one actor to listen to a particular piece of jazz, another to read a certain novel, another to see a psychiatrist, and another he would simply kiss. And more, though he never mentioned political people or ideas, it was assumed that he identified himself with the idealism of the left and that his emotional and intellectual loyalties lay with the workers and the simple and the poor. Like Odets, he wore the fading colors of the thirties into the forties and fifties, the resonances of the culture of antifascism that had once united artists everywhere in the world.

Kazan
and
Arthur
Miller

Kazan directed only three of Miller's plays, *All My Sons, Death of a Salesman,* and *After the Fall,* but their association is one of the splendid markers of twentieth-century achievement in drama. Kazan felt "it had the earmarks of the kind of production for which I'd become famous. The playwright whom it most influenced was Tennessee Williams, who thought it eloquent."

A Streetcar Named Desire (1947)
by Tennessee Williams

"Stanley is exactly like you in some ways. He's supremely indifferent to everything except his own pleasure and comfort. He is marvelously selfish, a miracle of sensuous self-centeredness. He builds a hedonist life, and fights to the death to defend it—but finally it is not enough to hold Stella. And this philosophy is not successful even for him—because every once in a while the silenced, frustrated part of Stanley breaks loose in unexpected and unpredictable ways and we suddenly see, as in a burst of lightning, his real frustrated self."

EDITOR: Blanche DuBois has been dismissed in mid term from her position as a high school English teacher in Laurel, Mississippi, and thrown out of the Hotel Flamingo for having a liaison with a seventeen-year-old boy. She has also lost the remnants of her family's estate, Belle Reve, through her inability to maintain the mortgage payments piled up by her dissolute forebears.

Desperate, on the verge of a complete collapse, she has sought refuge with her pregnant younger sister, Stella, and Stella's husband, Stanley Kowalski, in New Orleans. (Williams plays on the resonant symbolism of New Orleans public names, for when Blanche arrives she takes the streetcar named Desire, transfers to the Cemetery line, and gets off at Elysian Fields—in mythology the home of departed spirits—her sister's neighborhood.)

There is an immediate sexual charge and concomitant antipathy between Blanche and Stanley, for she has the naturally flirtatious airs of a delicate Southern belle and he is a preening peacock, wise in the ways of women. Blanche is threatened by Stanley's brutishness, and later Stanley overhears Blanche talking of him to Stella with repulsion at his low class and his vulgarity. He now understands her as an enemy to his marriage and to his ego.

Blanche flirts with Stanley's friend Mitch, hoping to snatch him as a husband, a last chance for her salvation. Stanley has heard rumors of her Laurel reputation for being immoral—she had entertained traveling salesmen and soldiers from the local base. Panicked by Stanley's hints of what he has learned, Blanche confides in Mitch her devastating guilt at the long-ago suicide of her young husband (Allan Grey). At a dance, she had taunted him as a homosexual after finding him with an older man, telling him she found him disgusting. He had fled the dance hall and shot himself. The remembered sound of the shot reverberates continually in her mind, as does the music the dance band was playing. After her confession, a plea for forgiveness and understanding, Mitch takes her in his arms and kisses her. She cries out: "Sometimes—there's God—so quickly!"

Later, Stanley warns Blanche that he has told Mitch of her past, and Blanche realizes that only disaster is ahead for her. At the confrontation between Stanley and Blanche, Stella's birth pangs begin and Stanley takes her to the hospital. He returns before the baby is delivered, and finds Blanche, lost in delusions, decked out in her phony finery, shifting in and out of a fantasy of meeting a wealthy protector. Stanley, half drunk and euphoric at his coming fatherhood, decides this is the moment to bring Blanche off her high horse, and he rapes her: "Come to think of it—maybe you wouldn't be bad to—interfere with. . . . We've had this date with each other from the beginning!" The "date" Blanche has had from the beginning was with her destruction.

After returning home, Stella fights off believing Blanche's tale since Blanche has only fragmented moments of sanity. Stella has her committed to a public mental institution, and when a doctor arrives to take Blanche away, Blanche wildly fights off his assistant, who pinions her to the ground, but the doctor speaks gently to her, raises her from the ground, and escorts her out the front door. Holding his arm, Blanche accepts him as her savior: "Whoever you are—I have always depended on the kindness of strangers."

FROM THE NOTEBOOK

AUGUST 1947

A *thought:* Directing finally consists of turning Psychology into Behavior.

Theme: This is a message from the dark interior. This little twisted, pathetic, confused bit of light and culture puts out a cry. It is snuffed out by the crude forces of violence, insensibility, and vulgarity that exist in our South—and this is the cry of the play.

Style: One reason a "style," a stylized production, is necessary is that Blanche's memories, inner life, emotions are a tangible, actual factor. We cannot understand her behavior unless we see the effect of her past on her present behavior.

This play is a poetic tragedy. We are shown the final dissolution of a person of worth, who once had great potential, and who, even as she is defeated, as she is destroyed, has a worth exceeding that of the "healthy," coarse-grained figures who kill her.

Blanche and Don Quixote are both emblems of the death of an old culture. This is a poetic tragedy, not a realistic, naturalistic one. The acting must be styled, not in the obvious sense. (Say nothing about this to the producer and actors.) But you will fail unless you find this kind of poetic realization for these people's behavior.

Blanche is a social type, an emblem of a dying civilization, making its last curlicued and romantic exit. All her behavior patterns are those of the dying civilization she represents. In other words, her behavior is social. Therefore find social modes! This is the source of the play's stylization and the production's style and color. Likewise, Stanley's behavior is social too. It is the basic animal cynicism of today. "Get what's coming to you! Don't waste a day! Eat, drink, get yours!" This is the basis of his stylization, of the choice of his props. All props should be stylized: They should have a color, shape, and weight that spell *style*.

An effort to put poetic names on scenes to edge me into stylizations and physicalizations. Try to keep each scene in terms of Blanche.

1. Blanche comes to the last stop at the end of the line.
2. Blanche tries to make a place for herself.
3. Blanche breaks them [Stanley and Stella] apart, but when they come together, Blanche is more alone than ever!
4. Blanche, more desperate because more excluded, tries the direct attack and creates the enemy who will finish her.
5. Blanche finds that she is being tracked down for the kill. She must work fast.
6. Blanche suddenly finds Mitch, suddenly makes for herself the only possible, perfect man for her.
7. Happy only for a moment, Blanche comes out of the bathroom to find that her doom has caught up with her.
8. Blanche fights her last fight. Breaks down. Even Stella deserts her.
9. Blanche's last desperate effort to save herself by telling the whole truth. The truth dooms her.
10. Blanche escapes out of this world. She is brought back by Stanley and destroyed.
11. Blanche is disposed of.

Find an entirely different character, a self-dramatized and self-romanticized character for Blanche to play in each scene, as if she were playing eleven different people. This will give the play the kind of changeable and shimmering surface it should have. And all these eleven self-dramatized and romantic characters should derive from the romantic tradition of the Pre-Bellum South. For example, in Scene 2 she is "Gay Miss Devil-May-Care."

The style—the real deep style—consists of one thing only: to find behavior that's truly social, significantly typical, at each moment. It's not so much what Blanche has done, it's how she does it—with such style, grace, manners, old-world trappings and effects, props, tricks, swirls, etc., that they seem anything but vulgar.

And for the other characters, too, you face the same problem, to find the Don Quixote character for them. Stylized acting and direction is to realistic acting and direction as poetry is to prose. This is a poetic tragedy, not a realistic or a naturalistic one. So you must find a Don Quixote scheme of things for each.

Blanche.

Blanche is desperate! This is the end of the line of the Streetcar Named Desire.

Her *Spine* is to find protection. The tradition of the old South says that protection comes through another person.

Her problem has its base in her tradition. Her notion of what a woman should be. She is stuck with this "ideal." It is her. It is her ego. Unless she lives by it, she cannot live; in fact, her whole life has been for nothing. Even the Allan Grey incident, as she now tells it and believes it to have happened, is a necessary piece of romanticism. Essentially, in outline, she tells what happened, but it also serves the demands of her notion of herself, to make her *special* and *different,* in line with the traditional romantic ladies of the past.

Because this image of herself cannot be made actual, given a real form, certainly not in the South of our day and time, it is her effort and practice to actualize it in fantasy. Blanche has constant daytime fantasies. Only in these does life turn out the way it should. Only in these can she live as she must. Everything that she does is colored by this necessity, this compulsion to be special (Stella Adler [actress, teacher, married to Harold Clurman]). So, in fact, *Reality becomes fantasy, too.* She makes it so!

A question: How did she lay those soldiers?

Another question: Is part of Blanche's suffering self-accusatory? Or is it a demonstration of suffering so she will be pitied and therefore given the attention, love, and understanding that she needs? Yes!

A tenet of Blanche's code is that a woman does not assert herself, does not even defend herself. A man is to do it for her. But the times have changed, and besides, Blanche has no such man. So there is a constant feeling of weakness and defenselessness. Both Stella Adler and Emma E. Thacher [Kazan's mother-in-law] are women out of another time, who go on, in our day, living in the old way and, since it no longer works, feeling helpless, frantic. One of the elements in this tradition is a lady's helplessness, especially in practical affairs. It is not only expected of a lady, it is a treasured, prized quality. Its original purpose was to make the man feel competent, managing. In a word: manly.

Marlon Brando and Jessica Tandy

Blanche at the beginning should be a heavy. Stella has, through Stanley's assertive masculinity, found her own strength and health. Blanche immediately tries to infantilize Stella. In effect, this works to break up her happy home. But gradually the audience should begin to feel that Blanche is a complex, sensitive woman, out of her environment, really rather helpless and in real difficulty. As this happens, the pain and the reality begin to appear—a democracy of pain and need, basic human tragedy begins to show, and slowly the audience should start to pity and admire her.

The variety essential to the play and to Blanche's playacting and to Jessica Tandy's achieving what the role demands is that she be a heavy at the start. For instance, contemplate the inner character contradiction: bossy yet helpless, domineering yet shaky. The audience at the beginning should see her negative effect on Stella and want Stanley to tell her off. He does, he exposes her, and then gradually as we see how genuinely in pain, how actually desperate she is, how warm, tender, and loving she can be (the Mitch story), how freighted with need she is—then we begin to go with her. The audience realizes that they are witnessing the death of something extraordinary—colorful, varied, passionate, lost, witty, imaginative, of her own integrity—and thus they feel the tragedy. In the playing too there can be a growing sincerity and directness.

Blanche, out of place, unappreciated, a stranger in the modern, rough, coarse South; yet despite sickness and unbalance, she has more warmth than any of them. It is important symbolically that Blanche is an English teacher. She is the last repository of culture, abandoned, not prized, deformed, destroyed, gone begging for protection. At the end, the grandeur and the nobility belong to Blanche, and the "victors," Stella and Stanley, are left with each other, a relationship of vulgar crudity and, for Stella, of growing emptiness and terror. (Also, Tennessee wants desperately to be with other people, yet be superior to them.)

The thing about "the tradition" in the nineteenth century was that *it worked then*. It made a woman feel important, with her own secure position and functions, her own special worth. At that time it also made a woman *one with her society*. But today the tradition is a nonfunctional anachronism. *It does not work.* So while Blanche must believe it because it makes her special, because it makes her sticking by Belle Reve an act of heroism, rather than an absurd romanticism, still it doesn't work. It enforces Blanche's loneliness, makes her feel a social outcast, insecure, shaky. The airs, the demands of the tradition, isolate her further. And every once in a while her resistance, weakened by drink, breaks down, and she seeks human warmth and contact where she can find it, not on her terms but on theirs: the merchant Kiefaber of Laurel, the traveling salesman, and the others, among whom the vulgar adolescent soldiers seem the most innocent. Since she cannot integrate these episodes, she rejects them, begins to forget them, lives in fantasy, rationalizes and then explains to herself: "I never was hard or self-sufficient enough . . . men don't see women unless they are in bed with them. They don't admit their existence except when they're love-making. You've got to have your existence admitted by someone if you are going to receive someone's protection," etc. As if you had to apologize for needing human contact! Protection, that is what she so desperately needs. That's what she comes to Stella for, Stella and her husband. Not finding it from them, she tries to get it from Mitch. *Protection.* A haven, a *harbor.* She is a refugee, punch drunk, and on the ropes, making her last stand, trying to keep up a gallant front, because she is a proud person. But really if Stella doesn't provide her haven, *where is she to go?* She's a misfit, alien, her "airs" alienate people, she must act superior to them, which alienates them further. She doesn't know how to work, so she can't make a living. She's helpless. She needs someone to protect her. She's a dying relic of the last century now adrift in our unfriendly day. From time to time, for reasons of simple human loneliness and need, she goes to pieces, smashes her tradition . . . then goes back to it. This conflict has developed into a terrible crisis. All she wants is safety: "I want to rest! I want to breathe quietly again . . . just think! If it happens! I can leave here and not be anyone's problem."

Blanche as doomed. She won't adapt herself. She's too fine on the one hand. She is too committed on the other. Unless she maintains her tradition, what else is there that she can hold to that makes her feel her special worth, that makes a place for her as a cultural light? For, wounded and crippled as she is, she remains yet the little point of pure light in a muddy and vulgar turmoil of the South today. She is Tennessee, out of place, not accepted, given to vast and sudden sinning, but still proud and building her ego on the only basis she can: her special worth, her apartness. But since her ego is built on this apartness, her growing loneliness is built on the same thing. As she builds what her ego needs, she also builds what will destroy her: loneliness and the other qualities that make Stanley destroy her.

If this is a romantic tragedy, what is its inevitability and what is the tragic flaw? In the Aristotelian sense, the flaw is the need to be superior/special, or her need for protection and what it means to her, the "tradition." This creates an intense solitude. A loneliness so gnawing that only a complete breakdown, a refusal, as it were, to contemplate what she's doing, a destruction of all standards, only a desperate violent ride on the streetcar named Desire can break through the walls of her tradition. Inevitably, the tragic flaw creates the circumstances that destroy her.

Consider the inner conflict. She needs a safe harbor, yet she cannot leave any man alone (why did this boy prefer a fairy to her—and everybody knew it—is there something wrong with her as a woman? No!) and furthermore, although her last hope for a safe harbor is her sister, still she cannot resist making a pass at her sister's husband. She can't help it. Just as she must prove she's a better girl than her sister. She can't leave any man alone. Each man is a challenge. She is so insecure as a woman. So she is doomed by her own inner contradiction. Her anxiety and its defense in action make it impossible for her to get what she needs most desperately.

A tragedy is where a character is doomed by the inevitable contradiction in her character. Blanche's character makes it impossible for her to achieve the one thing she wants and needs most in the world: a home and protection, and the support of another. Rather, and inevitably, she strives to accomplish her death. She is doomed in this society.

There is another simpler and equally terrible contradiction in her own nature. She can't face her physical or sensual side. She calls it "brutal desire." She thinks she sins when she gives in to it, yet she does give in to it, only from loneliness; but by calling it "brutal desire," she is able to separate it from her "real self," her "cultured, refined" self. Her tradition makes no allowance, allows no space for this very real part of herself. So she is constantly in conflict, not at ease, sinning. She's still looking for something that doesn't exist today, a Gentleman, who will treat her like a virgin, marry her, protect her, defend and maintain and establish her home. She wants an old-fashioned virgin-white wedding dress, and still she does things out of "brutal desire" that makes this impossible. All this too is Tradition.

She has worth too. She is better than Stella. She says, "There has been *some* progress since then! Such things as art—as poetry and music—such kinds of new light have come into the world since then!

In some kinds of people some tenderer feelings have had some little beginning! That we have to make *grow*! And *cling* to, and hold as our flag! In this dark march toward whatever it is we're approaching. . . . Don't—don't hang back with the brutes!" And though the direct psychological motivation for this is jealousy and personal frustrations, still she, alone and abandoned in the crude society of our Southern states today, is *the only voice of light. It is flickering and, in the course of this play, goes out.* But it is valuable because it is unique.

Blanche's history up to the moment the play opens: Blanche and Stella are members of the Southern landed aristocracy, brought up on the ladylike genteel standards of the cream of Southern society. Blanche was sheltered within the tradition, although all around her, her men folks were fucking their fortunes and lives away. They—her grandfathers, fathers, uncles, etc.—were already out of place, doomed. They held on to their standards and deeds, which their actual lives hardly corresponded to. The Southern aristocracy considered it their duty, their prerogative to safeguard art, music, tender feelings in the world. But the whole possibility of such a supported landed leisure class no longer existed. They were dead (as is Blanche). But wouldn't admit it till it overtook them. The tradition of Blanche's childhood upbringing then is that a girl should be raised to be pure and innocent, the center of culture in a man's world, delicate, a conversationalist, dewy-eyed, like E.E.T. [Kazan's mother-in-law], always a child, dependent on servants, wary of them, never soiling her lily white fingers, bred for idealistic love.

At the age of sixteen she fell in love with Allan Grey, a pure, poetic creature who married the purest and most innocent and unknowing girl he could find, in a desperate effort to save himself from a homosexuality that frightened and gradually overwhelmed him. Allan Grey came to Blanche for help. She didn't know how to give him any, or how to help anyone with any problem. Her upbringing, her techniques and standards, were those of helplessness and passivity. When the boy blew off the top of his head, she felt guilty for something she still didn't understand. So did the townspeople, who blamed her. The light went off in the world, never to go on again. Nothing in her education enabled her to assimilate this tragedy. She felt inadequate and despised as a woman.

There is a simple way to look at Blanche . . . the objective, superficial, town-view aspect that must be there also: the town lay who puts on airs. The airs are especially aggravating because they are more than skin deep and so so superior and even a little superior. Everyone, practically, who meets her wants to bring her down to a human level. Stanley does. He makes her as common as shit.

Blanche is not a whore. To a whore, a professional, love for a man and sex mean little. To Blanche, everything! She's hungry for it. But as Williams says, all that appears to be sex is not sex. The sex act proves to Blanche that she is a woman, that men need her, will protect her. The sex act is the opposite of alone-ness. Desire is the opposite of Death. And in the heart of the embrace, the constant obstacle, namely her need to be superior and special, is forgotten. She feels, if only for a moment, a completed woman.

The only thing she can do about her loneliness is to degrade herself.

The contradiction, the difficulty, is that while she's got to cling to someone, suck her strength from someone else's, still the demands of her "aristocratic" tradition are that she be superior to them. This too is the demand of her intelligence, sensitivity, superior nature. Mitch is the only person who fits the demands of this contradiction. His mother raised him to need, positively need, a dominant woman. He wants to be treated like a child ("slap me if I go too far"). But her past is chasing her, catching up with her.

You've got a "nice girl" playing Blanche. But there is no play if Blanche is a nice girl. The "sympathy" she gets finally must be earned . . . and complex. At the beginning Jessica Tandy must be presented as the villain, the troublemaker. . . . Blanche in first four scenes is, in effect, *destructing*.

Blanche is a stylized character, she should be played, should be dressed, should move like a stylized figure. What is the physicalization of an aristocratic woman pregnant with her own doom?

Blanche is the only *light* in the dark world around her. True, it is a wavering and feeble light, but it is the only one. It is sullied and soiled, complex and sick, but the only solution that Southern society can find for its challenge is to stamp it out, destroy it and dispose of it. Make the challenger disappear. The complexity can't be understood.

Blanche is a butterfly in a jungle looking for just a little momentary protection, doomed to a sudden, early violent death. The more I work on Blanche, incidentally, the less insane she seems. She is caught in a fatal inner contradiction, but in another society, she would work; in Stanley's society, no.

This is like a classic tragedy. Blanche is Medea or someone pursued by the Harpies, the Harpies being *her own nature.* Her inner sickness pursues her like *doom* and makes it impossible for her to attain the one thing she needs, the only thing she needs: a safe place.

An effort to phrase Blanche's spine: to find protection, to find something to hold on to, some strength in whose protection she can live, like a sucker shark or a parasite. The tradition of woman (or all women) can only live through the strength of someone else. Blanche is entirely dependent. Finally, the doctor!

Blanche is an outdated creature, approaching extinction, like the dinosaur. She is about to be pushed off the edge of the world. On the other hand, she is a heightened version, an artistic intensification, of all women. That is what makes the play universal. Blanche's special relation to all women is that she is at that critical point *where the one thing above all else that she is dependent on—her physical attractiveness, what men find appealing about her—is beginning to fade.* Blanche is like all women, dependent on a man, looking for someone to hang on to: *only more so!*

So beyond her frenzied desperation, Blanche is in a hurry. She carries her doom in her character. Is it any wonder that she tries to attract each and every man she meets? She'll even take that protected feeling, that needed feeling, that superior feeling, for a moment. Because, at least for a moment, her anxiety, hurt, and pain will be stilled. For a moment the anxiety is quieted, for a moment the complete desire and concentration of a man is on her. He clings to you. He may say I love you. All else is anxiety, loneliness, and being adrift.

Compelled by her nature (her need to be superior), she makes life with Stanley and Stella impossible. But there is a possible last bit of luck. She finds the only man on earth whom she suits. A man who is looking for a dominant woman. For an instant, she is happy. But Stanley, whom she's antagonized by her destructiveness, but especially by her need to be superior, uses her past to destroy her. Finally, she takes refuge in fantasy. The only place she can obtain peace is in her own mind. She "goes crazy."

Why does the "Blues" fit the play? The blue piano is an expression of the loneliness and rejection, the exclusion and isolation of the Negro and their longing for love and connection. Blanche too is "looking for a home," abandoned, friendless. "I don't know where I'm going, but I'm going." The blue piano catches the soul of Blanche, the miserable

A Streetcar Named Desire, set design by Jo Mielziner

unusual human side of the girl that underlies her frenetic duplicity, her lies. It tells, it emotionally reminds you, what all the fireworks are caused by.

Physically, Blanche must always present an unchanging impression: Her social mask is the High Bred Genteel Lady in Distress. Her past, her destiny, her falling from grace is just a surprise . . . then a tragic contradiction. But the mask never cracks.

The only way to understand any character is through yourself. Everyone is much more alike than they willingly admit. Even as frantic and fantastic a creature as Blanche is, she is made up of things you have felt and known, if you'll dig for them and are honest about what you see.

Stanley.
A kind of naïveté, even slowness. He means no harm. He wants to knock no one down. Only he doesn't want to be taken advantage of. His code is simple and simple-minded. He is adjusted—now. Later, as the power of his penis dies, so will he, the trouble will come later, the "problems."

But what's the chink in his armor now, the contradiction? Why does Blanche get so completely under his skin? Why does he want to bring Blanche, as he brought Stella, down to his level? It's as if he said: "I know I haven't got much, but no one has more and no one's going to have more." He's the hoodlum aristocrat, and he's deeply dissatisfied, deeply hopeless, deeply cynical. The physical immediate pleasures, if they come in a steady enough stream, quiet his resentments, as long as no one else gets more than he does. If they do, then his bitterness spills out and he trashes the pretender. But he can't seem to do anything with Blanche, so he levels her with his sex. He pulls her down and crushes her.

One of the important things about Stanley is that Blanche would wreck his home. Blanche is dangerous. She is destructive (like Stella Adler). Soon she would have him and Stella fighting. He's got the things the way he wants them around there, and he does not want them upset by a phony, corrupt, sick, destructive woman. *This makes Stanley right!* Are we going into the era of Stanley? He may be practical and right, but what the hell does it leave us? Make this a personal objective characterization for Marlon Brando. Choose Marlon's objects. The things he loves and prizes, all sensuous and sensual: the shirt, the cigar, the beer (how it's poured and nursed).

Stanley is exactly like you in some ways. He's supremely indifferent to everything except his own pleasure and comfort. He is marvelously selfish, a miracle of sensuous self-centeredness. He builds a hedonist life, and fights to the death to defend it—but finally it is not enough to hold Stella. And this philosophy is not successful even for him— because every once in a while the silenced, frustrated part of Stanley breaks loose in unexpected and unpredictable ways and we suddenly see, as in a burst of lightning, his real frustrated self. Usually his frustration is worked off by eating a lot, drinking a lot, gambling a lot, fornicating a lot. He's going to get very fat later. He's desperately trying to squeeze out happiness by living by *ball and jowl,* and it really doesn't work because it simply stores up violence until *every bar in the nation is full of Stanleys ready to explode.* He's desperately trying to drug his senses, overwhelming them with a constant round of sensation so that he will feel nothing else.

For Stanley sex goes under a disguise. Nothing is more erotic and arousing to him than "airs." "She thinks she's better than me. I'll show her." Sex equals domination, anything that challenges him—like calling him "common"—arouses him sexually.

In the case of Brando, the question of enjoyment is particularly important. Stanley feeds himself. His world is hedonistic. But what does he enjoy? Sex equals sadism. He conquers with his prick. But objects too: drink, conquest in poker, food, sweat, exercise. But enjoy. Not just cruelly unpleasant, but he never matured, never grew up from the baby who wants a constant nipple in his mouth. He yells when it is taken away.

Stanley has got things his way. He fits into his environment. The culture and the civilization, even the neighborhood, the food, the drink, etc., are all his way. And he's got a great girl, with just enough hidden neuroticism for him—yet not enough to threaten a real fight. Also, their history is right: He conquered her. Their relationship is right: She waits up for him. Finally, God and Nature gave him a fine sensory apparatus . . . he enjoys! The main thing the actor has to do in the early scenes is make the physical environment of Stanley, the *props,* come to life.

Stanley is deeply indifferent. When he first meets Blanche, he doesn't really seem to care if she stays or not. Stanley is interested in his own pleasures. He is completely self-absorbed to the point of fascination. To physicalize this: He has a most annoying way of being preoccupied—or of busying himself with something else while people are talking with him, at him it becomes. Example, first couple of pages, Scene Two.

Stanley thinks Stella is very badly brought up. She can't do any of the ordinary things—he had a girl before her who could really cook, but she drank an awful lot. Also she, Stella, has a lot of airs, most of which he's knocked out of her by now, but which still crop up. Emphasize Stanley's love for Stella. It is rough, embarrassed, and he rather truculently won't show it. But it is there. He's proud of her. When he's not on guard and looking at her, his eyes suddenly shine. He is grateful too, proud, satisfied. But he'd never show it, demonstrate it.

As a character, Stanley is most interesting in his contradictions. His soft moments, his sudden pathetic little tough boy tenderness toward Stella. In Scene Three he cries like a baby. Somewhere in Scene Eight he almost makes it up with Blanche. In Scene Ten he does try to make it up with her—and except for her doing the one thing that most arouses him, both in anger and sex, he might have.

The one thing that Stanley can't bear is someone who thinks that he or she is better than he is. His only way of explaining himself—he thinks he stinks—is that everyone else stinks. This is symbolic. True of our National State of Cynicism. No values. There is nothing to command his loyalty. Stanley rapes Blanche because he has tried and tried to keep her down to his level. This way is the last. For a moment he succeeds. And then in Scene Eleven, he has failed!

Stella.

Stella's *spine:* to hold on to Stanley. Blanche is the antagonist.

One reason Stella is perfectly ready to submit to Stanley's solution at the end is that she is unconsciously hostile toward Blanche. Blanche is so patronizing, demanding, and superior toward her, makes her feel so useless, old-fashioned, and helpless. Everything that Stanley has rid her of. Stanley has made her a woman. Blanche immediately returns her to childhood, to younger-sister-ness. *Stella would have been Blanche except for Stanley.* She now knows how much Stanley means to her health. So no matter what Stanley does, she must cling to him, as she does to life itself. To return to Blanche would be to return to the subjugation of the tradition.

The play is a triangle. Stella is the Apex. Unconsciously, Stella wants Blanche to go to Mitch because that will relieve her of Blanche.

And there is a terrific conflict between Blanche and Stella, especially in Stella's feelings. Blanche in effect in Scene One resubjugates Stella. Stella loves her, fears her, pities her, and is really through with her. Finally, Stella rejects Blanche for Stanley.

All this, of course, Stella is aware of only unconsciously. It becomes a matter of conscious choice only in Scene Eleven, the climax of the play, as it is the climax of the triangle story.

Stella is a refined girl who has found a kind of salvation or realization but at a terrific cost. She keeps her eyes closed, even stays in bed as much as possible so that she won't realize, won't feel the pain of the price she has paid. She walks around as if in a daze. She's waiting for the dark where Stanley makes her feel only him, and she has no reminder of what she has given up. She does not want the other world to intrude. She's in a sensual stupor. She shuts out all challenge all day long. She loafs, does her hair, her nails, fixes a dress, doesn't eat much, only prepares Stanley's dinner and waits for Stanley. She searches for no other meaning from life. Her pregnancy just makes it more so. She is buried alive in her flesh. She doesn't seem to see much. She laughs incessantly like a child tickled and stops abruptly as the stimuli, the tickling, stops, and returns to the condition of a pleasantly drugged child. Give her all kinds of narcotized business.

EDITOR: On the fourth day of rehearsals Tennessee Williams sent Kazan the following note, which Kazan incorporated into his notebook:

> Gadge. I am a bit concerned over Stella [Kim Hunter] in Scene One. It seems to me that she has too much vivacity; at times, she is bouncing around in a way that suggests a co-ed on a benzedrine kick. I know it is impossible to be literal about the description "narcotized tranquillity," but I do think there is an important value in suggesting it, in contrast to Blanche's rather feverish excitability. Blanche is the quick, light one. Stella is relatively slow and indo-lent. Blanche mentions her "Chinese philosophy"—the way she sits with her little hands folded like a cherub in the choir, etc. I think her natural passivity is one of the things that make her acceptance of Stanley understandable. She naturally "gives in," accepts, lets things slide, she does not make much of an effort.

She is in a paradise, a serene limited paradise, when Blanche enters— but Blanche makes her consider Stanley, judge Stanley and for the first time, she finds him wanting. But it is too late. In the end, she returns to Stanley.

Stella, like Blanche, is doomed. She has sold herself for a temporary solution. She's given up all hope, everything, just to live for Stanley's pleasures. So she is dependent on Stanley's least whim. But this can last only as long as Stanley wants her. And Stella cannot live this way for-ever. She begins to feel, even in the sex act, taken, unfulfilled—not rec-ognized, and besides, she's deeper, requires more variety from life. Her only hope is her children, and like so many women, she will begin to live more and more for her children.

She tries to conceal from herself her true needs through hiding her-self in a sex relationship. But her real needs—for tenderness, for the several aspects of living, for self-realization—still live, and she can't kill them by ignoring them. She hugs Stanley in Scene Four out of desper-ation and out of a need to silence her doubts by the violence of sexual love (the old reliable), but Blanche has succeeded in calling Stella's attention to her own "sell-out," and she can never see Stanley or their relationship in the same way again.

At the beginning of the play Stella won't face her hostility (con-cealed from herself and unrecognized) toward Stanley. She is so dependent on him, so compulsively compliant. She is giving up so much of herself, quieting so many voices of protest. Latent in Stella is rebellion, and Blanche arouses it.

Stella is plain out of her head about Stanley. She has to keep herself from constantly touching him. She can hardly keep her hands off him. She is setting little traps all the time to conquer his pretended indiffer-ence (he talks differently at night, in bed). She embarrasses him (though he is secretly proud) by following him places. They have a game where he tries to shake her all the time and she pursues him, etc. He makes her a panther in bed. He fulfilled her more than she knew possible, and she has to stop herself from crawling after him. She's utterly blind as to what's wrong with Stanley, and she doesn't care, until Blanche arrives. At the end of the play, her life is entirely different. It will never be the same with Stanley again.

Mitch.

Mitch's *spine:* to get away from his mother. Blanche is the lever.

He wants the perfection his mother gave him—everything is approving, protective, perfect for him. Naturally no girl today, no sen-sible, decent girl, will give him this. But the tradition will.

Like Stella, Mitch hides from his own problems through mother-love.

Mitch is the end product of a matriarchy. His mother has robbed him of all daring, initiative, self-reliance. He does not confront his own needs.

Mitch is Blanche's ideal in a comic form, 150 years late. He is big, tough, burly, has a rough Southern voice and a homespun manner. Coarse, awkward, overgrown boy, with a heart of mush. He's like that character (who cries easily) in *Sing Out, Sweet Land* [a musical Kazan directed without credit in 1944 that starred Burl Ives and Alfred Drake]. He is a little embarrassed by his strength in front of women. He is straight out of a Mack Sennett comedy—but [Karl] Malden [Mitch] has to create the reality of it, the truth behind the corny image. "Lennie" in *Of Mice and Men* [the tragic, simpleminded lug of John Steinbeck's short novel and play]. Against his blundering strength there is contrasted the fragility and fragrance of a girl. Her delicacy.

Mitch, too, is most interesting in his basic contradictions. He doesn't want to be Mother's boy. Goddammit, he just can't help it. He does love his mother but is a little embarrassed at how much. Blanche makes a man out of him, makes him important and grown-up. His mother—he dimly realizes—keeps him eternally adolescent, forever dependent.

Violence—he's full of sperm, energy, strength. The reason he's so clumsy with women is that he's so damn full of violent desire for them.

Mitch's mask: he-man mama's boy. This mask is a traditional, "corny" one in American dramatic literature. But it is true.

This play contains the crucial struggle of Mitch's life. Mitch instinctively, and even to a degree consciously, knows what's wrong with him. He is jibed at often enough. And in his guts he knows they're right. Mitch, in his guts, hates his mother. He loves her in a way—partially out of *early habit*, partially because she is clever—but much more fundamentally he *hates* her. It is a tragedy for him when he returns to her absolute sovereignty at the end. He will never meet another woman who will need him as much as Blanche and will also need him to be a man.

EDITOR

After seeing *All My Sons,* Tennessee Williams wanted only Elia Kazan for director of his new play, but Kazan's terms were stiff, and Williams's agent Audrey Wood and producer Irene Selznick threatened to begin negotiations elsewhere. (Candidates included film director John Huston and British director Tyrone Guthrie.) Also, Kazan had been reluctant at first and held off reading the play because "I wasn't sure Williams and I were the same kind of theatre animal" and he didn't want to compete with fellow director Joshua Logan, who had broadcast his enthusiasm. The more Kazan resisted, the more Williams became convinced this was the man *Streetcar* needed. Fearing that Kazan's hesitancy might involve doubts about the script, Williams sent Kazan a private letter, dated April 19, 1947, that gave Kazan the key to the production:

> I will try to clarify my intentions in this play. I think its best quality is its authenticity or its fidelity to life. There are no "good" or "bad" people. Some are a little better or a little worse but all are activated more by misunderstanding than malice. A blindness to what is going on in each other's hearts. Stanley sees Blanche not as a desperate, driven creature backed into a last corner to make a last desperate stand—but as a calculating bitch with "round heels." Mitch accepts first her own false projection of herself as a refined young virgin, saving herself for the one eventual mate—then jumps way over to Stanley's conception of her. Nobody sees anybody truly, but all through the flaws of their own ego. That is the way we all see each other in life. Vanity, fear, desire, competition—all such distortions within our own egos—condition our vision of those in relation to us. Add to those distortions in our own egos, the corresponding distortions in the egos of the others—and you see how cloudy the glass must become through which we look at each other. . . . I remember you asked me what should an audience feel for Blanche. Certainly pity. It is a tragedy with the classic aim of producing a catharsis of pity and terror, and in order to do that Blanche must finally have the understanding and compassion of the audience. This without creating a black-dyed villain in Stanley. It is a thing (misunderstanding) not a person (Stanley) that destroys her in the end. In the end you should feel—"If only they all had known about each other!"—But there was always the paper lantern or the naked bulb!

Kazan began preparations for *Streetcar* in the late spring of 1947 while directing the film *Gentleman's Agreement* in California. His first tasks were a rabbinical, meticulous study of the script and, of prime importance, a tunneling out the personal consequences for him of the theme and an exploration of the similarities between his background and personality and that of the characters—that is, to find the character basis within himself. He strove to make himself one with the play, and without this integration of self and play, he could not proceed with assurance. (This grasp would elude him on the next Williams play he directed, *Camino Real*.)

Preferred candidates for the roles of Blanche and Stanley were the film stars Margaret Sullavan and John Garfield, but Williams and Kazan found Sullavan's reading mild-mannered and pedestrian; and Garfield would sign for six months only and demanded a guarantee that he would play Stanley in any eventual film version. Hume Cronyn, Jessica Tandy's husband, urged Kazan and producer Irene Selznick while in Los Angeles to see Tandy in a local production of Tennessee Williams's one-act *Portrait of a Madonna*, whose central figure was a semidraft for the character of Blanche. After the performance everyone knew that their Blanche had been found. "Here she was, we all agreed, in a leap of relief and gratitude," said Kazan.

In the mid-1940s Marlon Brando had been acclaimed as one of Broadway's most promising young actors, winning a Donaldson Award for Best Supporting Performance for a brief scene in *Truckline Café*. He had earlier received positive notice in the sentimental play *I Remember Mama*, and as Marchbanks opposite Katharine Cornell in George Bernard Shaw's *Candida*. During the pre-Broadway tryouts of a calamitous production of Jean Cocteau's *The Eagle Had Two Heads*, Tallulah Bankhead had had him fired. This probably ingratiated him with Kazan, who spoke of Bankhead as the only actor he had ever hated.

By all accounts, Brando astounded everyone at his first reading. When Kazan sent him off to read for Williams in Provincetown, Massachusetts, Brando famously pocketed the bus fare and hitchhiked. After Brando read for him, Williams wrote his agent, Audrey Wood, of Brando's fitness for the part:

> I can't tell you what a relief it is that we have found such a God-sent Stanley in the person of Brando. It had not occurred to me before what an excellent value would come through casting a very young actor in this part. It humanizes the character of Stanley in that it becomes the brutality or callousness of youth rather than a vicious older man. I don't want to focus guilt or blame particularly on any one character but to have it a tragedy of misunderstandings and insensitivity to others. A new value came out of Brando's reading, which was by far the best reading I have ever heard. He seemed to have already created a dimensional character, of the sort that the war has produced among young veterans.

Some critics (among them Harold Clurman; see pages 66–67.) thought that Williams reconceived Stanley to conform him to Brando's charisma. However, Brando's performance, a triumphant fulfillment of the Stanislavsky-based method, redefined and set a still-continuing standard for American acting.

In *Great Directors at Work* David Richard Jones exhaustively compared the first version of the script; the stage manager's prompt book, published as the Acting Version; Williams's published version; and the screenplay. In addition to "adjusting rhythm, emotion and texture by changing mood, speed, brightness, and loudness" and inventing stage action (an offstage mugging and pursuit), Kazan, according to Jones, "revised *Streetcar* substantially. . . . He reworded hundreds of speeches, though he often did little more than change 'Now let's cut the rebop' to 'All right! How about cutting the rebop.' A few scenes, especially scenes 5 and 9, he rewrote almost entirely between first rehearsal and opening night."

Brenda Murphy describes another famed production element. Kazan and Mielziner designed a steady beam of light (a follow spot), a halo of subjectivity, to focus on Blanche throughout the play "in either blue or amber, depending on whether the light supposedly derived from daylight, moonlight, or candlelight." It isolated Blanche from the other characters and from the action, suggesting her increasing panic and inability to separate fantasy from reality.

Kazan and
Tennessee
Williams

Karl Malden, who had previously been directed by Kazan in *All My Sons* and the film *Boomerang!*, played Mitch in both the stage and film versions of *Streetcar.* He recalled Kazan's precise care and molding of each moment, his acute sense of making the actor embody word and gesture with reverberant implication. Malden worried over giving dramatic heft to Mitch's reply to Blanche's question about his mother, "You love her very much, don't you?" Mitch struggles with his admission, the monosyllable "Yes."

> Now, the first week of rehearsal I couldn't do anything with that, it was a nothing line. And one day I'm going through it again when I look up and see Gadg pull the most terrible teeth-gnashing face. I said, "What's the matter?" And he said, "Did you watch me? That's how you should feel when you say that line. Because you hate your bloody mother. Sure, you have to say you love her—you even have to think you do. But deep inside you know she's got a double nelson on all your emotions and she's the reason you can't develop and mature."
>
> As soon as I understood that, I'd licked not only the line but the whole character. He didn't bawl me out like a great director because my approach was wrong. He just pulled a funny face like a buddy with a sense of humor giving me a tip.

In his introduction to the 2004 edition of *A Streetcar Named Desire*, Arthur Miller remembered the revelation of new genius when he saw the play in New Haven before its Broadway opening.

> It took only a few minutes to realize that the play and production had thrown open doors to another theatre world. . . . A writer's soul, a single voice was almost miraculously enveloping the stage. But remarkably, each character's speech seemed at the same time uncannily his own, they seemed free to declare their contradictory selves rather than being harnessed to the play's story-telling needs. But at the same time that story marched inexorably forward, shaped as it was by Kazan's hand and a cast that was nothing short of superb. In fact, this production was the fullest bloom of the vanished Group Theatre's intense, decade-long investigation into the Stanislavski Method; it was a form of realism so deeply felt as to emerge as a stylization. . . . Along with Williams the other great revelation of the performance was of course Brando, a tiger on the loose, a sexual terrorist. Nobody had seen anything like him before because that kind of freedom on the stage had not existed before. He roared out Williams' celebratory terror of sex, its awful truthfulness and its inexorable judgments, and did so with an authority

that swept everything before it, Brando was a brute but he bore the truth. . . . The play cannot be disparaged, but this production, like few others of any play I ever saw, *became the play*, it was impossible to separate them, the cast had left themselves behind, became the characters. . . . And it was the good fortune of play and playwright to have been guided by a Kazan who understood the New York audience and kept intact the play's link with the familiar realistic tradition while allowing its language free play.

A year later Miller incorporated many of *Streetcar*'s stage devices—the lead character's confusion of reality, memory, and delusion, the diaphanous sets, the heightened poetic language—into his masterwork, *Death of a Salesman*, also directed by Kazan.

Not everyone was enthusiastic about the play or the production. Some responses were like Blanche's to Stanley—a panicked need to fight off the sexy beast, to fend off an attraction that threatened to overwhelm their finer instincts. On the right, many thought the play sensational and disgusting: sex was rampant, Marlon Brando in a torn T-shirt raped the heroine onstage and slapped his wife who moaned for sex. It was a dirty play, right up there with the recent Broadway scandals about ladies of the night, Jean-Paul Sartre's *The Respectful Prostitute* and Philip Yordan's *Anna Lucasta*. Naturally, this made it Box Office. But this time it was the loudmouth with the biceps who was the scandal.

On the left was the criticism that the play's dreamy production disguised a crude social drama of the destruction of the genteel old South by an immigrant "Polack." Mary McCarthy, in *Partisan Review*, found it a pack of pretensions, missing the better chance to be a soap opera comedy about hogging the bathroom: "If art, as Mr. Williams appears to believe, is a lie, then anything goes, but Mr. Williams' lies, like Blanche's, are so old and shopworn that the very truth upon which he rests them becomes garish and ugly, just as the Kowalskis' apartment becomes the more squalid for Blanche's attempts at decoration."

The two reviews of greatest interest to Kazan were from Eric Bentley (critic, teacher, and translator of Bertolt Brecht) and from Kazan's old mentor, colleague, former partner, and persistent competitor, Harold Clurman. Bentley thought Brando "quite wrong for the part. Brando has muscular arms but his eyes give them the lie. . . . Presumably Kazan must take some of the responsibility for the changes made when the play went into production. Was he trying to make it more sensational? The early audiences, one recalls, fairly licked their chops over the sexiness of the play."

Clurman's assessment of the play and Kazan's direction was more pernicious; the subjects appear to be Williams and the actors, but the target is Kazan.

In *Streetcar* all the actors are good, but their performances do not truly convey Tennessee Williams' play. By virtue of its power and completeness the play pretty nearly succeeds in acting the actors, but the nature of the play's reception indicates a prevailing sentiment of excitement and glowing enthusiasm dissociated from any specific meaning.

Jessica Tandy's Blanche suffers from the actress's narrow emotional range. One of the greatest parts ever written for a woman in the American theatre, it demands the fullness and variety of an orchestra. Miss Tandy's register is that of a violin's A string. . . . When Blanche appeals to her sister in the name of these values (yearning for tenderness and the desire to reach beyond one's personal appetites) Miss Tandy is unable to make it clear whether she means what she says and whether we are supposed to attach any importance to her speech or whether she is merely spinning another fantasy. . . . Through [Marlon Brando's] own intense concentration on what he is thinking or doing at each moment he is on the stage, all our attention focuses on him. Brando's quality is one of acute sensitivity. None of the brutishness of the part is native to him: it is a characteristic he has to "invent." The combination of an intense, introspective, and almost lyric personality under the mask of a bully endows the character with something almost touchingly painful. . . . For what is Stanley Kowalski? He is the embodiment of animal force, of brute life unconcerned and even consciously scornful of every value that does not come within the scope of his life. . . . The play becomes the triumph of Stanley Kowalski with the collusion of the audience, which is no longer on the side of the angels. This is natural because Miss Tandy is fragile without being touching (except when the author is beyond being overpowered by an actress), and Mr. Brando is tough without being irredeemably coarse.

By way of challenge and argument, Kazan invited Clurman to direct the Chicago company of *Streetcar*, headed by Uta Hagen and Anthony Quinn (understudied by Jack Palance). "There you go, Harold; come on, get it on, do it your way, let's see," said Kazan. And Kazan found what he expected at a rehearsal. In his autobiography, Kazan summed up the difference in their approaches, insinuating that Clurman was a liberal sentimentalist:

Tennessee in this version became the poet of frustration and his play said that "aspiration, sensitivity, departure from the norm are battered, bruised and disgraced in our world today." Those are Harold's words and his belief, and they accurately describe the effect of what I saw on stage. Since all of us in the Group Theatre thought of ourselves, at the time we were banded together, as aspiring, sensitive, and departing from society's norm, wasn't this mode of thinking self-favoring, even self-pitying? What I saw recalled our old wishful thinking in the thirties, the belief that the good and the true in our time were inevitably taken advantage of by the villains of capitalism and money corruption—an idea I now believe to be sentimental malarkey. The play, with Harold, had become a moral fable, presenting the people we believed ourselves to be, with ethical values so clear and so simple that the audience could not doubt where the sympathies and allegiances should be placed. . . .

Was my conception of *Streetcar* what Harold declared it to be—"unresolved"? The answer is yes. Life is a puzzle, unresolved, and as we enter it, no one is there to hand us a book of instructions, the kind you get when you buy a new car. And "thematically disruptive"? Yes to that too, Harold. I wanted to thwart an audience, not flatter them by too quickly and too easily admitting them to the company of "angels." That elevation they should have to struggle to reach.

Death of a Salesman (1949)
by Arthur Miller

"Of all the plays I have directed, Death of a Salesman *is my favorite."*

EDITOR: The action of the play shifts between sometime in the late 1940s—shortly after the end of World War II—and fifteen years before. Often the two periods interweave, the past actions reflecting the movement of the protagonist's obsessions, memories, and fantasies.

Traveling salesman Willy Loman, in his early sixties, returns to his small Brooklyn home late at night after suffering terrifying losses of concentration while driving to Boston on a selling trip. He has only narrowly avoided fatal accidents, for some inner compulsion and vaguely formulated solution to the dilemma of his existence is moving him to suicide. Distracted, tormented, and agonizingly depressed, Willy is unable to control his thoughts, imagining himself in the past, often talking aloud to those who inhabit his memories.

He is now paid sales commission only, and the present owner of his firm, Howard, the son of the man who had hired Willy many years before, wants to be rid of him, refusing to give the exhausted Willy a job in the New York office.

His wife, Linda, fusses over him, trying to assure him that all will work out. Later she defends him against his son's contempt: "Willy Loman never made a lot of money. His name was never in the paper. He's not the finest character that ever lived. But he's a human being and a terrible thing is happening to him. So attention must be paid. He's not to be allowed to fall into his grave like an old dog. Attention, attention must be finally paid to such a person."

In a room above, their two sons, Biff and Hap, overhear their parents' conversations. Biff, now in his early thirties, has just returned from an itinerant, pointless existence out west, and Hap, who has an apartment nearby, has come home to spend time with his older brother.

Willy is struggling to find the reason why, and the moment when, his life took a wrong turn, why everything he tried to accomplish failed, and why his elder son, his "golden boy," who seemed destined for a triumphant life, has achieved nothing.

He reexamines the time of Biff's senior high school year. When Biff failed his math final and refused to go to summer school to retake the course, he threw away the chance of a college football scholarship. Since then Biff's life has been a miasma of lost ambition and unsure goals, lacking substantial identity. He has become a compulsive petty thief, as if thievery were a way of pacifying his panic, of grabbing what life has denied him.

Biff and Hap plot a senseless scheme to sell sports equipment with the backing of someone who had once employed Biff as a clerk—and from whom Biff had stolen some goods years before. Biff's rejection by his former employer, who barely remembers him, forces him to face the insubstantial and baseless goals of his life (dreams of building success on being "well liked," of beating the competition, the corrupt ideals of his father) and compels him to force his father to recognize that all the hopes Willy had for his son were insidious delusions.

The decisively destructive moment in the past was Biff's discovery of his father with a strange woman in a Boston hotel room. For Biff, this act represented the betrayal of his mother and caused the collapse of his hero worship of his father.

At the end of the play Willy's solution to the terror of his existence is to commit suicide, trusting that his life insurance money will fund his son's future. Hoping that his death will appear accidental, he crashes his car.

FROM THE NOTEBOOK

SEPTEMBER 1948

The play is about Willy Loman.

It is a tragedy, in a classic style, with the drive of an inner inevitability that springs from a single fatal flaw. Willy is a good man, he has worth, but he is a salesman with a salesman's philosophy. Therefore, he dooms himself.

This is a love story, the end of a tragic love story between Willy and Biff. He builds his life on his son, but he taught the son wrong. The result: The son crashes and he with him. Without Willy loving Biff and Biff loving Willy, there is no conflict. The whole play is about love, love and competition. The boy loves him. The only way Willy can give anything back is through $20,000 [the insurance money Biff will receive on Willy's death].

Directing: You = Willy = All people. These people are not aware. What the audience should feel at the end of the performance is: pity, compassion, and terror for Willy. Every dramatic value should serve this end. (Your feeling for your own father!) This Willy is a fine, tender, capable, potentially useful human. He's just socially mistaught.

It is essential to highly contrast the behavior and confidence of Willy and the Boys "before and after." Cause and effect. Thus you can make very clear what happened. Why it is Social versus Nature: i.e., it is happening all over!

It is essential to transfer your emotional feeling through the play to Willy. Find Willy in you. It is the portrait of the fall of a man, at the crash-end of a tragic love affair with his son Biff and what leads up to his suicide (in terms of inner emotional events).

It is essential to find Willy in you. You'll never do this play by mechanical direction, or by "forcing the energy," or pounding as you have been doing lately (*Sundown Beach* and home life)—where a scene hasn't seemed "effective" you have "pushed."

Now in this play all movement must come from *character* impulses. No crosses, etc. Martin Ritt in *Set My People Free* gave a horrible example of Kazan direction at its emptiest: clean crosses and pound pound pound. <u>WITH ENERGY SUBSTITUTED FOR EMOTION.</u> General energy instead of particular emotion.

This play has a line that is all down the inside of Willy's spine. This man goes crazy right before your eyes and commits suicide, and Miller shows you the logic behind the "insane" act. You have to find this line in you.

For instance, when Art [Arthur Miller] said, if this man is doing one thing and the person across from him is doing the opposite (ex., Willy is talking, the other person maintaining a silence), Willy will suddenly change his behavior and do what the other person is doing ("the trouble with me is I talk too much!"). That is how insecure he is. He is swimming in guilt like you, completely uncertain like you; like you, he is completely uncertain; like you, with no real anchor, needing constant love as reassurance therefore unreliable because he will finally accept it from any quarter.

You can have simultaneous action quite often. Overlap all scenes. Stay "ahead" of the audience.

Follow Willy's internal line. A man finally gains his objective through killing himself. *Subjective* is the word. He has to be directed from the point of view of what *happens* in Willy's head. The inner impulse and the emotions that lead to those impulses. The things he suspects, imagines, makes up, his defenses.

This play takes place as an arena of people watching the events, sometimes internal and invisible, other times external and visible, and sometimes *both*. The world is the world of Willy and the way he sees it. In the end, it is completely in his world. His eyes glaze over as he seems to be talking to them, but he is really talking within his own mind. The people watching have an emotional relation to Willy, trying to reach out to him. But by the end of the play, there is no one there for him to reach out to. He is living entirely within himself; the people watching this spectacle are horrified. The man simply isn't with them anymore.

The You in Willy, the guilt, the uncertainty, the constant need of an atmosphere of approval and love at all costs. The turning on people violently and then crawling to regain their love. The need for success, that approval too.

The opposition in the two opposing emotions. The need to be pre-eminent versus the need to be loved and together.

Stylize the action of the flashbacks. Sudden vivid moments caught at peaks of high intensity, the way people are caught in a dream.

Make a ballet of it. Theatricalize it! Don't, for chrissake, be afraid. Make a piece of theatre out of it! It must have the vividness of an OPPRESSIVE NIGHTMARE!

In such a nightmare or even an ordinary dream there is an insistent or repetitive quality to certain of the details—which are the significant details—the whole scene of each of these flashbacks can be built around the insistent repetitions of a detail; for example, Linda with the wash basket and the stocking trailing out of one pocket.

This play has to be directed with COMPASSION, which simply means with a quick and intense realization of the PAIN of each of the characters and the true import of the SPINE, its living or emotional consequence.

But the director, as he directs from day to day, as he lives and grows with the actors on stage from day to day, must have his heart filled with COMPASSION, a fellow feeling, an empathy, a projection for and into the PAIN of each character.

1. Willy: guilt and shame, defeat, abandonment and humiliation. HE HAS FAILED. George Kazan Sr. Spine: He must win out finally, because he is too proud to admit his defeat.
2. Biff too—his pain, bewilderment and disgust with himself. This poor bastard hates himself, would destroy himself. Through this very hating of himself, because of it, the pain of it, he is ready to face who he is, find out who he is! This is the first step toward truth and help.
3. Hap: pain: the excluded. The stepson, the greatest danger with

this character is to direct him externally and get a "characteriza-tion" effect. But the job is to feel out how the things he does, false and outlandish, come from his pain, from his life-long rejection. This poor miserable bastard is compelled to be some-thing he won't like when he achieves it. IF! But he is consumed with the desire to make the grade, which is, translated, match someone else's standard.

4. Linda wants the nice normal things and in a sense has them! She has a husband she loves desperately. She has two fine sons. But there is something, something, she really doesn't under-stand that is killing her husband before her very eyes. Since it is within him, she can't fix it, discover it, ever realize quite what it is. Her mortal enemy is living within Willy. It is one half Willy's philosophy. So she is fighting an invisible, intangible, increas-ingly powerful enemy within her husband, and this enemy is killing him. Her life is to protect Willy.

Willy.

5. His fatal error (this is an "inevitable tragedy," our Greek tragedy) is that he built his life and his sense of self-worth on something completely false: the Opinion of Others. This is the error of our whole capitalist system—we build our sense of worth not within but in our besting others and at the same time having their constant approval. A boy, Biff, must be both pre-eminent and still adored, conquering all and still loved by all. What an impossibility!

6. Consequently, he both hates and loves the same people and can neither really love or really hate anyone. If they perfectly approve of him, they are great. If, on some issue, they don't, they are his enemies. But completely, like Bob Lewis [director and teacher]. They are sudden complete shits. Suddenly he'll fall in love with someone, but this is meaningless, since it is nothing more than the expression of his need for their love. Or he'll suddenly hate. This too is meaningless!

7. A personality, for Willy, is that magical thing which some people are born with, and which makes them both pre-eminent, best-ing all others, and still liked.

8. Even his relationship to his children was based on their perfect, unquestioning approval of him. On this basis, he loved them. When they stopped adoring him, he hated them. In the early

scenes Biff and Hap *worship the old man.* They are merely extensions, tools for self-worship, of his ego, When they grew up, they found they have been raised with only one point, to win their father's praise. When this didn't work, they hated their father, and he them.

9. A person "talks to himself"; in this case, has imaginary conversations with other people because of some *compulsive* reason. Usually, to defend himself, reenact some scene to prove himself, to attack someone that he failed to defend himself against properly in the real world. The *action* behind each of these imaginary conversations should be found.

10. Compare George Kazan [Kazan's father]; human potential for love and friendship (remember the warm old days at Atesh farms, consider how he does the shish kabob) and the business side of him. How much less of a man that makes him. Walter Fried [producer] ditto, vainly trying to be something he's not and how this eviscerates and disfigures him. Still, he has real talent for human love, and this charming side of him is aborted and crushed by his own efforts to live by the competitive principle.

And the horrible things Willy Loman taught his children.

The philosophy of Aggression, Competition, and Pre-eminence. "You are loved only if you are successful," which kills, and this is the central philosophy of our Civilization.

Another similarity to you: He finds "criticism" where none is intended. He sees imputation of guilt where none is intended. So he is constantly defending himself where there is no attack. He is drowning in guilt, and at the same time he attacks Linda. He wants her absolute and uncritical love: "You do love me completely and still uncritically, don't you, even though I have just been slamming hell out of you?"

Biff and Willy.
Bound in love. They are each other's shame. (They are the worst of themselves by what terrible things they see much more clearly in each other.) Biff especially is embarrassed constantly by what terrible things he learns about himself by looking at his father. It's terrifying. That's what Biff means when he says he can't look him in the face.

None of the dream figures are in the past. They are as much in the present. They are as Willy needs to think of them for reasons of personal dignity, self-esteem, etc.

Linda in the past is a figure fashioned out of Willy's guilt. Hardworking, sweet, always true, admiring. "I shouldn't cheat on a woman like that. Dumb, Slaving, Loyal. Tender, Innocent." In reality, she is much much tougher. She has consciously made her peace with her fate. She has chosen Willy! Fuck everyone else. She is terrifyingly tough. Why? She senses Willy is in danger. And she just can't have him hurt.

FROM SCRIPT NOTES

In the first scene, Willy tells Linda in thorough detail exactly what happens in a car—or later with Howard. He gets so compelled, passionate, and involved that he loses himself and gets terribly frightened that he has lost the source of love he so badly needs and so he crawls back and begs for it!

Linda has unconsciously been expecting a suicide—in a rush to make sure nothing is wrong. Last time it was an Accident.

Boys' scene:
Premise: They are together. Love each other. They are not aware that each has changed. That things are completely different. That is the dramatic discovery of the scene.

Biff is fighting out loud the same old battle that he's been shadow-boxing for months, years. He is stuck in a rut of bewilderment. And he can't get rid of it because he doesn't know who he is, where he is, what he wants. His father has really fucked him up. He can't accept who he is because it conflicts with his father's idea of Pre-eminence.

Hap has a simple aim: to get Biff to stay home. The truth is he approaches it with the techniques of a Salesman—since he is one—by winning the confidence of the Customer. Selling his personality, getting on the same side, and then giving him the old harpoon fast.

Resolution: So it takes Biff time to discover that Hap is "taking" him, that Hap is different, that he no longer feels close to Hap and that it's over between them.

Willy at the refrigerator: In the first fantasy sequence the PLOT DEVELOPMENT is that Willy faces the question: Was it my fault? Did I louse up my son? That is why he brings Ben back. For the first time he faces the question or the challenge: "It was your fault Willy!" "You ruined Biff." The scene should have a Stylized Unity, which is based on Insistent Detail.

The Woman: The women he had met on the road he remembers in the way most flattering to him: Crazy about him! Cute, pretty, so proper! Whoever would have thought she was laying him? But boy was she sexy, and she couldn't wait to have him again!! And yet the joke, the wonderful joke, she looked so well mannered, neat, clean.

EDITOR: Some months after the opening Kazan was displeased with the performances. He sent a letter specifying his complaints to the four leading members of the cast: Lee J. Cobb, Mildred Dunnock, Arthur Kennedy, and Cameron Mitchell.

People ask me how a performance can be kept up. It can only be kept up in one way: by being made better. There is still plenty to do on this show and on your performances. You are an exceptionally fine company, sincere and well-meaning. I can see that you have all been thinking about your parts. And there have been changes made. But the changes are not for the good. And I have to say something about each one of you, and then next week I will have some rehearsals to see if we can really get the show firmly on the right track.

You gather I was disappointed in what I saw last night.

But first I want to say something about the show as a whole. There is a quality gone out of the show, and that is a central one, an intangible one, and one that is hard to keep up, and one that cannot be faked. The play is about a family. A family, at its most simple, is a group of people bound together not only in a tie of blood. That is not the important thing. The important thing is the tie of LOVE. That is what makes it a family. And when a family is torn apart by dissension and conflict, what is being lost is the most precious thing, the love of these people for each other. That is what is in jeopardy, nothing else. A bitter argument on a street between two men is an object of only passing concern. But if you know about these people, know they are bound together in a bond of love, and above all if you feel, even while they're quarreling, that they really and deeply love each other; well, then something is at stake there that concerns and interests every single human.

This is what I felt absent last night on the stage. The play, to begin with, got off to a most unfortunate start. You will forgive me if I'm blunt. Something has died that existed between Lee [Lee J. Cobb, as Willy] and Milly [Mildred Dunnock, as Linda], and something central has gone out of that relationship. It is absurd of a director to say that he doesn't care what your relationship is off the stage. I do care. It shows on stage. What there is now are two very accomplished actors. We do not see a man and wife.

The impression I had was that the main feeling Lee had was one of annoyance with Milly, and that the main feeling Milly had was a stalwart kind of being on guard: the result for her being a clear, crisp, bright, and thoroughly professional exterior, like a good simonizing job, not a scratch on it.

I have no intention of going way back to fundamentals. You are as intelligent a group of actors as a director could be thankful for. And you can remember what I stressed originally, and you can work together to get it back. You have an obligation to each other—you can only be good *together,* remember that—and of course, you have an obligation to the play and to me which I don't need to stress.

But let me say one fundamental thing. The main thing you have to create, each of you, in that first scene is something that you have to create not on stage but off stage, before you come on. Milly, for instance, is a woman who has alone carried the pain and the weariness and the discouragement of a lifetime with Willy: She is worn to the hub [nub?]. Physically exhausted and carrying on on nerve alone. She wouldn't ever show this to Willy, and this makes her more and more tired. Above all, she is frightened to death. The central fact is that she loves him and that from day to day she expects his suicide, news of his death. She would never show this to him, or show pity to him, and this makes her tired, too. She is holding on, waiting for a disaster that is sure to come. What happens now is that we have a charming, successful, and thoroughly professional performance, one that she knows is good. Much of the play is being played as if you know it's good. It's not nearly as naked and disarmed as it was.

And Willy, too, when he comes in, should enter as if from a nightmare. He is not just annoyed at Milly for asking questions he considers silly. That is a color, a secondary color. He too has frightened himself to death, as he realizes that he's unconsciously trying to kill himself. He's shaken. He is old. He is thoroughly and completely depleted. Lee Cobb is a man in excellent health, at the top of his career and his personal powers. You simply have to do a tremendous job—more, much more than you can possibly realize before you can show yourself on stage and dare to pretend that you are Willy Loman. And when you're there in the room with your wife, you do not, I mean you should not, talk to her. There should be very little awareness of her as someone who loves you utterly and without qualification and who spells home to you. And when you growl at her a bit and contradict her a bit, that is home too, for a wife means among other things someone to grouse at freely.

Now I have taken the liberty of using Milly and Lee as examples to expand upon, but I don't feel Howard loves Willy as much as he did, and I don't feel Johnny Kennedy [Arthur Kennedy, as Biff] adores him the way he used to, and I don't feel that Tom Pedi [as Stanley] hero-worships Cameron Mitchell [as Happy], and all in all you seemed last night like a company of Equity actors, and goddamn it, the soul has gone out of this show.

I tried during rehearsals to give each one of you a single hook to kind of hang on to. For instance, with Milly I said it was to protect Willy. That's all she's doing. It's as if her husband was dying of cancer and god-damn it, she was going to protect him from any least possible injury and insult. She was going to protect him. That's a different thing from protecting herself, or putting her sons in their place. For instance, the point of the brightness at the beginning of Act Two is to send Willy off full of confidence so that he can knock Howard for a loop. She is not bright, doesn't feel right. It is all for Willy's sake. And withal, this woman who is protecting Willy, with her life and what is left of her body, is worn out; she is a little mouse of a woman. She is not capable of big scenes. Until the last couple of years she never raised her voice in the house. The interesting part of it is that Milly is better than she was in the young parts because those qualities she has gained from the deserved acclaim her performance has received, her confidence in her-self, her very right pleasure with herself, and her general rested state all contribute to a new excellence in the younger scenes but have a bad effect in the main ones.

And speaking again of the little handles I tried to give each of you, mottos as it were that you can hang on to (spines we used to call them), I told Lee that he was trying to win out. That he was a proud person and that he was finally successful: He won out. The man is not aware of his own pain, and above all he is not aware of his own significance or of the significance of his pain. Now there is a subtly intruded but finally a vast difference in his performance. This man last night suffered and was aware of it. He took time for it. Willy is much more naïve, and he always fights back. Willy never feels sorry for himself. He always fights back, if it's only by blaming someone else. The character is always more naïve. He is in fact childish. We watch him with wonder because, despite every reasonable conclusion he might draw from events, he goes on

Arthur Kennedy, Lee J. Cobb, and Mildred Dunnock

behaving the same way. The best example is: "That boy is going to be magnificent." Nothing has penetrated. Nothing ever penetrates. He is bound to win out, and he does. He never thinks of himself as wrong. He is not as smart as Lee, nor as subtle, nor as aware, nor as understanding. He is dumb, almost blind. He is an energy, a force. He is unbalanced. He is crazy, to put it on one final, all-inclusive word. When he tries to convince Biff in the restaurant scene that Oliver greeted him warmly and so forth, he is not being tricky, the poor son of a bitch believes it, and he does it with full-hearted giving of himself. He forces Biff to quaver and waver and finally begins to say things that didn't happen. Biff, a young strong man, is thrown off the line of the truth that he is desperately clinging to by Willy's force. There is nothing subtle about this force. It brooks no denial. A man has to bow to it. It is insane.

And just to cite another example of Willy's insanity, for that's what it amounts to—there is no point in thinking of him as rational, because that leads to rational behavior on stage, and Willy's behavior does not bear a true correspondence to the causes we see. In the Boston hotel room a sensible man would simply admit to his son what his son just saw with his own two eyes. But our friend Willy tries to carry it off. He tries his briskness, he calls on his palsy relationship with his son, and only when this fails does he get down on his knees and hug his son and beg his understanding based on their love. And as the boy leaves the room, he is calling after him, not taking pauses to suffer, but calling after him, trying to order him now (as insane an act as possible), and he is never aware of his own position. He doesn't in fact know where he is until Stanley the waiter comes in. He is lost in his own desire to go back through fantasy into the crucial scene in his life and to make right that terrible thing with his son. He is lost in this desire. He is not lost in his own grief for himself. He has no awareness of himself. And when Stanley comes in, he is nothing but shocked. He tries to pull himself together and finally does so through the seeds! [Willy tells Stanley the waiter that he is looking for a store where he can buy plant seeds.]

Willy is unaware. Willy is insane. Willy is naïve. And Willy is always trying to win out. That's it in a nutshell.

And now about Johnny Kennedy. You have kept the form of your performance better than anyone else. But the intensity of your performance is on a level that sometimes is too low for me. For you really have me and my taste to deal with. It gets down to that. So let's admit it. I'm aware that there were certain commentators, and one extremely able one, who commented that they thought your performance was overwrought. Well, I liked it. I thought it helped put the play over, but that isn't the main thing. It corresponded to the way life seems to me, as I have seen young men, my brothers, strangers in corresponding crises. I don't know whether these same critics wouldn't draw back a little. And as for the one [it was Harold Clurman] who made the point about you—I have heard him give louder performances in private life with less cause.

But if you feel more comfortable not taking everything at full bent the way I had you, that's up to you. You're doing the right things and you've kept the main outlines of your performance. For me, it's lost its thrilling edge, the feeling it had that here was a man who had been through hell, who had been really kicked around, tried everything, met defeat many times, never found his way, and had a real thorn in the side of his soul that he was now making a last desperate effort to pluck out. I gave you, Johnny, a rather scholarly and unphysical spine. I said you were going to find out who you were, and face it. But again here the start of the character is so important. Remember in Hollywood when we first talked about the part, I told you there was something gangsterish about the first view we had of him, and by that I meant something dangerous, mean, disappointed, not to be crossed, a jailbird, a man of great inner torture. Well, all this is not present now in the first scene with Cam. It is suggested, as I say, the outlines are there, but you are not really dangerous anymore. The impression is of two nice boys, one a little troubled. Well, in life Biff has been through what

Art says, and your first job every performance is to create that, to bring that on with you. That's hard work, and in my opinion, since it is so difficult, more your obligation to the performance than saying your lines. That's why I forbid visiting back in the dressing rooms, and that goes for author and producers and company managers. No one can walk out onstage for this show with a hastily gulped sandwich inside him. You have to be full when you go on. The form is not enough.

Cameron, you are a less experienced actor than the others here playing important parts, and you are trying harder and conscientiously. The word with you is *sell.* Somehow you are no longer Hap on stage, and the change is that you no longer sell. You lack just that, that kind of action or behavior. The part cannot be played straight. It is a hot-air kid. He is sincere and has become a hot-air kid without his knowing it or meaning to, and it's because he has been injected with a lethal dose of the *selling* poison. He tries to accomplish everything—sincere, serious, or trivial—that way, and he sells sincerely, and he sells believing in what he's selling, but he sells. And then you have another fault that many young actors have. You "indicate," that is, you show the audience what you want them to get from your performance rather than just doing it and having faith that they will get it. Believe me, you do it, and they will get it. For instance, when you come downstairs with Johnny for the scene with Milly at the end of Act One, you don't have to keep rubbing your head to show that you're sleepy. Just be sleepy, sit still the way a person does when he's sleepy, and even doze a little, be half awake, and they will get it.

And when you see Charlie come in when Pop is yelling about your jobs and your women and so on, just see Charlie and try to call Pop's attention to Charlie, but don't <u>show</u> the audience that you're trying to call Willy's attention to the neighbor. And at the end I wanted you to cry at the funeral, but now you are straining every nerve to show the audience that you are grief-stricken. If you can cry, do so, silently and honestly; cry and mourn your father. A good rule for actors: DON'T SHOW MORE THAN YOU'VE GOT. It will be false. It is sure to be false. And what you're supposed to be doing there is not crying or mourning. A person feels in life despite himself. A man doesn't try to cry; that is only an actor. What you're doing is defending yourself against an imaginary accusation and a very real guilt. And out of this guilt comes a resolve that you will still come out number-one man, that you will make it up to Willy. But even this you sell. Your goal is not to become number-one man, but to sell the idea that you will, to Charley and to your brother and TO YOURSELF. A week later he will forget all about it, but his selling, at the moment he makes it, is completely sincere, and meant.

Let me say a word about Bob Simon [the stage manager]. Bob sat through every rehearsal. He took down everything central I said. When he comes up and speaks to you, he is there representing me and is doing his level best to suggest where you might have gone off the track. He is not me. He is Bob Simon. But I insisted that he be here, and he has my respect, and he knows the facts and the salient points of my direction. In fact, last night he reminded me of something that I had forgotten myself. And I ask that you pay attention to him and pay respect to him as being what he is. We are anxious, no less than you, to keep this show up. It is not easy to keep up, as you see. Bob might be wrong. He likely isn't. There is almost certainly something in what he says to you. He may very well remember what I said better than me. He's paid to remember. That is his job. And he is here in an official capacity. He is not a friend. He is a functionary whose job it is to help keep the show up. Look at it this way: He can be a great help to you. If you feel you may be off, talk with him, ask him, consult with him. You will at the very least get what I once said on the point and you'll probably get much more.

That's all for now, I'm only sending this to four people: Lee, Johnny, Milly, Cam. So please keep it to yourselves. The reason I send it is that you may have a permanent record of the probable dangers around your performances. If I have anywhere seemed harsh, you will know without my saying so that it's only as you might be plain or blunt with someone in your own family. I love you all, and am very proud to have been your director. You know that.

Gadge

EDITOR

For Kazan, *Death of a Salesman* had overtones of his conflicted relationship with his father, George Kazan. "Studying the play, as I was preparing to direct it, I began to see my father differently; I stopped being angry at him. . . . Like Willy, my father considered his eldest son a special failure and, oh, God, this hurt him! And me! But how could I blame him for what he expected of me and didn't get?"

Death of a Salesman, set design by Jo Mielziner

In his direction Kazan stressed the disappointment, confused aims, and misconceptions between Biff and Willy, and made their relationship the central love affair of the play. Absent from his discussion is the tagline that was sometimes derisively attached to the play: "What did you do in Boston, Willy?" Biff's discovery of his father with a strange woman in a hotel room as the critical disjunction of their relationship is the play's main structural weakness, for it skews by melodrama the themes of personality, ambition, and ideals. It makes Biff seem prudish and self-exculpatory.

Kazan's analysis of the play propelled him into merciless and steely self-criticism, an examination that was misread in the critical response to his autobiography, *A Life,* as self-justification, but was for him a form of confession. In his notes for the play he confesses to possessing the materialist characteristics the play decries: aggressiveness, competitiveness, selfishness, destructiveness, deep and uncomprehending rage. "I came to believe the point [of the play] was far more lethal than anything Art put into words. It's in the very fabric of the work, in the legend itself, which is where a theme should be. The Christian faith of this God-fearing civilization says we should love our brother as ourselves. Miller's story tells us that actually—as we have to live—we live by an opposite law, by which the purpose of life is to get the better of your brother, destroying him if necessary, yes, by in effect killing him. Even sex becomes a kind of aggression—to best your boss by taking his woman!"

Kazan credited Jo Mielziner with providing the scenic element that gave the complex structure of the drama dynamic coherence:

> The concept of a house standing like a specter behind all the scenes of the play, always present as it might be always present in Willy's mind, wherever his travels take him, even behind the office he visits, even behind the Boston hotel room and above his grave plot, is not even suggested in the original script. Although the spectral home is a directorial vision, it was not my idea any more than it was Art's. It was urged on us by the scenic designer, Jo Mielziner. I went for it—it solved many problems for me— and when we took it to Miller, he approved of it. In this production, it was the single most critically important contribution and the key to the way I directed the play. Both Miller and I were praised for what Jo had conceived.

The producers had proposed the film and stage star Walter Huston for the role of Willy, but Kazan held out for Lee J. Cobb, who had appeared in Kazan's film *Boomerang!* and had been a member of the Group Theatre. "Huston is not deeply anxious, Cobb is! Willy Loman is an anxious man = Lee J. Cobb," insisted Kazan. He personally appealed to Twentieth Century–Fox film executive Darryl Zanuck to grant Cobb leave from his movie contract. In rehearsals, Kazan pushed Cobb (whose performance is now legendary) to avoid any display of self-pity; he wanted from Cobb "rage, frustration, pride, bewilderment."

Kazan was masterly not only at mining the personal traits of the actor but working on external actions that made the character legible for both the player and the audience. In his autobiography *Timebends,* Arthur Miller describes Kazan "syncopating the speech rhythms of the actors."

> He made Mildred Dunnock deliver her long first-act speeches to the boys at double her normal speed, then he doubled that, and finally she—until recently a speech teacher—was standing there drumming out words as fast as her very capable tongue could manage. Gradually, he slacked off, but the drill straightened her spine, and her Linda filled up with outrage and protest rather than self-pity and mere perplexity. Similarly, to express the play's inner life, the speech rate in some scenes or sections was unnaturally speeded or slowed.

Dunnock remembered this exercise even more vividly:

> He took an old broomstick, I think it was the piece of an old broomstick, and he began to use it like a baton. And as I did the scene, he kept beating it and saying, "More! More! More! More!" Finally I was screaming at the top of my lungs and I burst into tears and I said, "I can't! I *won't* do it that way," and he said, "That's *exactly* the way you'll do it." . . . "But what about the nuances?" And he said, "Nuances? We'll come to those in a couple of months." I always say that the greatest director I worked with is Kazan, and it is because of this play. He has the capacity to make you use yourself to your fullest extent—and to fall flat on your face, but he always takes the blame for anything that's not right; you never lose face with Kazan. He also lets you be free of yourself. Linda Loman was a part I had to struggle to get, because I'm not a natural Linda Loman. His descriptions of the character helped me to be able to play her. He said Linda Loman is an old-fashioned woman; she would let her husband use her like a doormat, but never feel that he was using her. She *exists* in somebody else always; she never exists in herself.

Death of a Salesman achieved the kind of popular Broadway success usually only accorded musicals, and the play was hailed immediately as one of the great American dramas. In an early review Brooks Atkinson wrote in the *New York Times:* "By common consent, this is one of the finest dramas in the whole range of the American theatre. . . . Although Elia Kazan has done some memorable jobs of direction in the past few years, he has never equaled the selfless but vibrant expression of this epic drama which has force, clarity, rhythm and order in the performing."

With this play Miller joined Tennessee Williams as the foremost young American playwrights, the only inheritors of Eugene O'Neill's eminence— they were the American Ibsen and Chekhov—and it was a virtually unanimous decision that with *Streetcar* and *Salesman* contemporary American drama had achieved international standing; in fact, only France, with Sartre, Anouilh, and Giraudoux, could rival it. Concurrent with this was a recognition that this cast of American actors, who were the fulfillment of the promise of training in the Stanislavsky method, rivaled the great actors of any nation. Cobb's Willy gave Cobb for a time the repute of *the* great American actor, a reputation, Kazan thought, that Cobb later let slip away.

Throughout his career Kazan maintained Harold Clurman as his adviser and mentor and sparring partner, and Clurman always had lessons and criticisms for Kazan. In his review of *Salesman,* Clurman once again resisted giving Kazan total approval.

Elia Kazan's production is first rate. It is true to Miller's qualities, and adds to them a swift directness, muscularity, and vehemence of conviction. If any further criticism is in order I should say the production might have gained a supplementary dimension if it had more of the aroma of individual characterizations, more of the quiet music of specific humanity—small, as the people in the play are small, and yet suggestive of those larger truths their lives signify.

Mildred Dunnock as the mother embodies the production's best features: its precision, clarity, purity of motive. Someone has said that the part might have been more moving if it has been played by an actress like Pauline Lord with all the magic overtones and "quarter-tones" of her subtle sensibility. Concretely such a suggestion is, of course, irrelevant, but it points to a need I feel in the production as a whole more than to Miss Dunnock's particular performance.

Lee Cobb as the salesman is massively powerful and a commanding actor every step of the way. Yet I cannot help feeling that Cobb's interpretation is more akin to the prototype of King Lear than to Willy Loman. What differentiates Willy from some similarly abused figure is his utter unconsciousness—even where the author gives him conscious lines—his battered pride, querulous innocence, wan bewilderment even within the context of protest and angry vociferation. . . . Arthur Kennedy, who plays the older son, is a truly fine actor, who loses some of his edge because the general high pitch of the production forces him to blunt his natural delicacy.

Jo Mielziner's scene design seems to me too complex in shape and too diverse in style to be wholly satisfactory for a functional set or for beautiful decoration.

Kazan challenged Clurman's hesitations and, in this case, as he had done with *Streetcar*, he granted Clurman the direction of the road company, which starred Thomas Mitchell. Mitchell proved director-proof, and Clurman resorted to directing all the other actors to behave in a way Mitchell was forced to respond to. The critical consensus was that Clurman domesticated the play, muting the high pitch ("epic level," Dunnock called it) of Kazan's production.

Camino Real (1953)
by Tennessee Williams

"I didn't touch this play. I didn't find this play."

EDITOR: Kilroy arrives in the plaza of a seaport town. For some travelers, it is a way station; for others, a final destination. Some set out from here to freedom, some to death; most are stranded. At the back of the stage is a flight of stairs leading to the unknown, either to death or to ascendency into legend. On one side of the plaza is a luxury hotel whose proprietor, Gutman (the name taken from the role Sydney Greenstreet plays in the film *The Maltese Falcon*—urbane, hard-nosed, and amusingly sinister), provides commentary on the action. On the opposite side, separated by a fountain, is a flophouse.

The characters are either literary, legendary, or folkloric types. Kilroy the American is the adventurous loser, hapless, innocent, and good-hearted. His name derives from the tag "Kilroy was here," graffiti scribbled on walls and surfaces wherever American soldiers served during the Second World War. Kazan wrote in his autobiography that all the characters are doomed "but Kilroy has a quality the others lost: He can struggle to get up when he's knocked down."

The first to appear are Don Quixote and Sancho Panza, who enter from the audience. Throughout the play the characters engage the audience by direct address, and much of the action occurs in the auditorium space, with entrances from the orchestra and chases across the balcony and boxes. The great romance of the drama is between a frail and desperate Marguerite Gautier (the "Camille" of Dumas's play) and the notorious lover Jacques Casanova. Kilroy's momentary love is the Gypsy girl Esmeralda (the name but not much else taken from Victor Hugo's novel *The Hunchback of Notre Dame*—a hunchback makes a mute appearance), whose virginity is renewed in a moonlit ritual. At the end Kilroy heads off with Don Quixote into the unknown.

In late 1949 Kazan directed a workshop production of Williams's short play *Ten Blocks on the Camino Real* at the Actors Studio. Seeking an appropriate directorial approach, Kazan asked Williams to spell out his intentions. Williams wrote him from Key West:

As I said over the phone, the people are nearly all archetypes of various human attitudes toward life, which is the Camino Real. Marguerite Gautier is the romantic sensualist, and her friend Casanova is an out-and-out rake but with romantic yearnings that promiscuity did not satisfy. Baron de Charlus is the completely cynical voluptuary and hedonist. They belong together because they have pursued a fairly similar course, so they all stay at the hotel, which is the "haut monde," the prosperous side of the street. The Gypsy's establishment is the brutal enigma of existence. Her daughter is the eternal object of desire. Kilroy, like Don Quixote, who he eventually joins, is the simple, innocent adventurer into life, the knight-errant who has preserved his dignity, his sincerity and his honor, though greatly baffled and subjected to much indignity and grief. I am not sure how precisely all this adds up, but perhaps it doesn't have to, so long as the essential effect, of poetic mystery, is realized. I wrote it without figuring it out very logically in advance.

FROM THE JOURNAL

In working on *The Camino Real* I have just realized something—that my analytical thinking on plays has been for a long long time fouled up on a kind of pseudo-Marxist ethics. In other words, I tried to find in each play that I did a kind of allegory or a dramatized illustration of the working out of an ethics. According to this, I lined up each and every figure on the side of "good" or "bad." If the play did not adhere to this stricture, I would bloody well force it. Martin Ritt does worse: by him there are Communists or "progressive figures," and there are reactionaries. But worse than either is the figure in between. He is called a Social Democrat. The effect is to reduce each play to a ridiculous and poverty-stricken "meaning," out of which all the contradictions have been ground out. And to a parable or allegory in which we see reflected nothing but our own prejudices and dogmas. And the very stuff of life, the contradictions, is ground out in the process. And I did not really see the stuff that the author has set down, the real "material" of life. The Marxist glasses I put on in 1934 permit me to see only Marxist dogma. There go the contradictions. There go the facts. There goes the most important effort: What is the author really saying? Even now I keep thinking: "Kilroy is right. Kilroy is good." Well, the fact is that Kilroy is neither. Kilroy is Kilroy. Marguerite does not stand for or represent any force or theme. She needs no ethical label. And it is not illuminating to make an ethical judgment or evaluation of her. In fact, if you do, you will find it pretty well impossible to do the other and necessary thing: find out who the hell she is and what the hell she really is like. The purpose of the director's analysis of the labor of imagination and of the marshalling of the director's means is only to reveal <u>her as herself.</u>

Consider in the play, TW [Tennessee Williams] says: The lawful, in our civilization, are cruel. The outcasts are imaginative, or colorful; also weak and cannot help each other, except by clinging together for a short minute. He does not say whether or not he approves of this. In fact, he both admires and despises himself. He would say, apparently, that it is better to live by your dreams, and at the same time he says that people who do so are doomed and even cowardly. The world is ruled by the people who live by aggression, and they are indeed colorful and attractive, have humor, or they are relaxed enough to have humor. The romantics, on the other hand, have little humor. And are phony as hell. But phoniness is not bad. Nothing is either good or bad. And as for society's role: Never heard of it? "The castanets click mysteriously." And probably he never intended the vendors to be the people: even though there is a lot of symbolism in the play. And is Kilroy's friendliness good? Or silly? Both! No! <u>Neither!</u> That's the point. He just shows him as inevitably and unswervingly friendly. Obviously, TW both loves Kilroy (himself) and despises him. He is a wanderer, homeless (but TW wants a home). He is doomed by his own bigheartedness. He lives in his dreams, etc. (But what would TW's attitude be?) N.B. that in *Streetcar* TW (Blanche) is shown both sick to death and loveable and TW obviously loves Stanley Kowalski. No ethics involved here, except in the most contradictory sense. What is shown however is the POR-TRAIT OF TENNESSEE WILLIAMS AND OF HIS WORLD. That is the effort and the job of every good playwright, every good artist. Belles Lettres, Letters to the World: saying: This is what I see. What do you see?

Yours for a new <u>Realism</u> in your thinking, and from it, a new Radicalism.

EDITOR: *Camino Real*'s "magic realism" is a form readily accommodated by present-day audiences, conditioned by the novels of Gabriel García Márquez and the films of David Lynch. Kazan was so challenged by the job of realizing the short version (*Ten Blocks on the Camino Real*) onstage that he asked Williams to expand it to full length. Over the next three years Williams sent Kazan piecemeal revisions, and Kazan urged Williams to greater clarity of intention. Kazan worked extensively on reordering the episodes to give the play theatrical progression and thematic unity, and he suggested changes within the episodes on each rewrite.

JULY 24, 1952

Dear Tenn,

I have been searching and searching for the unity that an audience is supposed to find and follow in all this material. What is *the* story? And what particular story are we telling? There is one story element that seems to be the essential one. It is the basis for every big scene that is "right," and every time I feel that something is wrong, off center, and doesn't belong, it is because it doesn't concern itself with the problem that all these people face, namely: How to get out of this place! This is the problem of everybody in this show. Symbolically this means: how to die with dignity and honor and gallantry! And since death is the final fact of living, it also must mean How to love with dignity! The rearrangement and reorganization that I am suggesting below was founded basically on the idea that this is the story of a group of charac-ters who find themselves in the imminent and inescapable presence of death and all have to find their way of going to it. Or to put it more actively and dramatically, how to get out as Themselves and not as just Meat.

EDITOR: On August 20, 1952, Williams wrote in his journal: "Yesterday eve we read over the work I've done on *Camino* under Gadg's direction. He kept snorting and exclaiming, Oh, this is wonderful! The way a doctor tells a dying man what perfect condition he's in. It seemed to me like one long agonized wail and I couldn't go out to eat with him. Said excuse me but I think I'll go cruising now."

The play baffled the designer Jo Mielziner, who was privy to the corcorespon-dence between Kazan and Williams, and when the production was finally being readied, he withdrew. Kazan turned to Lemuel Ayres, with whom he had worked on the Helen Hayes vehicle *Harriet*.

Dear Lem,

Here are some notes on the setting for *Camino*.

The place where the play takes place is a port of departure. (Gutman says: "This is a port of arrival and departure and we have no permanent guests.") It is further a port of departure into the unknown.

Obviously the play is completely unrealistic—a fantasy, it is called. But beyond this, there is one other factor that makes a real problem that other fantasies don't have. That is that the play is directed by the author to be played largely in a Theatrical or presentational side. Generally, therefore, while the back areas of the stage are illusionistic, the front area should be presentational, and the actors should have at least as much contact with the audience as do revue or even burlesque performers. This fascinating going from a fairy land, remote, eerie, and forbidding, to a close and most direct contact with the audience is one of the main problems, as it is one of the main virtues of the play. It is also absolutely brand new stylistically speaking and gives both you and me a problem that neither we nor anyone else has ever faced before. The only theatre I know where this kind of combination of supposedly stylistic elements exists is in the Japanese theatre, but I believe that they work too formally for the illusionistic parts of this play.

This is a place where people arrive without knowing how they got there. The author describes it once most beautifully as that it takes place "on the far moonlit end of the Camino Real." It is the end, then, of a series of converging roads. They come in, it would seem to me, from more or less one direction. In the opposite direction there is space, terror, mystery, the unknown, death. This is a jumping-off place.

I've always felt that the set should sweep from the known—which is the direction of the audience, up and up and then away in back to the unknown, which is seen through the arch (which can either be the arch of death or the arch of triumph) and beyond the arch toward space that is so unknown that it is limitless and unknowable.

In other words, I think the entrances to the place should be generally from the direction of the audience. That doesn't mean through the audience, though this should be continued too. It does mean that people enter more or less from the direction of the audience. The players move between the audience which is known and the back of the stage which is mysterious and unknown. Kilroy identifies the members of the audience as his friends. Most often he talks directly to them. He consults with them, and again and again asks for their sympathy and understanding in the way one should be able to approach a close friend in a crisis. Generally, the audience get their understanding and feeling for the play through Kilroy. When Kilroy disappears into apotheosis as a legend, he goes up and away into the mystery beyond the arch.

There are other actors, notably Gutman, who deal directly with the audience. Gutman regards the audience as he does everything else, as people that are there to be "taken" and sources for enjoyment, his particular kind of enjoyment.

Basically, there should be an ascending progression from the "reality" (not really real at all, but highly theatric) of the downstage and forestage areas up to the mystery and potentially awesome and majestic and "timeless" areas in the back. I see this as a great sweep up.

Then I would say that the main design job is to make this place come to beautiful life. Mostly I see the proportions of the houses, porches, entrances, doorways, windows (as Tenn has described them) quite small. The feeling should be a lyric one. That is, it should be allusive and suggestive rather than heavy. The "feel" of the set should be one of evanescence. It should constantly seem to change. The lighting should never be "nailed down" into one mood.

The first look at the entire set can be just a tiny bit realistic. Perhaps those square pieces of cloth on a frame and mounted on a single pole that one sees in Mexican markets can be used to advantage here. After this opening suggestion of a poetic type of realism, there is only increasing fantasy and increasing theatricality.

EDITOR: In his autobiography Kazan wrote of his disappointment with the production and particularly with the set:

I wrote the designer we'd chosen a long note explaining what I hoped for in the set. I didn't get it. What I got was a lugubrious realistic setting that was, in a word, heavy-handed. And too real. It made the fantasies that took place inside it seem silly. I should have ordered a new setting, but I didn't. I betrayed myself by not sticking to my guns. I'd buried my original—and I believe correct—intention in talk. And good fellowship. The designer was a friend.

FROM SCRIPT NOTES

GUTMAN gives light and music cues on stage as part of play (somewhat like Dowling).* This has advantage of correcting technical mis-

---

* Eddie Dowling played the narrator, Tom Wingfield, in the original production of Tennessee Williams's *The Glass Menagerie*, who similarly makes direct address to the audience.

Jo Van Fleet in *Camino Real*

takes at openings. ("Hey lightman, where's your number five spot? Bring it up five points!") He can also say "Pick it up!" when the tempo lags. Or "We're getting some coughs in the house!" Someone in the cast who is a little outside the play, a mediator between audience and play who can be used to advantage. Incidentally, a good Gutman would be George Sanders or Melvyn Douglas. He doesn't have to be fat. Charles Laughton would be the ideal. Charlie Feldman, who is Charles Boyer's agent, says that Boyer, who would be available, is not tied up! He would add at least two thousand a week to grossing potential, not just his name but his absolute perfection in the part.

The only theatre in history that treats people, personages, (rather) in this way is the oriental theatre, and above all the Theatre of Japan. Here the personages come out in full panoply. Here they are dressed to kill as it were. They are legends. They are finally and completely what they are. Nobody could be it more. They are not ordinary. They are not every day. And it isn't only their clothes. It is their behavior. Their "spines" and actions are chosen with a close eye to the most characteristic. Their props are their final props. The props that never leave them. Jacques's cane. Kilroy's leather wrist strap? Marguerite's parasol?

Work on this: These characters, if they are dressed right and properly activated, can be the scenery of the show. "Don't [run?] the arguments with the actors—get the performances right." [Years later Kazan scribbled in the margin: "But I didn't do this."]

Tennessee says the play is about how to live with honor and gallantry in the world today. But it is most personal. Tenn altogether shrinks from the world of 1952. It affronts him. He has no place in it and is driven like the other characters to the dim moonlit end of the Camino. Since the problem of how to live in its most dramatic form is that of how to die, Tenn has so dramatized it here.

Your danger is that you will begin to think of the play as a struggle between people ethically right and those who are wrong. This does not go for Williams. They are all doomed. They are all interesting. They have the glamour of their crises.

EDITOR

When in late 1952 Kazan went to Hollywood to oversee the final cut of *Man on a Tightrope,* which he had filmed in Europe, he found that he had lost his privileged place on the Twentieth Century–Fox lot. Darryl Zanuck, believing *Tightrope* a flop, had severely edited the film without consulting him, and Kazan was shunted to a temporary office on the backlot. His sense of alienation increased when he returned to New York, for he found he was still ostracized by a substantial portion of the Broadway community, including members of the Actors Studio, for his HUAC testimony. Feeling like one of the play's discards, an outcast seeking his way back, he began staging *Camino Real.*

> I wanted a production that had the bizarre fantasy of the Mexican primitive artist José Posada. It was an idea to which my choreographer, Anna Sokolow, responded; she knew Mexico well. But the play didn't take place in Mexico or in any other land that can be found in an atlas. It happens in the topography inside the author's head. What it needed was the vision of the right artistic collaborator. I talked about Posada, yes, but it is not sufficient to have "brilliant" ideas and enthuse everyone concerned. Posada! Sounds great, doesn't it? Especially if you haven't seen his work. Candied skulls and skeletons! Great! But something beyond talk is required, in this case, the right help from the right designer.
>
> The other thing that went wrong was the casting. . . . What had encouraged Williams to rewrite and expand his original short play was the work I'd done at the Actors Studio with three of our

actors, experimenting on the grotesque comic ritual when, at the rise of the full moon, the Gypsy's daughter's virginity is restored. Williams was pleased with what the actors and I had done, and I cast the whole play from our number. They responded generously, with spirit, loyalty, devotion, and all the talent they had. But I knew when I read the play again that any of them, dear and good people, were—with the exception of Eli Wallach—not up to the needs of their parts. They were trained in a more realistic technique. So was I. . . . I was forcing the casting of *Camino Real* and distorting my own requirements to declare that the play must be played by members of the Actors Studio; it was artistically false. . . .

I believe that the reason for this insistence in the case of *Camino Real* had little to do with an artistic purpose. It came from a desire to again be accepted as their hero by the actors of that organization, to demonstrate my courage and my steadfast loyalty to them, and to live up to an ideal to which I'd pledged support again and again and for which I'd demanded theirs. By demonstrating that I had the power to force things to happen our way, I would make the Actors Studio mine again. In plainer language, I wanted to be liked. An unworthy end, and one I achieved at some cost to the Williams play.

Unfortunately the play has poetry and imagination but no cumulative dramatic drive. It had brilliant scenes but not a crescendo of tension, which would come from one scene leading into another into another and so on. In effect it had no third act and died, as the poem goes, with "a whimper." I felt that hidden in the folds of its

Kazan and
Tennessee
Williams

fabric was an element of self-pity, an emotion that appears now and then in Williams's work but not in his best plays.

The critic Eric Bentley ascribed to Kazan extensive creative contributions to Tennessee Williams's plays, implying not merely reshaping and emphatic staging but rewriting, a blistering issue for Kazan and Williams. In his review of *Camino Real* (one of the few positive ones—in the *New York Herald Tribune* Walter Kerr had written: "Williams is our greatest playwright, and this is his worst play"), Bentley gave Kazan perhaps too much credit for some of the work Kazan shared with the choreographer Anna Sokolow. And, though Bentley irritated Kazan to the point of a threatened lawsuit, he was an acute explicator of Kazan's staging acumen, Kazan's theater "magic."

> To me the evening was of interest chiefly as the latest essay of Elia. . . . At any rate, it is Mr. Kazan's presence we feel most strongly, Mr. Kazan's methods whose results we witness.
>
> Mr. Kazan's most commendable quality is a simple one: He is a showman. This is partly a matter of sheer efficiency; in his productions, everything is taken care of, second by second. . . . But Mr. Kazan's showmanship goes beyond efficiency into legerdemain. He is a wizard. Even if I knew I was to witness a hateful interpretation of a hateful play, I would await any Kazan production with considerable eagerness. For Mr. Kazan's name in the program guarantees an evening of—at the least—brilliant theatre work at a high emotional temperature.
>
> Perhaps the most memorable things in *Camino Real* are choreographic, and yet they could not have been done for Mr. Kazan by a choreographer because they are worked out in the terms of acting, not dance. One of these things is just a presentation of people rushing to catch a plane. Mr. Williams made the episode symbolic by calling the plane *il fugitivo* and having Marguerite Gautier and Jacques Casanova try to get aboard, but Mr. Kazan makes it symbolic in much finer fashion—by simple intensification of the event as we all know it. If we have sometimes to complain of neurasthenics and hysteria, there is no doubt that Mr. Kazan has found his own way of lifting a performance above the trivial and naturalistic. Conversely, when the action tends towards the artifice of dance or ceremony, he knows how to keep it anchored in everyday reality. When the others dance, Eli Wallach as Kilroy mixes dancing and boxing and embarrassed awkwardness quite magnificently. . . .
>
> Though *Camino Real* gives Mr. Kazan more power, I cannot agree with those who say it exacted from him a different style

because it is a fantasy. Even when confronted with "realistic" plays like *A Streetcar Named Desire* and *Death of a Salesman,* he gave us phantasmagoria. Blanche DuBois's background was diaphanous walls and voices disembodied as Saint Joan's. Willy Loman's life was shrouded in shadow and woodwinds and ghosts from Alaska. The only difference is that *Camino Real* doesn't pretend to realism. The unreal which formerly crept up on us here meets us head on. Whether New York will prefer this I do not know. Possibly the escape into unreality was welcome in the former plays only because it was disguised as its opposite; and now that it is overt the public will either reject it or declare it unintelligible; in which case the play is done for. Possibly, on the other hand, there are many besides myself who cannot resist the wicked fascination of Elia Kazan.

Cat on a Hot Tin Roof (1955)
by Tennessee Williams

"No living playwright that I can think of hasn't something valuable to learn about his own work from a director so keenly perceptive as Elia Kazan."   Tennessee Williams

EDITOR: Big Daddy's family has gathered at his Mississippi Delta mansion to celebrate his sixty-fifth birthday, but what is being withheld from him is the diagnosis of incurable cancer. Big Daddy's two sons are Gooper, the elder, whom Big Daddy dislikes (along with Gooper's mercenary and conniving wife, Mae, and their five children), and Brick (a former varsity football player and sports announcer who has turned to drink). Brick's wife is the indefatigable and willful Maggie, "Maggie the Cat."

The argument of the play concerns which son will inherit Big Daddy's plantation.

Brick has fallen into despondency over the death from alcohol and drugs of his close friend Skipper, whose homosexual feelings for him he refuses to acknowledge. His wife, Maggie, is determined to reignite her conjugal relationship with her husband. Complicating the situation is the revelation that Skipper and Maggie slept together, in a failed attempt on Skipper's part to disprove his sexual attraction for Brick.

The continuous action of the play is accentuated by three dramatic confrontations: in the first act, between Brick and Maggie; in the second, between Brick and Big Daddy, a passage that ranks at the pinnacle of Williams's achievements; and in the third act, the resolution of the legacy of Big Daddy.

Maggie is literally and symbolically the life force of the play, but it is Big Daddy who overwhelms the drama with his vitality, florid language, and rugged and often cruel bluntness.

Kazan's notebook for *Cat on a Hot Tin Roof* has been lost.

Williams sent Kazan a note attached to a preproduction rewrite explaining what he was after:

> The play was not just negative, since it was packed with rage, and rage is not a negative thing in life: It is positive, dynamic! . . . [Brick's] one of the rich and lucky! Got everything without begging, was admired and loved by all. Hero! Beauty!—Two people

fell in love with him beyond all bounds. Skipper and Maggie. He built up one side of his life around Skipper, another around Maggie.—Conflict: Disaster!—One love ate up the other, naturally, humanly, without intention, just did! Hero is faced with truth and collapses before it. . . . Maggie, the cat, has to give him some instruction in how to hold your position on a hot tin roof, which is human existence which you've got to accept on any terms whatsoever. . . . Vitality is the hero of the play!—The character you can "root for" . . . is not a person but a quality in people that makes them survive.

Williams published two third acts, his preproduction text, and a substantial revision that he wrote at Kazan's suggestion. The revision brings Big Daddy back into the action—he had been absent from the third act in the earlier version—expands Brick's role, and offers a less ambiguous, more promising ending. Recent performances have returned to Williams's original version.

In a 1964 interview Kazan recalled his conception of how the play should be staged:

In *Cat on a Hot Tin Roof* I had everybody address the audience continually. Every time they had one of those long speeches they'd turn and say it to the audience. Nobody thought anything of it once we opened. But there was a hell of a lot of bitching about it before. . . . The whole of the second act of *Cat* was a long address by Burl Ives to the audience. I had him address various members of the audience . . . "What would you do?" is implicit in this kind of staging. It sucks the audience into the experience and emotion of that moment.

EDITOR: In his memoir, Kazan wrote:

Jo Mielziner and I had read the play in the same way; we saw that its great merit was its brilliant rhetoric and its theatricality. I didn't see the play as realistic any more than he did. If it was to be done realistically, I would have to contrive stage business to keep the old man talking those great second act speeches turned out front and pretend that it was just another day in the life of the Pollitt family. This would, it seemed to me, amount to an apology to the audience for the glory of the author's language. . . . So I caused Jo to design our setting as I wished, a large triangular platform, tipped toward the audience and holding only one piece of furniture, an ornate bed. This brought the play down to its

Cat on a Hot Tin Roof, set design by Jo Mielziner

essentials and made it impossible for it to be played any way except as I preferred.

Kazan was enraptured by the extravagance of Williams's language, luxurious, poetic, piercingly aphoristic, rich in imagery. Williams thought of his plays as fundamentally realistic, and it was Kazan who emphasized their allusive, suggestive atmosphere, their very theatricality, by the precision of stage movement and gesture, of music and sound effects. Kazan depended on the master designer Jo Mielziner for a nonliteral use of space and setting, and for extraordinarily sensitive and meticulous lighting. With reluctance, Williams deferred to the American theatre's boldest craftsmen. In hindsight, it is remarkable that the conceptual originality of Kazan/Mielziner productions were the aspects least remarked on—*Streetcar, Salesman, Cat on a Hot Tin Roof,* and *Sweet Bird* were similar in production method: bold and extremely complex combinations of realism and theatricality in the playing, setting, and lighting.

Kazan knew that he was reconceiving, or rather "translating for the stage," Williams's work, and he meant to present the plays "as he saw them." Williams was wary but acquiescent; what he gained, he believed, was worth more than what he had to yield. And then there was the paradox that Kazan was more lucid in giving an exposition of a play's intent than Williams, and Kazan could not for long suppress his own creative impulses. The fuzziness of *Sweet Bird* and *Cat* (in both, the conception of the male protagonist and the shifting and fluid fields of objective reality and subjectivity) were focused by Kazan in ways that supplied what Williams for a time was unable or unwilling to articulate. Kazan did not betray Williams's meaning, but Kazan was always clear, definite, and precise in intention even when ambiguity was the goal, and Williams felt the world a mystery. In the published version of *Cat*, Williams included a defensive authorial note about the delineation of Brick: "Some mystery should be left in the revelation of character in a play, just as a great deal of mystery is always left in the revelation of character in life, even one's own character to himself in life." For Kazan beauty was palpable; for Williams it was evanescent and therefore tragic. And with all that, Williams knew that Kazan was his best interpreter, that he was the director most capable of illuminating Williams's work, that the tension between their different approaches was the catalyst to realizing best on a stage the play's metaphysical vision.

Kazan proposed three major changes for *Cat on a Hot Tin Roof*. The first was to strengthen sympathy for Maggie by softening her character. In Williams's 1952 source short story, "Three Players of a Summer Game," the Maggie character is conniving and devious. The second and third changes involved adding a sense of development in Brick's character after the extended second-act confrontation between Brick and Big Daddy (yielding a less pessimistic ending) and bringing Big Daddy into the third act. Williams made the changes reluctantly—he feared losing his director over the issue.

As with *Camino Real*, Kazan sent lengthy letters to Williams with instructions for possible alterations. After one such letter, Williams noted in his journal on November 29, 1954: "Got a 5 page letter from Gadg elucidating, not too lucidly, his remaining objection to play. I do get his point but I'm afraid he doesn't quite get mine. Things are not always explained. Situations are not always resolved. Characters don't always 'progress.' But I shall, of course, try to arrive at another compromise with him."

In response, Williams gave Kazan revised dialogue for two of Brick's scenes and offered this analysis of Brick's character:

NOVEMBER 31, 1954

> I "buy" a lot of your letter but of course not all: Possibly I "buy" more than half, and after a couple of nights studying it out, I think I understand it.
>
> To be brief: The part I buy is that there has to be a reason for

Brick's impasse (his drinking is only an expression of it) that will "hold water."

Why does a man drink: in quotes "Drink." There's two reasons, separate or together. 1. He's scared shitless of something. 2. He can't face the truth about something.—Then of course there's the natural degenerates that just fall into any weak, indulgent habit that comes along but we are not dealing with that sad but unimportant category in Brick.—Here's the conclusion I've come to. Brick <u>did</u> love Skipper, "the one great good thing in his life which was 'true.' " He identified Skipper with sports, the romantic world of adolescence which he couldn't go past. Further: To reverse my original (somewhat tentative) premise, I now believe that, in the deeper sense, not the literal sense, Brick is homosexual with a heterosexual adjustment: a thing I've suspected of several others, such as Brando, for instance. (He hasn't cracked up but I think he bears watching, he strikes me as being a compulsive eccentric.) I think these people are often undersexed, prefer pet raccoons or sports or something to sex with either gender. They have deep attachments, idealistic, romantic: sublimated loves! They are terrible Puritans. (Marlon dislikes me. Why? I'm corrupt.) . . . Take Brando again. He's smoldering with something, and I don't think it's Josanne! Sorry to make him my guinea pig in this analysis (Please give this letter back to me!) but he's the nearest thing to Brick that we both know. Their innocence, their blindness, makes them very, very touching, very beautiful and sad. Often they make fine artists, having to sublimate so much of their love, and believe me, homosexual love is something that also requires more than a physical expression. But if a mask is ripped off, suddenly, roughly, that's quite enough to blast the whole Mechanism, the whole adjustment, knock the world out from under their feet, and leave them no alternative but—owning up to the truth or retreat into something like liquor.

In the published version Williams continued to defend Brick's passivity and the absence of Big Daddy in the third act:

I didn't want Big Daddy to reappear in Act Three and I felt that the moral paralysis of Brick was a root thing in his tragedy, and to show a dramatic progression would obscure the meaning of that tragedy in him and because I don't believe that a conversation, however revelatory, ever effects so immediate a change in the heart or even conduct of a person in Brick's state of spiritual disrepair.

Williams implies that Kazan gently forced Williams's hand in order to ensure a commercial success, and Williams's accusation would be a smoldering irritant for Kazan.

> I especially resented Tennessee's calling "my" third act—which I didn't write, plan, or edit—the "commercial" third act. I'd had no such purpose in mind. It was Williams who wanted the commercial success, and he wanted it passionately. All he'd had to say was: "Put it back the way I had it first," and I would have. Apart from friendship and devotion, I'd have had to restore his original by the mandate of the Dramatists Guild.

Less remarked on are more significant changes from the production script to the published one. In the published second act there is more explicit talk of Brick's suppressed homosexuality, as well as Big Daddy's acknowledgment both of the patrons' homosexuality—it is their mansion he inherited and in their old bedroom in which the action is set—and his non-judgmental acceptance of a possible sexual relationship between Brick and Skipper. It is the insinuation of denied homosexuality that infuriates Brick. Brenda Murphy writes, "Significantly, the reading version for *Cat* was prepared from the pre-production version and an even earlier version of Act Three rather than from the production script, as the reading version of *Camino Real* had been. In the early version of *Cat*, Big Daddy has a tolerance for homosexuality that Brick lacks, and it is Brick's refusal to listen to Skipper that gnaws at him—all this was eliminated." Without evidence of Kazan's influence, Murphy concludes, in a private letter to this editor, "that Williams thought better of including this overtly sympathetic treatment of gay characters himself, cutting it back to what he knew the Broadway audience would tolerate."

Of the contemporary reviews, only Eric Bentley, as with his review of *Camino Real*, was alert to the meticulous details of Kazan's staging techniques. Despite threats of a lawsuit from Williams and a denial from Kazan over Bentley's proposal that Kazan wrote some of Williams's dialogue, Bentley persisted in describing Kazan's unique directorial mannerisms as substantive alterations of the plays themselves:

> The general scheme [of the set and stage arrangement] is that not only of *A Streetcar Named Desire* but also of *Death of a Salesman:* an exterior that is also an interior—but, more importantly, a view of man's exterior that is also a view of his interior, the habitat of his body and the country of his memories and dreams. A theatre historian would probably call this world a combination of naturalism and expressionism, yet one has no impression that it was arrived at

by mixture, or even by choice, of styles: it is a by-product, or perhaps end product, of a certain sort of work which has its own history and identity. It is one of the distinctive creations of American theatre.

He [Kazan] has departed further from naturalism: just as there is less furniture and less scenery, so there is a less natural handling of actors, a more conscious concern with stagecraft, with pattern, with form. Attention is constantly called to the tableau, to what, in movies, is called the individual "frame." You feel that Burl Ives has been *placed* center stage, not merely that he is there; in the absence of most of the furniture, a man's body is furnishing the room. When the man lifts his crippled son off the floor, the position is held a long moment as for a time exposure. . . .

All the groupings are formalized. My reviews should probably be accompanied by diagrams showing where Mr. Kazan put everybody, by twos, by threes, this one over there moon-gazing through the imaginary window, all fixed to the spot until the director's signal is given to move. . . . A follow spot from the back of the balcony chases the actors around, picking out the center of the action for a kind of emphasis resembling a movie close-up; one is often reminded that this stage director is also a movie director.

And with the means of the new American theatre (school of Lee Strasberg and Harold Clurman) . . . it does reach the most cherished end of the older theatre—true grandeur of performance. . . . I do not think the reason for this resides in the formality itself. The effectiveness of this grandeur resides, in my opinion, from the interaction between formality in the setting, lighting, and grouping and an opposite quality—informality is hardly the word—in the individual performances. The externals of the physical production belong, as it were, to the old theatre, but the acting is internal, "Stanislavskyite." Within the formal setting, from the fixed positions in which they are made to stand, the actors live their roles with that vigilant, concentrated, uninterrupted nervous intensity which Mr. Kazan always manages to give.

J.B. (1958)
by Archibald MacLeish

*"The best work I had ever done had come out of an emotion of
some kind. I'd solved* J.B. *technically, but my true voice was
never heard."*

EDITOR: The J.B. of the title is the modern counterpart of Job, and the
drama tests his fidelity to God in terms of twentieth-century calamities. *J.B.*
is set in a circus tent with an upper platform that represents heaven, and a
performing ring in the floor that represents earth. God (Mr. Zuss) and Satan
(Nickles) are played in masks by two old circus vendors who once were
actors, and the story of modern Job is a play within a play.

In the first scene J.B. is a happy, prosperous businessman surrounded
by his family, whom he loves, and grateful to God for his abundant good
fortune. God proceeds to enlighten him about the nature of life with a
series of afflictions—the death of his oldest son in a gratuitous postwar
accident, the murder of a daughter by a psychopath, the deaths of two other
children, the destruction of his factory in a bombing, the loss of his wealth
and home, the attack of boils, the desertion of his wife.*

This verse play was published before it was produced onstage. It was first
performed by the Yale School of Drama in April 1958. Bosley Crowther's
enthusiastic review ("*J.B.* ranks with the finest work in American drama")
persuaded Alfred de Liagre to bring the play to Broadway, and he invited
Kazan to direct. Kazan had numerous suggestions for revision: rearranging
episodes and some cutting to eliminate the disjunction of action and dialogue, mostly in the first act. He wrote De Liagre, "In general my idea
would be to produce the play in two acts of completely continuous
action. . . . I believe that the staging should be basically Shakespearean. It
should acknowledge the presence of the audience and, by this, the relevance of what's being said to the audience's present concerns. In other
words, it is not a play about Job; it's a play about the mid-century American
and mid-century America. The question you ask is: 'Will America be able to
take it when it comes?' I think the play should be staged so it says: 'Will you,
the audience, be able to take it?' "

---

* This summary is adapted from Bosley Crowther's review of the Yale production,
New York Times, April 24, 1958.

FROM THE NOTEBOOK

EDITOR: Kazan gave Boris Aronson, with whom he had worked on the musical *Love Life*, detailed instructions for the set, compensating, perhaps, for his doubts about the play.

SPRING–DECEMBER 1958

1. It is not a circus. It looks like a circus. It is not an illustration of anything. It is the plastic rendition of essences. Ex. The family "circle." The restricted area within which the family functions. This is a circle, bound by a perimeter, a wall. The platform above is "above," the place where man, to still his fear and anxiety, imagines God dwells, waiting and judging. The circus too has a platform at its upper reaches. So that here too at first glance the set looks like a circus. The stand or platform for the acrobats also looks like the small balcony of St. Peter's in Rome from which the Pope addresses the faithful, where he plays "god."

2. There is another circle, a bigger one, which includes the restricted area of the family and which is the World (where Satan walks back and forth). This "world," a circle too, includes the audience and in fact tips down toward them. Satan walking about on the earth, walks up to the people in the audience, the people in the world, is among them, connects with them. The small circle of the family is within the large circle of the world. Here too essences rendered plastically.

3. This is a show. It is a circus or vaudeville show. It does not take place in a make-believe place bound by a picture frame. We may never use a curtain to begin with. The actors do not act as if the audience does not exist—except for those actors at the beginning, J.B. and family, who are contained within the circle of the family. The style of direction and the acting is vaudeville-like, big, presentational, out front. People represent essences, they are not individuals. They are large characteristics, all meaningful and significant of essences, not the small and local characteristics of individuals. They are what the Russians call "Masks"—broad types, significantly rendered. The behavior of the Comforters, for instance, is, in each case, characteristic of the essence of what each one represents.

4. The course or action of the play is the spiritual history of the American, and America of our time and within our memory. From

J.B., set design by Boris Aronson

1912 to 1958 and on into the immediate future, as we anxiously await the next war or cataclysm. The symbols of the story and the events are all from our recent history—achieved by recognizable signs and images of our time. The play is, in a way, the dream or nightmare of an American starting from Anxiety about what our fate is to be and ending in an affirmation of life.

5. The tent is the whole apparatus which man put up to stand over his head to protect him and shelter him and which, in fact, stood between him and god. The ecclesiastical claptrap, the churches, the pagan and Oriental and Eastern and Western religions, from the cavemen till today, of the whole apparatus which man put up to shut out the black, mysterious, and frightening void, but which also blocked man's view from the hard, stern, frightening questions of Where am I? How small am I really? Is anyone aware of me? Is there anyone else? Is there any meaning to it all? Within this tent, from time immemorial the drama of Man's relation to God has been played. The symbols on the tent represent security, solidity, etc., but man has created them out of his fears, just as he has created Zuss's image.

6. Visually, the play progresses by Nickles tearing down, segment by

segment, these symbols of security and solidity and safety. And as each piece is torn down, he reveals the locale of a coming disaster.

It is the circus of the world—a phrase which suggests the ESSEN-TIALS—which are torn down. Man's world is torn down. Nickles leaves man naked and alone, helpless, defenseless. That is man's actual condition today. His gods are gone. There is no more tent. There is no more protection. There are no more illusions. Man is up against his own cosmic isolation and insignificance. Above is black void. The final disaster that Nickles perpetrates on J.B. is to leave him this way, isolated and alone.

Man starts in 1912 protected. He finishes in 1958 or so stark naked, completely unprotected. This range is the one we must visualize.

This is a circus where magic is combined with meaning.

Visually. The setting should be spare and suggestive, "simple," abstracted. The bits of props, the working props, the costumes, the types of actors, the makeup, the sounds, the business, the dances, the songs, the movement, the clothes all must be terrifically saturated in the color and meaning of what they are designed to represent.

The set is the circus of the world. The props, costumes, and the characters, the acting and the direction convey the New England part of it. The set is the universe, step by step revealed. The props and personalities are the American in the universe.

The POLE is the signifier of the question which man hurls into the impersonal void. It is not dramatically prominent at the beginning. It may not even be noticed. But it is made prominent and dramatic and meaningful by the stripping down of the tent of standards—it then stands alone, as *the* question.

The people of the disasters come out of little vignettes from which Nickles pulls them. Each vignette is tied into an American memory of a particular period or disaster: 1. After the wars. 2. Hell raising before the Crash. 3. Delinquency period, as now. 4. The coming atom bomb. 5. The radiation sickness that follows.

These are the magics that we have to create by a few quick strokes, each in a different style and only partially seen. It can be terribly effective if we don't see whole figures.

Visual progression. By the end of Act One the tent has collapsed. The protection of drama, etc., is no longer there. Act Two is set under an open sky on a couple of platforms.

EDITOR: At the first reading, Kazan addressed the cast before MacLeish read his play aloud to them:

This is a play in verse.

That is not the most important thing about it, but it is an important thing about it. I've asked the author to start our rehearsals by reading it aloud to us. I've never done this before. In fact, at one time I used to be rough on authors. I used to suggest to them early—and not always by indirection—that they attend rehearsals at fixed intervals. And I'd throw a fit if they'd ever once talk to an actor. The fact is that I've asked him to speak to you, indirectly, by reading his verse. I want you to feel, and I believe you will feel, as you listen to him, that this verse, this line of his is not a problem and is not a burden. It is an asset. Not only will the audience enjoy the language, but you actors will find it good to work with, a help and support. That's how I felt when he read the play to me.

There is a story of a director—this man an Englishman, inciden- tally—who commenced rehearsals of a verse play by saying: "This is a verse play. It is written in verse, but if anyone in the audience knows it's poetry, we're sunk."

Well, as it happened, that was a bad play, written in bad verse and they were sunk before they started. But the reason I tell you that story is to make the point that this is not my attitude toward verse and this particular verse play.

In fact, I think good poetry is not an affectation, an involution, a mannerism, a stylization even. When it is good, it is a necessity. It's the only way, quite possibly, that the author has found to say and say clearly and directly what he wants to say. I say "necessity" because one feels that the author has been forced to find a way, a language, a technique to say things that are ordinarily so difficult to say that they remain in the world of the unarticulated. In this category there are thoughts newly discovered, experiences still in the half twilight of intuition, ideas that still have around them the husk of the experience from which they sprang, all things difficult, subtle, new, unsaid before. And if the verse is good, the audience, listening, is able to grasp immedi- ately the concepts and images, and experience them with the pleasure that comes from sudden, unexpected illumination.

This play is not a thesis play. It doesn't prove a point about either God or Man. What it does is illuminate an experience of living today. A

Raymond
Massey and
Christopher
Plummer

poet, by telling us what's happening to him, helps us to feel what's happening to us, and since the experience explored is an inward one, the poetic language is a necessity, not a flourish.

To find how to read this verse correctly not only includes the important questions of breath and voice, stress, cadence and rhythm, but to find in our parts the inner impulse of the author to express what he was feeling. If we create within ourselves the right experience, the rest will come. The rest is just work.

EDITOR

Just before its out-of-town Washington engagement, MacLeish invited friends to attend a run-through. They weren't entirely pleased, and MacLeish wrote to Kazan, November 15:

> Lil [Lillian Hellman] thought the play—what she saw of it—had been "hypo-ed" up to a considerable degree—enough so that the play itself was in danger of getting lost in its own business. But this, she felt, was not serious because—as she put it—"Gadg, like

other great directors, likes to begin high and work down." I remembered your telling me a couple of months ago that you would do things neither of us would like in order to sandpaper them down to what we would like.

Ellen [Ellen Barry, the widow of the playwright Philip Barry] thought the play had been snowed under.

Ada [Mrs. MacLeish] said that she too was bothered, confused, deafened, by the little inter-scenes and particularly by the noises after the bombing.

I agree that those inter-scenes do intrude on the play. They started as punctuation and they have become new scenes—and scenes which are not in the play itself. . . . It seems to me there is a contradiction of styles in these inter-scenes. The set is not realistic in any way; it indicates, it suggests. But the inter-scenes are in a different and to me jarring dimension. I'd be grateful if they could come down, fall back—and if silence could replace all those coughing cries after the bombing.

Variety reported on the play's Washington opening: "The primary trouble with *J.B.* is the fierceness of its writing and staging. It needs relief either in a slackening of pace or comedy. The audience response at the finale seemed to indicate a feeling of let-down."

The company knew the play was in trouble, and Kazan said later: "A wave of depression hit the whole group." He felt they had the audience in the first act and lost them in the second. Two days later he awoke knowing where the trouble was. "We had left out Aristotle's 'recognition scene.' The very turning point in the history of our protagonist had been left undramatized." The next day MacLeish brought in a revision, which Kazan thought solved the problem: "Then we had it."

It seems that a man keeps learning the same lessons over and over, all his life long. Of course, I should have caught an error of that size months earlier. I had studied the play all summer and hadn't seen, till almost too late, that the one scene the audience must have was that one: the moment when J.B., having accepted his insignificance and impotence in the face of the scale and majesty of the universe, passes from dependence and humbleness to independence and dignity and pride in his own manliness.

In his autobiography Kazan admitted (something he hadn't told the actors or MacLeish) that he had had no faith in the play: "I must confess that the merits of that play eluded me. I must also confess that I have no ear. Poetry makes me impatient, even Shakespeare. . . . As for *J.B.* I am not convinced that it is poetry. It looks like poetry on a page, but doesn't 'rise.' I didn't believe it was poetry when I directed it. I staged *J.B.*, which is different from 'direct,' and did it with my eye, which is pretty good, not my ear."

Sweet Bird of Youth (1959)
by Tennessee Williams

"It necessitated a setting that was even less realistic than the setting of Cat on a Hot Tin Roof, *and again I had the feeling that I was violating the author and that there was a gap between us."*

EDITOR: Chance Wayne is the paid companion of the aging actress Alexandra Del Lago, the Princess Kosmonopolis, and the two are sharing a suite at the Palms Hotel, in St. Cloud on the Gulf of Mexico. The Princess is hiding out after the screening of her comeback film, which she believes is a disaster. She has picked up Chance, a sometime gigolo and aspiring actor, at a Palm Springs hotel, and they are traveling cross-country, fueled by drugs and alcohol. By making tapes of their stoned conversations, Chance plots to blackmail the Princess into getting him a movie contract.

St. Cloud is Chance's hometown, and he has returned in the hope of reconnecting with his girlfriend, Heavenly Finley. The local doctor, George Scudder, warns him to leave town as quickly as possible, for Heavenly's father, Boss Finley, a powerful Southern politico, has threatened to castrate Chance if he ever returns. Finley believes Chance infected Heavenly with syphilis, and the diagnosis came so late in the stage of the disease that Heavenly was given a hysterectomy.

During Boss Finley's political rally of the second act, a Heckler threatens to expose Heavenly's history and Finley's attempt to cover up the scandal. At the play's conclusion, Finley's threat of castration is about to be enacted by his son, Tom Junior, and the Princess is thrown out of the hotel because of her relationship to Chance. For both the Princess and Chance, "the sweet bird of youth" is the bird that has fled.

Like many of Williams's full-length plays, *Sweet Bird of Youth* was a combining and reworking of some of his early one-act plays, and after its tryout performance in 1956, Williams worked on revisions for three years before it opened on Broadway in the spring of 1959. In the interval Williams had offered *Orpheus Descending*, directed by Harold Clurman, whose failure unnerved Williams and also affected the reception of *Sweet Bird;* critics complained of overwrought melodrama, decadent characters, gratuitous violence, and hallucinogenic ambiance. During the same period Kazan made the film *A Face in the Crowd* and had two Broadway hits, William

Inge's *The Dark at the Top of the Stairs,* and Archibald MacLeish's verse play *J.B.*

Sweet Bird, like *Camino Real,* was subjected to Kazan's minute and elaborate editorial suggestions for revisions; Williams accepted some of Kazan's suggestions, ignored others, and was irritated by all of them. The dissolute golden youth (Chance), the faded movie star (Alexandra Del Lago), and the ruthless political boss (Boss Finley) were a tough combination, and the play's overload of plot threads and the characters' antecedent history made revision mainly a job of focusing the plot, clarifying intent, and modifying characterization.

In its first production at George Keathley's Studio M in Coral Gables, Florida (April 1956), the play was billed as a "work in progress." Williams made daily changes and asked Kazan and designer Jo Mielziner to wait a few weeks before attending a performance, with the hope that the three would eventually collaborate on a Broadway production. Though Kazan had offered rigorous notes on *The Rose Tattoo* and *Orpheus Descending,* he had not committed to these productions, and since both were financial failures, Williams was increasingly convinced that only Kazan, notwithstanding *Camino Real,* brought him the chance of success. To Williams's relief, Kazan and Mielziner thought the play promising enough to agree to direct and design. All three had prior commitments, which caused the three-year delay, though throughout that time Kazan kept up his effort to get Williams to revise the play. A year before the scheduled Broadway opening, Kazan worried over unresolved questions about the main character.

MAY 20, 1958

Dear Tennessee:

First I want to say that *Chance* has the potential of being a character as memorable as any you have written. That's saying a lot. Maybe it is going too far. I don't think so. He is a sort of grotesque mid-twentieth-century Hamlet. I agree with you that all the sickness of our time is contained in him. His anxiety about keeping up with the parade, his pathetic, desperate measures to achieve recognition, his clumsy blackmail, his bizarre big shot behavior are all heartbreaking and tragic and meaningful. He is also a great stage figure. I mean that the audience will watch him with a combination of recognition and concern and identification, the way they do other great stage figures.

You see, I am in a complimentary mood, but I do mean it. The potential is there for something really wonderful.

I also think you have for the first time since *Streetcar* the setup for a genuine tragedy. I won't go into a lot of theory about it, but I do mean this and I do mean it in the most classic sense. Chance has a tragic flaw in the same way that Blanche did, in the same way that Oedipus did, in the same way that Willy Loman did. And he dies as a result of this tragic flaw. I think you are dead wrong to have the same ending to this play that you did to *Orpheus,* for that is what you do have, Tennessee, no matter how skillfully you try to disguise it by underwriting the stage direction. I see through the stage direction.* I see that some shadowy, underlit villains will come out and take the boy out into the wings, presumably to castrate him. I didn't believe it in *Orpheus,* and I don't believe it as I read it in this script.

Let me tell you a story. I had a friend in the thirties. A man named Manny Eisenberg who was half artist, half homosexual. He did publicity for the Group Theatre. He was full of pretensions, yet I liked him very much. Indeed, I was touched by his pretensions. He was talented in many ways, but in every field the degree of his talent was very small. He was a writer, a photographer, a producer, a wit, a poet—all just a little bit. But he aspired. He wanted to be big and recognized. And of course the city didn't. It looked scornfully at him. Manny Eisenberg was doomed from the day I met him. One day he came to recognize that everybody was laughing at him behind his back and that he was a figure of ridicule. He was losing his hair by then, getting fat, and was losing jobs because he had begun to drink too much. I began to be oppressed by a feeling that within the near future this man was going to kill himself. Here's how he did it. He chartered a small airplane and instructed the pilot to fly over the Broadway theatrical district, and to fly rather low. The pilot did this, circling several times. At a certain point Manny stepped out of the plane and dived out on the city that had scorned him. He reminds me of your character. I thought from the very beginning Chance was doomed. In fact, Chance smells of doom. It comes out of him like sweat or like a radiation. When you showed me in the first act that he had a pistol, I thought, "This man will kill himself." Early in Act Two he says to the Princess, either I will make a good thing of it, or else! I think he should kill himself. It seems dead right for

---

* *Orpheus Descending* was a reworking of Williams's 1940 *Battle of Angels.* Directed by Harold Clurman, it opened on Broadway in March 1957 and featured Maureen Stapleton and Cliff Robertson. The 1960 film version, *The Fugitive Kind,* directed by Sidney Lumet, starred the actors Williams had wanted for the stage, Anna Magnani and Marlon Brando.

him. How he does it I have no suggestion for, and if I had it would be no damn good. But all through the play I felt Chance was bringing on his own end.

And he dies because of what he is and because of what society has made him and because of the way he has twisted himself to fit what he thinks society demands of him. He dies for profound and inner reasons, not because there are a few monsters in a certain part of this country. Tennessee, I don't believe people in the South are any more cruel than the people in the North. I think you are unfair to the South. In many ways the people I met down there are more human than the people on Broadway, or in Hollywood, or on Madison Avenue, or in New England, or in the Bible belt of the Midwest. You pick on the South, son, because your own personal nightmares are set there. Southern bullies frightened you once, or something. I don't know. But it seems to me that it's possible for you now to take a more "balanced" view of it. I was embarrassed by the villains at the end of *Orpheus,* although I did think Harold staged that scene miserably. But the story of Chance is completely all-American.

There are Chances all over the place—all phenomena of this particular time, this particular society. All of them doomed because of their own natures and because they have gone with the false ideals of our society. Chance is significant because he is trying to go with the system, succeed by its standards, which are false standards. Somehow making him a victim, not of his own nature and not of a broad social ideal, but a bit of a "heavy," makes your play much smaller than it really is.

Remember my old joke with you that whenever you were in difficulties you got lyrical and whenever I was in difficulties I got loud? When I see you getting lyrical at the end of a play and trying to make an ending around Heavenly, when all of the audience should be feeling, and will be feeling, is What Happens To Chance?—then I know that something unsatisfactory is going on with you and that in your heart you know it. I think the end of the play has to do with Chance, and you must really conclude his story. I thought the lyricism about Heavenly becoming a nun, although much, much better in the rewriting, and I believe an excellent end for her, should not have the emphasis it has now.

Anyway, I am going on and on about the same thing. You, by now, have my feeling on this point. On to the next. In general, I feel there is a little too much of the Grand Guignol in your play. It's as though you didn't trust your own material and felt obliged by the particular anxiety a playwright feels to hop it up with a lot of sensational bits. For example, I think it is marvelous that the Princess is losing her memory. That in fact she has none when she wakes on this particular morning. Further, I think the new stuff you have written on why she smokes hash is wonderful and will make the audience feel themselves into The Princess. But the oxygen mask business seems over gruesome, as though it were an end in itself. And I felt the same way about the line, "Make love to her with your knife." And a number of other things. We get it all without having it rubbed in our faces. Again I say it's as if you don't trust your own legitimate dramatic powers and resorted to these external shockers to jazz up the audience. It's as though Shakespeare had decided to be the author of *The Duchess of Malfi*—Webster, I believe.

Another suggestion about Chance. I suggest that at several points in Act 2, Scene 1, we put in the tooting of Cadillac horns, as if Chance were driving around and around the block where Boss Finley's home was, tooting the horn to call attention to his presence in town and to his new affluence and power. This would solve the technical fault that our leading man is not in this scene. And of course, the Cadillac horn could be cued in at appropriate moments and commented upon.

Now here is the suggestion that you are going to hate. I hope you don't. I think the suggestion is an awfully good one, but I have a feeling I will be running into a very strong conviction of yours here. I like Act 3, Scene 1, but I don't like playing it as you do, pretending that the theatre is a meeting hall where this rally is taking place, pretending that the audience is an audience of Southerners, who are attending this rally and spotting characters around the hall, etc. This all seems to me stylistically gauche, and I have a suggestion which I think is a good one.

I suggest that in the cocktail lounge there be a big TV set. If the show is produced and directed, as it should be, larger than life, this TV set could be larger than life too. In fact, at a point in the action of the last scene of the present second act, it could become even bigger, opening up at the corners as you sometimes see screens doing in motion picture theatres. The rally should be presented filmically on this enlarged television screen. We could show a real Southern audience in a real Southern hall with believable supernumeraries going into believable events in a believable environment. At a certain moment, all our audience should see on the stage is an enormous screen with this grotesque rally going on, the camera cutting from enormous close-ups of the Boss's face to shots of the audience, etc. At the same time Chance is placed prominently on our stage, watching what seems like a preview of his own fate. As the riot begins in the televised rally, we see figures exiting from the hall pursuing the heckler. Just as this happens, they enter the cocktail lounge and the "live" vision of our audience. The beating takes place in the cocktail lounge by the reflected light of the TV screens, in front of Chance and with Boss Finley on the TV screen in close-up, still bellowing away. This, Tennessee, would be entirely in style and would be really New Theatre. What you have now seems old-fashioned to me and I think it is terribly true as a theatre image to have this enormous image of Boss Finley bellowing away while some hoodlums are beating up a heckler, and Chance is watching, frightened to death, a witness to a preview of his own fate.

I like the character of Heavenly. I do not think she should be more prominent. I am not "more interested in the young people of the play." I think Heavenly is perfectly in place and in proportion. I thought the Princess's final betrayal of Chance is excellent, and I think the form of the play as you have it now is basically right. My main points are about the end of Act 2, or the beginning of Act 3, and about the end of the play, and I have made them. I think what is presently Act 3, Scene 2, is enough for a whole act.

I think the style of the play is an advance of what you did on *Cat*. I think the arias are wonderfully done and will be most effective and can be staged even more frankly than we did on *Cat*. I think your writing is as good as it ever was. I think the psychoanalysis has done you good and you should go back. The only thing that disturbs me from this point of view is your insistence on what I call Grand Guignol. You don't need it, my dear, dear friend. So cut it out. Let up on us.

I have some other notes, but they are all detailed. I am not going into them. I have been awfully rough on you, but please put it down to the fact that I like the play a lot, and its author, and I feel that utter candor is the least I can give you. I haven't held anything back. I have said just what I think. I would like to do the play, if after reading this letter you still want me to. There is a practical problem, which I talked to Audrey [Wood] about. I cannot do anything till after the first of the year. I am already committed for the fall and was when I first read your play. But if you want to wait for me, I'll be your boy. As I say, if you still want me after reading this letter. Incidentally, there is now going on the worst jam for theatres that there has been within my memory. According to Roger Stevens, there are no theatres available till February.

Love,
Gadg

EDITOR: In the early fall of 1958, months before rehearsals were to begin, Kazan became more aggressive in urging Williams to complete the revisions.

SEPTEMBER 2, 1958

Dear Tenn:

As I see it, the play is about Chance. It's about Chance's desperate return to St. Cloud, desperately undertaken, desperately timed. It is about his return to St. Cloud in search of his youth and in search of what his youth means to him, his purity. You might say he is trying to regain his purity. Conversely, you might say he wants to be punished for his sins and thus be cleansed and purified. He hopes, first of all, to embrace the symbols of his youth and the cleanliness he has lost, to wit: Heavenly and His Mother.

But there is a joker, and the joker has several sides. 1. His mother is dead. 2. Heavenly is not Heavenly anymore. 3. His position, his own position, is one of extreme danger. He is psychically sick and crippled. Chance, you might say, is not Chance anymore. 4. Things have changed. He doesn't know it, but what he has come back for is impossible.

But he cannot leave. He has a chance to leave, albeit in a degraded position, and to escape with his "life." But he knows it wouldn't really be his "life," so he doesn't escape. He stays and he takes his punishment, be it castration or death.

In other words, the plot of the play, as I see it, is simple, straight, and sound. Now I'll oversimplify it. A man comes back to his home town. He is warned. He is warned again to get out of town. We see, and he discovers, that the threat is serious. And more serious. And still he doesn't go. And the threat looms. The knife is at his throat. The scissors at his balls. And finally, he has one last chance to go. And he lets this chance go. He allows his last chance to get away. Suddenly, we see he wants to be destroyed. He walks up to his destruction. Or rather, he allows it to come to him.

This is a good plot. It is as simple as Oedipus. It has a strong, simple line. And above all, it has its terror "built in." The terror is in the story.

Now, I don't mention the Princess in the above outline. You can tell Chance's story without her.

But this does not mean she is an unimportant character. She is a most important character. But the play is basically not about her. It is about Chance. Hers is a parallel fate. Hers is a deep understanding of his fate. She provides an illumination. She is as important as hell. But the play is not about her.

A parallel. In *Streetcar*, which is a masterpiece of construction, the play is about Blanche. Her arrival starts it. Her "death" finishes it. It's about her. This does not make Stanley unimportant. He is most important, brilliant, and unforgettable. But the play is about Blanche.

Now the seventh scene of *Streetcar* is a two-character scene. The two characters being Stanley and Stella. Blanche is not in the scene, but it's all about Blanche. Do you remember the scene? It is not off the point. It does not break the unity. It is not a diffusion. It is about the relationship between Stella and Stanley, but as seen in the light of the conflagration that Blanche caused. And what happens in the scene affects Blanche's fate.

So here I say, this play is about Chance, and every scene should be about Chance. But it doesn't mean Chance should be in every scene. Every scene should either have Chance in it or be about Chance and have an effect on Chance's fate.

I think Act One is perfect, with one small exception that I'll make later on.

Your trouble, as you very clearly point out, is in Act Two, and may I say this? You have trouble there and it is serious trouble, but it is not like *Camino Real*. It can be and will be fixed. And when it is, you'll have a wonderful and sound play and a play that will be recognized as one of your best. You have never written better than you have in this play, Tennessee, or more honestly. Not only did I not lose faith in the play as I examined it more, but my admiration for it increased with rereading.

What's wrong with the Boss Finley scene? It goes off into several stories that are irrelevant. There is a spreading or diffusion onto stories or relationships that don't pertain or relate to the main story, which has to do with Chance's return to St. Cloud. For example, the story between Boss Finley and Tom Jr. is irrelevant. For example, Heavenly's miracle you can keep, but I consider it irrelevant.° The story between Miss Lucy and Boss Finley, when given that much time and space and feeling, seems irrelevant. And the story between Boss Tom and his wife, even though it is the foundation on which you mount one of the most brilliant speeches you have ever written, is also irrelevant.

° The "miracle" was Heavenly's restored virginity. This was dropped, as was the tale of Heavenly being raped in the Hollywood hotel the Garden of Allah. This would have exonerated Chance of the charge of infecting Heavenly with syphilis.

I think I mean *seems* irrelevant because sometimes if the number of speeches is cut down, if the proportion of story is changed, or (and this is the most important thing) if they are related to the main story fully, elements that seem irrelevant become relevant. I don't think you should eliminate Tom Jr. He just should be there to the extent that he functions in the Chance story. I don't think you should eliminate Lucy, but she should be brought down in proportion too.

And you must never consider eliminating Aunt Nonnie. She is completely on the line. She is about Chance's past. She dramatizes what Chance once was. What he lost. What he is suffering from.

Now I'll go into more detail, I'll act like a "strong director."

As I say, Act One is perfect except for one thing. I believe George Scudder should be convinced it was Chance who infected Heavenly. He should be dead sure of this and therefore his hatred of Chance is not only stronger but more human, more understandable. Chance is aghast and denies Scudder's accusation. But Scudder can't even begin to try to believe anything Chance says, and we, the audience, don't know at this point in the play what the true fact is. The author saves (i.e., should) the true information as to what happened till Act Two. We're not sure Chance isn't a liar. We may even think he is. After all, he reveals himself as a desperate but pathetic blackmailer. And we are not at all sure that Scudder is not right, despite the fact that we don't like him.

Now Act Two. In Act One we have been shown Chance's desperate scheme, his need to return to regain his youth, and what his youth means—that is, his purity, his need to be punished and cleansed and to rise again on this Easter morning. Now in Act Two we are shown the trap that Chance is in. The catastrophe that is mounting to overwhelm him. In simple talk, we are shown that if Chance doesn't go, he will be killed or castrated.

Now, concretely, about Act Two, I agree about the Boss Finley scene. It is, as you say, "cluttered with irrelevant bits," and I agree that we should as soon as possible get into the meat of the scene between Boss Finley and Heavenly. Aunt Nonnie has to be introduced, but the Boss Finley–Heavenly scene is the scene that ties into Chance's story and moves it ahead.

I have a daring suggestion, and it may not be any good, but maybe it is. The suggestion is that Heavenly tells her father that the Heckler is right. Boss Finley has been going on the basis that there is not one drop of truth in what the Heckler has been saying. The Boss has been denying the Heckler's accusation with the fullest conviction. He has been regarding the Heckler as crazy.

Now Heavenly, in desperation and a kind of psychic terror, asserts to her father that the Heckler is right. And she tells him about her in the Garden of Allah. She tells him about her past relationship with Chance and through her and at this point we find out what really happened. This, of course, is an overwhelming blow to her father. But his reaction to it is characteristic. Now he insists that she go on the platform with him as a symbol of pure Southern white virginity. Now he insists she mustn't see Chance and if she does Chance will go out of St. Cloud "on the garbage scow." And now, without telling her, his hatred of Chance reaches a level of violence that is uncontrollable.

And of course, now he has good reason to hate Chance.

Now a word about Boss Finley. There is a tendency here to caricature him. Forgive me for trying to tell you anything about the South, but I must say this. When I was down in Benoit on *Baby Doll,* I met a lot of fellows on those "Citizen's Committees," and my impression was that they believed it. In fact, they saw themselves as heroes, heroically fighting against terrible odds, fighting for what they thought was right. I even liked some of the men. As soon as I read your stage direction about the arpeggios on the organ, I knew I was in for caricature sketch. Tennessee, you can turn these out by the yard. They are very funny, they are brilliant, in fact, and seductive as hell. Big Daddy was a great figure because he was deeply felt. Boss Finley is perfect when Heavenly is talking and tells him that he should have let her marry Chance long ago. There are many other places where he is brilliantly written, but he verges on the stage heavy. Enough said.

Once Heavenly has told him about her history with Chance, the true facts, this old man is in a spot. And this is aggravated by the fact that this is the first time he will be going on a big regional TV hookup, with the chance of the Heckler making an appearance. I assume that up till then the Heckler has just appeared at meetings that weren't being broadcast. So the old man determines to go ahead with the daring scheme to put his daughter on the platform dressed in white. When Heavenly refuses, he makes the assertion that if she sees Chance, or doesn't do what he says, Chance will go out of town on a garbage scow. At the end of the scene, Heavenly agrees. She will go through with it. She has no choice. It isn't so much that she wants to see Chance again. That is all over and she has changed. But simply, she doesn't want Chance murdered.

Briefly, during Act Two, Scene One, we meet Scudder and Tom Jr. and Nonnie, but only briefly and only in re the main story. Tom Jr. is part of Boss Finley's "Muscle." Boss Finley has "reliable Muscle" under the command of his own son. We can also meet Aunt Nonnie briefly in this scene because she has the great scene in the cocktail lounge to come.

Now I agree with you about eliminating the phone conversation. It is a worn device, and it is bad stagecraft. It won't be necessary now if you agree that the information about the Garden of Allah might come in the Finley home scene. This would make the phone conversation unnecessary.

Nonnie, by the way, might easily eavesdrop (bringing in coffee, newspapers, etc.) on some of the scene between Boss Finley and Heavenly, or she could sit there through all of it. Above all, she hears the Boss's threat to kill Chance and she could feel murder in Boss Finley's threat toward Chance. By the way, any father would feel murderous toward a boy who had done to his daughter what Chance has done.

EDITOR: A week later Kazan wrote Mielziner with detailed suggestions for the stage design, including sketches of scenic ideas.

SEPTEMBER 9, 1958

Dear Jo:

I had a good weekend on SBY. I've put in a lot of time on it and, I believe, finally figured out what I want to do with it. And, therefore, at last I know how I want to proceed. I didn't the last time I met with you, and I was wobbling pretty badly the time before. It is a tough play to do and could go so many ways and the important thing is to go the organic "route."

So I am rushing this letter to you. For one thing, to tell you to STOP. I know how you are. I know that in between lighting sessions you will be opening your dispatch case and taking out the folder marked SBY, and the little revolving stage, and your colored pencils, and by the time you get back to New York, it will all be done. Therefore, this letter post haste. Please, Jo, stop! I think we are on the wrong track. We are certainly up the wrong tree, if we are up a tree. In effect, we have to start over. That doesn't mean a lot of the things we discussed aren't completely right. But basically—basically there was no basis—I never solved the play from the point of view of the director. I never told you what I needed to make the play "work" for me. I think you've solved it from the designer's point of view up to a point. Up to the point, that is, where I stopped helping you. I mean, I think it will look beautiful in the theatre and it will work quickly and well. But something about this show makes it necessary for me to have more help from the production scheme. It needs a production scheme, in other words, one that is organic and really dramatizes the play. It has to be done just right. It will only make sense if the production makes the RIGHT sense.

A lot of what is in this letter, Jo, is thinking aloud. But I can think aloud in an uninhibited fashion with an old friend, so just bear with me.

I think this is the most truly autobiographic play Williams ever wrote. Not in the way *Menagerie* [*The Glass Menagerie*] was autobiographical—not a memory, softened and romanticized by time, of his youth, but Tennessee trying to describe his state of soul and state of being today and now. It is the frankest play he has written, dealing as it does with his own corruption and his wish to return to the purity he once had. And while we again have the central romanticized figure of the boy surrounded by threatening and murderous forces, this time this central figure is not romanticized as it was in *Orpheus* [*Orpheus Descending*], but male, partly corrupted and true. . . . I believe it is Tennessee in disguise, right down to the thinning hair. Chance is in a trap, or he is in a pit, and he is surrounded by murderous forces that want to do away with him or castrate him. He has the choice of either leaving town and cutting himself off forever from his pure "roots" or of staying and being killed. He is not strong enough to fight these murderous forces. And perhaps he doesn't even want to escape. I increasingly feel that unconsciously he wants to stay there, be punished, pay for his sins, meet his deserts, painful though they be, deadly though they be, cleanse himself through penance of the most awful physical and mental kind. It was as though Tennessee felt that after all he has done he should be punished or castrated. This is the strangely and unexpectedly puritanical side of Williams. He is obsessed with his own sin, and I suppose it is this sense of guilt that makes his vision so universal.

We all have it to some degree or other.

Now, whatever else the director does or does not do, he absolutely must dramatize and directly put on the stage in physical form this basic situation. We have to picturize Chance in this trap, or pit, finally having no escape or just one degrading escape possible. Like the bull in the pit surrounded by hostile and jeering crowds who cheer at his betrayers and murderers and await his death with the pleasure of vengeance.

Gruesome? Well, when I did *Baby Doll* in Greenville, Mississippi, Williams came down to visit me. He stayed at the Greenville Hotel for three days, and there, if ever I saw one, was a trapped man. He felt quite clearly that the people of the town hated him. He complained that no one called him. He smarted over snubs, real or imaginary, from people he passed on the street. He began to feel that he was trapped. In one obsessive drunken moment he said he hoped he could get out of town alive, and he began to be panic stricken. I couldn't find him a swimming pool, and this lack of physical outlet made him more panicky. After three days he disappeared without warning. He had even felt, and I have felt this, trapped in his hotel room. That in case of an emergency or of sudden danger, there was no way out of the hotel room. And after all, there was only one way out for him. Down through the lobby full of people that knew him and, as he saw it, hated him.

You get the idea. It's all in the play. The scene in the cocktail lounge is exactly this. And furthermore, I am only treating the matter superficially. He feels the whole world is against him as an artist and as a homosexual both. Well, you are familiar with the man, and you know the situation that he thinks he is in. Sometimes I wonder how the hell he lives!

Now, that is one thing that somehow should be caught in a production scheme. Here comes the other.

How does Williams get out of the trap? For on certain occasions he does. On certain occasions, for temporary short terms of time. Well, for one thing, which is like Chance, increasingly by drink. This makes him suddenly confident, light, fearless, social, gay. It is temporary. But he must drink. He is compelled to. I suppose he has taken dope, though I doubt if he is given to this a great deal. But still Tennessee only writes what he has been through. And then by the act of loving. Tennessee complains that as he gets older this is a decreasingly frequent escape for him. And then by the greatest of all, an act of imagination. Through the act of memory recall, for instance, and either written down or not, through the process which is the artistic process. In this way he is able, every morning as he shuts himself up in his room and looks through the door at the wolves outside waiting to devour him, he is able to go into the land that John Keats describes and to be free and happy again, pure again, free again.

I don't think Tennessee could live if he were unable to function as a writer. His art is necessary for him.

You recall how often in his plays the idea of flight is dwelt upon.

Geraldine Page and Paul Newman

Now I say, Jo, that these two worlds, the threatening, hostile, murderous, real world, from which Chance (Tennessee) can transport himself into the imaginary world by an act of art, or by some extraordinary stimulus, that the two worlds are the <u>alternating environments of this play</u>. The fact that one of the traps is a hotel room and the other a cocktail lounge is important, but not central. Tennessee has gone past realism. The realistic trimmings are peripheral. The core is what has to be made to live in concrete terms of stage art.

And as these two worlds are the environments of the play, the process of the play is again and again how Chance passes from one world to the other. And this is done more frankly and plainly and directly than the author has ever done it before. We see Chance and the Princess and even the Boss come forward under the author's direction and re-create for themselves and for us their wish-dreams, their romanticized pasts, their lost glory. And as this happens, the author, now confident in the capabilities of the new stage, says in his stage direction that "Room changes." "Bar disappears." "They are alone in the Palm Garden." "He is alone with himself." In other words, the TRAPPED ONE is transported on the wings of this spiritual experience—drink, dope, romance, sex, longing, imagination, memory, what-ever—OUT OF THIS WORLD.

I am very leery these days, Jo, of highly colored words that remain words. This is Harold Clurman's great deficiency. He does not take his own eloquence seriously enough. He does not turn it into movement, scenery, costumes, and behavior. I want to be very bold on this show, more probably than Tennessee may wish for. I want to physicalize this going from "reality into the world of dreams." This back-and-forth process. I say we have to physicalize this quite literally, in the literal-ness, that is, of art. We have to show the background, threatening and hostile, and suddenly they are swimming in another environment, an environment which is created by their imaginations or their overstimu-lated senses. And the point is that this imagined environment is realer than the so-called real one. The Princess lives in her memory, like many an old actress we know. Chance lives in his imaginings, like many a person we know who "walks around in a fog all day." And who only comes down to earth when he is writing or loving or drinking. I see the figures of Chance, of the Princess, bathed in this environment, which they have created and where they feel at home and without fear. Of course, this is exactly what drink and dope and love and memory and the exercise of the artistic faculties do. Some people would add to this list religion. My point is that I want to find a theatrical form for this, and this is the help I need from you. We have to create a set which changes magically the chairs and furniture and objects in hand. They have to simply disappear. Suddenly the threatening picture is gone. Suddenly the overbearing physical relationships have eased. Suddenly the people, the strange people, are in a world of their own making. A nonspecific world, a nonliteral world, a world of the imagination.

Well, after I have figured out what the core of this thing is, I began to figure out how this could be done. The show is peculiar. There aren't a lot of sets; three sets. But in a way you can do it so there are a lot of environments—memory environments, dream environments. If you begin to think of the scenery as subjective scenery, and if you begin to think of Chance's world as the world that an artist inhabits, then per-haps there are more than three sets.

For example, this scheme makes our idea of the TV picture on the big screen absolutely in style. Of course, Chance sees nothing at that time in the room except the enormous, threatening, animated photo-graph of Boss Finley. You might say as Chance watches the TV "he doesn't know where he is." That is all that exists for him in the world.

Sometimes when you are drunk, you really literally do forget where you are. You are living in a world of your own. I would like to try, Jo, to think of the scenery in this way, that is, as subjective scenery.

At the end of Act Two, as I see it, Chance is caught in a pit which is in the shape and with the "trim" of a cocktail lounge, and here in the proxy of the Heckler he is beaten up. In Act Three, Chance is left behind. He allows himself to be left behind in a pit which is the Princess's room, and as he lies there finally the murderous figures begin to converge on him. He is caught there for the last time. He won't walk out of that pit, or that trap, alive. In other words, both these sets have to be designed so you feel the boy is in some sort of declivity and at the mercy, because of the very nature of a pit or trap, of his hostile fellow humans. But all through both acts and in the first act too, he is getting out of it and the set must make this change possible and physical.

Other changes, like bringing the bed nearer or further, or shifting the furniture by means of a revolving stage, must not be made. They are unimportant. The only important changes are the ones I have tried to describe above, and they should be the only changes made. And these changes that are unimportant must be made before our eyes and magically and by lights. Nothing else must shift. It confuses things to have other movement and other changes. The changes in the subjective scenery, changes made by lights, are the only changes to be made. I have become convinced of this, and that is why I am writing you now, not even waiting for you to return to New York to tell you to stop working on the revolving stage idea.

Now, how can all this be done? What physical arrangements, mechanics, equipment, design, will solve this? I had to ask myself this question before I asked it of you. And to an extent, as a director, I had to solve it as a designer. I think I have. It is not much designwise, but I have an arrangement idea, a basic picture idea, and also a mechanical idea. I have sketched out four little ground plans, which I am attaching, which you can read perfectly well. They are crudely done, so you will have questions on them, and ask me. And then there are some notes which also are attached as to how these things can work. I hope the ground plans are clear, but if they are not, pick up a phone, or let me know when you are coming to New York next and first thing is for us to get together and talk this thing out.

Love,
Gadg

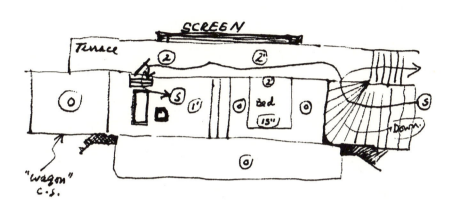

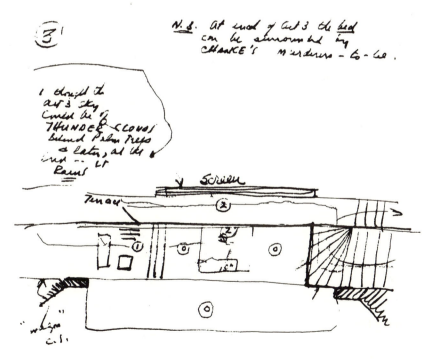

Screen

(2')

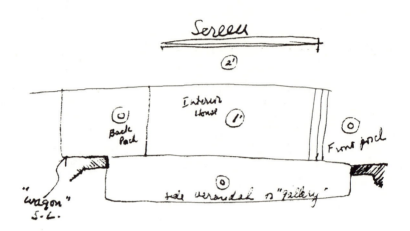

Interior House (1')

(0)
Back Porch

(0)
Front porch

(0)

the verandah or "gallery"

"wagon"
S.L.

(H) Path of Heckler

Screen

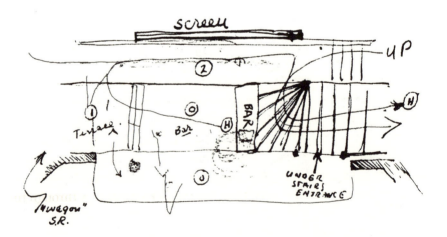

UP

(2)

(1)

(0)

(H)

(H)

BAR

Terrace

wc   Bar

(0)

UNDER
STAIRS
ENTRANCE

"wagon"
S.R.

EDITOR: The next day Kazan added an addendum to the letter:

The next day I read this letter over and it certainly is long and you are a very patient friend for reading it. The funny part is that next day I agree with it. I think it needs cutting but I think it is exactly what I wanted to say. Only thing that did strike me was that my poor little ground plans look very modest and simple after all my trumpeting and theorizing in the letter. However, don't take the ground plans too literally. They have an idea to them. You will see in Act Three, for instance, that there is a darn good opportunity for a final picture of this boy lying on the bed and all the hostile people around him on levels and in a sort of circular enveloping movement coming down the stairs behind the room on what I call the terrace, and finally around and into his room. In other words, the basic idea here is crudely done, but still you will feel, I think, that it is there.

Now, you will notice behind each set there is this screen, and I want to ask you a question about it. I have been looking at a lot of prints of the Japanese theatre. They always have a frame in back of their scenery, within which is hung a painted drop. The painted drop is sort of deceptively realistic. I mean it looks real, but of course it isn't at all. No more than their painting is. But it's definitely art pretending to be art, and not pretending to be real. Is it possible to paint such a drop from the rear and light it from there so that it only becomes visible when it is lit from the rear? And then when the backlights go out, projections could come on from the first pipe, and in this way, we could have a sort of lap dissolve. You must have fooled around with this kind of thing, and you would know the answer better than I would. I have always thought that projections to back up a scene brightly lit for actors didn't work. That is, either the actors suffered or the projections seemed dim. But here we have a chance to go from a sort of painted formalized "realism" to a projected nonrealistic, nonliteral imagery. And if the transition from one to the other could be done "magically," maybe we would have exactly what I was looking for.

Otherwise, the set, as I see it, in plan is simple. It's just a long wagon made up of various levels and that is stationed in various places. There is a staircase at one side, as you see, into which we can look through the stair rail.

Of course, I have not attempted any elevation ideas. I have been looking at the paintings of Sheeler and Bloom, and I have often thought of your idea of making the whole set in some light color. I don't know whether you still think this way. There is something about the world of Charley Sheeler and Peter Bloom, Feininger, etc., that seems right in feeling to me, but this, of course, is your problem and I probably shouldn't even mention these fellows to you.

Tennessee does have an idea. He says the hotel is in a sort of Grand Hotel gothic style. This could provide what decorative elements you need for the frame. In some of these old summer resorts on the Gulf Coast like Pascagoula and Biloxi, where I visited, there are these ghosts of old Grand Hotels done in a style from the very end of the last century. The paint by now well peeling, the colors thoroughly tamed by the hot sun. Sort of like an old, old actress with clothes from another time and a monster of a hat, who is forced to come out into the bright sunlight where every bit of makeup and jewelry and apparel will look at its worst.

It's also possible, of course, that the whole town was built in a flurry of inspiration and all built in more or less the same style, at more or less the same time. What I am trying to put more simply is that Boss Finley's house could be in the same style as the hotel.

I have probably talked you to death, Jo, and I will stop right now. But I do suggest that you read the play again with the thoughts in this letter in mind, and of course, I will be awfully anxious to see you. I'll be in town Friday, if you are back by then, and I'll certainly be here next Monday, my family with me, back for good.

Love,
Gadg

EDITOR

Though Williams made constant revisions, Chance's significance remained unclear. Williams admitted years later that he was never able to give Chance a vivid personality to fit his symbolic function in the play—a dilemma similar to the one that dogged the concept of Brick in *Cat on a Hot Tin Roof.* Later, Williams admitted that Chance was used "in a symbolic manner. It is a ritualistic death, a metaphor. He had to be real to be important. You cannot use a character as a dramatic symbol if he is important. You cannot use a character as a dramatic symbol if he is not first real for you. I didn't discover his real value until the end." Contrary to Kazan's reading of the play and Williams's first intent, the character who evoked Williams's most compassionate and theatrically urgent response was the Princess; this identification and allegiance served to bifurcate the play.

Just before the first rehearsal, Williams wrote a new final curtain speech for Chance. He sent it to Kazan and Mielziner on November 11, 1958:

> And so I am trying like hell to work into the last few minutes of this play some kind of summation comparable to Blanche's last line in *Streetcar*: "Whoever you are—I have always depended on the kindness of strangers." I think the audience, even the intelligent audience, and the good critics, will want something out of the main protagonist, Chance, besides his destruction. They'll want it to mean something to him. And to them. Otherwise it may seem like shooting cat fish in a barrel. . . . I think that can only come out of a moment of dignity in him, which, if I can find the words for it, he should express. I'm just letting you know that I am aware of a problem that I'm sure you are aware of also. Chance's last words are: "I don't ask for your pity, but just for your understanding—not even that—no. Just for your recognition of me in you. And the enemy, time, in us all."

Williams, Kazan, and Mielziner agreed on a nonrealistic set, with few but telling props—a cyclorama backed all scenes, the lighting was dramatically designed, the actors addressed the audience directly, sound effects coursed through the action (as they had in *Streetcar* and *Cat*), and a projection of a political rally as if on an enormous TV screen doubled the action in the second act. Only Mielziner succeeded in integrating these elements; and he later admitted that the projection of the TV screen was a technical failure: "a lack of cohesion in what was otherwise a stunning performance and a wonderful production." The script veers too extremely among realism, and poetic effect, and political satire, and defeats what was Kazan's craft genius for merging elements of nonrealistic and realist staging, the underlying strength of the productions of *Streetcar* and *Salesman*.

Kazan's concerns about the stage violence in Williams's plays, what Kazan termed Grand Guignol, were addressed in a defensive article Williams wrote for the *New York Times* even before the play opened:

> If there is any truth in the Aristotelian idea that violence is purged by its poetic representation on a stage, then it may be that my cycle of violent plays have had a moral justification after all. I know that I have felt it. I have always felt a release from the sense of meaninglessness and death when a work of tragic intention has seemed to me to have achieved that intention, even if only approximately, nearly.

The play received mostly negative reviews—*Time* magazine called it "close to parody, but the wonder is that Williams should be so inept at imitating himself"—but Brooks Atkinson in the *New York Times* welcomed it as one of Williams's finest dramas, and the pre-Broadway sale of the movie rights, and the drawing power of Williams and Kazan and stars Paul Newman and Geraldine Page, guaranteed a financial success. It ran for 375 performances.

For revivals, Williams revised the play, beginning this process even while the original production was on tour. On April 4, 1960, he wrote to his close friend and onetime collaborator Donald Windham:

> Right now I have put aside new work to re-write a play already produced and finished on Broadway and limping about the country on tour, "Sweet Bird of Youth." It violated an essential rule: the rule of the straight line, the rule of poetic limits of simpleness and wholeness, because when I first wrote it, crisis after crisis, of nervous and physical and mental nature, had castrated me nearly. Now I am cutting it down to size: keeping it on the two protagonists with, in Act Two, only one or two suitable elements beside the joined deaths of the male and female heroes, so that instead of being an over-length play it will be under-length (conventionally) and the first and third act will not be disastrously interrupted by so many non-integrated, barely even peripheral, concerns, with a social background already made clearly implicit, not needing to be explicit.

The team of Williams, Kazan, and Mielziner planned to reunite on Williams's next play, the comedy *Period of Adjustment* (eventually Jo Mielziner did the set, but George Roy Hill directed). When Kazan, heavily committed to film projects (and without enthusiasm for the play), withdrew, Williams blasted Kazan in a phone call for both current and past offenses. Kazan responded by letter, spewing up his own smothered resentments.

APRIL 22, 1960

Dear Tenn:

I'm furious at the way you spoke to me on the phone. You haven't a right in the world to infer that I'm lying to you. I have never lied to you. And have I ever asked you to crawl? Has our relationship ever dealt in pity? We have a clean relationship and I did my share to keep it clean.

I don't believe you can listen now. But I want to put down a few facts and maybe they will sink in. You're right: I did promise to do your play. I did because I wanted to do it, and I wanted to do it because I think it's a beautiful play and a deep one. At that time I intended to get out of the [William] Inge movie [*Splendor in the*

Grass]. I'm in psychoanalysis again and I found myself especially harassed and discouraged and weary. I still am, incidentally, but that is no concern in this now.

But when it got right down to it, I couldn't get out of Bill's movie. Not because of any contractual reason. But because I had initiated the project. I had made him write it. The date on his first complete script is April 1958. That means we were having conversations about it at least nine months before. How the hell can you pull out of a project that has cost a writer that much work and thought? Especially when I started the whole thing. I couldn't. I didn't.

NEXT, as to how much work it is. That again was my fault. I underestimated it. I thought I could do both. I guess I could—but at terrific cost to myself. Example. I finished shooting *Wild River* on the fourth of January. I will finish putting the score on it May 2. That means I did four months' work on it after I was through shooting. Charles Maguire estimates I will finish shooting Inge's film August 7. I should then, by all indications, finish putting the score on this one December 5. Furthermore, since I am producing Inge's script, as well as directing it, I will be responsible for the ad campaign, the promotion, the booking of the first theatre, the exploitation, the selling, etc. In other words, I will have much more work to do on this one than on *Wild River.*

I'm not Otto Preminger [Hollywood producer and director of *Laura, Anatomy of a Murder, Advise and Consent*]. I can but don't glory in doing several things at once, I've done too much of it. I haven't done justice to your play at the readings I've attended. I think your play is a very fine one, but I've been half-there at the readings. I haven't yet really worked with Jo Mielziner. I should have. Generally I've felt like I was heavily overloaded, and the fall especially looked like sheer hell, with my being so busy that I could neither do your play well nor do the job I should on Inge's film. If your play had been a difficult one, and if I felt that it really needed some extraordinary "treatment," why then I would somehow have done it and to hell with the cost to me in energy, etc. But I think it's a play that could be done very well by a lot of directors. If it's cast right with good actors, it will almost play itself. I'm not even sure that a lighter hand than mine wouldn't be better. I might overdramatize it, I'm not sure I'm just exactly right for it.

I knew you were bound to think that I didn't really like your play. I expected that. But I didn't expect the insults. Frankly, it appears to me that the loyalties in our relationship have run more from me to you than the other way. I stuck onto *Baby Doll* through the thick and thin of your indifferences and disappearing. . . . I stuck with *Sweet Bird* when you thought it was crap. I insisted on Gerry Page [Geraldine Page, who appeared in the film version as well] when you thought she was wrong. And I have taken for four years a whole campaign of vilification in the press to the effect that I was distorting your work. You started this line with your preface on *Cat* [in the published version]. As you wrote it down, that was an honest preface. But in context and in effect it was not. It gave people generally the idea that I had forced you to rewrite *Cat*. I can't force you to rewrite anything, first because you are strong, secondly because you are protected by your Guild. The contrary is the true fact: that I offered ten days before the New York opening to put in your original third act. You never stated that in your preface; nor did you note that I offered repeatedly to put your original third act into the road company. You made the decision not to.

Since then a host of people, unleashed by your preface, have been attacking me for distorting your work. . . . I've come to the conclusion that somehow you were willing to have me blamed for the faults in your plays, while you are praised for their virtues. Why otherwise have you never said one word in the press in my defense? Is that fair? Did I make you rewrite the second act of *Sweet Bird of Youth*? You know goddamn well that if the shoe was on the other foot, if you were being blamed unrelentingly for my faults, I would have spoken up long ago. What other conclusion can I come to except that consciously or unconsciously you agree with them? It's been four years now that this horse shit has been in the press: Hewes, Atkinson, Cassidy, and all of them, and YOU HAVE NEVER ONCE SAID A WORD!!°

I went to Milwaukee to see *Sweet Bird of Youth* [on tour], I needed every day here, but Audrey [Audrey Wood, Williams's agent] and through her, you, pleaded with me to go out. I did. And I saw the play, and took notes and gave notes. All the time I was there I felt taxed and overworked, I felt that I was being unfair to Bill [Inge] and to myself in re his movie. At the same time I went very carefully through *Period of Adjustment,* planning the direction so that I knew how it would move on the stage so that I could give Jo Mielziner a ground plan before he left for Europe. I thought many times I should quit *P. of A.* But never seriously because I have always put you first. Then came Cassidy's piece, and I began to think. It isn't that I care what she thinks. I truly

---

° Howard Hewes in the *Saturday Review,* Brooks Atkinson in the *New York Times,* Claudia Cassidy in the *Chicago Tribune.*

don't. And Hewes is an ass. And Atkinson is a man whose opinions I'm indifferent to. I only cared that YOU were silent. And I was forced to think that really and truly you felt the same way.

Then I thought, why does he want me to direct his plays? The answer: Because of some superstition that I bring commercial success. Which you terrifyingly want. But that is part of the same distasteful picture. Just as I can't help but think you agree with Cassidy, I also think that you think of me as the person who can make your plays "go" and that you are willing to make some sacrifice in integrity and personal values to get the commercial success which I bring you. Well, Tennessee, fuck that! That is a hell of a humiliating position, and I don't want any goddamn part of it. You should have come to my defense long ago. Ask yourself the reason why you didn't.

I'm not going to break my neck, slough off Inge's movie, do a half-ass job on *Period of Adjustment* only to be told in time, again, that I had misdirected your play into a hit. And then, to wait and wait for you to say something and wait for nothing. What the hell kind of position is that for a man? It's not for me.

Anyway, baby, you really don't need me on this one, I know it will work without me (Cheryl, incidentally, agrees) [Cheryl Crawford, the producer]. Get a new boy and a new relationship. This play will work with another director. This is a beautiful, funny, human play, but it's also unified and well constructed. I think a lot of it and I think a lot of you. I truly wish you all success. And I love you,

Gadg

The quarrel ended with this exchange—and though Kazan never worked with Williams again, Williams continued to show him his new plays in the hope of tempting him back. In the early 1960s, Kazan asked Williams for a play for the first season of the Lincoln Center Repertory Theatre, and Williams offered the one-act *Kingdom of Heaven,* but Kazan felt the makeshift Washington Square facility too spacious for this small-scale work. A revival of *Streetcar* was considered, a project Kazan claimed to be delaying until he could find the right actress—though it is difficult to believe he would have prepared a production that would inevitably be compared to his classic stage and film versions.

Short Takes

The Young Go First (1935)
by Arthur Vogel

This was a play I did when I was a Communist and it protests the social situation and specifically the situation in the Civilian Conservation Corps, one of the "alphabet soup" social services that were set up in the New Deal by Franklin Roosevelt. It was played by a theatre group, of which I was a member when I was a Communist, called the Theatre of Action. A member of the cast was Nicholas Ray, who became a famous film director twenty years later. Another member of the Theatre of Action was Martin Ritt, who also won a great deal of fame and respect later as a director of film features. The most interesting memory I have of the production was that when we discovered we had no third act, I gave the actors "beats" of action to improvise on, had a stenographer in the front row taking down what the actors said, had those notes typed and made a third act from what I had. It worked too. Those were the days!

Casey Jones (1938)
by Robert Ardrey

Casey Jones was written by a man who was not to achieve any fame as a playwright but a good deal as an author. Robert Ardrey wrote *African Genesis* and several other books about the origin of man. He was from the Midwest and was a man who esteemed the solitary, "stand up" hero, who was fast fading from the American scene. It was a rather feeble play with a basically sentimental premise. It was, however, notable for its setting, a locomotive which seemed to move onstage. This was by a designer who never achieved the recognition he should have, Mordecai Gorelik. An early espouser of Bertolt Brecht, his own work was spare realism, not "epic" in any of that much misused word's meanings. I learned a valuable lesson from "Max" Gorelik: A play should take place not BEFORE a setting but INSIDE a setting. He meant by this that a stage setting should be an environment not a backdrop.

It's Up to You (1941)
by Arthur Arent

During the Second World War, I worked for our Department of Agriculture. One of their problems was to make the American public aware of the importance of rationing—sympathetic to its necessity. My task was to cook up a play performance in the style of the so-called Living Newspaper about rationing. So I did. We had some novelties there, such as a woman onstage having a dialogue scene with her image, projected on a motion picture screen of great size behind her. Another was casting the fine "revolutionary dancer" Helen Tamiris as a steak. She did it very well. I enjoyed myself.

One Touch of Venus (1943)
by S. J. Perelman, Ogden Nash, and Kurt Weill

I had three tries at the musical theatre form and I'm not proud of my work in any of the three. *One Touch of Venus* was a great success, but mostly if not altogether because of the work and presence of Mary Martin, Agnes de Mille, and the dancer Sono Osato. These women were remarkable talents. I learned a great lesson from the *corps de ballet* in the production, watching how hard they worked, how disciplined they were. Actors now don't work nearly as hard nor are they as ambitious artistically—I don't mean in their careers but in their artistic potential and capabilities. I believe Miss de Mille, whose dances were brilliant, was the most dominating personality I ever worked with, so dominating in fact that I was reduced to a kind of stage manager who watched her work in amazement and arranged the lights and stage space to her bidding. I soon became weary of this kind of subservient role, and after my next musical I decided to admit that this was not my best field.

Jacobowsky and the Colonel (1944)
by S. N. Behrman

This was a play written originally by Franz Werfel, adapted (whatever that means) for the theatre by Clifford Odets and then rewritten with humor and a skillful human touch by S. N. Behrman. The production was quite good and it was inhabited by a genius, Oscar Karlweis. He was at his best in this production. He had a deftness and a charm which does not presently exist in our theatre. He played the role of a Jew, Jacobowsky, fleeing south in France before the advancing Nazis. His companion in the ride to freedom is a Polish colonel who shares many of the less attractive qualities of the Nazis. How Jacobowsky—that is Karlweis, for the two soon become synonymous—tantalizes and slips away from the Nazis and his more immediate tormentor, the Polish colonel, is the body of the play. The direction had its merits too.

Deep Are the Roots (1945)
by Arnaud d'Usseau and James Gow

Deep Are the Roots is the first play I did when I came back from the war and is a play—now completely old-fashioned—of social protest. The set-up, a black coming to self-awareness in an environment of the deep South, is now of no interest. We've gone past its message and its drama. The leading role was well played by an actress with a luminous quality, Barbara Bel Geddes, and all that I remember from the play is her face at certain moments. It was, I believe, the high point of her professional life and she was never to surpass it.*

Tea and Sympathy (1953)
by Robert Anderson

Tea and Sympathy is a perfect play, small, modest, tender, sensitive, and beautifully constructed. These plays, the fruit of the first intense experience of a lifetime—*Glass Menagerie* of Tennessee Williams is another, Clifford Odets's *Awake and Sing!* still another—pop up as if by some divine accident. All I had to do was not make bad mistakes— such as over-dramatizing, over-theatricalizing the play. And to provide it with correct setting in the scale and size suited to a play of modest intimate action. And, above all, perhaps, cast it right. Robert Anderson provided us with the right actress for the role in Deborah Kerr, who gave a performance of sympathetic sensitivity equal to the best features and scenes of the play. From first to last, the experience was the simplest, the quickest, and the easiest I had in the theatre and it left me wondering why can't every play be as easy to produce? I've done two other perfectly constructed plays but of a much grander scale, *Streetcar Named Desire* and *Death of a Salesman*. Anderson's play is that of a miniaturist and he doesn't make one false step.

The Dark at the Top of the Stairs (1957)
by William Inge

The Dark at the Top of the Stairs is a childhood memory play by William Inge. This is a sensitively written play in a minor key, a play of deceptive depth. The first impression it makes is not distinguished—it seems like the kind of story featured in women's magazines, those intended to pass the time for housewives. But slowly it gets deeper and

---

* Kazan includes in this proviso his production of *Cat on a Hot Tin Roof,* in which she played Maggie. Bel Geddes also appeared in Kazan's 1950 film *Panic in the Streets.*

more poignant until we can't help feeling, as we sit before it, that the author has tapped a vein of the most genuine emotion. Again it was played by actors not of star caliber but perfect for their roles. This had become my trademark. The value of the evening did not rest on a supercharged performer. It was, in all, a quiet and most affecting night in the theatre—but it is rarely revived now because that kind of offering has been overwhelmed by what's on TV.

After the Fall (1964)
by Arthur Miller

After the Fall was the first Lincoln Center Repertory Theatre production that I did and the only one that was worth a damn. We mounted it in a temporary theatre on the campus of New York University. We carved out an amphitheatre shape, poured in concrete and covered it with a pre-fabricated steel roof. It was a striking theatre occasion. I found the first act very dull. There was a character whom Miller identified with me in relation to my testimony; he was not unsympathetically portrayed. The leading figure, Quentin, who could pass for Miller, talked to the audience endlessly, and, I thought, without much interest. Then came the second act and on stage came the character based on Marilyn Monroe, Miller's second wife, played brilliantly by Barbara Loden. Miller here was amazingly honest; he put in the mouth of this

Arthur Miller, Barbara Loden, Jason Robards, and Kazan

character all the anger that Marilyn had against him at the end. Miss Loden played the gamut of emotions from the naïve but manipulative young flirt to the drug-obsessed, fading woman with murderous feelings.

The Changeling (1964)
by Thomas Middleton and William Rowley

The Changeling is a play of Jacobean England and I thought it a good play, a strong play. But my production was miserable, it didn't work at all. It discouraged me, once and for all, from doing classical theatre. I decided after my experience with this production that I had no feeling or genuine interest for any but contemporary plays on contemporary subjects. I still believe this. It's my failing.

The Chain (1983)
by Elia Kazan

I finally tried to write a play. It taught me to value playwrights. I failed.

FILMS

A Tree Grows in Brooklyn (1945)

"Bud" Lighton [the producer] surrounded me with help in the various areas where I was uncertain, like the camera, where I did not know one lens from another. At the beginning Leon Shamroy [the cameraman] seemed sort of harsh; after we shot a couple of days, he proposed to Lighton that he should codirect with me. I refused, but there was some justice in what he said, because I just staged the scene as I would a theatre scene and then he determined where to put the camera and so on.

The scenery was rather good, but there was something essentially false. If we had shot in New York on the East Side, it would have been truer to life. But much worse than the scenery—the rooms were too clean, too nice, too much the work of the property man—were the hairdressing and costumes. They looked like magazine illustrations. The only true correct thing on the visual side was the face of the little girl, Peggy Ann Garner. Because her father was overseas in the war, because her mother had problems, because she herself was going through a lot of pain and uncertainties, Peggy's face was drawn and pale and worried. It looked exactly right. She was not pretty at all, or cute or picturesque, only true. There wasn't anything Peggy had to do as Francie that I couldn't somehow awaken because it was all going on inside of her. It was also my idea not to have any background music but just source music—the sound of an organ grinder and so on.

Peggy Ann Garner, Joan Blondell, and the director
on his first Hollywood film

We soon had a good unit with Dorothy McGuire, who liked me—and I liked her—with Jimmy Dunn, who was uncertain enough and so dependent on me, and the little girl, and Joan Blondell.

Essentially *A Tree* is a tiny story. In the same way as *East of Eden* is the scale of Julie Harris's face and the little flicker in her eyes, so *A Tree,* too, is an intimate, interior story. The outside has to be there, but what is important is that I get the light in that little girl's eyes, the expression on her face, the feeling in her soul.

At that time I was separated from my wife, I missed the children and my own little girl, so I had an extra feeling about a child's love for her father, which you find in the film. My wife was puritanical and so was the character played by Dorothy McGuire. But I wouldn't direct this movie at all in the same way now, I haven't got the same vocabulary now—it is a sentimental story and I don't believe in that now. I would never have made Dorothy McGuire as sympathetic as she was. Although she did well, she was miscast: She is an upper-middle-class girl. The mother should have been a working-class Catholic Irish girl, much tougher and more narrow in her values.

Boomerang! (1947)

We shot that entirely on location—not a set in the picture. We used only a few actors, and the rest were all people from Stamford, Connecticut—members of the police force, for example. Cops act good, by the way. I don't know why it is, but something about that profession makes them all good actors. We shot on the streets at night with as many as five thousand people watching. The picture was a terrific thrill that way—it made me see my identity. I really enjoyed that life, whereas I was miserable on the MGM set [for *Sea of Grass*]. For one thing, I was miserable living in Hollywood—I never liked the place. I never unpacked my bags. Another thing I learned from *Boomerang!* was that it cut through a lot of bullshit about photography—"beauty" photography. On *Sea of Grass* I was initiated into all that careful backlighting and halo-lighting and line-lighting and so on. But the cameraman on *Boomerang!* was an old guy [Norbert Brodine] who just put the camera down and turned the box on. And it looked better to me than the other! I think the film is thin. I think it's a good film, I thought everything worked. It was a piece of mechanism, a fairly effective piece of storytelling mechanism. But I wouldn't do that now. Not a goddamned thing in it would I do now.

I cast the movie from my New York brood, many of whom were soon to come into the Actors Studio, plus Ed Begley, a reformed drunk and a fine man who had precisely the heavy load of guilt his part needed; plus Dana Andrews, who could learn seven pages of dialogue for a courtroom scene in an hour over black coffee, after he'd been up all night drinking something else.

I selected all the locations, and not a single scene was shot in a studio set. We used the streets of Stamford, Connecticut, and the county courthouse in White Plains, New York. Dick Murphy [the scriptwriter] was always at my elbow; if a scene didn't work, we made it work. We didn't have to consult anybody about anything. I had a cutter with me, Harmon Jones, who also became a friend and quickly convinced me that making films wasn't so difficult—"Look at the dodos who made them!" I'd soon master the technique of film editing, he said, and would be able to rely on myself; meantime, I should rely on him.

I've called *Boomerang!* my cure. It was. I walked the Stamford streets—they were my stage—as master of it all. Call it arrogance, I call it confidence, and it had come flooding back, filling the cavity that was emptied in Culver City.* There was a lovely harmony in Stamford and in that White Plains courthouse. Work was joy again. I'd found my way of making films.

On *Boomerang!* I learned a lot of techniques, a lot of little tricks, but more importantly, ever since then I've felt, I can do a film anywhere. I don't need sets or movie stars. In *Boomerang!* is, I think, the basis for *Panic in the Streets*, and in *Panic in the Streets* is the basis for *On the Waterfront*. If you see those three films together, you'll see the development. There are no sets whatsoever in *Panic* or *Waterfront*. They were shot entirely on location.

Unfortunately a lot of *Boomerang!* is the same studio machinery—brought indoors. Most of the actors were stage actors, like Jane Wyatt. She plays an oversweet version of what a wife should be. Dana Andrews was actorish. He was not like a real lawyer. The same thing with Ed Begley. He was a terrific old hand and a wonderful man, but he was, again, an "Actor." It's not just that they were stage actors—they were actors not out of my training, but out of another world.

The difference between an actor and an "Actor" is finally a different view of humanity in the theatre, in film, in art, and in life. Ours is a nonartificial view. It's a realism of personality. It's an ordinariness in people. It's a feeling of ambivalence within people. It's a nonhero and nonheroine tradition. In our school, individuals are people first and actors second.

There was very little you could do with Dana Andrews. He'd come to work, dress up, and we'd roll him out. His style was okay in that movie because he was playing a lawyer, and essentially there wasn't supposed to be too much going on inside him. But unfortunately that kind of acting leaves you with the feeling that there was nothing really personally at stake. When you're not really touching something within the actor, you're not conveying the feeling that "This is life."

EDITOR

Boomerang! was Kazan's third film; his second was *Sea of Grass*, for MGM, which starred a tremulous, weepy Katharine Hepburn and a distracted Spencer Tracy. "It was a phony. One of the reasons I felt so resentful was

* Culver City was the location of MGM Studios, where Kazan's misadventures with *Sea of Grass* took place.

that I felt that I should have quit and I didn't. We were never to leave California, and my whole idea was to shoot the film out where there was still tall grass—Wyoming, Colorado, wherever. Instead I was stuck with the opposite approach to filmmaking. It was terrible, just awful." Differently, *Boomerang!* was filmed on location, and Kazan's distinctive directorial manner is clear and forceful—the naturalism and grit of the performances, the economy and pointedness of each scene, his predilection for realistic setting and method actors, and the sharp thematic focus are all hallmarks of Kazan.

Darryl Zanuck [Executive Producer] was pleased with the rushes. He telegraphed Kazan: "You have performed like an efficient veteran disregarding neither quality nor economy and I am really grateful." He was less satisfied when he saw the finished film, but the fault was not Kazan's:

> The direction and acting were absolutely superb but the story line lacked any suspense or sustained conflict. . . . By planting "Crossman" definitely as the murderer in the first reel we eliminate all suspense. By revising the early continuity and making some deft eliminations, the transformation is really astounding and the audience has a chance to enjoy the developments as they occur and they are finding out things at the same time the characters are finding them out.

Final cut was Zanuck's prerogative, but story construction was a Zanuck specialty, and Kazan always valued Zanuck's canny intelligence.

Kazan invited Arthur Miller, whose play *All My Sons* Kazan was to produce later that year in partnership with Harold Clurman, to the Stamford location, probably to seduce him away from Clurman, who was slated to direct *Sons*. Further enticement came when Kazan placed Miller in the line-up scene. Miller particularly admired the New York actors of the cast—"they looked like his own characters, ordinary human beings, instead of Sardi's 'Little Bar' hangers-on," and Kazan credited Miller with urging that *Boomerang!* actors Ed Begley, Arthur Kennedy, and Karl Malden be cast in *All My Sons*.

Gentleman's Agreement (1947)

No matter what I think of it today, what I remember most about *Gentleman's Agreement* is that at the time no one said *Jew*. When it was being made, all the rich Jews in California were against it. And the Catholic Church was against it, because they didn't want the heroine to be a divorcée. There were a hell of a lot of people who said to Zanuck, "We're getting along all right. Why bring this up?" And in that sense, it was a step forward at the time. On the other hand, it was, as far as it went, essentially a *Cosmopolitan* story, wasn't it? It was dressed up with these overtones, but essentially it was a very familiar, easily digestible story with conventional figures going through it. There isn't anything unpleasant in that picture. It was kept on a level of acceptability. It surprised people, but it didn't shock them.

There's one part of it I like, when I look back on it, which is where Dorothy McGuire is telling Garfield how she couldn't stand all this bigotry she overheard. And Garfield says, "What did you do about it?" There's a scene I liked. The rest of it just looks Hollywood to me. They're all dressed up, and they're all going through these well-read maneuvers of social behavior. Whenever I see it, it reminds me of the illustrations in ladies' magazines in those days. I mean, those people don't shit.

Kazan and Gregory Peck in New York

They don't do any of the natural functions. They'd walk through, and their dress was always perfect. That was just before I began kicking the hairdresser and the wardrobe people off the set. I wasn't doing that then. But I think that film is directed, again, like a stage play, and it's rather well directed. I think the movement in the scenes, and the way the scenes are paced and staged and so on—it's good stage direction. I'm not particularly fond of it. I was awful glad when it got over.

EDITOR

Based on a popular novel by Laura Z. Hobson, a screed against covert anti-Semitism, *Gentleman's Agreement* was the most commercially successful and prestigious of Hollywood's post–World War II socially conscious "statement" movies. Others of the genre were *Lost Boundaries,* a docudrama of a black family "passing" as white; *Crossfire,* another film dealing with anti-Semitism; and *Home of the Brave,* a study of racism in the military. In *Gentleman's Agreement* a reporter takes on the assignment of pretending to be Jewish and is rebuffed at hotels and discovers anti-Semitism in the workplace. Why a Jewish writer is not assigned this task is a question never bothered about, and Gregory Peck staring in the mirror and wondering if his looks are sufficiently Jewish is not the film's finest moment. Kazan never commented on a chilling scene when McGuire comforts Peck's son that, though his schoolmates taunt him because of his father's assignment, he really isn't Jewish. Peck, roused out of his earnest and dull performance, rounds on her, and their argument is the liveliest scene in the film. Too bad he doesn't dump her.

Zanuck, on the lookout for entertainment value, stressed the romance of Peck and Dorothy McGuire, "an adult and interesting love story." At the end McGuire, an upper-class Wasp from Darien, repents her casual and unthinking anti-Semitism—in fact, she should have been the tale's true villain. Kazan realized this but was powerless to control the script's and Zanuck's evasions.

Panic in the Streets (1950)

Well, by the time I got through with *Pinky* and *Gentleman's Agreement*, I said to myself, "Look, I'm not making films, I'm photographing plays." I began to study films again, especially Jack [John] Ford. And I said, "I'm going to make a film that's all action, and I'm going to start using the camera to tell the story. I want to make a film like a silent, as close to a silent as I can. I'm going to try to make something that is specifically filmic." Then I read this script. It wasn't much, but we rewrote it every day on location. That was the fun of it. We were shooting in New Orleans, and we had a hell of a time. I hung around the harbor, and I felt the wind on my face, and I thought, "I've been indoors all my life! I've got to get out of the theatre and into film!" It just freed me of all that inside-a-set tension and just directing minuscule little bits of acting. And it's funny, because I got into film because of outdoor films—*Potemkin* and *Aerograd. Aerograd* particularly has this terrific air of the forest and the cold and the leaves.

I don't think I could have made *On the Waterfront* like I did if I hadn't done *Panic in the Streets.* For one thing, I got to love the waterfront. I still love it. I'd like to make another picture about it. I love water. I really have a thing about that. I love harbors. My favorite shot in all my pictures is the shot of Ellis Island in *America America.* I love that shot—when they're lying around with the American flag up there. *Panic* might seem conventional to critics, but it was a big change for me, for my attitude toward everything. It was a liberation for me, I also think it's the only perfect film I made, because it's essentially a piece of mechanism, and it doesn't deal in any ambivalences at all, really. It just fits together in the sequence of storytelling rather perfectly. But that's really why I did it, and I got a hell of a lot out of it for future films. My other critical film for big change is *Zapata!* That changed everything.

Kazan expanded his use of the vocabulary of film with *Panic in the Streets*.

A *Streetcar Named Desire* (1951)

NOTES FROM THE FINAL DRAFT
OF THE FILMSCRIPT, JULY 1950

I'd say that the one thing is to direct these next three movies [perhaps *Streetcar, Viva Zapata!,* and Arthur Miller's unproduced script about longshoremen, *The Hook*] with your emotions and invent whatever style (visual) necessary to bring out of these stories (not scripts) the concealed and real emotion that is there! Feeling, pity, anger, protest, loyalty, love, life and death! That's what these pieces are about! They are all heightened experiences and need to be "realized" by you emotionally.

The danger is that the more proficient, experienced, rich, well fed you become, the greater the danger that you will become a "technician." Harmon Jones [editor of many of Kazan's films at Twentieth Century–Fox] and cameramen generally are all influences in the wrong direction. Their "rules" are good to know but are emotionally empty, or rather irrelevant. Neither here nor there. In fact, their smoothness is an enemy, and you must break away from it. That's why it's a damned good thing now on *Streetcar* that you have a fresh deal.

The job is to realize in film terms what you have only discovered in your last two pictures [chronologically, those films would have been *Pinky* and *Panic in the Streets*], the pain and violence of this story. It can only be realized that way—because otherwise it will become a gabfest. The emotion within this woman, her suffering, her pain, her inner life, can be much better revealed by film than it was on the stage. To the degree that we feel her pain, to that degree will we feel the compassion we must to realize this story. Otherwise: a melodrama. We must always feel that she hurts herself more than she does others.

So crawl into her with your camera. Be free. Don't listen to cutters. You explain to them what you want to get over. Talk talk talk to them all. They may think you're nuts, but be nuts enough to get over what you want to get over.

There is no use in the world in doing *Streetcar* unless you really make work your idea about "subjective photography," using the camera to penetrate Blanche and then showing the SUBJECTIVIZED source of the emotion. To make present her inner life you must use the camera and MUSIC as the explorers, reveal her. . . .

This will make for a new kind of storytelling. You tell not the literal facts, as an observer might see them. You bring directly to the screen BLANCHE'S WORLD!!!

Incidentally, the only way not to have scenic monotony is this way. You should never know quite where you are (in the realistic sense, especially in the last three scenes).

So crawl into her with your camera and your sound. See and hear as she hears and sees. Not only the distortions but also Stella putting her head on Stanley's shoulder (after she rejects him in her Scene Five exit) as a gesture of helpless love.

Photograph everything that hurts her. Everything that makes her feel lonely, abandoned, bewildered, helpless, lost, left out. Give the audience the pain she feels.

HEAT!!!!

Dresses diaphanous. Everybody fanning. Everybody unbuttoning. Or wanting to. Electric fans everywhere, girls wiping their chests, everyone drinking Cokes and other liquids, ICE, kids stealing ice. Dogs asleep in the shade, people rocking to create a little breeze. Perfume to combat the heat and the odor of sweat. Sounds of life, sounds of music, sounds of water running, sounds of fighting. NIGHT LIFE: Everyone walking slowly. Everyone lives outside. People sleep outside because of the heat.

Costumes; fussiness. Attempt at daintiness, femininity of sportswear. No bold patterns, organdy, chiffon, small prints, rayons, silks, fussy collars, high-heeled shoes. Blanche has lace on her underwear; Stella has no lace on her underwear. Props: fans everywhere, beauty accessories, cold cream, perfume, pins and curlers, sandpaper depilitator.

SOUNDS:

Cathedral bells, chickens, 4-Deuces, distant fights. Bowling pins. Drunks going home at night. Auto horns. Babies crying. Factory whistles. Trains, all kinds. Bells.

BLANCHE:

Blanche is extra aware of sounds. They connote all and evoke emotions. They simply affect her extra high-strung nature. She is always taking care of her clothes, like a craftsman with his tools, ironing, washing, dressing. Her trunk is full of tissue paper and carefully selected accessories. Part of her identity.

With
Vivien
Leigh
and
Kim
Hunter

Blanche is intelligent and has HUMOR. Accent this for chrissake or else she will become a tear jerker. She can be lovable, full of humor, of sudden intelligences.

Why is she drawn to Stanley? 1. There is no doubt she is drawn to what will kill her. She has a death wish. She is drawn to her "executioner." It is suicide. 2. Competitiveness with Stella. 3. Stella's description of her sexual fulfillment arouses her. She's without a man. 4. His strength and masculinity play on her traditional notion that a man must be a protector and a rescuer and strength itself. 5. She loves Belle Reve but hates it too, violently. She loves the cavalier tradition but hates it because her life has been bled away on that altar and she knows it is futile and sterile.

The general source of Blanche's character is the rejection by Allan Grey and the anxiety within her that this aroused. The result, a year later, is that every man she meets is a challenge. He must like her, he must desire her, or she's a failure. (Reminder of the story that David Selznick told about Joan Fontaine—she played with the fly of every man, couldn't help it, until he desired her, and then she lost interest.) The more he dislikes her, the greater the challenge, the harder she works, the more she needs to attract him. In effect, therefore, she appears to be trying to "make" every man that she meets. And especially, and most anxiously, if he does not like her. In short, Blanche is an

With
Karl
Malden
and
Vivien
Leigh

emotional parasite who can only live by being WANTED and NEEDED and LOVED by someone stronger than she is, so her whole activity is to attach herself for safety and for reassurance of the eternally running wound of her anxiety to someone stronger. Even a woman, it doesn't matter, or else SHE PERISHES.

EDITOR

In a 1971 interview Kazan undervalued one of his best films, a classic of American cinema:

> *Streetcar* is a beautiful theatre piece that I shot without softening it, without deepening it, filming it as it was because there was nothing in it to change. But I never set out to do that again, and I no longer believe in it.
>
> My main concern was working on the performances. I was good at that kind of thing then—I don't think I'm so good at it anymore. I was much more meticulous then about directing acting. My only problem in that film was that Vivien Leigh had played *Streetcar* in London, directed by Larry Olivier. So when she came over here, she had the whole performance worked out, and it wasn't anything like what I like. Larry's direction was an Englishman's idea of the

American South—seen from a distance—and Vivien's conception of the role was a bit of a stereotype, just as my direction of a British character might be. So for the first couple of weeks I had a lot of problems. Then gradually I won her over, and she began to cook. And I think that in the last half of the picture she's a hell of a lot better than she is in the first half.

Some people say I made Brando the hero. I didn't mean to make Brando the hero. But I wanted to show exactly what Williams meant, which is that he, as a homosexual, is attracted to the person he thinks is going to destroy him—the attraction you have for someone who's on the other side, supposedly dead against you, but whose violence and force attract you. Now, that's the essence of ambivalence. And that's what I tried to do, so that you felt sorry for her but could see, however, that his force was healthier.

After *Streetcar*'s Broadway success, there had been a number of exploratory offers for film rights. Zanuck wanted to make the film, but Spyros Skouras, board chairman of Twentieth Century–Fox, would have nothing to do with what he thought was a piece of filth. If Zanuck had cast from studio contract players we might have had Gene Tierney as Blanche, Linda Darnell as Stella, Cesar Romero as Stanley, and Paul Douglas as Mitch. Kazan had thought about producing it independently, but as with *Death of a Salesman* (a film version produced by Stanley Kramer is now forgotten, and later Kazan regretted he hadn't made it himself) this never happened. William Wyler was tempted, and a rumor was floated that he would reunite with Bette Davis for it, but he withdrew, intimidated by the censorship problems. Charles Feldman, an agent and producer, snagged the rights, with Warner Bros. providing the financing. This would be the only time Kazan directed a film version of a play he had directed for the stage; he reasoned that he did not like to repeat himself. In this case, the staginess of the film works to the advantage of the play's undercurrent of claustrophobia and hallucination.

In the film Kazan preserved most of his staging design, but the script was considerably modified to satisfy the Production Code of the Motion Picture Association of America. The most anxious questions concerned (1) Blanche DuBois's husband's homosexuality—her taunting of having found him in the arms of another man is what drives him to suicide; (2) Blanche's nymphomania as pacifier for her guilt; (3) Stanley's rape of Blanche; (4) the sexual attraction of Stella and Stanley; (5) the language. A filmscript was prepared by Oscar Saul, then revised by Williams, and Kazan melded elements from the playscript, the adaptation, and the revision into the final version.

During filming both Kazan and Williams appealed directly to Joseph Breen, administrator of the Production Code, who had heard rumors that

Kim Hunter and Kazan

Kazan was filming objectionable material that had not been shown him. Kazan's letter is cannily misleading but provides a gullible Breen with justification for Code approval.

Dear Joe,

Just a note. I don't ever mind honest differences, but I hate misunderstandings. They're dangerous, and the quicker they're quashed the better. Jack Vizzard [of the Breen office] said that it seemed like from your side there was some possible breach of faith (or attempt at same) on ours. So let me assure you, I wouldn't put homosexuality back in the picture, even if the Code had been revised last night and it was now permissible. I wouldn't want it. I prefer the delicately suggested impotence [of Allan Grey] there; I prefer debility and weakness over any kind of suggestion of perversion. The revisions in the long speech [Blanche's confession to Mitch, which Williams rewrote for the film] came from three sources. There was a suggestion that she "despised" her husband because he couldn't hold a job, or because his poems were returned or something. Secondly, after shooting for four weeks I became oppressed with the feeling that the script was very, very talky. Everyone had been warning me about it, and I finally began to feel it strongly myself. Gab gab gab. And most of it from Leigh. I have cut enormous hunks (in one case two-thirds) out of other long speeches. And finally I felt that the punch of the speech was more diluted than it needed to be. I never hope to get any shock in the movie comparable to her walking into a room and finding her husband with another man. But The Speech is in a strategic position in the show, and has got to do its job in that spot, or else. I didn't think it did. And I am responsible for the show, responsible to everyone. That's why the blue page [a blank which suggested there was material Breen was not being shown]. Unfortunately, it took a little time and work on the actual shooting to bring me to the strong awareness necessary to sitting down and making a change. But I don't want you to think that I was trying to slip a third strike past you or anyone else. That I don't do.

I'm working on the rape thing too, I think I've got sight of a real solution and when I have it developed a little further, I'd like to discuss it too.

Yours,
Gadg Kazan

The "rape thing" continued to be a problem, and Kazan threatened to walk out if it was cut. Tennessee Williams appealed directly to Breen.

OCTOBER 29, 1950

Dear Mr. Breen:

Mr. Kazan has just informed me that objections have been raised about the rape scene in *Streetcar* and I think perhaps it might be helpful for me to clarify the meaning and importance of this scene. . . .

The rape of Blanche by Stanley is a pivotal, integral truth in the play. Without which the play loses its meaning, which is the ravishment of the tender, the sensitive, the delicate by the savage and brutal forces in modern society. It is a poetic plea for comprehension. I did not beg the issue by making Blanche a totally "good" person, nor Stanley a totally "bad" one. But to those who have made some rational effort to understand the play, it is apparent that Blanche is neither a "dipsomaniac" nor a "nymphomaniac" but a person of intense loneliness, fallibility, and a longing which is mostly spiritual for warmth and protection. I did not, of course, disavow what I think is one of the primary things of beauty and depth in human existence, which is the warmth between two people, the so-called sensuality in the love-relationship. If nature and God chose this to be the means of life's continuance on earth, I see no reason to disavow it in creative work.... Elia Kazan has directed *Streetcar* both on the stage and the screen with inspired understanding of its finest values and an absolute regard for taste and propriety.

Sincerely,
Tennessee Williams

Charles Feldman suggested that Stanley only beat up Blanche, opening the possibility that any actual rape might be a figment of Blanche's "broken mind." Another Feldman proposal was that in the film's final moments Mitch should chase after the car taking Blanche off to the asylum, offering the hope that he'll be anxiously awaiting her release. He said it might be "a lift for the film." At the least, it had to be made clear that Stanley received some punishment. Williams came up with a solution. Stella would mete out Stanley's sentence. Williams telegraphed to Kazan what would be Stella's verdict: "Dear Gadg, As Stella is crying she whispers to the baby these words of promise and reassurance stop we're not going back in there stop not this time stop we're never going back stop never, never back, never back again."

The rape is now symbolic. The back of Blanche's head crashes against a splintered mirror, leaving to the most naïve the question of whether a rape actually took place and giving credence, for the benefit of the blind, to Stanley's denial. In her long confession speech to Mitch, Blanche talks about something "strange" about her husband, his poetic manner—what it does is obfuscate the tale for someone who didn't know the play; for those who did, it seems as if Blanche is unwilling to tell all—that she discovered her husband in bed with another man is left out; the taunt is made into something about her husband being a bit too dreamy.

Most of the Broadway cast, with the notable exception of Jessica Tandy, appeared in the film. At the insistence of Jack Warner, who wanted a star for the lead role, Tandy was replaced by Vivien Leigh, who had appeared as Blanche in London, directed by her husband, Laurence Olivier. Vivien Leigh won the Academy Award for her performance, but Kazan and Karl Malden preferred Tandy, believing Leigh was compromised by retaining too much of her London performance in the early scenes. Brando was a dissenter from that opinion: He liked Leigh, and everyone agreed Leigh was sexier. Many critics thought Leigh superb. *The New Yorker*'s Pauline Kael wrote: "Vivien Leigh gives one of the rare performances that can truly be said to evoke pity and terror.... Elia Kazan's direction is often stagy, the sets and arrangements of actors are frequently too transparently 'worked out'; but who cares when you're looking at just the best feminine performance you're ever going to see, as well as an interpretation by Brando that is just about perfection." Kael undervalued, as Kazan did, Kazan's eliciting and shaping Leigh's agonized, fierce performance.

Without Kazan's approval or consultation, there were edits, amounting to three minutes (a lascivious look from Hunter, a smirk from Leigh), to mollify the threatened condemnation by the Catholic Legion of Decency. In a letter to the *New York Times* soon after the film's New York premiere, Kazan made public his complaints about Warner Bros.' treatment of him and the strictures of the Legion of Decency. In 1993, the cuts were restored to new prints, and Kazan confided to friends that the restored material didn't seem to make any difference.

Viva Zapata! (1952)

"Of all the films that I have made it is certainly one of those that are most dear to me."

EDITOR: In 1909 Emiliano Zapata heads a delegation of mestizo farmers from the southern Mexican state of Morelos to appeal to President Porfirio Díaz for the return of land confiscated by large landholders. Zapata's pleas are virtually disregarded, but he is marked as an enemy of the state.

In Morelos, Zapata is hounded for protesting the brutal treatment of protesting peasants by the government forces, the Federales. He hides in the mountains and is reluctantly conscripted by a political activist, Fernando Aguirre (an invention of Steinbeck and Kazan's), to back the overthrow of Díaz by Francisco Madero. During this period Zapata woos Josefa, the daughter of a bourgeois storekeeper.

When Madero succeeds, he names Zapata general of his southern army and designates Pancho Villa general of his northern forces, serving under General Victoriano Huerta. Madero proves a disappointment when he is reluctant to implement Zapata's plans for agrarian reform and redistribution of the land. Fearing Zapata's threat of an uprising, Huerta advises Madero to have Zapata eliminated, but Madero hesitates, and in 1913 Huerta deposes and assassinates Madero. In turn, the repressive Huerta is forced into exile by pressure from the United States and rebellious forces headed by Zapata and Villa. For a brief time, Zapata heads a provisional government, but he soon returns to his village, to confront his brother Eufemio, who has abused his authority.

Venustiano Carranza organizes a constitutional government, but is urged by Aguirre to have Zapata, still a powerful figure, assassinated. Zapata is entrapped and his body riddled with bullets. His mutilated remains are thrown on the lid of a hollow well in the center of a village square, and when the soldiers leave, mourning women surround the body. His white horse has escaped and runs free in the mountains, creating the myth that Zapata did not die, that the body is that of an impostor, and that Zapata will return when his people's need is greatest.

Marlon delighted me. In *Streetcar* he'd been playing a version of himself, but in *Viva Zapata!* he had to create a characterization. He was playing a peasant, a man out of another world. I don't know how he did, but he did it; his gifts go beyond his knowledge. It was more than makeup and costuming—that was easy, despite Zanuck's [the producer's] quibbling about his moustache. (Should it turn up or down? Was it too long or too short?) I spoke a few words of help: "A peasant does not reveal what he thinks. Things happen to him and he shows no reaction. He knows if he shows certain reactions, he'll be marked 'bad' and may be killed." And so on. But no one altogether directs Brando: You release his instinct and give it a shove in the right direction. I told him the goal we had to reach, and before I'd done talking, he'd nod and walk away. He had the idea, knew what he had to do, and was, as usual, ahead of me. His talent in those days used to fly.

It was simple for Marlon to understand that Zapata's relationship to women was not what men in our society feel—or are supposed to feel. "Don't be misled by all that shit in the script about how he loves his wife," I said to him. "He has no need for a special woman. Women are to be used, knocked up and left. The men fighting the revolution were constantly leaving them behind for months at a time. The woman he woos, Josefa, is middle-class; perhaps she represents a secret aspiration of his. She may also be some sort of idealization. There are plenty of other women available to satisfy his simpler needs. Don't mix it up with love, as we use the word. He loves his *compadres*. They are ready to die for him, and he would do anything for them." I was telling him not to play the scenes with his wife in the kind of romantic stupor American actors pretend. For these peasants, I told Marlon, fucking is not a big deal; it's become a big deal for us in America. But our kind of romantic love (if it is romantic, if you can call it love) is a product of our middle class. Zapata's social concerns are his real concerns.

Once I saw that Marlon had found the man in himself, I gave him less and less direction. In certain scenes I didn't say a word. When you start giving too much direction to an actor like Brando, you are likely to throw him off the track he's instinctively found and harm the scene. "If it isn't broke, don't fix it," the saying goes. I learned from working with this man that when a director deals with a really talented actor, he has to know when to stop talking. The first thing for a director is to see what a talent does on its own. It may be, as it frequently was with Marlon, better than anything you can describe. I also learned with him to try to capture the first flight of his instinct; I "shot the rehearsal." If you don't get what you want, then start directing—but not until then. Above all, don't show off how smart you are and what a brilliant director. Sometimes the best direction consists of reading an actor's face and, when you see the right thing there, simply nodding to him. A few

With
Brando
and
Anthony
Quinn

words, a touch, and a smile will do it. Then wait for a miracle. With Marlon, it often happened.

The competition between Brando and Quinn [who played Zapata's brother] was wonderfully fruitful and creative. By the way, there's nothing wrong with actors competing, as long as they're competing to be good and not to be stars. In fact, I sometimes try to arouse competition. For example, I often praise an actor openly. That makes every other actor on the set want the same praise.

My favorite scene is one without either of my stars [Brando and Quinn]. It takes place at the end, in the town square on a hot day, with the sun beating straight down. The women are hardly visible, because they sit against the sides of the buildings that outline the square, in a strip of shade. A troop of horsemen rides up and dumps the body of the murdered Zapata on a cistern top in the middle of the square. It is hollow underneath, and the fall of the corpse makes a heavy, thudding sound. The horsemen ride off. For a moment, the women, almost invisible in the black shadow, don't move. They have seen the dead bodies of their best men many times before. Slowly, the women approach Zapata. They wash and compose his body as they might have the body of their Lord. I kept the camera at a distance, and since what is shown is not in close-up detail, the viewer's imagination is free. This short sequence meant to me that at last I'd moved past the stage and its techniques to become a filmmaker.

Even in a film like *East of Eden* I was influenced by the theatre, where it's carried along by a scene of conflict expressed by dialogue conflict; there's an interchange of positions with one person having an objective in relation to another person, then the response, and all that interplay. I became less interested in that. But as I say, that started back in *Zapata,* which is all in shots—the two things are concurrent. Brando's character is not elaborated, and it's not interesting qua psychology. My interest in that picture was in the sweep of the events. And the characters are introduced at the top of their crises, and then dropped and changed. This is a result of handling time in a much swifter way, the way it is in life—it seems to go along smoothly, but violent and quick changes are happening underneath the surface, and suddenly you realize, "Christ, I'm not where I was two weeks ago!"

The first thing that attracted me to Zapata was his sense that power was corrupting him. He didn't want it. That's how I felt a lot. The other thing was that John [Steinbeck] and I were both ex-Communists, and Zapata's story allowed us to show metaphorically what had happened to the Communists in the Soviet Union—how their leaders became reactionary and repressive rather than forward thinking and progressive.

In the scene when Zapata (Brando) falls over his dead brother's body (Quinn), I gave the actors no direction whatsoever. Not one word. By the time we shot that scene they had a good relationship. If you start giving directions to any actor like Brando in a scene like that you're very liable to hurt yourself. One thing a director has to know is when to keep his mouth shut, to wait and see what the actor does instinctively, personally, without trying to fill any preconceived patterns. That's good director-to-director advice. If I had said something, I would have spoiled it. That's an elemental scene between two people who love each other. Brando fussed with Quinn's dead body, he did something with his face. Then he brought Quinn's dead hands up to his own face. That was all Brando. Only if you're not getting what you want do you start giving directions.

Well, everybody influences everybody, but the film that made a big impression on me was *Paisan,* particularly the last episode. Rossellini does a marvelous thing there when he gets to the climax—he leaps, he doesn't walk to the climax. He jumps to something and then he jumps over something, he jumps to something and then he jumps over something. It's a fantastic thing. I learned to try to jump crag to crag, rather than going all through the valleys.

I love *Viva Zapata!* The visual style of the film was taken from five books by two Mexican still cameramen, the Casasola photographs—this was the most photographed war up to that time, I guess. Some of those photographs I imitated pretty exactly. When Zapata and Pancho Villa meet, and their staffs gather around then—that's an exact reproduction right down to the casting.

With the precedent of the success of the 1934 film *Viva Villa,* MGM commissioned over succeeding years a number of treatments of the story of Villa's companion revolutionary, Emiliano Zapata, one with Robert Taylor in the lead, and a later one for Ricardo Montalban. In the mid-1940s, John Steinbeck had discussed developing a screenplay on Zapata's life with a Mexican studio, but the project came to nothing. Kazan too thought of Zapata, and in the late 1940s he joined with Steinbeck to produce a story treatment that would satisfy Darryl Zanuck. (The project and collaboration may have been instigated by Zanuck.) Zanuck liked the idea—it might be something for his biggest star, Tyrone Power. "It can make a great show with all of the excitement of *The Mark of Zorro* [Zanuck had produced a version that starred Power in 1940] and with a wonderful theme that will shine through." In 1949 he bought the development material from MGM, and at the end of the year Kazan and Steinbeck gave Zanuck a treatment.

While Kazan was directing the film of *A Streetcar Named Desire,* Steinbeck completed a script, but Zanuck began to have doubts about the political climate, for the House Un-American Activities Committee had been rabidly and noisily exposing Communists and Communist influence in the movie industry, and Kazan knew that soon he would be subpoenaed. Zanuck wondered, "Is this the right time to tell this story? Is this the moment to tell the story of a Mexican revolutionary hero? . . . In *Zapata,* we have to make certain that our entertainment will carry the added responsibility of answering the question: 'Exactly what is this all about? And what was the purpose in making it?' " Did the story of Zapata have an entertaining theme? Did America want such a serious tale? Zanuck was strong on commercial possibility but less prescient on what qualified as a masterpiece. "*Sunset Boulevard* was a masterpiece until it was released throughout the country and failed to do business. It is not so big a masterpiece today."

And how was it to be cast? "The big problem lies in the man who plays Zapata. If a Mexican is used, then we should use all Mexican players and let them all speak with their own natural accent. But, if we use Brando, or any other American, we face the problem of either dubbing his voice or letting him speak with a fake accent, or dubbing all of the other Mexican actors in English." Brando had been Kazan's choice from the start, and Zanuck did not finally object. But he would not accept Kazan's choice to play Zapata's wife, Julie Harris, already a celebrated Broadway star. Instead, he wanted contract player Jean Peters. The film's casting is an odd straddle of Hollywood regulars (Peters, Margo), Kazan favorites from New York (Brando, Mildred Dunnock, Joseph Wiseman, Frank Silvera), Mexican extras, and, providing a smooth and authoritative link of all styles, Anthony Quinn, who won the Academy Award for his role as Zapata's brother Eufemio. But the result, in spite of Zanuck's cautions, was not too dissimilar to the biopics produced by Warner Bros. in the 1930s, particularly the decidedly odd-sounding Frenchmen of *The Story of Louis Pasteur* and *The Life of Emile Zola* or the even odder Hollywood/French village inhabitants in the Zanuck-produced *Song of Bernadette* who would seem to have been more familiar with bagels and Irish stew than baguettes.

A singular contribution by Zanuck was Zapata's white horse. It will give us, said Zanuck, "an opportunity to have some fine warm scenes between Zapata and the horse." Zanuck consulted with the Mexican censorship bureau, which sent an official to advise on the script. Changes were made, but the production ran afoul of Mexican unions, controlled according to Kazan by Communists, who demanded even more changes, in addition to being irritated that a Mexican hero was being played by a gringo. Instead of being filmed in Mexico, the production was moved north of the Mexican border.

Just before the film opened Kazan addressed Zanuck's worries about the film's politics.

JANUARY 29, 1952

Dear Darryl:

It has occurred to me that the very best answer you could give to anyone who has doubts or questions about the politics of our picture is to point to the figure of Fernando Aguirre. This personage was put in there as an embodiment of our feeling about the Communists, and two points are made. They are destructive of the very point of Communism. First, it is emphasized repeatedly that the man's chief drive is toward power. In the interests of power, he turns against his best friend and sponsor, Francisco Madero. Secondly, at a point where he sees that there is no advancement for him with Zapata, he not only leaves Zapata but joins the palace group, who are plotting Zapata's death. The only recognizable figure at the death of Zapata is the Communist, Fernando Aguirre.

If this character is not completely destructive of the Communist as he operates in politics and in society, I don't know what is. Please remember, dear Darryl, that we put this man in with an eye toward possible attacks in the future. This picture is not only pro-democratic, but it is specifically, strongly, and incontrovertibly anti-Communist.

Just one more point. Our hero at the climax of his political career does something that no Communist would ever do. In this act, there is the whole meaning of his character and his life. I am referring to the moment when he picks up his hat and walks out of the palace, and thus walks away from power. No Communist has ever done it, nor ever will.

Love,
Gadg

The film opened well to positive reviews, but after the first weeks business was sluggish, and ultimately the film did not earn back its cost. Zanuck knew what had gone wrong. They should have told the same story without using Zapata's name and made him "a sort of Mexican Robin Hood."

We tell exactly the same story that we told in the film except that we leave out the political and historical aspects and emphasize more the Robin Hood aspect of his character. I believe that we would have turned out an enormous box office attraction. We were defeated in advance by the critics who praised it but referred to the picture as "historical" etc. We had two strikes against us before the public ever viewed the picture. . . . For my money you did an enormous job on the location of *Viva Zapata!* But here again apparently the subject matter did not have the appeal that we anticipated. It came out at a time when audiences were reaching for pure escapist entertainment and not willing to listen to any messages or historical lessons even about an exciting and colorful Mexican bandit.

On the Waterfront (1954)

*"On the Waterfront was my own story; every day I worked on
that film I was telling the world where I stood and my critics
to go and fuck themselves."*

EDITOR: Terry Malloy, ex-boxer, now works as a longshoreman and receives handouts and small jobs from mob boss Johnny Friendly, who con-
trols the corrupt dockworkers' union. Terry's brother, Charley Malloy,
lawyer and accountant to Friendly, had managed his brother's failed fight
career.

Unwittingly, Terry is inveigled by Friendly to lure a fellow longshoreman, Joey Doyle, to the roof of his apartment building, from which Doyle
is thrown to his death by Friendly's goons as punishment for testifying
before the New York Crime Commission on dock corruption. Guilt-ridden
by his complicity in Doyle's murder, Terry is attracted to Edie Doyle, Joey's
young sister, who demands that her brother's murderers be brought to justice. His love for Edie causes him to realize how compromised his existence
is, and the vicious injustice of the mob's domination of the waterfront.
Fearing that Terry will betray him by revealing the true facts of Doyle's
murder, Friendly orders Charley to either bring his brother into line or kill
him.

In a taxicab confrontation, Terry ignores his brother's threats; instead, he
accuses Charley of betraying him by derailing his boxing career. But for
Charley's mishandling, he might have had a fight career. "I could have been
a contender; I could have been something," he tells him.

For not dealing brutally with Terry, Charley is killed by Friendly's men.
Terry finds his brother's body impaled on a meat hook on a side street. This
brutal act pushes Terry to testify before the New York Crime Commission,
while in the hearing room Friendly shouts out his contempt. When Terry
appears for work the next day, Friendly and his henchmen viciously attack
him, beating him close to death. Refusing to accept defeat, Terry staggers
along the dock, with his fellow longshoremen finally lining up behind him
and protecting him from further intimidation. Without physical support, he
walks into the warehouse, ready to work.

During the rehearsal period, Marlon Brando asked Kazan to spell out the differences between the personalities of *Waterfront*'s Terry Malloy and *A Streetcar Named Desire*'s Stanley Kowalski.

Dear Marlon:

Perhaps it will be more useful if I put down what I think of Terry, rather than just talking about it. Then you can have it to look at. Then too, we can talk about it all after you've had a chance to think it all over. What the guy is, how he behaves, how he thinks, what he wants, is much more important here than usual because I really hope to be photographing the kid's insides as much as exterior events. The story of this kid's regaining his dignity or self-esteem—in a word, "regeneration"— happens inside the man and has to be done by you so I can photograph it. Terry's is also a more complex or divided character than Stanley, and the inner conflict is going on all the time—in even the smallest episodes—and it is not resolved till the end.

At any rate let me list, in the order that they come to me, the elements that are important for you to think about.

Crucial is the fact that he is an orphan. As a kid, he felt homeless, unwanted, even scorned, inferior to the rest of mankind. Perhaps he remembers couples looking for kids to adopt passing him by. Why is Friendly his idol? Because Friendly did pick him up, made a fighter of him, lavished concern and aid and friendship on him. Only Mickey [the name was changed to Johnny before filming commenced] "adopted" him and brought him to the point where he was desired and even "famous."

Fighting was his move for recognition. It was his bid for a place in the sun against a world from which he had been shut out from birth. It was his revenge on a world that had rejected him. When he fought, he was "someone," not an orphan. Mickey gave him this.

At the beginning of our story he had not been about to face the fact that Mickey "took" him. He cannot give up his idol. If he turns against Mickey he would be giving up the only friend he ever really had. Deprived of this one loyalty, he would have nothing. He knows in his heart that Mickey did him dirt. He just cannot look at it, he cannot face it. It would destroy too much in his inner structure.

And to tell the truth Mickey still gives him a little gratitude and flattery. He's still enjoying a tiny part of the favor that he used to have one hundred percent when he was Mickey's PET.

When he looks at Mickey, his eyes change from adoration to resentment, from a betrayed look to a worshipping look. He's like a rejected lover who after years still hasn't quite given up. There is no health and

With Brando and Eva Marie Saint

strength for him till he kills Mickey completely—which he symbolically does in the last sequence of the picture. It is crucial that this idolatry of Mickey be built up so that the final payoff can mean what it should.

The orphan re-orphanized. The lover betrayed, but still not giving up.

The next important thing is that Terry is terribly sad and fundamentally lonely. Consider that he lives alone in one small room with one small window. There is something of the ascetic about him. Consider: He has no girl. His best friend is the boy Jimmy and the other Golden Warriors (they still idolize him). He cannot consider Mickey really his friend. His best friends are the pigeons.

An awful lot of famous athletes don't do so well with girls. Whether it's that they've never grown past adolescence or what, they are notoriously unconfident lovers. They just don't seem to be able to make a satisfactory or permanent connection with a girl. I don't need to expand on this. You must know plenty of examples. If you don't, ask me. In our case, there it is: He lives alone in a room at twenty-eight.

His experience with girls has been an occasional whore—the girls from Mickey's entourage. He never could trust himself to them. He might have felt always that the girls were out to take him, and that, in turn, they were legitimate prey. Never before Edie had he had a chance to be close to a girl with gentleness and tenderness.

I suppose along with everything else there must be something of the narcissist in most fighters. Boxing is Terry's armor, and his defense. I thought that his greatest solace in times of stress or pain or confusion might be shadow boxing. I thought of him shadow boxing, when he's confused, with tears in his eyes.

This is completely different from Kowalski. Stanley is undivided. He is confident. He is on top. He has no self-doubts. He has no sex problem. He is not conceivably lonely. He is brash, gregarious, convivial by nature.

Terry seems to swagger and sometimes affects a jauntiness. But his eyes betray him. The swagger is a cover. When he is not being watched or living up to the pictures on the fight cards in the ticket brokers' offices—why then he is terribly gentle and withdrawing. You will find most fighters are this way, especially the young ones. Jimmy the kid seems tougher, more aggressive, more dominant than he is. Jimmy seems like HIS supreme commander. Jimmy is undivided and is confirmed in his values. Terry cannot seem sure because he is divided and in inner conflict.

Marlon, this part is much closer to you and to myself too. It is a complex part. He says cynical, arrogant things to the girl. But the next moment we should see that he's not that cynical or confident or sure— and that in his eyes there is a questioning. Kowalski had no self-doubt. Even at the end, he leaves Stella in the yard and returns to his poker game.

The great thing about this part is that it has an inner story. He starts one way. He ends up another. He does something at the beginning that drives home to him that he has become a bum. He meets a girl who for the first time is on the side of the good in him. All through the events and because of his love for her he finds that somewhere along the line he had lost his self-esteem and inner dignity. He finds out that he doesn't think much of himself. He finds that he hasn't faced the fact that Mickey and Charlie have used and degraded him. That he was afraid to face this. And now that he does, he must agree that he has become a bum. Then he, with the unspoken encouragement of the girl, through the priest's antagonism (the priest never gets to like him in the story), he goes out to regain his dignity and self-esteem and he does— the HARD way. That is the personal story.

A bum becomes a man. That's it.

He says all this cynical stuff to Edie. He makes fun of her idealism, in fact, of her sappy loftiness. But he is listening and sizing her up. He is deeply troubled inside, alone, abandoned, betrayed, and he needs help. Kowalski needs nothing. Until he loses Stella.

Kowalski's toughness is real. Terry's is an imitation of Mickey's, a way of responding to how the world values or devalues him. Kowalski's world is not unfriendly. It is MADE for him. Terry often sits quietly in a corner, alone.

The unusual part of all this is that the kid is not a thinker. His perceptions and his emotions both are on a primitive level. He is a primitive. He really can only half read. If he thinks too much, it gets painful. And then he shakes his head to shake it off like a fighter might shake off a crushing right cross.

If you have met Tony Mike DeVincenzo, you will have an idea of what I mean; Tony thinks in strictly Mafia terms.* A murder can only

---

* DeVincenzo had testified before the Waterfront Crime Commission about corruption. As Kazan said in his autobiography, "He named names. When he did that he broke the hoodlum law of silence. . . . I did see Tony Mike's story as my own, and that connection did lend the tone of irrefutable anger to the scenes I photographed and to my work with actors."

be answered by a death. If someone insults him, HE (not someone else, not the law) must answer. It is strictly gang code stuff. What is the source? Pride. Your pride is insulted, you must redeem it. I showed you Tony Mike's gesture for "somebody gave me a fucking!" This is close to an international gesture. I'll show you the Greek version. You know the Italian version (the uppercut).

I think his angers are deeper and more animal-like, more superstitious, more unanswerable than Stanley's. Stanley's anger flares up; Terry's angers are suppressed, nursed, grow to a point where they cannot be satisfied except with murder. Terry is truly dangerous. Stanley just fights a lot. Stanley is secure in his group. He is the center of his world. He is never challenged in the ultimate sense. Because he is king of his dung heap beyond challenge.

EDITOR

In the late 1940s Kazan collaborated with Arthur Miller on a filmscript, *The Hook,* dealing with labor organizing among the longshoremen of Brooklyn's Red Hook, a neighborhood Miller returned to later in the play *A View from the Bridge.* Ultimately, Miller withdrew from the project after, according to Kazan, Harry Cohn, the head of production at Columbia Pictures, asked Miller to skew the script toward exposure of Communist infiltration of the union rather than mob corruption, changes that for Miller robbed the story of factual validity. Although Kazan wrote that he was unsure of Miller's underlying reasons, Miller claimed that he felt pressure from Harry Cohn, Roy Brewer (head of the stagehands' union), and the FBI to substitute Reds for racketeers. When Miller quit, Cohn fired off a telegram to Kazan: "Strange how the minute we want to make a script pro-American, Miller pulls out."

Kazan knew that the novelist and playwright Budd Schulberg had also been preparing a waterfront film, this one based on a series of newspaper articles by Malcolm Johnson that in book form won the Pulitzer Prize for local reporting. After Miller quit the *Hook* project, Kazan asked to see Schulberg's script, then joined forces with him. Schulberg and Kazan confronted the same big-studio opposition that Miller and Kazan had. Darryl Zanuck considered *Waterfront,* but cautioned Schulberg and Kazan that waterfront corruption should merely provide a background to the personal story: "I believe that the evil of the waterfront situation should be the background . . . and the personal story must predominate. There is no use in making a wonderful picture like *Zapata* which nobody comes to see except the intelligentsia." Before agreeing to a profit participation rather than

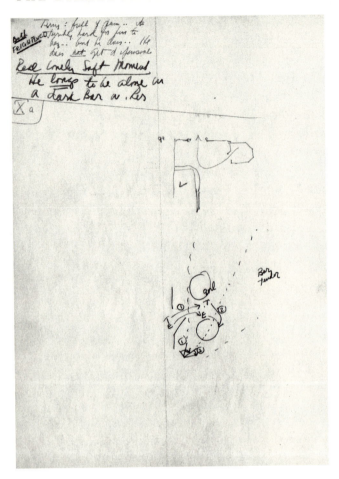

working out a flat fee for Kazan and Schulberg, Zanuck wanted either a finished script or a guarantee that Brando would star: "I think he will do the picture and that you can get him, but you have got to get him for me." After lengthy meetings and correspondence, however, Zanuck ultimately turned down the project. Later he explained, "At that time I felt that since we had overnight committed to a program of CinemaScope 'spectacles' I had no alternative but to back away from intimate stories even though these were good stories." (The next project Kazan would propose to Zanuck was, bewilderingly, *Oedipus Rex*. Zanuck responded, "This of course is a great subject . . . personally I am so fed up with material of this sort that it is difficult for me to become interested.")

Before arriving at a final script, Kazan and Schulberg went through at least ten versions, and Leo Braudy in his rigorous and acute monograph on the film, when considering Schulberg's later novelization, explores the energizing underlying ambiguities of the film's intentions: "Schulberg's story is

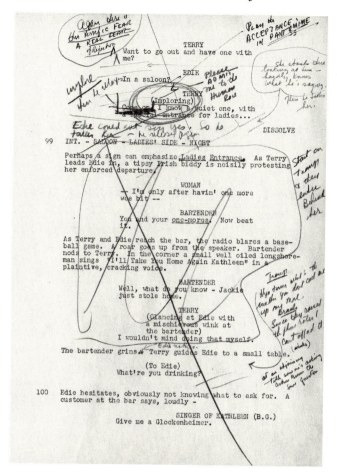

Facing pages of Kazan's shooting script—the bar scene with Edie and Terry—showing his drawings of camera angles, dialogue rewriting, and other notes.

the intellectual emerging from isolation and engaging with the world, Kazan's the physical unreflective person who finds a conscience and love—an inner self. Kazan is attracted to the story of the scorned and even despised man who proves himself, Schulberg to the disengaged intellectual who has to realize that the world is hard but justice is still worth fighting for."

At a chance encounter at the Beverly Hills Hotel, Schulberg and Kazan cornered the independent producer Sam Spiegel and convinced him *Waterfront* was a viable project. Spiegel packaged a distribution deal with United Artists that guaranteed a small budget of $500,000 on the understanding that Frank Sinatra would play Terry Malloy, but at the same time Spiegel continued to pursue Marlon Brando, who had earlier turned down the project. Brando's participation would guarantee a bigger budget.

When Brando finally agreed, Spiegel revised the budget upward, and United Artists withdrew. Spiegel arranged a new distribution deal with

Columbia's Harry Cohn, who agreed to bankroll the production for $880,000. Sinatra, who had already done wardrobe tests, threatened to sue, and Spiegel settled with him out of court. Production began in New York City and Hoboken, where the film was made in its entirety, in the winter of 1953–54.

Kazan later described the shooting:

> We shot *On the Waterfront* surrounded by people, by spectators. It was great; it was like a public trial. We photographed scenes in front of a line of longshoremen who were watching their lives being filmed. Once I was grabbed by the neck, thrown up against a wall, and the guy was going to beat me up. This was just outside a bar, and a little longshoreman inside saw it and came out. He got a hold of the guy who was going to hit me, and he murdered him, he beat the shit out of him. The atmosphere was that violent. There were things I can't tell about corruption, about our paying off people—little black sacks, things like that. We were right in the midst of life on that picture, and it shows, doesn't it?

Brando was adept at improvising and inventing business (and preferred those to following the script or getting advice from directors other than Kazan). Kazan has given him credit for the actor's best moments: his gait, holding on to Edie's glove when she drops it, turning the gun away that his brother points at him, stumbling through the tale he tells Edie of his childhood. In a 1954 interview Kazan told the *New York Post* film critic Archer Winston of his regard for Brando's creativity:

> No, I didn't tell him how. He's a genius. For me, it's the greatest performance since Johnny Huston's old man [Walter] in *Treasure of Sierra Madre*. He did things that weren't in the script, not in my direction. You know the way he walked like an ex-boxer, on his toes, his arms held down, close to his body. I had Marlon meet an ex-boxer, Roger Donoghue, who once killed an opponent. The guilty feeling. It was wonderful the way Brando seemed to absorb it. He's just a genius. He gets it by a kind of osmosis.

Brando's performance is the glory of the film, but Kazan's direction keeps the action taut and compelling, each scene played as if life depended upon it. Perhaps it was the limited production time and harsh conditions that urged the director and actors to energy and sharpness. Kazan had his cadre of Actors Studio–trained performers, and since he filmed in Hoboken, he was able to use as extras those who had lived the story. In spite of some clumsy writing, the scenes have a feeling of spontaneity that is the reward of Kazan's incisive sense of motivation and point.

The most contested aspect of the film is its implied vindication of Schulberg and Kazan's testimonies before HUAC, its justification for "squealing." "Maybe I did wrong, probably did," Kazan told Jeff Young. But the film's propulsive dramatic power is not compromised by any strained implication, especially since giving names of Communist Party members to HUAC is not a neat parallel to informing on corruption and murder. The film's salient themes are tyranny and self-assertion. If anything, any unspoken agenda would have derived from Kazan's anger at his ostracism by the theatre and film communities. "The whole story is about the fact that he's going to lose all of his old friends by testifying but he's really not with the reformists either. He's mistrusted by all sides," Kazan said. The brutal beating that Friendly and his henchmen give Terry might be its most "Kazan" moment, his complaint and his pained expression of injustice. Schulberg's rancor was more at the disregard of Hollywood producers than at the liberal revulsion to his testimony. The financial and critical success of the film was Schulberg and Kazan's revenge on the "Hollywood system," and they were particularly happy to accept their Academy Awards in New York rather than in Hollywood.

A little-known contribution to the film came to light in an interview that cinematographer James Wong Howe gave at the American Film Institute on April 14, 1973. Nowhere else is Howe's work on *On the Waterfront* acknowledged. Asked if he had ever worked with Kazan (a leading question), Howe replied that he had, one time only.

> Kazan said, "You know I got an ending to this picture, where Brando is fighting, I need more shots of fighting. Would you do that for me?" I said yes. The production manager asked me how many lights I wanted. I said, "No lights." So we went down and shot, and it got later and later and it was getting darker and darker. Finally I said, "Gee, Gadg, this is about it." He said, "I need a shot of Brando. He's beaten up so dizzy and he's walking into the warehouse. The door opens here." We used a handheld camera. It was an Eyemo that I gave to the operator. I put a piece of chalk down on the cement and said, "Now look through that camera and walk around that chalk mark." He kept walking and walking and said, "Gee I'm getting a little dizzy." I said, "Keep walking. Keep walking. Okay. Now point the camera at that door and hit the trigger and walk." He couldn't walk very steady, so it made a wonderful shot from Brando's perspective. If I hadn't spun the operator around and got him really dizzy, it wouldn't have worked.

East of Eden (1955)

"East of Eden is more personal to me; it is more my own story. One hates one's father; then rebels against him; finally one cares for him and recovers oneself, understanding and forgiving him, and you say to yourself, 'Yes, he is like that,' and you are no longer afraid."

EDITOR: On the eve of America's entry into World War I, tormented and rebellious young Cal Trask discovers that his mother, Kate, whom his father, Adam, had told him was dead, is the drug-addled madam of a brothel in Monterey, not far from his hometown of Salinas, California. He confronts her, and though she has no sentimental interest in this son or his brother, Aron, she gives him seed money for a business venture.

Pained by his father's preference for Aron, Cal's self-righteous and pious brother, Cal anguishes over Adam's stern coldness to him. Abra, Aron's girlfriend, feels sympathy for Cal's dilemma since she too has a troubled relationship with her father. She fights off her recognition that it is Cal she truly loves.

When Adam's scheme to transport vegetables in iced railroad cars fails, Cal, using the money his mother gave him, secretly invests in a bean-growing enterprise, which succeeds because of the wartime economy. Cal earns enough to recover the money his father lost in the transportation scheme, but Adam cruelly and contemptuously rejects the cash as the tarnished profits of war. Again, Cal has found only disapproval and rebuff from his father.

In retaliation, Cal drags his brother, Aron, who has idolized the memory of his mother, to the whorehouse to show him what she has become. Aron, his illusion shattered, goes into a drunken rage and runs away to enlist in the army. Adam, because of Aron's breakdown, suffers a stroke. At his bedside Abra pleads with Adam to show forgiveness and compassionate affection for Cal. Without a sign from him, she tells Adam, Cal will never recover from his sense of abandonment and loss but will remain doomed. A weakened Adam signals to Cal to come to his side, and with great effort he asks Cal to stay with him, to take care of him.

East of Eden was Kazan's first color film, his first in a wide-screen process, a true lavish Hollywood production. Budgetary and artistic freedom was the benefit of *On the Waterfront*'s success.

Jack Warner hadn't read the book, didn't propose to, didn't even ask what it was about, and didn't ask whom I was going to cast. What he did ask was: "What'll it cost?" "About one six," I said. "You've got it," he said. I doubt Warner ever read our screenplay; he was a hunch-bettor. I was his hunch that year. I told him that since it was about young people, I might use "newcomers." He stood up. "Come have lunch with me," he said. "Cast who you want." I was on my own.

Being an Anatolian, I knew that all this beneficence was as temporary as anything else in life, including life itself. It would last as long as I brought in the money. A few years later, after two box office busts in a row, I no longer had final cut. After another losing effort, I couldn't get backing at all.

EDITOR: Steinbeck and Kazan worked on a treatment, trying to whittle down the epic scale of the novel, but the effort proved to be a slog. Kazan was secretly worried about Steinbeck's stolid way with dialogue. He didn't want to repeat the mistakes of their previous collaboration, *Viva Zapata!,* and yet he didn't want to offend Steinbeck, who (as Steinbeck suffered from knowing) was no longer a critical favorite.

MAY 18, 1953

Dear John,

It must seem strange me writing you. Doing it because I've got something tough to say and it's not easy to say it. On the other hand, I want to put it exactly as I feel it, no more, no less.

I spent the last three days in the country going over and over our outline. I tried to look at it as a producer. It says in the contract that I'm a producer. Beyond that, as I've told you many times, I feel a tremendous responsibility doing *Eden* especially under the compensation partly by profit arrangement. And beyond that, I just got to do you real proud this time. I'll be in my own private dog house for years if I don't bring this one off completely.

I blame myself for what happened to *Zapata.* I'm supposed to be the moviemaker of the combine. And the moviemaking was what was wrong with *Zapata.* It ended up in the "It sure has wonderful things in it" category. The attack we took on it was just not right. And the mistake we made was right at this stage of the work. Nothing we did (or could have done) subsequently helped, once we made the basic mistake in planning.

As you know, I've been terribly concerned that I might make the same kind of mistake here. I'm a damned good director on the set. At the planning stage. I think I could still use a year or two of "class A" ball. I made the same kind of mistake on *Tightrope,* for instance. And again right at this point. I let get by two no-good love stories that didn't tie in. I figured I could somehow cover everything with a big sauce of direction. Well, I poured it on. I swam in mountain ice-cold streams, and I gave out songs and I held kisses longer than necessary for all practical purposes—and still the bloody scenes stank on film. My fault. I was responsible.

Now I think absolutely every choice we've made thus far on *Eden* was right. But I don't think we're home yet planning-wise or in this outline stage.

Even when you were up in Connecticut ten days ago, I felt something was wrong with our outline. Remember the morning you left I suggested that we start with Cal and stick with him all through. This was to pitch the audience immediately into our story on the main track.

Now I think Cal should be centralized even more.

The more I studied it during these last days, the more serious I felt the work we still had to do. I still think we're diffuse. *Zapata* was diffuse. I know we've chosen the right part of your material to work with. I know we've made excellent and even daring eliminations—but to use and use an old and honorable word, we need a much better <u>continuity</u> before we write a line of dialogue.

So this led to the next step in my thinking. I think we ought to get you a better and more experienced movie constructionist than Gadg Kazan. Put it another way, Kazan the producer would not hire Kazan the writer to work with you on this job.

I have no false modesty. I'm a fertile director, but stress *director.* The ideas I have are basically director's ideas. I'm not a first-rate constructionist—I know that. And a first-rate novelist and a first-rate novel should have a first-rate screen technician. . . .

What I'd like to do is bring in a really first-class screen artisan or craftsman. I'd like to take this man our line-up of material and develop it into a first-draft screenplay. His job would be basically simplification and unification and continuity—singleness! He would work in consultation with you, and he would work in consultation with me.

Thinking of someone like a couple of guys you've met, Bob Ardrey or Paul Osborn. These guys aren't up to your ankles as writers or artists. They're not. But they are specialists. Screenwriting is a special field. It is not your forte and it is not mine. . . .

This man would write a first draft, a rough one, but one that would embody his ideas on unity and simplification, and singleness. Once we had this draft, we would find ourselves with plenty of time before our Warner Bros. deadline. We'd have real objectivity. We'd be outside.

Gadg

EDITOR: Kazan's great casting hunch was James Dean, a young actor who had played the tantalizing Arab boy in a stage adaptation of André Gide's *The Immoralist* and succeeded in seducing critics in addition to the play's protagonist. Screenwriter Paul Osborn suggested Dean, and after a brief interview, Kazan was sure this guy *was* Cal. Steinbeck agreed, "said he sure as hell was, and that was it."

An acting tyro, Dean had not much technique. "Jimmy would either get the scene right immediately, without any detailed direction—that was ninety-five percent of the time—or he couldn't get it at all." Animosity between players would sometimes be a useful tool for Kazan, and Dean and Raymond Massey's mutual dislike is the most famous instance of Kazan's bad-cop direction.

Ray Massey, the old-timer who'd played Lincoln enough times to establish a franchise and was now playing Jimmy's father, anticipated that Jimmy would quickly spoil rotten. He simply couldn't stand the sight of the kid, dreaded every day he worked with him. "You never know what he's going to say or do!" Ray said. "Make him read the lines the way they're written." Jimmy knew that Ray was scornful of him, and he responded with sullenness he didn't cover. This was an antagonism I didn't try to heal; I aggravated it. I'm ashamed to say—well, not ashamed; everything goes in directing movies—I didn't conceal from Jimmy or from Ray what they thought of each other, made it plain to each of them. The screen was alive with precisely what I wanted; they detested each other. Casting should tell the story of a film without words; this casting did. It was a problem that went on to the end, and I made use of it to the end.

I felt that Dean's body was very graphic; it was almost writhing in pain sometimes. He was very twisted, almost like a cripple or a spastic of some kind. He couldn't do anything straight. He even walked like a crab, as if he were cringing all the time. I felt that, and that doesn't come across in close-up. Dean was a cripple, anyway, inside—he was not like Brando. People compared them, but there was no similarity. He was a far, far sicker kid, and Brando's not sick, he's just troubled. But I also think there was a value in Dean's face. His face is so desolate and lonely and strange. And there are moments in it when you say, "Oh, God, he's handsome—what's being lost here! What goodness is being lost here!"

Dean had the most natural talent after Marlon. But he lacked technique; he had no proper training. He could not play a part outside his range. He often hit a scene immediately and instinctively right. Sometimes he did not and then there would be problems. Nor was his intelligence of a high order. Directing him was gratifying because he always caught something of the spirit of the youth which considered itself disenfranchised by the preceding generation, their parts. But there was an element of self-pity here and I found this irksome. He had considerable innocence but not as an adjunct of strength or courage, but of hatred and a kind of despair. His imagination was limited; it was like a child's. To direct him was somewhat like directing Lassie the dog; the director dealt in a series of rewards and threats and played a psychological game with him. He had to be coddled and hugged or threatened with abandonment. His own favorite actor was Brando, and the only word possible here is hero-worship. When Brando came to visit my set of *East of Eden,* Jimmy was awestruck and nearly shriveled with

Albert Dekker, Raymond Massey, and James Dean, at right

Kazan invited Dean's hero Brando to the *East of Eden* set,
here with Julie Harris.

respect. But I cannot concur in an impression that has some currency,
that he fell into Marlon's mannerisms; he had his own and they were
ample.

He was fortunate in *East of Eden* that he had with him one of the
young saints of the American theatre, Julie Harris, an actress who had
all of Marlon's gifts but on a miniature scale. She also had emotional
force wedded, as Marlon's was, to gentleness. Two of the most gentle
scenes in my films are the scenes Marlon played with Eva Marie Saint
(another angel) in *On the Waterfront* and the one Julie played at the
end of *East of Eden*, which is—I speak of her performance—of surprising beauty. She also brought to that production the quality I
needed most to help with Jimmy Dean, kindly patience. I believe that
most any other actress would have time and again become restless and
even resentful of the psychological games Dean played. But not Julie.
She made Jimmy feel that he was a first-class artist, and he flowered
under her encouragement.

EDITOR: In a stray note Kazan appended to his journal, Kazan reconsidered
the unconvincing final scene of *East of Eden:*

There is no real drama unless you have situations that push the main
character to the extreme frontier of his nature. You must finally so
arrange it that the leading character's back is to the wall. There he has
no exit. He must face the music.

Don't let him off easy. In *East of Eden* you let Dean off easy. Therefore the end is false! You must never be able to ask the question: Then what happens? What happens in a dramatic piece must be *final*! No exit.

Drama is the most dynamic of all arts. And the filmstrip, by its very nature—it runs! it is run!—is the most dynamic of the dramatic arts. You start a movement in the first feet that must gain momentum and charge till it crashes against an immovable wall in the last feet and that is it.

Sentimentality is the enemy of drama. It waters down the conflict. It is the sister of self-pity.

Last five minutes of *East of Eden.* Now you know that the old man would have died without a kind word for Dean—and that the kid would have to spend a long time climbing back.

Toughness fills an audience with the greatest of all theatre emotions—awe!

EDITOR

Kazan and Steinbeck had planned to dramatize the whole novel, but they soon realized they were developing a movie that would run for ten hours.[*] They narrowed the focus to a tale of father and sons and finally concentrated on Cal. The loss of the back material, however, created a lack of narrative impulse. (We are too far into *medias res,* especially since there is no confrontation between the mother and father.) Also, the often-described and encouraged animosity between Dean and Raymond Massey left no implicit premise and development for the concluding reconciliation. It was, as Kazan knew, unsubstantiated. The film seems not to conclude but to peter out. It would have made a better tale if one had killed the other. In addition, Richard Davalos as the preferred son offers no counterweight to Dean's Dostoyevskian angst, but that might be the script's fault. As lovely and sympathetic as Julie Harris is, she appears too old for Dean's baby-faced Cal, and the implication that she can't have a fulfilling relationship with Cal until he makes peace with his father is never given dramatic form. Kazan's uneasiness with Dean's lack of discipline was probably exasperated by Dean stealing the movie not only from the other actors but from Kazan. Only in his moments with Jo Van Fleet is Dean challenged by anyone else on screen. When Dean is not in sharp focus, one is anxious to have him back—he is

[*] An eight-hour, three-part television miniseries that was shown in 1981 was an adaptation of the whole novel.

watchable because nothing, nothing, he does can be anticipated. But Kazan "made" that performance. (As Kazan said, Dean is much less good and often irritating in *Rebel Without a Cause* and *Giant.*)

The film is beautifully, even showily, photographed and, typically, brilliantly staged. Kazan is infallible with place and ambience. It does not fail scene by scene—great set pieces for everyone—but it feels incomplete, the episodes not pushing ineluctably toward some epiphany. Kazan was too ambitious and personal an artist to consider what would have provided him with a structural model for this kind of epic, cross-generational tale: *Gone With the Wind.*

Baby Doll (1956)

"It is the best film, I believe, that anyone has made from Williams."

SUMMARY, FROM KAZAN'S *A LIFE*: A penny-ante entrepreneur, Silva Vacarro bulls his way into a community of the Deep South and sets up a modern gin to process cotton. One night the gin burns down. Vacarro suspects arson and has a hunch that the man whose business he's taken away, Archie Lee Meighan, did it. To make sure, he drives his pickup to Archie Lee's home, a crumbling white mansion, and questions Archie Lee's wife, Baby Doll. She is a nineteen-year-old infant who still sleeps in her childhood crib. Vacarro finds that the marriage, arranged by her father on his deathbed to ensure his daughter's protection, has not been consummated. Baby Doll, as she regularly informs her impatient husband, is not ready for marriage. She is very "ready"—but not for him. Vacarro's revenge is to begin to seduce the

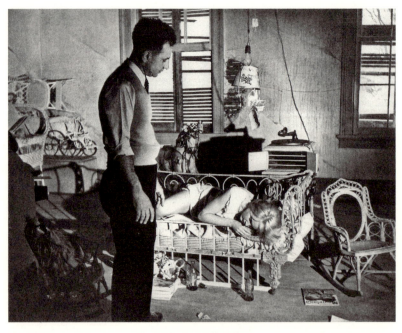

With Carroll Baker

girl, whereupon she blurts out a confession that her husband did burn down the gin. The film never makes clear whether the seduction is consummated. Waiting for Archie Lee to come home, Vacarro naps in Baby Doll's crib. When Archie Lee arrives, after a hard day's work ginning out Vacarro's cotton in his own gin, he finds Vacarro waiting for him. Vacarro leads him to believe that he's had Baby Doll. That is his revenge.

EDITOR: Censorship storm clouds hovered over *Baby Doll* from the beginning. A week before filming began on location in Greenville, Mississippi, Kazan was still wrestling with the script—and with the fears of Warner Bros. executives Jack Warner and Steve Trilling. Geoffrey Shurlock of the Production Code office had sent Warner Bros. a list of changes required to qualify for a Production Code certificate. "The first of these," wrote Shurlock, "was the justified adultery that the script seemed to indicate." Kazan told Jack Warner what he would and wouldn't do and provided him with a reading of the film that might pacify the censors.

NOVEMBER 14, 1955
HOTEL GREENVILLE
GREENVILLE, MISS.

Dear Jack,

I will do everything the Shurlock office wants, except one thing that I cannot do. If I did, I'd have to throw away the whole picture.

I have eliminated everything except the points I note below.

Assure [Geoffrey] Shurlock and [Jack] Vizzard once more that both Williams and I specifically do not want there to have been a "sex-affair" between our two people. I have eliminated the lines about her skin breaking out entirely. I have eliminated the stage direction about her hurt expression when Silva says that nothing happened between them.

But this film is about one thing and only one thing. It's about a middle-aged man who is held at arm's length by his young wife. It's a false marriage, falsely made, and it's bound to collapse because the basis of it is false. Actually, we don't show her going with another man.

Inform Shurlock and Vizzard that at the end of the picture Silva is going to walk away from her. Having forced justice on a reluctant community, he has what he wants. He doesn't really want Baby Doll. She is terribly attracted to him. He is not to her. He wants one thing only: to avenge the burning of his gin. He wants to put Archie so incontrovert-

On location,
directing
Eli Wallach
and Carroll
Baker

ibly on the guilty spot that even friendship can't save him, the friendship of the local authorities, that is.

I think Silva's dropping her at the end of the film will make the adultery issue quite clear. There wasn't any, and actually while Silva has aroused her, he isn't particularly interested in her, once Archie Lee has been taken away.

Tell the boys that the hero of this film, for me, is Archie Lee. He is a pathetic, misguided, confused, desperate man. Sin and violence and so forth come out of fear and desperation. Archie Lee should be pathetic. And will be, and amusingly so.

I cannot reduce the element of Archie Lee's sex frustration. I don't know how you want to handle this. I will, you can be sure, handle it delicately and in good taste. And since it will all be done comically and amusingly, the sordid side of it will be eliminated. There will be nothing sordid about it. Archie Lee will be pathetically amusing. The boys know that when I say something, I make good on it. The audience will only feel how absurd his awkward and misarranged passion is. How funny! How sad! Jack and Steve and Geoff and I all being firmly bogged down in middle years will understand this.

In line with this thinking, tell the boys that I cannot eliminate Archie's going into the bathroom after his wife, I cannot eliminate the dialogue about Archie's sex frustration, I cannot change the doctor scene and furthermore assert unequivocally that it has nothing to do with sex frustration, since every middle-aged man is familiar with the sudden slump of ALL his powers that comes (dismayingly) in his late forties. Furthermore, I must make the scene of Archie Lee trying to make love to his wife deeply tender and loving. I do not direct vulgar sex scenes. The request they make that I eliminate Archie slugging his wife is pure bull. I won't pay any attention to that point. I, above all, cannot eliminate the dialogue starting "How long did he have to wait?" etc. This is the whole nub of the story, and if I eliminate this passage or curtail it, the audience won't have the vaguest idea what the hell the film is about. This is the essence of the plot. And there is nothing wrong with it except that it violates the dictates—not of the American public—but of the Catholic Church ONLY.*

Furthermore, Baby Doll does grow up in the story, but I will make it clear that her growing up has nothing to do with her having her first vaginal orgasm. The lines they want eliminated are essential to the story and I have no intention of eliminating them. But I will cut out Baby Doll's hurt expression when Silva tells Archie Lee (truthfully) that nothing has happened between them.

In general, Jack, it seems to me that with fewer and fewer people leaving their TV sets and their homes after supper, we must, we MUST strike out for exceptional subject matters and really unusual treatments of these subject matters. In one sentence, we are now obliged AS A MATTER OF SELF-PRESERVATION to put on the screen of motion picture theatres only what they cannot and will never see on their TV screens at home. Our industry now is in a desperate situation, and we must be bold and fight for our lives. TV is improving fast, and getting bolder every day. The wide-screen gimmick cannot keep our heads above the water much longer. We've got to break our own taboos and strike out for increasingly unusual material.

There is now nothing indecent about this subject. It is a comic por-

---

* The last sentence was cut at the suggestion of Jack Warner's assistant before the letter was shown to Jack Warner.

trait of middle-aged ardor. It has grotesque and even tragic elements, but essentially the viewpoint is comic and affectionate. It will certainly not be sordid. They'll have to take my word for that. But where I think we must fight and fight hard is the admissibility of the grown-up subject at the core of this script. If we can and do, why then we may well have a picture that will really interest everyone and which people will leave their homes to see.

EDITOR: After completing location work, the interior scenes were filmed at Warner Bros.' Brooklyn studios. Frederick Morton reported on Kazan in action for a 1957 *Esquire* profile, "Gadg." Morton vividly details Kazan coaxing and bullying performances from Eli Wallach and Carroll Baker in the attic scene in which Silva seduces Baby Doll into signing a confirmation of Malden's guilt.

Carroll stretched herself trembling along one of the few solid beams visible and clung to it.

"You poor darling," Kazan said, and with a playful stroke brushed a bit of her hair onto her face.

"I can't see, Gadg," Carroll cried.

"That's why I said you're poor." He laughed, and shouted to a stagehand, "Ready to make with the dust, Logan?"

"Ready," said Logan, holding a bowl of dust.

"Lock it up, fellas," Kazan said.

"Lock it up," yelled Charlie Maguire, the first assistant director, and the red light flashed on over all the doors.

A buzzer sounded three times. The hammering ceased, the talking died, even the faint clicking of the typewriter from the office upstairs stopped like an abruptly broken watch. The entire building, with its high-powered personnel and fantastic illusion-making machinery, was in the palm of his hand.

"Action," Kazan shouted, and opened his arms wide, winglike [three stagehands released nine pigeons], and then a stand-in started to throw dust against the attic roof. And, amidst a flutter of wings and rustle of particles and a moaning and sighing from the prostrate, blinded Miss Baker, Wallach, standing a few feet away from his victim, began to stamp and earthquake the old attic and to demand that she sign the statement. He tacked a piece of paper onto a nail at the end of a pole, attached a pencil to it, and reached it over toward the girl.

All the while, Kazan repeated in soundless pantomime Wallach's snarls and stomps, Carroll's squirmings and jerks. With finger motions he directed the stagehands shaking the "attic" springs. He nodded to the sound man, who moved the mike boom suspended above the action. He encouraged or soft-pedaled the dust thrower.

Carroll meanwhile had signed the paper. Wallach retrieved it, kissed it exultantly. Then suddenly the scene became less fierce, more tender. Wallach took a long look at the girl; the dust drizzled down like gentle rain; Kazan's lips moved in a sweet, slow, silent rhythm. Wallach tacked a clean handkerchief to the pole, reached it to Carroll with a gallant gesture. She hesitated, gave a ghost of a smile, took it, and dabbed her eyes with it.

"Cut," said Kazan. He suddenly threw himself down headlong on an attic beam parallel to Carroll's. "Baby Doll," he said as one prostrate person to another (he even pushed some of his hair into his eyes), "Baby Doll, when he reaches you that handkerchief, it's like something very nice but unexpected. It's like something out of your childhood, something beautiful and unexpected like an Easter egg you suddenly found. Even touch it like an Easter egg— careful, so you won't break it, see?"

He stroked her cheek, then jumped up and called to Wallach in a rough man-to-man voice, "Eli, you old bastard, let's do it like you kiss that piece of paper not because you're grateful to her, but because that signature of hers is gonna break her husband. That kiss means 'Now I got him by the testicles!' And do some business that shows it."

"Some business?" Wallach asked.

"Yeah, you'll figure out something," Kazan said with a confident shrug.

Wallach kissed an imaginary piece of paper with a gloating growl that came up from his guts, and then spat.

"Great!" Kazan said with jubilation. "Roll it."

The scene was shot again. This time Wallach spat (and Kazan spat soundlessly with him), and Carroll took the handkerchief with marveling wonder while Kazan's hands cupped tenderly to form an Easter egg.

"Cut!" Kazan said, and instantly began to throw tiny pieces of mortar at Wallach's feet. "I want to annoy you, Eli boy. I want to get you mad. Come on everybody, that first shot again!" He grinned and continued to throw bits in Wallach's direction. "I'm gonna bombard the hell out of you until you show us you're really fighting crazy for that signature. I'm gonna stone you. . . . Action!"

He kept up his fierce throwing motions while his leading man went through the attic-stamping part of the scene again, but more intensely now under the waggish volleys. "Cut," Kazan shouted. "Perfect! Print 3 and 4. Lunch!"

EDITOR

For *Baby Doll*, Kazan drew up an initial film scenario based on two Tennessee Williams one-act plays, "27 Wagons Full of Cotton" and "The Unsatisfactory Supper." When Kazan showed the draft to Williams, Williams found the ending a vulgar trafficking in the sensational: Kazan had proposed that a rampaging Archie Lee mortally pierce Silva with a frog-sticking pole in a swamp battle and accidentally shoot a Negro before being dragged off by the local sheriff. This conclusion was far from Williams's concept of a "grotesque folk-comedy." "You say," Williams wrote to Kazan, "that whenever I am in trouble I go poetic. I say whenever you are in trouble you start building up a 'SMASH!' finish.—As if you didn't really trust the story that goes before it."

Some of Williams's displeasure was a spillover from resentments that had arisen during the preparation for the Broadway production of *Cat on a Hot Tin Roof*, during which Williams had felt bullied into revising the third act. Concerned about *Baby Doll*, Williams wrote his agent, Audrey Wood, of his gnawing wariness of Kazan:

> He sent me a five-page outline for the film play which would have meant starting over from scratch even if I thought it was right, and it was corny as hell and old-fashioned melodrama that just wouldn't come off. I've stopped trying to work on it, at least until further word from him. If he's got any sense, he'll come to his senses, and leave me alone with the script to work it out my own way. I think he cheapened *Cat*, still think so, despite the prizes. That doesn't mean I doubt his good intentions, or don't like him, now, it's just that I don't want to work with him again on a basis in which [he] will tell me what to do and I will be so intimidated, and so anxious to please him, that I will be gutlessly willing to go against my own taste and convictions.

Though Kazan gratefully accepted all Williams's suggestions for the filmscript, Williams worked on it only intermittently and kept a distance from the production. He spent a reclusive day or two at the Benoit, Mississippi, location, and then fled, excusing himself by claiming that the locals were hostile to him. All this latent anger at Kazan resurfaced years later, when Kazan at a late stage withdrew from directing Williams's *Period of Adjustment*.

The completed film was given a Production Code certificate on September 14, 1956, while receiving a Condemned rating from the Legion of Decency, the first film to get a split decision. The legion judged: "The subject matter of this film is morally repellent both in theme and treatment. It dwells almost without variation or relief upon carnal suggestiveness in action, dialogue and costuming. Its unmitigated emphasis on lust and the various scenes of cruelty are degrading and corruptive. As such it is grievously offensive to Christian and traditional standards of morality and decency."

Though he hadn't seen the film, from the pulpit of New York's St. Patrick's Cathedral a revolted Francis Cardinal Spellman cautioned all Catholics to stay away or risk damnation. A riposte came from another churchman, the dean of the Episcopalian St. John the Divine, the Very Reverend Dr. James Pike: "Those who do not want the sexual aspect of life included in the portrayal of a real-life situation had better burn their Bibles as well as abstain from the movies. . . . The movie is not pornographic." He went on to confess that he didn't think he "had sinned in viewing it."

Despite all of Kazan's and Williams's disclaimers, and from what is shown in the film and what isn't, it seemed then and seems now naïve to assume that intercourse hadn't taken place. The conclusion that "nothing happened" weakens the impact of the story. Surely Baby Doll has experienced more than an enlightened thought, and Silva, though callow and vengeful, must be something more than a tease. Whatever the discretion of the filmmaker, the performers tell us an undeniable fact.

A Face in the Crowd (1957)

"The film has an external story, but there is also a secondary story, running concurrently and hiding, as it were, behind the objective one. This 'hidden' story has an intimate reference to the emotional life of the author and the director. It is the story of women as conscience."

[Jackie] Gleason is out because he is not warm, not pure, not wise, not natural, not country. Especially now since all he's doing is going down to Florida to watch the ball teams train, especially now that we are stressing a certain innocence and childlikeness. This (as it did in Julie [John] Garfield, in Arthur Godfrey himself) can and does become venal and calculating and tough-minded and fiercely competitive. But Gleason is that way already.

If you cast [Andy] Griffith, you have to cast the girl like Judy Kazan [Kazan's eldest daughter], more unschooled, purer than he is. Griffith's hair, three stages: 1. Rumpled and uncombed, 2. High pompadour. 3. Thinned out and combed flat.

Lonesome's charms: When he's off, he's very much like Brando, soft spoken, deeply independent, smiling, gentle, no aggression, subtly humorous, cat-like, lazy, not easy to frighten, or rush; amused at others, secure and confident.

About sex, he's like MB [Brando], mostly mischievous too: "That's what girls are for, ain't it so?" For instance, in his bewilderment and naïveté, he is really just a country boy in a big city. And his simple manner does get everybody with him, does break down all barriers. Cast everyone to build this up, to make LR [Lonesome Rhodes] look good.

At the end, when Marcia goes to LR's penthouse apartment and tells him never again, she's doing it with Mel's pistol in her back—it is not her instinct to do this, her instinct is to forgive again and she is right to—Mel [the character played by Walter Matthau] is almost like a gangster, forcing her.

And finally she feels guilty and ashamed of her part in killing him,

With
Andy
Griffith

and she really means it. She is really attacking Mel when she tells him "I should have left him in jail." She is attacking all the system that she and Mel are part of. She and Mel are never entirely right together. One must feel that too much has been poured into a weak vessel.

In the last part, Andy Griffith should be really mature, powerful, menacing. His acting should be powerful and simple. Not tricked, fussy, or elaborated. His TV technique, which in the middle part was like Tennessee Ernie Ford, is now more like Arthur Godfrey, more high pressure, more given to sexual innuendo.

This story is of love and betrayal between LR and the people of the country. He speaks for them and at first is their partisan. So they fall in love with him. They reward him with their love and then their esteem and dollars. These spoil him. He begins to despise them. They find this out and turn against him. They withdraw their love: Love turns to hate. Like a man spurned by a lover, he commits suicide as a sort of revenge.*

This is the CENTRAL STORY, all the other stories are subordinate. The Marcia story is a part of the main story. It is not the main story.

Somewhere in the first part LR should sing a hymn touchingly and beautifully. The audience should be moved to tears. Immediately fol-

---

* In all versions of the script Lonesome Rhodes commits suicide; in the finished film he is left ranting drunkenly, an ending Kazan and Schulberg decided was more effective because less melodramatic. Still, Kazan was not satisfied how that worked out: "But until its very last moments, when the satire falls to earth, it is successful and great fun." (Kazan, *A Life,* 568.)

lowing, we are given a radio commercial—a rather crass one. When the commercial is over, LR comes on and immediately says, "They might have given it a moment, but just a moment before that hair wash. It would have gotten just as much attention a moment later, maybe a little more."

AUGUST 25, 1956

Last day shooting in Memphis. Must face one thing. I'm being careless and being rushed too much.

Actually, I'm not giving myself a chance to rehearse. Last night I actually did not rehearse the scene with Mrs. Coaley and LR. I had a line rehearsal, gave a hint or two, but I actually did not direct an acting rehearsal. The machinery and Harry Stradling's speed has overwhelmed me. I am not getting the benefit of my directing ability. Each scene does not contain my conviction about its content, enough of you. Budd Schulberg swayed me last night because I was swayable, because I had not found my connection. Don't let these people control the pace for you. Don't satisfy Budd or Stradling or the schedule. Satisfy yourself. Grow up and become a man!!

EDITOR: Some six months after the film's release, Kazan reconsidered the film's structure:

JANUARY 4, 1958

A work of art should not show. It should not teach.

IT SHOULD BE.

It should be like a fact that has many meanings, all as complex and mixed up as life itself, contradictory, unfathomable, mysterious. The meanings should be here. But the audience should feel—as they do in the presence of a work of nature, that they have to find them, dig them out, and interpret them for themselves, each putting on each his own meaning.

We conceived *Face in the Crowd* as a "warning to the American people." This was the complete give away. The movie was conceived, written, directed, and acted to show, to teach. Therefore it was oversimplified. It was mental. The complexity that we knew was left out. Above all, we were out to show what a son of a bitch LR was—where we should have been showing that LR was us.

The big thing that would have made that story true and a piece of the contemporary scene would have been if LR at a point had reversed. If he had made the discovery: I am becoming a shit, this is not what I started out to do. I am no longer the master of my own destiny. They'd got me. They've got me. I've got to get out. I've got to get out I've got to get out of it . . . AND THEN HE CANNOT.

This would have been what would have happened to a human in that situation. But our fellow was a puppet designed to show what a son of a bitch he was. But the fact is more dangerous (because somebody "nice," like you, is involved). And funnier and more complex, therefore more interesting.

And this contradictory set up, this inner conflict in a man, is the basis for real good story-telling because there is a back-and-forth play within a man that leads you to many, many incidents, and interesting unpredictable behavior under all circumstances.

In other words, it is life. It is a true story. The real LR is both good and bad.

This discovery and reversal are heartbreaking, recognizable. It is pain, within a soul.

And when you do this, your work of art is, it exists. It is not a contrivance, a contraption to teach.

EDITOR

For a tribute book for Kazan prepared by Wesleyan University, Budd Schulberg told of Kazan's getting what he needed from an actor:

> Again as with the *Waterfront*, he had a mixed bag of actors in *Face*. There were fine tried performers like Pat Neal and Walter Matthau, there were neophytes like Lee Remick and Tony Franciosa. There was Andy Griffith, who had played effective rural Southern comedy, but had never faced the challenge of a heavy dramatic role like that of Lonesome Rhodes. There was even a big tough customer named Big Jeff Bess, who we had plucked from a border country roadhouse and who had never faced a camera before. He had one scene in which he is supposed to be so furious at Andy (Lonesome) that angry tears came to his eyes. That was asking too much of the untrained talents of Big Jeff. After a series of futile takes, Gadg suddenly went up, and unexpectedly slapped Mr. Bess in the face as hard as he could, then cried "Roll 'em!" and stepped back of the camera to watch the results. Big Jeff came forward with angry tears in his eyes, ready to murder Kazan. When

he saw how convincing he was in that scene, his anger subsided. "Wow, that's real Stanislavski," I said to Gadg when the take was in the can. And Gadg said, "Budd, you take it any way you can get it."

Patricia Neal had come in contact with Kazan before but at a distance, when she was a member of the Actors Studio and as a replacement in the role of Maggie in *Cat on a Hot Tin Roof.* She was gratified by the intensity of Kazan's direction, even when she was a victim of his getting it any way he could:

> When I first was given the role I somehow thought that Gadg would do everything for his actors. How wrong I was. You, yourself, have to bring something with you to the set—it is from this point that he takes over. He is very friendly and treats you very considerately—almost like cotton wool. He is also very honest. He will tell you if a thing falls short of your capacity . . . even after he has told the cameraman to go ahead and print it. He prints quite a number of takes—far more than would be allowed in one of the big Hollywood studios.
>
> One of my big scenes is the betrayal of Lonesome Rhodes, the hillbilly singer who becomes a national figure, by throwing the switch that puts on the air his comments after he thinks he has been faded out. For this scene I had to hold on to the switchboard, crying, while about six men had to drag me away. For the first couple of takes, I could not register quite what Kazan wanted. He told me to hold on as hard and as long as I could. He left me and went over to the men who were to drag me away. (I was not supposed to hear him tell them to pull me away from the board as quickly as they could!) We did the scene again, my hands bled and I sobbed as the men pulled me away. Gadg had his scene—and the way he wanted it.

Wild River (1960)

"I love Wild River*—just the ease of it, the simplicity. I tried to deal with my own sense of beauty, rather than what I did in* Baby Doll *where I made things a bit grotesque. I tried not to do that here; it's purer, one of the two purest films I've made."*

The thing that's been stomping the film is not knowing exactly what one thing it is about. WHAT ONE THING. It's about Dave [called Chuck in the film], no doubt. If it's about the old woman, why the love story? If about the girl, why the dam, etc.? A man in the right, sure of being in the right, and out to do right, discovers that people can be in the wrong from his viewpoint. And still be right. And awesomely right from a moral and human angle. This discovery that they are right and he is callow comes as a terrific shock to him. The scene in which he is painfully bewildered at discovering they are right is the big left-out scene. It is necessary because it tells what the film is about. It is necessary because right here the action is *reversed and a new course set out.* He has done terrible harm while theoretically doing long-term good. The rights of the state against the rights of the individual, and he finds that for the first time he's humanly involved. And he reverses his course, sets out to salvage the human pieces. And make peace with his conscience.

Lee Strasberg agreed with Molly that I reversed the process. Which means that I made up my mind to do a story on a certain theme and cooked up a story to illustrate the theme, rather than finding a story that excited me as a story and a theme that I liked. The thing to start with being the treatment or entertainment, the artistic dramatic elements, rather than the theme. And how did this happen? You chose a theme that draws out of you some compulsive urges: of habit, guilt, ego, and the need to prove yourself. Then you jack it up and run a story under it. In this process the final story does not match the size of the theme or subject. Result here as elsewhere, your story is conventional.

Before I start on this third draft, it is terribly important that I become Dave. If I could tap into some unconscious memory, so that Dave will flow out of me it would be so much truer. Actually, I was Dave once. I remember when I taught a class in Directing downtown at the New Theatre League. I was about twenty-five, and Jack Garfein at his most cocky was nothing to what I was like. I was the hero of the young insurgent working-class art movement. I knew about directing, and I could teach anybody. It was easy. And there were certain things you had to know, which could be taught. I was convinced that I knew more than anyone else because I had had (the only one who had) the benefit of the external training at the Group. I spoke without fear of contradiction. I had done nothing to prove my position. But I simply did not suffer from self-doubt. I was doing everyone a favor in coming down there, and I went as the "taxi driver" of *Waiting for Lefty.* A hero, an original. The only one of a kind. I was that rare thing, the first of the Communist intellectuals in the dramatic arts.

I bulled the class, showed off, made them laugh, dazzled them with my speed and wit. And knowledge. I knew more than the Group. I knew things Clurman didn't know and Strasberg would never know. I told everyone what was wrong. I took gym sessions and dancing lessons and was in great physical shape. I was admired by women but was too superior to take any of it. Women were not my problem. I was too narcissistic for that. Everything was easy for me. I was even superior to the Communists. And when they didn't go along with me, I quit them. Finding all the inhibitions of the party insufferable, I went on my own. I was the future.

Remember Irwin Shaw. He had his life figured out. It was work in the morning, then a light lunch, then handball, everyday handball, tremendous compulsion to keep himself in shape, then cocktails, dinner, fucking. It was all one solid piece. He was not plagued with doubts. All in all, things were clearer in those days. You had notes and plans for twenty years ahead.

What happened? What upset those people? Their certitude went. They weren't so damn sure of everything. They Grew Up! But here I am, writing about them before they grew up. Those were the days. This boy Dave has plans, plans for books; he's going to write a play. He's got an offer to tour Europe and write about its decadence. He never stays with one girl too long. He's too good and too much for any one

With
Montgomery
Clift

girl. He thinks of his life as a series of contacts, where he sows good deeds, wisdom, semen, and then he passes on. Life for him is a series of limited engagements.

He is the instrument of history. He does the tough work. He breaks the eggs, confident in the surety that it is good for them to be part of the omelet.

EDITOR

In the mid-1930s Kazan traveled the South to witness at first hand the social conditions of rural America. During that time he worked as an assistant director on a film documentary, *People of the Cumberland,* which depicted the impoverished lives, and the benefits of collective action, of Tennessee strip miners. These experiences provided him with the ambition to someday tell a tale of the TVA's alteration of the landscape and of the lives of its people.

Twenty years later Spyros Skouras of Twentieth Century–Fox gave the go-ahead to Kazan's proposal for a TVA story, and the production was overseen by executive producer Buddy Adler. This was his chance, Kazan hoped, to write an original screenplay; but unsure how to tack a plot onto his setting and period, Kazan asked Ben Maddow to develop a scenario. Maddow's outline allowed Kazan to gauge precisely what he didn't want. He tried three drafts of a screenplay on his own, and none of them pleased his first critic, his wife, Molly, or producer Buddy Adler. Perhaps the problem was that he had thought too long on the subject, had accumulated too many ideas. In his autobiography he writes that over the years he had suffered a change of heart. In the 1930s, he wanted to celebrate the New Deal spirit of Franklin Roosevelt "engaged in the difficult task of convincing 'reactionary' country people . . . to move off their land. . . . Now I found my sympathies were with the obdurate old lady. . . . Something more than the shreds of my liberal ideology was at work now. . . . While my man from Washington had the social right on his side, the picture I made was in sympathy with the old woman obstructing progress." In that statement there is a flickering shadow of his anger at the liberal response to his HUAC testimony.

Calder Willingham tried his hand at a script that didn't please, and Kazan then turned to Paul Osborn, who had whittled John Steinbeck's saga *East of Eden* to manageable proportions. Two novels served for atmosphere and background material, William Bradford Huie's *Mud on the Stars* and Borden Deal's *Dunbar's Cove*. Jettisoned along the way, in addition to the liberal bias, was the religious background of the TVA supervisor sent to facilitate the relocation: "The Jew was all right with Ben Maddow, but not particularly good for Calder Willingham, and all right for me, but not good for Paul Osborn. Paul Osborn describes every leading man like he's Henry Fonda. . . . I said to myself, well, there's justice in what Paul is doing, because the other conflict is a mechanical one: Jew vs. Gentile. It's too obvious; it's even a cliché. So Jews and Gentiles don't get along—bullshit!" Osborn concentrated on the matriarch's stonewalling, as an emblem of what was lost, and a romance between the official (Montgomery Clift) and the matriarch's granddaughter, Carol (Lee Remick). The screenplay remained clotted. At its core, it was to be about the tension between tradition and progress, leavened by the protagonist's realization of the dubiety of his task. But Carol's widowhood and the rivalry of another suitor, the relationship of Ella [Jo Van Fleet as the Old Lady] to her black field hands, bigotry, the violence of a disgruntled cotton farmer, are vestiges of rejected screenplays. The film nervously wanders from subject to subject, episodes appearing like isolated events of a withheld organizing principle.

Minute by minute the film is fine, with stunning landscape effects. The ambience and detail are telling, and the performances conscientious to a fault. Jo Van Fleet verges on the overemphatic, with a brush of Lionel Barrymore scene-chewing; though when she glances with narrowed eyes at the other players, she seems resentful that they are stomping not on her homestead but through her movie. Lee Remick's character is given so much back biography and extended place that she seems not so much a foil as the displaced main protagonist. The problem, though he isn't *all* the problem, is Montgomery Clift, a family intimate whom Kazan had directed in the 1942 play *The Skin of Our Teeth.* He just barely holds his own, compromised by an ambiguous identity (how did this nervous guy get this job? you wonder). Kazan always did his best with a Kazan surrogate, a rebel and iconoclast:

With Jo Van Fleet

Brando in *Streetcar, Zapata,* and *Waterfront;* Eli Wallach in *Baby Doll;* James Dean in *East of Eden;* Warren Beatty in *Splendor;* Stathis Giallelis in *America America;* even Kirk Douglas in *The Arrangement.* Clift does not provide the focal point Kazan needs to find his way into the story. To a degree, *A Face in the Crowd* suffers from the same problem, and this accounts for the odd impersonality of both *Wild River* and *Face.* Of course, Kazan had wanted Brando, but Brando had sworn never to work with Kazan again, and Kazan couldn't come up with a replacement. Kazan claimed that Spyros Skouras insisted on Clift, who had been tragically debilitated by a car accident. It was Kazan's worst miscasting. Clift is physically weak, looks haggard, and is so shy with Remick that one wonders why she bothers. The best male performance is from Albert Salmi as the villain. Villains become especially likable when you are uneasy about the indecisiveness of the lead characters.

Kazan, aware of the absence of a determining hub, jacked up *Face* with a violent drunken finale; he resists that here and has Clift and Remick in the last scene peer out a plane window at the flooded land. It looks less like a conclusion than a flight from the film's shapelessness.

Kazan did not get the movie he wanted, but all of it is noble and honorable, and our sympathy is held by the sense that something of consequence is just around the bend. What followed, the next film but one, is a companion film to *Wild River* in scope and personal ambition, but one that avoids all *River*'s shoals, the film that is the capstone to his film career, *America America.*

Splendor in the Grass (1961)

"I think that's the most mature ending I've got on any picture I ever did. When she visits him at his place, and he's married — there's something there that is so beautiful. I don't really understand it. It's beyond anything I did — it just came out."

The basic story and characters were all beautifully provided by Inge in the manuscript; and then I wrote the script. I sent it to Inge, and I said: "Here's the script I made out of what you sent me," which was a very rough first draft, almost like a novel, "and now, study it and make adjustments in it." He didn't make many; there weren't many to make. It was a pretty good job.

FROM THE NOTEBOOK

APRIL 2, 1958

Romeo in the Age of Business, Style: A Romantic Tragedy

Deanie is being prevented from giving herself to Bud ostensibly on moral grounds, but really because Mr. and Mrs. Loomis know that "if you give it away then he won't buy it."

A poem in praise of young love. Take time (and make the script short enough) so that it can be a poem, so you will have time and the room for poetry, the boy and the girl laughing, eating fruit, juice of peaches running down the faces. In the sunlight. Dramatize the young love so the audience feels and knows that this is the best time of their lives.

They are not aware! They're not aware! They're not aware of what's happening to them or the significance of what's happening to them. Also, Bill Inge holds all his characters at arm's length. They should not be directed subjectively. They are all observed as characters.

FEBRUARY 6, 1960

I guess I made up my mind this morning to do the Inge movie. What I mean is that I made up my mind, and I guess I made it up this morning. What made up your mind? Something to do with the parents, Mrs. Loomis and Ace. The fact, first of all, that they are right throughout, that they mean well, and that they are nevertheless murderers. They murder a rare and fine thing, namely romantic love, a most precious thing. And they do it throughout repeatedly and consistently in the name of the Eisenhower virtues. They do it for their children's good. They do it with a sense of not being appreciated and understood. They do it also with a sense of self-righteousness, that only they are holding the fort for what is right. They do it to SAVE their children. They do it firmly, without self-doubt, completely within their tradition. They are the great American middle class. They are absolutely perfect in the middle of this tradition. They are the killers. All their rules are business rules, what is practical, what will make the most money. They are the dominators and the castrators. And you'd never know it to look at them; to look at them they are the image, the perfect image, of paternal and maternal concern and love, right down the middle of the tradition.

They are the ones who are ruining this generation and this country. They are the ones who with their dying breath still affirm the same values, and therefore they are the ones who have to be beaten, who have to lose.

The children are between them, bewildered at first, painfully discovering what they're up against, what is killing them, coming to hate their parents just after it is too late (Romeo and Juliet), only realizing what hit them when it's too late, loving each other to the end, finally picking up the pieces and making a fair-to-middling life for themselves out of what is left.

What I like about it: The courage of the two young people, who continue, who pick up the pieces and, within what is possible, start again.

The two heavies must be carefully disguised, exactly as they are in life. Exactly, I say, because in life you do not notice them or see them, or feel them evil, and it's all over before you know it. I would give them every virtue: middle-class wisdom, patience, self-sacrifice, real love, real tears, real concern for their children, living their lives for their children and everything, everything, everything . . . so most of the audience like them at least half way through and only catch on later.

And the kids are kids. They listen respectfully to their parents. And the advice and urging they get from Mrs. Loomis and Ace, which is counter to their own feelings, fill them with a sense of confusion. These are good kids who want to do what their parents tell them to do. These are kids, so-called "nice" kids, and in the first half of this piece they are very obedient and subservient kids. They get troubled (like Nick Kazan might) by advice, which is completely counter to their own impulses and desires.

Alikes: Bud and Ace; Chris and You (Bud = Nick → Chris), Alan Baxter as a kid.[*] Bud is like a guy whose suit is too big for him, whose reputation is too big for him, like the sons of famous fathers, and who is sensitive enough not to believe his notices. He's like Chris Kazan, David Selznick's sons, Eugene O'Neill's sons.

Ace: Darryl Zanuck, Bud Lighton, Cliff Odets.

Deanie: Jeanne Crain, Ann Blythe.[†]

Mrs. Loomis: Mrs. Loomis is like Paula Strasberg, warm, seductive, feeding everyone, jolly, companionable, gossipy, intrusive, observant, political in re everything, consuming, lesbian, sexed but unsexed, expansive, embracing, babyish, making everyone else a baby.

Theme: The play is about true and false identity. Who am I? The images our society and parents make us live up to. Deanie says: "Don't they realize I'm ME!" Ace thinks the chorus girl = Deanie. Ace wants Bud to be what Bud is not. He forces this on Bud, creating a sense of failure, guilt, conflict. He never looks to see who Bud is. Deanie's last line: "Bud, all this time he's been a man, hasn't he? Like other men all over the world, trying to get along."[**] Take the case of Ginny. Ace wanted a boy. He was disappointed with her. She felt this. The little attention he did pay her stopped abruptly—he dropped her like a hot rock—when Bud was born. Her father is the focus of her life. He rejected her, and she's "showing" him. She looks at Ace as at a lover who betrayed her, dropped her, and whom she's going to make regret it. She'll never let him forget it.

Another note on the theme: the discrepancy between the fake middle-class picture of life and the way I naturally live.

---

[*] Alan Baxter, later a successful Hollywood supporting actor, was Kazan's closest friend at Williams College and Yale Drama School, and they continued to be close during the early Group Theatre years, even though Kazan stole Baxter's girlfriend, Molly Thacher, and married her.

[†] Bud Lighton was the producer of *A Tree Grows in Brooklyn.* Jeanne Crain was a film star of the mid-1940s and 1950s, whom Kazan directed in *Pinky.* Ann Blythe appeared as the bad daughter in *Mildred Pierce,* and later in MGM musicals.

[**] This line was not used. Instead, when asked whether she still loves Bud, Deanie does not reply and recalls, in a voice-over, William Wordsworth's lines from "Ode: Intimations of Immortality": "Though nothing can bring back the hour / Of splendour in the grass, of glory in the flower; / We will grieve not, rather find / Strength in what remains behind."

The worst fake identity is the "nice girl" burden under which Deanie labors, and which prevents Bud from treating her like a human. She is the properly brought-up middle-class girl. She is prim, priggish, proper, smug, proud, and afraid of sex. She keeps pulling her skirt down, sitting primly, etc. Being the model of an "engaged" girl. At the same time, she has only been brought up that way. She is already fighting it. When she acts human, Bud is frightened. He says, "You've lost your pride."

Her essence: She is the kind of girl to whom the loss of the right boy would ruin her life—forever! She can't really go on to another. That's it!!! He was the one.

Bud and Deanie really need each other. They are romantically in love. They are much bigger and better together than they are separate. Whenever he gets all worked up (which is frequently), all she has to do to calm him down is touch him in a certain way, in a certain place, and he immediately quiets down. They are awfully good kids, earnest to the point of stupidity. Everything that happens to them happens because they follow some moral tenet, because they try to do right. Because they love their parents and follow the moral rules of a materialistic and business-corrupted midwestern society.

Sex. Bud literally can't with Deanie. When the moment comes to do it, he just can't and won't, feels it's wrong, sinful, gets worried, anxious, self-conscious, doubting, weak—and all this, all this, that his father has put into him, prevents him from consummating his love for Deanie. His father's possessive love is not threatened by Bud's doing it to someone he doesn't love. Bud, like you, will never have trouble doing it EXCEPT TO PEOPLE HE LOVES. Then he thinks he's betraying his father and fucking his mother. Then he thinks he is spoiling a "nice girl," and he becomes anxious, guilty, or can't.

There is a wild streak in Bud as well as in Ginny. He has sadism, wildness, danger in him. The opposite face of puritanism. Sex is duty. So he either does nothing with the nice girl or wallows in it, deep!

What are you trying to make the Audience Feel? Admiration and love for Bud and Deanie. For a simple reason that you show again and again. You show anybody and everybody trying anything and everything to break these two apart. They fail. Our lovers succeed. At the end, they still love each other, are still spiritually together. Dramatize this.

But at the end the audience should feel that there is something heroic about them, that something honest, simple, true, kind, soft-spoken, wise, mature, understanding, and above all dignified has come out of the fearful events in these two people. The pain is still there at the end, but Deanie sits upright, like your mother. And Bud is very decent and kind to Angelina. (Think of you and Art Miller at the Beverly Hills Hotel, friendly, neither blaming the other, studying each other, reserved to a degree, forgiving, going on alone, not putting any sentimentality or blame on each other.)

Considering that at the end they are still in love with each other, and will never be otherwise, they conduct themselves with honor, leaving behind as little mess as possible. Their problem comes because they love, hero-worship, have been seduced by their parents. And they can only be adult when they are free of their parents by death (in Bud's case) or by psychoanalysis. It is necessary for Ace to die and for Deanie to forgive her mother. (Remember Judy [Kazan's elder daughter] saying how much easier her life would be if she could hate her parents: "We have nothing to revolt against.")

Ace too suffers from wrong identity. He has this image of himself as a success. He can't get down off it. Without money, his identity collapses. He seems nobody. Is full of SHAME. He is so ashamed of his unadorned identity that he kills himself. Ace is lame. He puts on the Hemingway act, of "Fine Sermon." His house should tell all: moose, salmon, deer heads, bearskins. He is like Hemingway and Bud Lighton—he is at base and unawares homosexual. He is only happy in the company of men. He resents women and doesn't miss a chance to put them down. Marriage is something that should be entered into because that's the way it is. He doesn't like it when he sees a man in love. It's a sign of weakness. Probably he does everything possible to show the world that he is not tied to his wife, under her thumb. It's all acted out for the world—this independence. He physically adores his son. His house is a temple to masculinity.

The wrong Ace does is the result of passionate concern and love for your boy (Chris and you). Ace worships Bud. He can hardly keep his hands off him. Ace is pathetically anxious that Bud like him too—so sometimes he begs.

The objective fact is that Ace and Mrs. Loomis are murderers. The false identities they put on their children forever cripple them and kill the most precious thing, romantic love. But the only thing they want is the happiness of their children. They are only doing the best they know how. They are not heavies. The depth of the piece depends on the compassion, humanity, love, the Director shows these two. The actors must think of the objectives as: to save, help, fulfill, protect, guide.

APRIL 11, 1960

Kansas City, an unvarying materialistic civilization. No illumination in people's faces. There is no spirituality, inner light, or humanity, on any of the faces. Nor are there marks or evidences of living for pleasure. No sensuality. The faces are dumpy, drab, and plain. Bill Inge: "I'd say they might be good neighbors but not good wives, friends or husbands." In other words, if very little was asked of them, they can fulfill. But what faces! You might say they were disappointed faces, if you could feel that they ever ravenously or even strongly desired anything. The women have reduced beautification to a sort of kitchen science. They apply rouge by rote. It's simply that rouge, much rouge, is warm on the cheeks. This is a custom so obeyed, but no one looks at her face to see if it suits her. The hair is worn in curls, but tight little captured curls, neat, tight, ordered, no careless rapture here. The men are over-potatoed, they show strong evidence of their diet. The middle-aged women are terribly unattractive, it's hard to believe the men do it to them. But the women don't want these men to do it to anyone else. They'd prefer them dead.

EDITOR: Kazan defended the film after Jack Warner and Benjamin Kalmenson of Warner Bros. suggested cuts. The Legion of Decency threatened a Condemned rating, and there were worries that the Production Code office of the Motion Picture Association of America wouldn't approve it. Warner also thought some of the film glum and therefore uncommercial.

From a letter to Warner and Kalmenson:

JANUARY 4, 1961

I have the highest hopes and the greatest confidence that *Splendor in the Grass* will be highly commercial. I think once this film does reach the public, they will take to it avidly. This is the most "familiar" picture I have made since *A Tree Grows in Brooklyn*. It is part of everybody's life.

You, Ben, made several requests to me that morning for eliminations. I took your requests (and Jack repeated them in a following wire) most seriously. The very next morning I ran the film just to look at the sections you had brought into question.

First of all I want you to know that I have made some good cuts.
Now in detail.

Let me take up the toughest problem first. That is the scene in the
parking lot with the hero's sister and the group of men. I studied this
scene most carefully and thought about it a lot. The problem with making cuts in this scene has nothing to do with length or overemphasis on
sensationalism. It has to do with motivation and audience belief. The
weakest link in our story is the sudden announcement immediately following the parking lot scene by our hero to our heroine that he doesn't
want to see her anymore. This was repeatedly criticized in the script by
a number of smart people. They asked why he suddenly told her that
he couldn't see her anymore—after all, he had just been kissing her at
the New Year's celebration. What gives?

My answer—one which I believe sound—is that the boy, still sexually innocent, is so shocked by what his sister brings on herself in the
parking lot that he is frightened to give expression or even a chance to
his own sexual impulses. What makes the boy's sudden announcement
believable is that he is *that* shocked. Now I can't show more than one
or two close-ups to register the boy's upset. But I can make the audience feel the horror and sin of what his sister has brought upon herself.
And I did. I did not want to make what was going on glamorous. I did
not want to make it attractive. I made it look ugly and cheap and brutal.
I took a most moral attitude toward it. Made it full of horror. And it is
important for the believability of our story that it remain this way, basically, because if we once thin it out, we will suddenly find that the next
necessary step in our story is unbelievable, and then we will be in real
trouble.

I admit it is a delicate subject, but it is done for a purpose, not for
sensationalism, and I think it is done in the most irreproachable taste.
It is wrong—in anticipation of criticism—to ruin one of the best and
potentially one of the most talked about sequences in the film.

Despite all I have said, though, I did make four short cuts here. But
I still kept the basic makeup of the scene—what's more important—I
still think the hero's announcement to the heroine that follows remains
completely believable.

And I'm also going to add a line here that will help. When the sister,
practically out on her feet, is approached by the first man, the one who
takes her into the car, I'm going to have her say in a low voice: "Get
away from me. I don't want you." From my experience, I know how

With
Warren
Beatty

much this will help with Vizzard and Shurlock [both on the Production Code staff].

I don't want censor problems. But when something is absolutely legitimate and harmless and pure like that four-foot cut of the naked girl (with her boy's body) in an extreme long shot running from the bathroom into her bedroom—well, why pull it out before anyone has even objected? That is a most innocent shot. Was she supposed to become calm, stop, and put on a robe?

I have, however, replaced the second shot of the naked girl lying on her bed sobbing with a shot that only shows her legs to just above her knees. We do not see any of her upper leg in the new shot, and I know that will help in the overall impression.

Now about the woman on the porch. As I explained to Jack in a previous letter, it is this old woman who, by contrast, dramatizes Deanie's liberation, her new-found health and hope of happiness to come. She is emblematic of the sick and wounded self that Deanie is finally leaving behind her. When Bill Inge and I talked, we gave great consideration to what was implied in Jack's request about the old woman on the porch—namely, that there might be some unnecessary ugliness in the film. And we decided to make two sizable cuts. We cut out Ace's dictating to the whore before his suicide. The preparation for the suicide now has no dialogue in it, and it is short and covered with music. It is not "rubbed in" or "too realistic." And secondly, what is more important, we cut down to almost nothing the first scene in the institution. This eliminates the crazy woman in the room next to Deanie's, the one whom the attendants have to subdue and lead away. This element is entirely out of the film now. As well as the spooky nurse. So, perhaps,

Jack, with so much out of the last reels, you won't mind the glimpse of the woman on the porch.

I am not trying to get by with anything. Vizzard and Shurlock know it, and everyone else knows it, including the Legion of Decency, who've seen all of my pictures. If there is any criticism of my film on a moral basis, I would like to deal with it myself, face to face, directly. By my contract with you, I've got to get a seal and, of course, I will. Even if I have to give up a cut or two. But maybe I won't. And I want a chance to defend this film because I believe in it, and don't want it hurt.

I have done four pictures for you. Two have been real successes [*Streetcar* and *East of Eden*], one will finally begin to make some money pretty soon now [*A Face in the Crowd*]. And the fourth was a disaster for which I am heartily sorry [*Baby Doll*]. But in each case we worked very well together. Our contracts reflect this faith you have in me, which I believe I have earned.

Finally, how can I make further cuts when I have seen, only during the last months, what was allowed to pass in *Butterfield 8, Suzie Wong, The Grass Is Greener,* and two of your own—*Bramble Bush* and *Girl of the Night*? These pictures make mine look tame.

EDITOR

On the strength of three successive hits—*Come Back Little Sheba, Picnic,* and *Bus Stop*—William Inge was deemed a playwright qualified to join the company of Arthur Miller and Tennessee Williams. In 1957 Kazan directed Inge's next success, *The Dark at the Top of the Stairs.* Kazan then encouraged Inge to write a screenplay, and the project—*Splendor in the Grass*—was developed over an extended period. "He told me a story idea that he had. He wrote it up, and it was like a long novel. Then I worked on it. Then he worked over it. It went back and forth between us constantly."

Natalie Wood had a difficult time making the transition from a child actress to an adult one, and though Warner Bros. gave her strong opportunities, including a prominent role in *Rebel Without a Cause*, she wasn't "box office," and Jane Fonda and Diane Varsi had been tested before she was. But the year of *Splendor* (for which she was nominated for an Academy Award) was also the year of *West Side Story;* her subsequent movies were not great box office hits. Warren Beatty has appeared in an unsuccessful William Inge play, *A Loss of Roses,* and Inge, impressed with his gifts, suggested him to Kazan. This was Beatty's first film, but his self-assurance and cockiness charmed Kazan. "Warren—it was obvious the first time—wanted it all and wanted it his way. Why not? He had the energy, a very keen intelligence, and more chutzpah than any Jew I've ever known. Even more than me. Bright as they come, intrepid, and with that thing all women secretly respect: complete confidence in his sexual powers, confidence so great that he never had to advertise himself, even by hints."

At the time Beatty was engaged to Joan Collins, and Wood was married to Robert Wagner. According to their biographies (and Warren Beatty), the stars were cool to each other during the filming but had a brief affair a year later, during the *Splendor* publicity tour. Kazan remembered this differently and believed their performances were infused with their personal attraction. "All of a sudden, he and Natalie became lovers. When did it happen? When I wasn't looking. I wasn't sorry; it helped their love scenes."

In a 1966 interview Kazan remarked on a little-discussed theme of the film: "I think the best thing in *Splendor* was not so much the love story or anything else, as the portrait of the mother. At the end, when she says, 'I have done my best. . . . How can I have done wrong? Tell me. . . .' That is the result of a very deep vision. But, you see, that is not a big effect. It is one of those little effects that one can quite well let pass without noticing. Yet it truly expresses reality, and not only that of the mother, but that of the entire era behind it, an entire style of life, seen through a certain America, static, anchored in the past and refusing change."

America America (1963)

"It's my favorite of all the films I've made, the first film that was entirely mine."

EDITOR: At the opening of the movie, Elia Kazan speaks a brief prologue: "My name is Elia Kazan. I am a Greek by blood, a Turk by birth, and an American because my uncle made a journey." *America America* is the epic story of the odyssey of Stavros Topouzoglou, a Greek boy living in Anatolia during Turkish oppression at the turn of the twentieth century whose dream is to immigrate to America. His family entrust him with all their valuables and send him to Constantinople (to his mind, a way station), in the hope that his uncle will take him on as a partner in his rug business, enabling him to establish a place so that his family can follow. Along the way he is cruelly tricked and brutalized and robbed—an act he avenges with murder.

When the bruised and disillusioned Stavros arrives in Constantinople, his uncle takes him in. Later the uncle advises him that the easiest way to a fortune is to marry a wealthy girl. For a time he resists the idea. Instead he joins a band of clandestine revolutionaries, who are discovered and slaughtered, and he works as a demeaned porter, a beast of burden, called a *hamal.* But his goal remains "America." After his pitiful earnings are stolen by a prostitute, he reconsiders his uncle's proposal and is affianced to a rich rug dealer's daughter. At the last moment he withdraws from the engagement—he cannot settle in Constantinople. He takes the small dowry and buys a ticket for a ship bound for New York. "I believe that in America I will be washed clean," he tells the fiancée he is to abandon.

On board, he has an affair with the wife of a New York rug dealer who is sponsoring his emigration. When the husband learns of the affair, he threatens to have Stavros returned to Turkey, but Stavros is saved when a companion, a tubercular boy indentured to a shoeshine company, commits suicide, and Stavros assumes his identity.

In the final scenes we see Stavros making his first American salary as a shoeshine boy and then his family waiting for him to bring them to America.

At the time of the film's release, Kazan contributed an article to the *New York Times.*

I asked my father why he came to America. But I think he had forgotten. For a long time, I had had the idea of making a film based on the saga of my family's migration. It was our legend. The big drama for so many Americans is "how we got here."

I sat him down in front of a tape recorder and got him talking about the old days. He had belonged to the Greek minority in Turkey. He came from a village in the interior; my mother was born in Constantinople (now Istanbul), as I was. What was it like in the old country? Why did he leave? How did he get here? What were his adventures?

That afternoon I realized how old he had become. The marks of time were on my father's face. His memory fluttered, now lighting up, now wavering. He told the old tales. He described the massacre of Armenians in his village. He told how his father had taken everything of value that they owned and tied it on the back of their donkey and entrusted it to his oldest son. This boy, my father's brother, was to go up the dry dangerous road to Constantinople to make a fresh start for the family. And so he did. These stories I used in *America America*.

But when I asked the deeper question, "Why America? What were you hoping for?" my father seemed confused and could not answer. Whatever his emotions of long ago, they had evaporated. I turned to my mother. She was sitting beside him, looking at him with gentleness and tolerance for his age. I asked her, "Why did we come here?" Her answer was simple enough. "A.E. brought us here."

"A.E." was my uncle Avraam Elia, the one who left the Anatolian village with the donkey. At twenty-eight, somehow—this was the wonder—he made his way to New York. He sent home money and in time brought my father over. Father sent for my mother and my baby brother and me when I was four. My uncle also brought his sister, his stepmother, five stepbrothers, and assorted cousins.

Neither my father nor my mother liked the idea of this picture. Unvoiced, uneasy recollections of the Turks, I suspect, made them feel the whole subject was better left alone. When I planned my first trip to do research, they were apprehensive. Greece? All right, but why Turkey?

I offered to take my parents with me for a visit. I had the feeling that my father should be spending his last years back there, under an olive tree, watching the harbors, drinking raki. He had no such notion. "What's the matter with New Rochelle?" he demanded. "We stay here," said my mother.

I visited the massive, terrible—and beautiful—city of Istanbul, where porters, called *hamals,* still work as beasts of burden. I went to where my father was born, in the shadow of the snowcapped Mount

Aergius. Smells, sounds, a way of life half-remembered from my infancy, seemed to me idyllic. I found myself wondering, "Why did they leave?" A great deal of red carpet was put out for me. The Turks are Oriental in their courtesies. For a few days in Istanbul, I was a famous man.

It was then that I began to hear over and over, like a chant, the cry "America America!"

I had supposed that all this belonged to the turn of the century, the era of my picture. But there it was. America still means something deep and important. The young men go today or hope to go to other countries also, to Germany, to Australia, to Italy. But the dream still centers on America. I heard it so often that it was woven into my story, "America America." The unemployed, the pitifully employed, in Greece and Turkey alike came at me, "How do you get in?" "Take me back with you!" "Take my son!"

I tried to make the film feel like a legend. That's why Stavros and Vartan are on a mountain cutting ice. The "clean" mountain was a symbol of their aspirations. Ice is a clean thing; snowfall is a clean thing. All of this contrasts with the hot, dirty, fifteenth- or sixteenth-century town below where the Turks were not only oppressing the Armenians and Greeks, they were oppressing their fellow countrymen. One of the first things you see [in the film] is a Turk crawl up on his hands and knees and kiss the hand of the little governor.

I used to say to myself when I was making the film that America was a dream of total freedom in all areas. I made two points about that. One was that America had a responsibility to the dream: The dream has a responsibility to the dreamer. And furthermore, what these people availed themselves of when they got here, what they turned the dream into, was the freedom to make money. Money became their weapon; it was the symbol of strength. The last thing you see in *America America* is Stavros being given a quarter tip, which he tosses in the air and catches. You feel he's on that track.

Everything this boy undertakes is motivated by the sole aim to bring his family to America. He arrives at his ends by means that seem bad, yes. But who can say whether they are good or bad? Do the categories mean anything? Is there a Value that lets one ask those questions?

The prime relationship in filmmaking is that between a director and his cameraman. I was to discover two things about [Haskell] "Pete" Wexler. He was a man of considerable talent, and he was a consider-

With
Stathis
Giallelis

able pain in the ass. This is often the case with people of talent in show business. I realized early on that I'd made a mistake in engaging him. But there we were, in Turkey, and how would I go about changing a cameraman, where would I interview alternate choices, and what would I do about the crew? They'd come with Wexler, they'd go with Wexler. So I decided to suffer it through, to treat Pete as a challenge, one I might learn from. And it happened that I did learn from him. He gave me my first experience with the hand-held camera. Pete could, with the smoothest motion, dip and turn, move in and out like a perfectly operated small crane, all the time making his focus-length adjustments. He was damned good, I had to admit. I admired him even as I begrudged him the respect I felt.

Later I was told he'd held my anti-Communist testimony against me. That would explain what went on between us, but why then had he accepted the job with me? On the last day of shooting, I accosted him. "Tell me, Pete," I said. "Now that we're through, what did you think of my script?" "I thought it was a piece of shit," he said. "Then why did you take the job?" I asked. His answer was: "I knew what a Kazan picture would do for my career."

I think that *America America* would have been better if I had had a professional actor endowed with the same qualities that my young amateur had in him. But that special form of virility that was his, no actor could give me. That young man had gone through the Greek civil war; his father had been wounded and had died in his arms. That boy, at fifteen, found himself the head of an entire family, and he acquired a kind of hardness, of avidity, of force of soul. . . . But on the other hand, he had serious limitations, because he was not an actor. You see, on the one hand, you gain, on the other you lose; it is for you to establish your own balance. As for me, I tried to obtain the thing that seemed primordial to me—the life that he had in him that should pass into the role. That is what I want, and it matters little to me whether I have it with a professional or with an amateur.

EDITOR

On April 16, 1965, after the film *Tom Jones* swept the Academy Awards, Henry Miller sent Kazan a note: "I don't think the film deserved so much. It was good but not great. Yours is great, but not always good." Others, though, find it both good and great. Its episodic structure yields a feel both of documentary and of anecdotal memory—facts enhanced and wondered at. Stavros is less a character than a will, a blind resolve, a force that won't be resisted; his goal is finally selfless, to redeem his family, to fulfill the task his father has set his eldest son—to save the lives of his parents, brothers, and sisters. He succeeds by miraculous acts, by accidents, by luck as well as by his refusal to be denied. The film is a ritual of self-realization, a ritual that is brutal and cruel, and a ritual in which the odds are stacked against you—and here the protagonist wins out, with terrible penalties.

The tale excited Kazan's greatest directing abilities: impeccable staging in both intimate, grand landscape and action sequences (abetted by a splendidly matched cameraman, Haskell Wexler, who paradoxically loathed him), intense characterizations, and sharp daggers of great cinema—the father's violent slap and embrace at the beginning has epiphanic power that resonates throughout the rest of the film.

It is not a perfect movie, but it is weak only in the last third, when Kazan compensates for a "male" story with two overindulged performances from the actresses playing Stavros's fiancée and mistress. The protracted finale, though, is a triumph, the ambiguous consequences of an odyssey that is viewed throughout ironically. Is what has been won worth the personal cost? Doesn't luck decide all? *America America* is a harsh, uncomfortable film. In the mid-1960s American film audiences were not so interested in heritage (a topic that would resurge in the seventies with *Roots*); in the midst of the Vietnam conflict, a movie about emigration appeared retrogressive. And it had no stars and was in black and white.

The Arrangement (1969)

"I feel certain that if Marlon had played the part, the film would have worked, but I was on a treadmill, and a frantic kind of activity gripped me."

EDITOR: Advertising executive Eddie Anderson is compulsively driven to attempt suicide by ramming his car into a truck on the Los Angeles Freeway. During his recovery he agonizes over the pained ending of his affair with a co-worker, Gwen. He confesses to his wife, Florence, his loathing for the "arrangements" of his life, his empty work successes, the extravagances of his comfortable lifestyle. Unable to find order or peace within himself and unsure of his mental stability, at the urging of his lawyer he gives his wife power of attorney over his assets. He travels to New York when he learns that his father, Sam, has been hospitalized, but distrusting the doctors, he takes his father to the abandoned family house. He asks for help from Gwen.

In turn, his family retrieves the father, and in a violent confrontation, they have Eddie institutionalized. With Gwen's help, he leaves the mental hospital to attend his father's funeral and there confronts his wife, who now is having a relationship with his lawyer, and his family.

The reception of the film *The Arrangement* was vitriolic. Kazan sent a defensive letter to the French critic and admirer Michel Ciment:

I've never been attacked as viciously and personally as I was on *The Arrangement*.

Why? This question is open. Was it the film they were attacking or me? If it was myself, that is not a matter for discussion. Prejudice cannot be treated rationally.

If it was the film, I would want to make a few points on its behalf and for its understanding.

The Arrangement has faults; it has my own deficiencies. But must we measure works in the field of art by their virtues? The only perfect film I may have made was a "chase" [probably *Panic in the Streets*], and it was only perfect, if it was, because it was perfectly mechanical. As soon as you begin to deal in ambivalences and in symbols of any complexity, and as soon as you begin to offer personal attitudes and views, you risk misunderstanding. And rejection.

The Arrangement is not autobiographical in its plot, but its values are as I see them. And its purpose is not the conventional one: to entertain.

The Arrangement was made to disturb people.

To this end, the personages depicted are not individual; they are prototypes.

They were intended to be the social masks of our day and of our country in our day.

Florence the wife, for instance, is the typical upper-middle-class wife. Her typicality is her tragedy. She has all the standards, values, and aspirations, all the virtues too, of the upper-middle-class wife. She wants to do good; her good intentions kill her and her husband. She is above all a class product, predetermined by her social training. She is an epitome.

Eddie, the central figure, is also a prototype. His character split, the "divided self," is classic. He wants to be a success, but he wants to be a rebel. He aspires to be a typical American, and yet he is inevitably an outsider. He wants to be commercial, and he wants to be in some way "artistic." He wants a secure domestic situation, and he wants to be sexually free. He wants to be able to pose as a situation requires, and he wants to be true to himself. He has two careers, pursued simultaneously. And he has three names, a different one for each side of him.

I was trying to deal with conceptual beings, not heroes and heroines.

This seems to me, at the moment, to be the most effective and true way to describe our social scene. In that sense, *The Arrangement* is the most social film I have made.

It does not seem valuable to me to photograph the demonstrators massed outside the Conrad Hilton, or fighting the police in Lincoln Park without doing something more: looking beneath their beards and beads and under their blanket rolls and recognizing them for what they are, the well-educated children of middle-class America. And devout idealists. To show them simply as rioters or eccentrics or even revolutionaries is to enforce a false impression.

I even think it's dangerous and ignorant to pass off the police as themselves rioters (which they were) and "pigs" without indicating something of what they are in class, in education, in ideals. To simply dismiss them as sadists doesn't increase our knowledge of them or of our country and time.

In this light, most "social" films seem to me to evade the problem they profess to attack.

Many of them—so say their makers—are metaphors. They are "Westerns," for instance, and their heroes are outlaws, sheriffs, and cowboys. But, say their authors, they are really about Vietnam and why we're there, or about the prevalence and dangers of violence, or perhaps about neo-McCarthyisms.

Or are they about hippies, gentle and cute and eccentric and violently alienated, or about urban derelicts, or about simple Italian peasants getting the better of the German Wehrmacht or what not? All metaphors!

But the audience sits there, enjoying the show or not enjoying the show, and its content and social meaning pass through them like morning coffee. Those are *those other fellows,* they say. What that film seems to be saying is not about us. Of course it's true! Violence is terrible. The Nazi were monsters as well as finally stupid. Forty-second Street is a terrible place—but very colorful.

But how does that apply to us? It doesn't. It's only about those freaks, those Wild West characters, about Nazis, about Italian peasants, about those depraved derelicts, about those other people, those special characters. Not about US!!

One critic said *The Arrangement* embarrassed her. Which was exactly what I intended. I did wonder how she could not have been embarrassed at what she saw in many other films she has looked at this season. The answer, I'm afraid, is that the "sordid" events in other films (incidentally far more luridly portrayed) were happening to people from whom she could separate herself or, to put it more bluntly, whom she could patronize. Yes, those awful things do happen among derelicts on Forty-second Street, or safely in the past, or among low life of other countries. But when they happen in the homes of people of the same culture and of the same class as herself, they embarrass. Well, they should.

I tried to make a film where the people on the screen are the epitomization of the people watching the screen. I tried to make everything as familiar and as typical as possible. I accepted the danger of banality. But above all I wanted the audience to jump a little, yes, to be embarrassed, to see themselves and ask: Is that what makes me tick too? Are those my own standards? My values? Is that my situation? Is that the truth about me?

And so—I suppose inevitably—"It can't be! Fuck Kazan!"

But for an instant the people in the audience may have asked the real questions.

I believe that now, in this time and in this situation, films should talk, particularly to Americans, but to your people as well, *without allowing them an exit*! They must not be able to say, "That's about those other fellows," or "That's that very special case," or "Those are *exceptional* people!"

They must not be able to patronize what's on the screen. They must not be able to escape the inferences of what's shown them.

I wanted my film to seem at first perfectly familiar. Which is one of the reasons I cast the film as I did. For instance, Deborah Kerr can no longer quite be, on the screen, an individual. She is *The Perfect Wife*, a living prototype. This is not actually the way Miss Kerr herself is; she is a charming and true woman. But I believed that the image she spent so many years building on the screen (often against her will) was in this case operating for me.

And so Eddie Anderson. Kirk is one of our bravest leading men; he has never lost a screen war, rarely a battle. He is one of a group of leading men who are the filmic symbols of our national invincibility. What do I now show? That this prototype, who has always reassured us, is in deep trouble, actually at the end of a road.

And so with the other figures: the immigrant father who came to America to be free to make a fortune, the girlfriend prototype of the Pill revolution, the lawyer, fair and friendly and completely "standard," who ironically wins it all in the end.

And the climax of my film simply says that our society condemns a

With
Kirk
Douglas

man who breaks the mold as erratic and finally dangerous, and therefore in one way or another restrains him. In this case within an institution for the mentally deranged. And who puts him away? His best friend, the lawyer, and his dearly beloved wife! And why? *For his own good!*

That is what the film is about. You will notice that no one in it is entirely likable and no one in it is dislikable. No one triumphs. The end too is uncertain. People simply break apart and go in opposite directions. It's what's happening in this country.

I'm forced to add, "As I see it." I don't think many others here did. Of course, I wonder if this is not my fault. But I also wonder if the film should not have been judged by those whose profession it is to entertain their readers by judging a film by what it was attempting—as well as by what it achieved.

I do not think the film is behind the times or, as some of the New York critics said, old-fashioned. It is ahead of its times, but not in its techniques. There isn't a shot in the film made with a zoom lens. There are no long tracking shots of people on motorbikes, and none of the people seem to run in place because they were photographed with a long lens.

Its novelty, a genuine one I think, was to make the personages UN-special. In the effort to say to the audience: That is you, like it or not, that dilemma is yours, accept it or not; that crisis is yours, turn away if you can!

The Last Tycoon (1976)

*"The ending I devised said more about me and my feelings
than it did about the film's hero . . . it was a kind of death for
me, the end of life in the art where I'd worked for so long. It
was all over and I knew it."*

Monroe [Stahr, the protagonist of the film and of F. Scott Fitzgerald's
novel] learned years ago that if he showed a weakness of any kind he
would be devoured. And the truth is he would be.

So he has donned this invulnerable coat of steel. There isn't an aper-
ture that any weapon can penetrate. He cannot be fazed. He sees the
power struggle and sees who his enemies are. He gives them the greatest defense of all, a pleasant front. Always polite, always plain and clear
and professional. He doesn't like any of them because to like one
would allow himself to be taken. Nor is he impolite or rude to them.
He is impersonal. If he were to show his disgust or occasional antagonism it would give them a chance to hit back at him, it would justify
their bad attitudes toward him.

But the result of all this is that he has a terrible need for tenderness
and love. Since he was not and cannot express or exercise any of it, he
is loaded down with desire, not for fucking, but for love. He then loves
excessively. And at the same time that he is feeling this extreme desire
for closeness, he is aware of its dangers. *It leaves him vulnerable to
hurt.* So he keeps trying to rein himself in, he keeps reconsidering.
Does he want to go that far, does he want to expose himself to hurt that
much, does he want to take off his coat of mail?

The part of the script that worries me most is not the big scenes nor
the psychological scenes. These are comparatively simple. What worries me is the love scene in the middle, particularly the scenes where
Pinter has suggested nudity. This is so banal by now. Who wants to be
diverted by genitalia? That is not what the story is about. The love in
this story is need for closeness and tenderness. It is a bottled-up goodness and love hunger. On both sides. The tragedy is that they could be

wonderful together and they can't quite make it because of his nature and because of the circumstance she brings with her and because of her need for a man who is not a "KING," for a safe, simple, good, reliable man.

JANUARY 5, 1975

Stahr is special, unique, monastic, a relic.

He walks alone. Occasionally men follow him waiting for orders.

He is in a daze of work and thought. He carries the whole studio operation in his head. And he wants it that way.

Zanuck was a tycoon too. He walked alone. He had nothing on his mind except business, the business of the studio operating! Only his relationship to women was different. But it was the same coin, other side. That generation divided women into whores and saints. Stahr-Edna vs. Kathleen. Zanuck, remember.

He has a vision of a perfect life and he operates from it. It's the only way he can. But the studio can't operate that way anymore, and the writers can't and won't, and women aren't that way anymore. Even Kathleen. She reads his hesitation right. How? He knows that something is making him hesitate, and she also knows that if it ever came down to a choice, he'd choose the studio, its operation. The movies are him. When he says, "I don't want to lose you!" it means the studio as well as Kathleen and perhaps the studio above all.

FEBRUARY 19, 1975

Spiegel [the producer] is concerned that I will "sentimentalize" Stahr. He keeps reminding me, every time I discuss it with him, that Stahr is ruthless. Yesterday he said he has a tendency to be power mad, or that he is. I've forgotten which distinction he made. I have thought about his point, and it has a certain validity. Stahr should be awful tough, "that little tin Vine Street Jesus." Perhaps it is necessary for a young man—Kubrick, for instance—to be ruthless when he comes to power so young. He has to command elders, and he can't help thinking that they resent his authority over them. And that he also develops a taste for it since he is and has been right so often and they have been wrong so often. And it is inevitable that he soon gets trapped in this power, that he enjoys it, that it becomes habitual with him. AT THE SAME TIME I have worked with Zanuck, and although he certainly enjoyed his power and while he was a "boy wonder" and while he ran the studio with an absoluteness that was overwhelming, nevertheless he "came

With
Ingrid
Boulting
and
Robert
De Niro

on" like a regular guy. He only acted all-powerful when he was challenged. And even then he didn't yell. He simply became unequivocal and somewhat steely. And he might wave his arms and reject challenge or qualification. Spiegel himself is a tycoon of this sort, and he certainly has a taste for power, but he comes on like a Dutch uncle and is also full of a kind of charming schmaltz and generosity and intelligence. He wants to be both, a human and an all-powerful tycoon, at the same time, which "bothness" is Stahr's problem at this period, it seems to me. Earlier on he had to develop an iron front, an unwavering toughness because he was a kid making adults take his orders. Cf. Billy Martin and the Texas Rangers.* But after his wife's death something happened to him, and he feels that he has frozen his heart and abandoned his humanity and has no warmth left, and he begins this effort that defeats and tumbles him down, the effort to regain his humanity.

The Ambivalence of Stahr

He is a hard-nosed businessman. He is precise and exact and most knowledgeable about his business actions. He is ruthless. He sees things in a clear balanced light. But when he first sees Kathleen, it is in a strange refracted light, twice reflected, that is, from the big units on stands that are rushed in to light the flood. And when he sees her in this light, she seems to be floating in the water. The upper half of her body is lit and the bottom half is not lit, so she is ethereal and floats in space.

---

* Billy Martin was a famous second baseman. In his subsequent career as a manager (particularly for the New York Yankees) he became notorious for battling not only umpires but his players. Here Kazan refers to Martin's managing the Texas Rangers, 1973–75.

The wind is blowing her hair, which makes her seem even more romantic and unreal and visionary. And when Stahr sees Kathleen the second time, he sees her just out of the door of the house where she lives. There is an arbor, a shallow one, but covered with leaves, etc., in front of the door, and the light is mottled and soft and the effect again is a romantic and unreal and visionary one. She looks like a spirit self-illuminated from within. And her face has a soft light that is tinted green and yellow. She is always a dream figure, an apparition, an ideal of beauty and romance.

Monroe has a sense of nobility and a sense of mission that promises us a tragedy. De Niro has to characterize Stahr this way. *He is a young king,* a prince with a moral mission, the chosen one, the one destined (as he saw it) to move films up to better things. And he deals with a mercenary and reactionary crowd.

Having realized how dried up and toughened and serene he has become, he reaches back to regain his humanity. When he does this he exposes what he has never exposed before, his vulnerability. His naked neck. When he exposes this, he is killed.

Short Takes

Sea of Grass (1947)

So now I had some power to choose what I'd do next and I immediately chose the wrong thing. I was naïve, which made it worse. I thought I was going to be doing a great epic of the great open country—like *Cimarron* or *Red River.* Instead I found myself a prisoner on the great closed MGM lot. I was always within walking distance of the Commissary and the barber shop. My problem was simple. I had two great stars and a couple more near great. Spencer Tracy, who played the lord of the house, never won the friendship of his horse, not even the tolerance. Katharine Hepburn came trotting out every morning in another designer period dress. They were both agreeable and entertaining people to be with and I enjoyed our conversations but I didn't enjoy the film-making. It received what it deserved—a very bad reception.

Pinky (1949)

Don't blame this one on me. I don't. I didn't help prepare the script. I didn't have the idea of casting a most genteel, middle-class white girl as a light-skin black. I didn't agree again to shoot real locations on studio sets. That was all Jack Ford's idea. After ten days of work he got sick and had to withdraw and Zanuck asked me to do him a favor and take over. I hadn't yet learned how to say no. Again, outdoor scenes inside a sound stage—even scenes of violence on a bridge. I was handsomely

paid for any little work and I bought a place in the Connecticut countryside. It was a painless experience—until I saw the result—which
was also painless, without the pain that true drama should cause. I was
becoming something I didn't want to be, "an actor's director." An
expert at moving anybody around for a camera. What I wanted to be
was a filmmaker.

Man on a Tightrope (1953)

I thought that with *Panic* and *Boomerang!* I'd learned the value and
the technique of shooting out in the open country. I had not. Was still a
stage-bound director. This film was my liberation. How? Because I
found myself incapable, and had to ask for help and guidance. Well, it
was a big joke. I'd never have a bigger, to photograph a whole circus,
albeit a small one, crossing a bridge between Communist Czechoslova-
kia and free Austria. I learned by shortcomings. I learned the uses of
fortitude, energy, courage, daring. I became, with this film, the man
who made *On the Waterfront*—and didn't need help on that.

The Visitors (1972)

The Arrangement was a financial disaster. So I went on writing novels.
They were all published immediately and the point of view, material,
and treatment were entirely my own. I thought the amount of money
spent on *The Arrangement,* three times more than on any other film I'd
ever made, was absurd and I wished to return to the purity of poverty,
in other words to show that filmmaking was basically a single and most
human endeavor and did not require an enormous structure of
machinery and equipment and the overhead costs which that brings
with it. My son Chris and I were discussing the effect of the war in
Vietnam on the United States' civilian population and a news item in a
newspaper struck us. Chris wrote an excellent shooting script and we

found five totally unknown actors and made it on the piece of land in Connecticut where we both live. Our film predates all other films with this theme. It also seems to have offended many critics and members of the audience in the United States. I don't understand why. It was a financial disaster, but I heartily recommend it to you.

Directing Steve Railsback and James Woods in *The Visitors*

THE PLEASURES OF
DIRECTING

Kazan addressing students at Wesleyan University

ON WHAT MAKES A DIRECTOR

Note: This is an address Kazan delivered at Wesleyan University on the occasion of a retrospective of his films, September 1973.

At the Yale Drama School and elsewhere I spent a valuable time as a backstage technician. I was a stage carpenter, and I lit shows. Then there was a tedious time as a radio actor, playing hoodlums for bread. I had a particularly educational four years as a stage manager, helping and watching directors and learning a great deal. And in between, I had a lively career as a stage actor in some good plays.

In time I was fortunate enough to have directed the works of the best dramatists of a couple of the decades. I was privileged to serve Tennessee Williams, Arthur Miller, Bill Inge, Archie MacLeish, Sam Behrman, and Bob Anderson and put some of their plays on the stage. I thought of my role with these men as that of a craftsman who tried to realize as well as he could the author's intentions in the author's vocabulary, working within his range, style, and purpose.

I have not thought of my film work that way.

The *auteur* theory is partly a critic's plaything. Something for them to spat over and use to fill a column. But it has its point, and that point is simply that the director is the true author of the film. The director TELLS the film, using a vocabulary the lesser part of which is an arrangement of words.

A screenplay's worth has to be measured less by its language than by its architecture and by how that dramatizes the theme. A screenplay, we directors soon enough learn, is not a piece of writing so much as it is a construction. We learn to feel for the skeleton under the skin of words.

Meyerhold, the great Russian stage director, said that words were the decoration on the skirts of action. He was talking about Theatre, but I've always thought his observations applied more aptly to film.

It occurred to me that it might be fun if I were to try to list for you and for my own sport what a film director needs to know, what personal characteristics and attributes he might advantageously possess.

How must he educate himself? What skills does his craft require?

Without elaborating, I will try to list the fields of knowledge necessary to him, and later those personal qualities that would best serve the role of director.

Literature. Of course. All periods, all languages, all forms. Naturally a film director is better equipped if he's well-read. Jack Ford, who introduced himself with the words, "I make Westerns," was an extremely well-read man.

The Literature of the Theatre. For one thing, so that the film director will appreciate the difference between film and literature. He should also study the classic theatre literature for construction, for exposition of theme, for the means of characterization, for dramatic poetry, for the elements of unity, especially that unity created by pointing to a climax and then for the climax as the essential and final embodiment of the theme.

The craft of screen dramaturgy. Every director, even in those rare instances when he doesn't work with a writer or two—Fellini works with a squadron—must take responsibility for the screenplay. He has not only to guide rewriting but to eliminate what's unnecessary, cover faults, appreciate nonverbal possibilities, ensure correct structure, have a sense of screen time, of how much will elapse, in what places, and for what purposes. Robert Frost's advice "Tell Everything a Little Faster" applies to all expositional parts. In the climaxes, time is unrealistically extended, "stretched," usually by close-ups.

The film director knows that beneath the surface of his screenplay there is a subtext, an undercurrent of intentions and feelings and inner events. What appears to be happening on the surface, he soon learns, is rarely the true substance of the action. This subtext is one of the film director's most valuable tools. It is what he directs. You will rarely see a veteran director holding a script as he works—or even looking at it. Beginners, yes.

Most directors' goal today is to write their own scripts. But that is our oldest tradition. Chaplin would hear that Griffith Park had been flooded by a heavy rainfall, and packing his crew, his standby actors, and his equipment in a few cars, he would rush there, making up the story of the two-reel comedy en route, the details on the spot.

The director of films should know comedy as well as drama. Jack Ford used to call most parts "comics." He meant, I suppose, a way of looking at people without false sentiment, through an objectivity that deflated false heroics and undercut self-favoring and finally revealed a saving humor in the most tense moments. The Human Comedy, one Frenchman called it. The fact that Billy Wilder is always amusing doesn't make his films less serious.

Quite simply, the screen director must know either by training or by instinct how to feed a joke and how to score with it, how to anticipate and protect laughs. He might well study Chaplin and the other great two-reel comedy-makers for what are called sight gags, nonverbal laughs, amusement derived from "business," stunts and moves, and simply from funny faces and odd bodies. This vulgar foundation—the banana peel and the custard pie—are basic to our craft and part of its health. William Wyler and George Stevens began by making two-reel Westerns and comedies, and I seem to remember Frank Capra did too.

American film directors would do well to know our vaudeville traditions. Just as Fellini adored the clowns, music hall performers, and the circuses of his country and paid them homage again and again in his work, our filmmaker would do well to study magic. I believe some of the wonderful cuts in *Citizen Kane* came from the fact that Orson Welles was a practicing magician and so understood the drama of sudden unexpected appearances and the startling change. Think, too, of Bergman, how often he uses magicians and sleight-of-hand.

The director should know opera, its effects and its absurdities, a subject in which Bernardo Bertolucci is schooled. He should know the American musical stage and its tradition, but even more important, the great American musical films. He must not look down on these; we love them for very good reasons.

Our man should know acrobatics, the art of juggling and tumbling, the techniques of the wry comic song. The techniques of the commedia dell'arte are used, it seems to me, in a film called *O Lucky Man!* Lindsay Anderson's master, Bertolt Brecht, adored the Berlin satirical cabaret of his time and adapted their techniques for his plays.

Painting and sculpture, their history, their revolutions and counter-revolutions. The painters of the Italian Renaissance used their mistresses as models for the Madonna, so who can blame a film director for using his girlfriend in a leading role—unless she does a bad job?

Many painters have worked in the Theatre. Bakst, Picasso, Aronson, and Matisse come to mind. More will. Here, we are still with Disney.

Which brings us to Dance. In my opinion, it's a considerable asset if the director's knowledge here is not only theoretical but practical and personal. Dance is an essential part of a screen director's education. It's a great advantage for him if he can "move." It will help him not only to move actors but move the camera. The film director, ideally, should be as able as a choreographer, quite literally so. I don't mean the tango in Bertolucci's *Last Tango in Paris* or the high school gym dance in *American Graffiti* as much as I do the battle scenes in D. W. Griffith's *Birth of a Nation*, which are pure choreography and very beautiful. Look at Ford's cavalry charges that way. Or Jim Cagney's dance of death on the long steps in *The Roaring Twenties*.

The film director must know music, classical, so-called—too much of an umbrella word, that! Let us say of all periods. And as with sculpture and painting, he must know what social situations and currents the music came out of.

Of course he must be particularly INTO the music of his own day— acid rock; Latin rock; blues and jazz; pop; Tin Pan Alley; barbershop; corn; country; Chicago; New Orleans; Nashville.

The film director should know the history of stage scenery, its development from background to environment and so to the settings *inside which* films are played out. Notice I stress "inside which" as opposed to "in front of." The construction of scenery for filmmaking was traditionally the work of architects. The film director must study from life, from newspaper clippings and from his own photographs, dramatic environments and particularly how they affect behavior.

I recommend to every young director that he start his own collection of clippings and photographs and, if he's able, his own sketches.

The film director must know costuming, its history through all periods, its techniques and what it can be as expression. Again, life is a prime source. We learn to study, as we enter each place, each room, how the people there have chosen to present themselves. "How he comes on," we say.

Costuming in films is so expressive a means that it is inevitably the basic choice of the director. Visconti is brilliant here. So is Bergman in a more modest vein. The best way to study this again is to notice how people dress as an expression of what they wish to gain from any occasion, what their intention is. Study your husband, study your wife, how their attire is an expression of each day's mood and hope, their good days, their days of low confidence, their time of stress and how it shows in clothing.

Lighting. Of course. The various natural effects, the cross light of morning, the heavy flat top light of midday—avoid it except for an effect—the magic hour, so called by cameramen, dusk. How do they affect mood? Obvious. We know it in life. How do they affect behavior? Study that. Five o'clock is a low time, let's have a drink! Directors choose the time of day for certain scenes with these expressive values in mind. The master here is Jack Ford, who used to plan his shots within a sequence to get the best use of certain natural effects that he could not create but could very advantageously wait for.

Colors? Their psychological effect. So obvious I will not expand. Favorite colors. Faded colors. The living grays. In *Baby Doll* you saw a master cameraman—Boris Kaufman—making great use of white on white, to help describe the washed-out Southern whites.

And of course, there are the instruments that catch all and should dramatize all; the tools the director speaks through, the CAMERA and the TAPE RECORDER. The film director obviously must know the camera and its lenses, which lens creates which effect, which one lies, which one tells the cruel truth. Which filters bring out the clouds. The director must know the various speeds at which the camera can roll and especially the effects of small variations in speed. He must also know the various camera mountings, the cranes and the dollies and the possible moves he can make, the configurations in space through which he can pass this instrument. He must know the zoom well enough so he won't use it or almost never.

He should be intimately acquainted with the tape recorder. Andy Warhol carries one everywhere he goes. Practice "bugging" yourself and your friends. Notice how often speech overlaps.

The film director must understand the weather, how it's made and where, how it moves, its warning signs, its crises, the kind of clouds and what they mean. Remember the clouds in *Shane*. He must know weather as dramatic expression, be on the alert to capitalize on changes in weather. He must study how heat and cold, rain and snow, a soft breeze, a driving wind affect people, and whether it's true that there are more expressions of group rage during a long hot summer and why.

The film director should know the City, ancient and modern, but particularly his city, the one he loves like De Sica loves Naples; Fellini, Rimini; Bergman, his island; Ray, Calcutta; Renoir, the French countryside; Clair, the city of Paris. His city, its features, its operation, its substructure, its scenes behind the scenes, its functionaries, its police, firefighters, garbage collectors, post office workers, commuters and what they ride, its cathedrals and its whorehouses.

The film director must know the country—no, that's too general a term. He must know the mountains and the plains, the deserts of our great Southwest, the heavy oily-bottom-soil of the Delta, the hills of New England. He must know the water off Marblehead and Old Orchard Beach, too cold for lingering, and the water off the Florida Keys, which invites dawdling. Again, these are means of expression that he has, and among them he must make his choices. He must know how a breeze from a fan can animate a dead-looking set by stirring a curtain.

He must know the sea, firsthand, chance a shipwreck so he'll appreciate its power. He must know the under surface of the sea; if he does, it may occur to him to play a scene there. He must have crossed our rivers and know the strength of their currents. He must have swum in our lakes and caught fish in our streams. You think I'm exaggerating. Why did old man [Robert] Flaherty and his Mrs. spend at least a year in an environment before they exposed a foot of negative? While you're young, you aspiring directors, hitchhike our country!

And topography, the various trees, flowers, ground cover, grasses. And the subsurface, shale, sand, gravel, New England ledge, six feet of old river bottom. What kind of man works each and how does it affect him?

Animals, too. How they resemble human beings. How to direct a chicken to enter a room on cue. I had that problem once and I'm ashamed to tell you how I did it. What a cat might mean to a love scene. The symbolism of horses. The family life of the lion, how tender! The patience of a cow.

Of course, the film director should know acting, its history and its techniques. The more he knows about acting, the more at ease he will be with actors. At one period of his development, he should force himself on stage or before the camera so he knows this experientially too. Some directors, and very famous ones, still fear actors instead of embracing them as comrades in a task. But, by contrast, there is the great Jean Renoir, see him in *Rules of the Game.* And his follower and lover, Truffaut, in *The Wild Child,* now in *Day for Night.*

The director must know how to stimulate, even inspire the actor. Needless to say, he must also know how to make an actor seem NOT to act. How to put him or her at their ease, bring them to that state of relaxation where their creative faculties are released.

The film director must understand the instrument known as the VOICE. He must also know SPEECH. And that they are not the same, as different as resonance and phrasing. He should also know the various regional accents of his country and what they tell about character.

All in all he must know enough in all these areas so his actors trust him completely. This is often achieved by giving the impression that any task he asks of them, he can perform, perhaps even better than they can. This may not be true, but it's not a bad impression to create.

The film director, of course, must be up on the psychology of behavior, "normal" and abnormal. He must know that they are linked, that one is often the extension or intensification of the other, and that under certain stresses, which the director will create within a scene as it's acted out, one kind of behavior can be seen becoming the other. And that is drama.

The film director must be prepared by knowledge and training to handle neurotics. Why? Because most actors are. Perhaps all. What makes it doubly interesting is that the film director often is. Stanley Kubrick won't get on a plane—well, maybe that isn't so neurotic. But we are all delicately balanced—isn't that a nice way to put it? Answer this: How many interesting people have you met who are not a little unbalanced?

Of course we work with the psychology of the audience. We know it differs from that of its individual members. In cutting films great comedy directors like Hawks and Preston Sturges allow for the reactions they expect from the audience, they play on these. Hitchcock has made this his art.

The film director must be learned in the erotic arts. The best way here is through personal experience. But there is a history here, an artistic technique. Pornography is not looked down upon. The film director will admit to a natural interest in how other people do it. Boredom, cruelty, banality are the only sins. Our man, for instance, might study the Chinese erotic prints and those scenes on Greek vases of the Golden Age that museum curators hide.

Of course, the film director must be an authority, even an expert, on the various attitudes of lovemaking, the postures and intertwining of the parts of the body, the expressive parts and those generally considered less expressive. He may well have, like Buñuel does have with feet, special fetishes. He is not concerned to hide these, rather he will probably express his inclinations with relish.

The director, here, may come to believe that suggestion is more erotic than show. Then study how to go about it.

Then there is war. Its weapons, its techniques, its machinery, its tactics, its history—oh my—where is the time to learn all this?

Do not think, as you were brought up to think, that education starts at six and stops at twenty-one, that we learn only from teachers, books, and classes. For us that is the least of it. The life of a film director is a totality and he learns as he lives. Everything is pertinent, there is nothing irrelevant or trivial. *O Lucky Man!,* to have such a profession! Every experience leaves its residue of knowledge behind. Every book we read applies to us. Everything we see and hear: if we like it, we steal it. Nothing is irrelevant. It all belongs to us.

So history becomes a living subject, full of dramatic characters, not a bore about treaties and battles. Religion is fascinating as a kind of poetry expressing fear and loneliness and hope. The film director reads *The Golden Bough* because sympathetic magic and superstition interest him—these beliefs of the ancients and the savages parallel those of his own time's people. He studies ritual because ritual as a source of stage and screen mise-en-scène is an increasingly important source.

Economics a bore? Not to us. Consider the demoralization of people in a labor pool, the panic in currency, the reliance of a nation on imports, and the leverage this gives the country supplying the needed imports. All these affect or can affect the characters and milieus with which our film is concerned. Consider the facts behind the drama of *On the Waterfront.* Wonder how we could have shown more of them.

The film director doesn't just eat. He studies food. He knows the meals of all nations and how they're served, how consumed, what the variations of taste are, the effect of the food, food as a soporific, food as an aphrodisiac, as a means of expression of character. Remember the scene in *Tom Jones? La Grande Bouffe?*

And, of course, the film director tries to keep up with the flow of life around him, the contemporary issues, who's pressuring whom, who's winning, who's losing, how pressure shows in the politician's body and face and gestures. Inevitably, the director will be a visitor at night court. And he will not duck jury duty. He studies advertising and goes to "product meetings" and spies on those who make the ads that influence people. He watches talk shows and marvels how Jackie Susann peddles it. He keeps up on the moves, as near as he can read them, of the secret underground societies. And skyjacking, what's the solution? He talks to pilots. It's the perfect drama—that situation—no exit.

Travel. Yes. As much as he can. Let's not get into that.

Sports? The best-directed shows on TV today are the professional football games. Why? Study them. You are shown not only the game, from far and middle distance and close-up; you are shown the bench, the way the two coaches sweat it out, the rejected sub, Craig Morton, waiting for Staubach to be hurt, and Woodall—does he really like Namath? Johnson, Snead? Watch the spectators too. Think how you might direct certain scenes playing with a ball, or swimming or sailing—even though that isn't indicated in the script. Or watch a ball game as Hepburn and Tracy do in George Stevens's film *Woman of the Year!*

I've undoubtedly left out a great number of things, and what I've left out is significant, no doubt, and exposes some of my own shortcomings.

Oh! Of course, I've left out the most important thing. The subject the film director must know most about, know best of all, see in the greatest detail and in the most pitiless light with the greatest appreciation of the ambivalences at play, is—what?

Right. Himself.

There is something of himself, after all, in every character he properly creates. He understands people through understanding himself.

The silent confession he makes to himself is his greatest source of wisdom. And of tolerance for others. And for love, even that. There is the admission of hatred to awareness and its relief through understanding and a kind of resolution in brotherhood.

What kind of person must a film director train himself to be?

What qualities does he need? Here are a few:

A white hunter leading a safari into dangerous and unknown country.

A construction gang foreman who knows his physical problems and their solutions and is ready, therefore, to insist on these solutions.

A psychoanalyst who keeps a patient functioning despite intolerable tensions and stresses, both professional and personal.

A hypnotist who works with the unconscious to achieve his ends.

A poet, a poet of the camera, able both to capture the decisive moment of Cartier-Bresson or to wait all day like Paul Strand for a single shot, which he makes with a bulky camera fixed to a tripod.

An outfielder for his legs. The director stands much of the day, dares not get tired, so he has strong legs. Think back and remember how the old-time directors dramatized themselves. By puttees, right.

The cunning of a trader in a Baghdad bazaar.

The firmness of an animal trainer. Obvious. Tigers!

A great host. At a sign from him, fine food and heartwarming drink appear.

The kindness of an old-fashioned mother who forgives all.

The authority and sternness of her husband, the father, who forgives nothing, expects obedience without question, brooks no nonsense.

And these alternatively:

The elusiveness of a jewel thief—no explanation, take my word for this one.

The blarney of a PR man, especially useful when the director is out in a strange and hostile location as I have been many times.

A very thick skin.

A very sensitive soul.

Simultaneously.

The patience, the persistence, the fortitude of a saint, the appreciation of pain, a taste for self-sacrifice, everything for the cause.

Cheeriness, jokes, playfulness, alternating with sternness, unwavering firmness. Pure doggedness.

An unwavering refusal to take less than he thinks right out of a scene, a performer, a co-worker, a member of his staff, himself.

Direction, finally, is the exertion of your will over other people—disguise it, gentle it, but that is the hard fact.

Above all—COURAGE. Courage, said Winston Churchill, is the greatest virtue; it makes all the others possible.

One final thing: the ability to say "I am wrong," or "I was wrong." Not as easy as it sounds. But in many situations, these three words, honestly spoken, will save the day. They are the words, very often, that the actors, struggling to give the director what he wants, most need to hear from him. Those words, "I was wrong, let's try it another way," the ability to say them, can be a lifesaver.

The director must accept the blame for everything. If the script stinks, he should have worked harder with the writers or himself before shooting. If the actor fails, the director failed him! Or made a mistake in choosing him. If the camera work is uninspired, whose idea was it to engage that cameraman? Or choose those setups? Even a costume—after all, the director passed on it. The settings. The music, even the goddamn ads. Why didn't he yell louder if he didn't like them? The director was there, wasn't he? Yes, he was there! He's always there!

That's why he gets all that money, to stand there, on that mound, unprotected, letting everybody shoot at him and deflecting the mortal fire from all the others who work with him.

The other people who work on a film can hide.

They have the director to hide behind.

And people deny the *auteur* theory!

After listening to this so patiently, you have a perfect right now to ask, "Oh, come on, aren't you exaggerating to make some kind of point?"

But only exaggerating a little.

The fact is that a director, from the moment a phone call gets him out of bed in the morning ("Rain today. What scene do you want to shoot?") until he escapes into the dark at the end of shooting, is called upon to answer an unrelenting string of questions, to make decision after decision in one after another of the fields I've listed. That's what a director is, the man with the answers.

Watch Truffaut playing Truffaut in *Day for Night,* watch him as he patiently, carefully, sometimes thoughtfully, other times very quickly, answers questions. You will see better than I can tell you how these answers keep his film going. Truffaut has caught our life on the set perfectly.

Do things get easier and simpler as you get older and have accumulated some or all of this savvy?

Not at all. The opposite. The more a director knows, the more he's aware how many different ways there are to do every film, every scene.

And the more he has to face that final awful limitation, not of knowledge but of character. Which is what? The final limitation and the most terrible one is the limitation of his own talent. You find, for instance, that you truly do have the faults of your virtues. And that limitation, you can't do much about. Even if you have the time.

One last postscript. The director, that miserable son of a bitch, as often as not these days has to get out and promote the dollars and the pounds, scrounge for the liras, francs, and marks, hock his family's home, his wife's jewels, and his own future, so he can make his film. This process of raising the wherewithal inevitably takes ten to a hundred times longer than making the film itself. But the director does it because he has to. Who else will? Who else loves the film that much?

So my friends, you've seen how much you have to know and what kind of a bastard you have to be. How hard you have to train yourself and in how many different ways. All of which I did. I've never stopped trying to educate myself and to improve myself.

So now pin me to the wall—this is your last chance. Ask me how with all that knowledge and all that wisdom, and all that training and all those capabilities, including the strong legs of a major league outfielder, how did I manage to mess up some of the films I've directed so badly?

Ah, but that's the charm of it!

THE PLEASURES OF DIRECTING

NOTE: As he was approaching his seventy-ninth year, Elia Kazan began writing the book on directing he had long been thinking about. He loathed textbooks and how-to books, didn't want to instruct anyone (as he himself had not wanted to be instructed), but instead hoped to convey, in the easy-going, reminiscing style of Somerset Maugham's *The Summing Up,* a book he admired, the joy and the fun of directing. His aim was to show readers the process of directing a film or a play, and the technical details were to be interwoven with his observations on the personalities and talents of the people he worked with and the ways they collaborated with him. He started by pulling together the notes on directing he had written over the years. He listed the technical and psychological preparations a director has to make ("props"; "lights"; "rehearsal process"; "first run-through"; "rough cut"; "morality, pride, honor" were some of the topics). Then he began his narrative—which moved between theatre and film—working and reworking essays and composing paragraphs he intended to expand later. At a certain point, he put the work-in-progress aside, and in 1995 he turned it over to his editor at Knopf. What follows is a combination of the pieces he had completed and fascinating fragments—interspersed, as Kazan had intended, with autobiographical material we have selected from his previously published writings and interviews.

There is only one way of looking at this trade: The filmmaker is responsible for everything. To rephrase that thought: Everything is your fault, and only rarely will you be praised for anything. But face it, if something goes wrong with your work, you the filmmaker (director), who fought for total control, as we all do, should not have allowed it to happen. If you're going to work in films, you must straight off accept total responsibility. That's why you have to know something about all aspects of the process, and that's why this book deals with those responsibilities as I have known them.

Final and absolute responsibility? That is not only a heavy obligation, but it is just the way we want it. It's not a burden, it's the rule of the game as we choose to play it. Making a film is an exercise in total control. My advice and my warning to people starting out in this field is to not surrender authority to anyone. Don't be nice, don't be cooperative, don't be obliging. Be sweet-tempered, of course, cordial, sure, pick up the checks and send flowers to the wife of your star, why not, but don't give in where it counts, not ever—and it counts, as I hope you'll see, in every area of the job.

In the hundred-year-and-counting history of the movies, there has always been a war for artistic control. Sometimes the men with the money held the power, sometimes the man who put it all together, the producer, now and then the star, and on rare occasions the writers.

We filmmakers have to know it all. All? Of course, that is asking too much. But I pride myself on my ability to know at least something of everything critical to the job. And certainly on my eagerness to learn more every day that I work.

I still think of myself as a beginner. I've only made twenty films. I had a floundering start. I know only what I could pick up wherever and whenever I could. I believe I still have lots to learn from the many filmmakers whose work I admire. At the same time I have nothing to learn. My work prejudices have the merit of being my very own. My brother and sister filmmakers have various gifts and I admire them, but the whole thing is to speak your own language, whatever it is and wherever you come from, to make your own choices and be ready to stand alone.

I believe that filmmaking is one of the great arts, potentially the greatest, and perhaps the ultimate one. It hasn't yet reached its full potential for artistic and social importance. You who labor in the field will find, as you progress, an ever deeper joy in this work. I think of filmmaking as a joyful privilege. Who could ask for anything more than to have the opportunity—and the wherewithal—to convey by film a meaningful personal sentiment? Not the kind of message expressed by words only, but to pass on an experience dear to the writer, with the force of a poem, a communication that combines every expressive art—photography, language, music, acting, movement—devised by man, coming out of your own feelings and seeking to reach not only the few people who are close to you but the whole world.

The films that I don't like are those where I don't feel any personality. It doesn't bother me that all Ingmar Bergman's movies are alike. They should be because he made them. If he's behind the camera I want to feel him, as I do in his films. The same with Antonioni and Fellini. I want to feel their own individual personalities; I don't want to be more eclectic or have fewer mannerisms (which I don't try to have). But I do think you can see that all my films are made by me; for better or worse, I do the best I can. I don't think any of them are perfect or wonderful, and some of the failures I like as well as, if not better than, the successes.

It is true that a director is a privileged person. I don't know of anything *more* pleasurable than working with a splendid group of people on a worthy project. The director is in a position to get close to a number of talented people of his own choosing, artists he admires and who open themselves to him as he will to them. There are very few communities of people that can compare with those a director can enjoy. That these relationships will be for the limited time of developing, shaping, and presenting a film or play makes them more precious, not less. What a pleasure to work with people from whom you can learn, who will stimulate your imagination and arouse your deepest emotions. How rare that is in life!

It is essential, be it a play or film, to quickly create among your collaborators an atmosphere of pleasure in work as well as openness and comradeship, a sense of common purpose to be enjoyed by people of equal talent. You are not to behave as a "boss," even though you chose them all and can replace them. It is your obligation, and your privilege, to establish the goals of the work and to help the others achieve these goals in collaboration with you. Furthermore, it is your duty to make the successful achievement of these goals pleasurable in anticipation. The actors and actresses must *long* to play the parts as you describe them.

You are the leader in a group search to reveal and create a work of art. The mood must be one of confidence that you build from day to day and joy in anticipation of what together you will achieve. The reward of good work, of achievement in art, is a greater reward than any I know and lasts longer. It continues to grace your life, and it affords you satisfaction and self-esteem and cause for pride. How few things in life do!

Does a director "fall" for members of his cast? Of course he does. How could it be otherwise? The director is on the most intimate terms with, a participant in the life experience of, each person involved with him in the effort. Even the most mechanical side of the work will relate to a fundamental choice of meaning and feeling. As to whether the director and the leading lady will fall in love, well, it's inevitable. How could it be otherwise? It is a relationship where everything is at stake and nothing can be concealed. The wise partners of the actor and director will expect this and understand and not resent whatever develops. The partner can be sure of one thing. The relationship between director and player will not last. What caused it to happen was the mutual effort to excel at any cost. And when the enterprise is completed, the effort will drain away and disappear. But while it goes on, the fact is this: My fate is in your hands, your fate in mine.

Nothing else, no other way of working on a project in art, is worth the time or the trouble. Totality, nothing held back, passion undiminished from beginning to end!

And that is the pleasure of it.

Committing Yourself Twice

A director commits himself to a project twice. The first time is from spontaneous enthusiasm. The second is after asking questions and overcoming doubts.

Don't talk yourself into it, question yourself. And write down your answers. If you abandon the project, you will know why. If you decide to go on with it, your written answers will help you later, in times of difficulty and stress.

Why did you like the script or the novel or the idea when it was first presented? What was it that attracted you? What was it about the theme that touched your innermost being? If it didn't stir you deeply, beware, because if you lack that kind of deep involvement, you may find halfway through that you have lost interest. You have become indifferent. The pleasure is gone.

Then get in trouble. Attack the project. That is often the best way to find out why you truly like it. Doubt yourself. Answer your worst questions. Don't be afraid.

There is only one person you must give a bad time to, yourself. It is said that if a man has talent, it is only because he tells himself, from time to time, the truth he's been trying to hide from himself. Do you truly like the project, or are you considering it for some curious, irrelevant reason? Be certain that your interest isn't based primarily on showing off your facility: "I can make that work. I know how to solve these problems." You are not building a house or doing summer stock. It's part of your life, not show business. This is when you must examine your own character, when you must force yourself to confront whether what you're considering expresses your deepest wishes, your hopes, your longing, your anger. Does it speak for you? Does it touch some fundamental strain in you? Tell yourself the truth; don't be an agreeable good guy. Be selfish. Be arrogant. Can it be made part of the current of your own life? You're paying a big price to involve yourself— months, even years of your life. Can the finished project be thought of as a chapter in your autobiography? Can you make it speak for you? Will it stand as an expression of your own existence? Truly? In what way? Will you be proud that you've done it? You can be 100 percent only rarely, but you should feel the enthusiasm necessary to try to give the work your whole being. Is the theme in some way your theme? Is the story your story?

If you can't find the *you* in the story, then it has no personal meaning for you. That's an important discovery, because then you should immediately walk away from it. Don't be lured into sticking with it by inertia or the sad faces of disappointed friends. They'll find someone else.

Suppose your questioning comes out positive, and you believe your first enthusiasm was well-founded. Your notes on this project that you are fool enough to start will rekindle, reenlist, and reenlighten you when you later ask yourself what did you ever see in it. I've known them to be lifesavers, dispelling weariness and the crippling effect of doubt. And you will remember the pleasure you once felt.

I am a mediocre director except when a play or a film touches a part of my life's experience.

I don't move unless I have some empathy with the basic theme. In some way the channel of the film should also be in my own life. I start with an instinct. With *East of Eden* I said, "I don't know why it is but the last ninety pages of Steinbeck's book turn me on." It's really the story of my father and me, and I didn't realize it for a long time. When Paul Osborn and I began to work on the screenplay, I realized that it's just the way I was. I was always the bad boy, but I thought I was the good boy. In some subtle or not-so-subtle way, every film is autobiographical. A thing in my life is expressed by the essence of the film. Then I know it experientially, not just mentally. I've got to feel that it's in some way about me, some way about my struggles, some way about my pain, my hopes.

I was accused of infusing my film *On the Waterfront* with my reaction to the response of my friends and colleagues to my testimony before the House Un-American Activities Committee. I plead guilty. That is what made the film strong. I did not duck the parallel, I admitted it and stressed it. I was not ashamed. I fed on my anger at being rejected by former friends.

A few years earlier I had made a film about anti-Semitism, *Gentleman's Agreement,* and got an Academy Award for it, but I had no personal experience to feed on. The film is polite and cool on a painful, devastatingly cruel subject. Moss Hart did the screenplay, and I don't think Moss was ever slurred or insulted as "kike" or "Jew bastard." He was always safe; he was insulated because he had money; he had wit, he had ability, he had intelligence. Darryl Zanuck, the producer, also had no deep personal stake in this story, but he was the only producer with courage to risk the subject of anti-Semitism in Hollywood even though he was the only non-Jew among the Hollywood moguls. The film lacks passion, though it is full of craft and mostly good intentions.

Indifference is not the essence of drama. To the contrary, *drama by its nature is partisan.*

I was separated from my wife when I was making my first film, *A Tree Grows in Brooklyn.* I missed my children very much, painfully. Also, I felt guilty. The father in *Tree* was a drunkard, and I was a lecher and a liar. We both betrayed our wives. The little girl in the film I treated as if she were the daughter I loved who was on the other side of the country. I think all this shows. It wasn't a perfect filmscript, but it was right for me. It was mine! And *America America,* not perfect either but good. I fitted it. It wasn't only the story of the yearning of a generation of people looking for a new life; it was my story.

What a theatre or film director is essentially doing is conveying an emotion he has, arousing an emotion he feels in a group of other people. You must from the beginning recognize what audience you are addressing and how you propose to move them. What precisely you want to make them feel. Once this is done, take care not to tell them plainly what they should believe about what they're being shown. Leave an element of doubt and mystery. Wonder is better than information. Don't patronize them. Don't be a whore for them. Don't tell them what they should think. But don't play up to them. Let them come to their own conclusions. But know yourself what you're reaching for in their feelings.

This means isolating the theme. What it's all about. What it should say in the end. But "say" is a dangerous word. "Convey" is better. Put down the theme, the meaning of the piece for you, in so many words.

The size of a film or play depends on the size of its theme. One can have all kinds of conflicts, but if the central thematic issue is a small one, or petty, the clashes will be of no significance.

Everything?

It bears repeating because you may think that I don't mean it. Directing is total. The director determines everything. Each choice you make, believe it or not, is equally important. The basic decisions are yours to make, but they need not be and usually are not yours to carry out. Other artists, the ones you have chosen, the ones you guide, will help to solve the problems you cannot. But you must know enough to point in a definite direction, to be able to ask the right questions. You should know the basics of each craft, enough to guide and determine— that is, to direct—the multifaceted process. For instance, the film director picks the locations. He tells the cameraman where to place his camera, how the camera is to be moved, and which lens to use. The stage director must give his designer ground plans, color schemes, and mood specifications.

I was brought up in a theatre tradition in which directing was thought of as primarily directing actors. If you had guided your actors well, you had in effect directed the play. This proved to be short-sighted. Psychology is one thing—psychological complexity can be explored. Movement is another. Directing can be thought of as rendering psychology into behavior, into action. What do the characters do because of their needs, their impulses, their desires, their wishes? Wish is the most important word for an actor, because he goes on stage to fulfill a wish. And then, what is the setting for this movement? How do the design, the circumstances in which the actor moves, contribute to the effect?

This broadside interest is total. Although you can't write music—few of us can—you must know what its effect will be, what purpose it serves. Think of music, like the sets, the costuming, the lighting, the sound effects, as friends you can call upon to help you. In this way, the music becomes yours as well as the composer's. It is your tool and your comrade. You will certainly need all the help you can get, and in the case of music, it is your function to determine its intent—or to determine that there should be no music, only the sounds of human life. You must be arrogant in selecting a composer who will work to fulfill your concept. The same can be said for every aspect of the production. You should have an urgent vision of the scenery, whether it serves as environment or background, what colors, what style, what changes, what movement. You should choose the design scheme of the scenery, and specify the ground plan, for the arrangement of elements will determine the movement of the actors you are about to direct.

Likewise the costumes. Don't let anyone question your authority. If they ask what you know about clothes, tell them, "Enough to know how I wish the characters to look and to be able to move in what they wear, what the dominant colors should be, what each costume should tell about each character." Then you will be surprised, for the costumer will not think you arrogant; she or he will appreciate the guidance. The most artistic liberty is enjoyed when there are demarcations, limits, frames within which one can explore and even be daring.

Train Yourself

Self-education should never stop. It drives wives crazy because the typical director never seems to have a free mind, it's always somewhere else. Everything is pertinent to a director: today's news, the study of the past, philosophy, aesthetics, the natural sciences, and the study of the human body, sports, dance, folk customs. As for the various functions of the craft you are involved with, the best way is to practice them yourself. It's less important to read about acting and to study the advice of great teachers than to act yourself. If you can, work in a summer theatre. Or get a part in a play or a movie and submit to the will of the director. Design a set for a production, create the costumes for another. Knuckle down and do it. Lighting is critical—you are creating another world, not a real world—and experience in this is absolutely necessary. You must know what the choices are and what the problems are and what the techniques are and what the available materials are before you can successfully guide others. Learn by doing. Fail, but try everything you can. Take subsidiary positions. Be an assistant director, a call boy, be a stage manager. Go to a dance class and learn how choreographers work and what keeps a dance moving, what the classical movements are. Everything is relevant.

Then read. What a pleasurable way of life it is that requires you to study everything! Collect books. Collect clippings. Cut out every illustration in papers or magazines that attracts you. It caught your eye for a reason. There are marvelous compositions in newspapers, especially the bad ones. They will stimulate your own compositions and movements.

Keep a diary. It will force you to articulate your observations, and it will train your eyes and ears to see and hear and notice. Carry a pocket notebook. Always have a pen with you. A half-hour's walk can be valuable. Every street in New York can provide an encounter, and all encounters that surprise you are precious. A bus or subway ride can be a treasure trip. Don't take taxis. You see nothing and learn nothing in a taxi—it's a waste of time.

Train yourself psychologically. Be on guard against cliché ways of thinking, like good guy, bad guy, nice guy, honest guy, or she's smart, tricky, a bitch, too clever, and all the rest. Above all, permit the disruptive and the vulgar and the shocking and the revolutionary and the hateful thought. Your mind should invite what will supplant the old and tired taken-for-granted thoughts. Clear your mind of censors. Don't believe that it's wrong to think anything. Later, when you are directing, if you think up a line or a piece of business and your first self-censoring reaction is "No! I mustn't say that or ask the actress to do that, it would hurt her image or my image or the way the audience is responding," then that is particularly what you should do! Don't avoid the thorny, the shocking thing. *Embrace* it, and find in it what shocked you. See if that thought doesn't help you to break down the clichés in your own mind or your own world. In you.

Avoid being a nice guy, a decent guy, a conforming guy—stifle him. The portrait I am painting of the director is a vision of a completely arrogant man. It is an accurate and necessary portrait. Everyone around you will try to *soften* you. Show no shame when you're accused of being arrogant. Say what you think no matter whom it might offend. You're not about to guide a children's summer camp. More likely you are related to a zoo-keeper. You need to have supreme confidence in the purpose, the intent, the content, the importance of your undertaking. Anyone who helps is a friend, everyone else an enemy who has to be won over. But if you can't, fuck them.

Remember that everyone has to bow to you and heed your every wish. They should. Without that degree of arrogance there will be chaos.

Writing for the Theatre, Writing for the Screen

A director should know everything about playwriting and/or screenplay writing, even if he is unable to write, is incapable of producing anything worth putting before an audience. He must be able to see the merits but also anticipate the problems involved in producing a script. The director is responsible for the script. Its faults are his responsibility. There is no evading this. He is there to guide the playwright to correct whatever faults the script has. At the same time he must respect the merits of the playwright's work during the tensions of production. He is responsible for the protection of the manuscript.

Note that the word is not "playwrite," it's "playwright." A play for the theatre is made as much as it is written. A film is made, not written. They are both constructions. The construction tells the story more than the words.

In the movies, the director should be co-author (ideally) because that is what inevitably he is. He should work on the screenplay with the writer from the very beginning. The manner in which the story is developed tells more than the words do. The problems that arise during production are almost always problems of construction. Since so much of the story of a film is told by visual images, the director is the co-creator. A screenplay is not literature—a film is constructed of pieces of film joined together during the editing process. The most memorable films are not usually treasured for their literary values. But in film as well as in works for the stage, story construction is a major component.

A filmscript is more architecture than literature. This will get my friends who are writers mad, but it's the truth: The director tells the movie story more than the man who writes the dialogue. The director

Polishing the script, on the set of *Wild River*

is the final author, which is the reason so many writers now want to become directors. It's all one piece. Many of the best films ever made can be seen without dialogue and be perfectly understood. The director tells the essential story with pictures. Dialogue, in most cases, is the gravy on the meat. It can be a tremendous "plus," but it rarely is. Acting, the art, helps; that too is the director's work. He finds the experience within the actor that makes his or her face and body come alive and so creates the photographs he needs. Pictures, shots, angles, images, "cuts," poetic long shots—these are his vocabulary. Not talk. What speaks to the eye is the director's vocabulary, his "tools," just as words are the author's. Until *Panic in the Streets,* I'd directed actors moving in and out of dramatic arrangements just as I might have done on stage, with the camera photographing them mostly in medium shot. My stage experience, which I'd thought of as an asset, I now regarded as a handicap. I had to learn a new art.

A true artistic partnership between a writer and a filmmaker is an excellent solution, but it's rarely arrived at. The dialogue remains an adjunct to the film rather than its central element. What can be told through images, through movement, through the expressiveness of the actor, what can be told without explicit and limiting dialogue, is best done that way. Reliance on the visual allows the ambiguity, the openness of life.

In the work of the best playwrights there is a mysterious, surprising quality. This play is unlike that of any other playwright. You may realize that the author is dealing with a strongly felt personal concern so important to him that it has been able to arouse the degree of energy necessary to produce a total manuscript. He has something to say; it is his message. The director of a screenplay has to appreciate what the writer is trying to say and stand up for it as surely as if he wrote the words himself. He is responsible for the writer's theme and must "realize" it, make it come to life for an audience. In film this consists of the choice and arrangement of images.

Most screenplays are adaptations of novels, stage plays, stories, news items, history. But the most interesting scripts verge on autobiography. The writer speaks to you, through the screen, using all the means of this form that are special to it, the succession of images as well as words. The best screen work has this element, even if the story appears to be objectively observed. The story is molded by the writer's beliefs and feelings.

The subject of writing for the theatre or screen defies easily formulated rules. The best rule of screen and play writing was given to me by John Howard Lawson,* a onetime friend. It's simple: unity from climax. Everything should build to the climax. But all I know about script preparation urges me to make no rules, although there are some hints, tools of the trade, that have been useful for me.

One of these is "Have your central character in every scene." This is a way of ensuring unity to the work and keeping the focus sharp. Another is: "Look for the contradictions in every character, especially in your heroes and villains. No one should be what they first seem to be. Surprise the audience."

It is essential that the viewer be able to follow the flow of events. If you keep trying to figure out who is who and where it's all happening and what is going on, you can't emotionally respond to what's being shown to you. But keep in mind that the greatest quality of a work of art may be its ability to surprise you, to make you wonder.

Another rule I have found useful is: Every time you make a cut, you improve a scene. Somerset Maugham, a wise old man, said that there

---

* Lawson was a playwright, screenwriter, and member of the Hollywood Ten; he headed the Hollywood division of the American Communist Party.

are two important rules of playwriting. "One, stick to the subject. Two, cut wherever you can." Another wise man said: "If it occurs to you that something *might* be cut, it should be cut."

Paul Osborn, an experienced and smart playwright and screen-writer, invited me to a screening of a movie made by the producer Sam Goldwyn. Sam asked Paul his opinion. "Needs cutting," said Paul. This made Sam frantic because he thought the same but didn't know what to do about it. "But where?" he asked. Paul answered, "Everywhere."

There's no such thing as realistic theatre. The very presence of the audience, the fact of selection of any kind, the very taking off of the fourth wall, makes it not realistic. I'm not interested in what's called realism. I don't believe I've worked "realistically" or "naturalistically" either. What our stage does is put a strong light on a person, on the inner life, the feelings of a person. These become monumental. You're not seeing the characters in two dimensions. They're out there living right in your midst. It puts a terrific emphasis on what's said too. You can no longer pretend a character is talking only to the partner he's playing with. He's talking in the midst of eleven hundred people and they're there to hear him. They can hear his breathing, so right off the bat, the theatrical exists. You can't duck it.

Stage operates through illusion. There's nothing between the actor and the audience. Only he—without help—can project the idea to the audience. In movies, the camera helps out—moves the idea along. Sometimes it can talk, as it closes in or backs up, helps express emotion, what a character is thinking; or it can anticipate action. The more words, usually the lousier a movie script. Movies must be the real thing. Camera gives the plot an assist, helps the story get there.

Improvisation

The irony is that improvisation needs structure.

One of the purposes of improvisation—and it's just as important in film as in theatre—is to free the wild impulses of people. It opens the possibility of surprises. It allows actors to surprise themselves.

The behavior of people is full of stereotypes. The danger is that an actor will behave in predictable ways. He will behave as expected. As is traditional. Correctly. Watch TV, watch the "soaps," and what I'm saying is apparent.

But life is full of surprises. "And then you know what he did?" "Then what do you think she did?"

Yes, that is all true, but the biggest surprises are where behavior has been most codified. The years and years of experience with theatre and film and books lead a performer to behave as would be expected in a given situation.

But within each person is the life of the unexpected. A good writer will surprise us, and that arouses our interest and challenges us and awakens our sense of truth. The surprise is the thing. Play for it. Fuck up if you have to. Surprise yourself!

A surprise will throw the movement off kilter, off the proper condition. And "proper" is a dangerous word in art—it has to be thrown out, and something beyond and altered has to be invited in.

The great writers, the great actors, the great artists have the capability and even the practice of surprising us. They open the door to the unexpected.

Look at it another way. Have you sat at the opera and heard Pavarotti singing an Italian song and said, "What intense feeling! Have I ever felt that way, felt that strongly? Or has my life always been more calm and controlled? Have I ever known the passion these men offer in their songs?"

Then you remember. It's usually something basic and simple, or some crisis of family or love where you surprised yourself, where your feeling was deep and you were carried away into a marriage that you vowed never, never to be led into, and you remember a thrill, usually sexual, that surprised you, and then—yes—the Italian tenor's resonance and fire was a bit familiar, you felt that way once, and it surprised you and finally overwhelmed you. And you were not, for that moment, commonsensical and orderly and well regulated.

And you know it's there; you once had the passion that damned Italian tenor glorified in, released.

Or another time when you began to laugh and couldn't stop, and you didn't really know why you found what was making you laugh so overwhelmingly funny.

What is the opposite? Good sense. Control. Civilization. And in the case of preparation for a play, adherence to the lines, saying them meaningfully and not overdoing the suggestion of feeling apparently called for by the text. Good sense, when it takes over, is deadly.

And *text* is a bad word. It is a binding word. It has no surprise in it. It says: Stick to the words, appropriately said.

That is one thing about Shakespeare: He calls for cries and moans and swells of anger beyond good sense.

How do we dig these swells of feeling out of the orderly run of words? How do we break out of what seems to be called for? How do we return to a more basic level of feeling, one less circumscribed and orderly? More surprising, more astounding, more true?

The first thing is to free ourselves of the words, get out from under the correct order of the sensible words, of the "text."

That is impossible if we concern ourselves and each other largely with the problem of presenting the words. We have to let it—whatever it is—run wild. And it can't if we are being obedient to the text.

During my days with the Group Theatre, we actors experimented with improvisations—animal sounds, for example; anything to loosen the hold of the text on us. *Text,* at that time, became a word I loathed. It was the expression of good sense.

Take a chance. Break the mold.

A Story About Vic Fleming

Victor Fleming is forgotten now, but when I went west to work in films, he was one of the most respected directors in the movie world. He made *The Wizard of Oz* and "saved" *Gone With the Wind.* Admired for his unshakable devotion to the job, he—along with John Ford—was the model of behavior for many other directors. Fleming was a proud man, socially remote, arrogant, and with a notoriously violent temper. There was nothing more important to him than making the best movie he could, and he would tolerate no obstacles.

Henry Hathaway told me a story about the filming of the first, and aborted, version of *The Yearling.*° They were in the South, and the star

---

° Another try at *The Yearling* was finished in 1946, directed by Clarence Brown and starring Gregory Peck, Jane Wyman, and Claude Jarman, Jr.

was Spencer Tracy. It was the kind of location Fleming liked, as remote from civilization as possible, so that the cast and crew would keep their minds on the job day and night.

A few days after production began, Fleming walked off the set and returned to his office in Culver City. The MGM executives were outraged but too frightened of Fleming's temper to confront him, except to ask gently why he had left without any apparent cause. Fleming told them the cause. He was down there, he said, making a film about love, about an impoverished family and a little boy with a pet deer, but no one in the cast was capable of any such feeling. The child actor and his parents could think of nothing but making him a star. The woman playing the mother was between a shit and a sweat about her costumes and why they couldn't be more flattering. And Spencer Tracy could only think of getting off weekends to go and fuck Katharine Hepburn. "With that bunch, how can I make a film about family love?"

That was all he had to say. There was a long silence, one they'd all remember. Then without another word, Fleming got up and left the room. No one detained him. The story got around. Other directors asked themselves and each other if ruthlessness and arrogance might be the only way to make a good film.

Scenic Matters

The scenery should tell the story—it should be the story, not only the environment in which the story takes place.

In the 1930s, when we were sure of things and doing plays of "social comment," we arrived at the theory of scenery as environment, not as decorative backdrop: The actors live and work within it, not in front of it. We wanted to show how it affected people. Theatrical environment will affect the actor's behavior, his performance, just as one's surroundings do in life. There is the inevitable intercourse between the environment and the actor that determines how he moves and the various points of emphasis, the obstacles, the cul-de-sacs, the ascent, and the descent. The environment must be chosen by the director to determine the way of life of the actors on stage.

We had another useful theory: scenery as metaphor, metaphor that determines the overall design pattern of the production and that gives the production its artistic unity. The production metaphor in some cases was a prize ring (*Golden Boy*), in another a womb, in a third a prison. Mordecai Gorelik put a mound of dirt in the middle of the front-yard set of Arthur Miller's *All My Sons*. Puzzled, we asked him if he could level it since the actors were stumbling over it. Not on your life, he said; the mound represented the grave of the dead son who was the linchpin of the play. The play was all about stepping over his grave.

We believed the director should choose the basic stage design and, later in my career, what is put in front of the camera. This is his first and basic critical choice. It sets the tone and style of the production and is the director's essential declaration of intent.

But we were to find that this theory of visual attack, while it suited the "progressive," left-wing social drama of the day, had limited application to that kind of theater only. Even then, we discovered it was too narrow, too absolute a concept. It limited the possibilities of artistic discovery. There were other theatrical styles, with other meanings and intentions, requiring different artistic solutions. The intent of the play dictates the scenic approach, and scenery as environment is only one among a multitude of options.

In opera and musical theatre the effective elements are songs and music. The opera singers look like opera singers, not characters in a drama, and it is necessary to aid them in projecting the arias, duets, quartets, and choruses. Inevitably, they have to be placed so that they project outward. There is no evading or disguising the fact that the form is close to an out-and-out concert. Efforts to make opera seem more "realistic" are absurd. The value is in the artifice. Scenery should not deflect from the singers; it should serve as background. It is a decoration, not an environment that surrounds and encloses them.

I have often considered what the ideal circumstances would be for me as a director. I'd like a permanently financed and staffed company of agreeable friends who are actors. The stage should be large and elastic. In the side and backstage areas, there would be a facility for storage and a workshop for scenery. Here there would be ramps, boxes, platforms, barriers, all manner of furniture, flats, drops and curtains, and buckets of paint—elements available to implement each of the director's intentions, and easily tried, moved, removed, and used as important design elements.

Rehearsals would start with hopes and plans and wishes, but without a ground or scenic plan. The atmosphere would be candidly and openly experimental. We would encourage mistakes and guesses and faults. There would be no time limit. The director and his actors would work until their basic intention had been brought as nearly as we thought possible to its end.

Once we refined our production concept, we would invite visual artists to see the proceedings. If they responded favorably to our efforts, we would ask them to bring their expertise to give shape and form to our work with a professional design and color scheme.

Both sides would be elastic because by this time the basic artistic concept would be clear to all. The director and his actors had taken the first essential design step, wedding the life of movement to various plastic elements as they had been tried and developed in the life of the play's performance. The designer might also have some astonishing suggestions to make but only on the basis of the essential production concept.

In film the search for the concept must be made by the director alone. He might give the so-called art director a portfolio of still photographs he has taken. Or he might offer as guide and stimulus plates of paintings in the style the director considers useful. The visual plan to the film is thus established—in the director's mind by his research and in the cameraman's eye by the director's visual suggestions.

My Chief Artistic Collaborators: Directors of Photography

In my film work the collaborators I valued most were the cameramen. Since I came from the theatre, where the spoken word is so essential, I had to be jolted into realizing that the eye, not the ear, was the most important sense, that a film's story is told by a sequence of images, and that very often, the less dialogue there is the better, that if a film could be told entirely by pictures, that would be best of all. I was forced to learn this lesson straight off in my very first film, *A Tree Grows in Brooklyn*. There I experienced the essential shock. My cameraman was a grumpy fellow whom I came to love. His name was Leon Shamroy, and his nickname with the crew was "Grumble-gut." He immediately set back the cocky young fellow from the New York stage (me) by arriving for work every morning with only the vaguest acquaintance with the text for that day's work. "What's the garbage for today?" he'd ask in his rasping voice. "Why the hell didn't you read the script?" I'd come back. "I'd rather watch a rehearsal," he'd say. "That will tell the story." I soon came to see that his point of view, while extreme, was essentially the correct one, that I should photograph behavior, not "talking heads." With this realization in mind, I began to study the work of the great directors. I marveled at how long Jack Ford would hold a long shot and how much it would tell, what imagination and daring he had. Watching his work and that of other directors I admired, I realized that all I'd been doing was photographing action of a kind that predominates the stage, staying mostly in medium shots with a close-up now and then to "punch home" a point or make an emphasis. In every difficulty, I'd rely on the spoken word rather than a revealing image.

So the cameramen became my friends in California. I thought most producers ignorant, inept bluffers. I thought the same of many directors, noting how heavily they relied on their cameramen to tell them where to put the camera down and what to do with it. Also, despite my reputation as an "actors' director," I did not find most actors stimulating artistic collaborators. There were exceptions, but if I were to choose a generalization that would be true to me, I'd say that my allegiance shifted from words to the camera and to the cameramen. I felt that, even more than the director, they were "on the spot," they had to produce a piece of film every day that would be used in the final picture. They had to make good, as we say, and no excuse would be accepted.

I also responded with affection and enthusiasm to their vitality and their pleasure-ability. They would experience what I would, the challenge and the fun of filmmaking, not budget making. They were handymen, and I admired that too—they would work in any weather, hot, cold, rain, snow, or under a burning sun. They were also enthusiastic improvisers and would get through any and all difficult times, one way or another. Nothing could set them back. When I was "stuck," they would suggest solutions, and I came to rely on them more and more and to confide in them increasingly. Only to them would I confide my ultimate intentions and dreams with relation to a film; to them and not to anyone else. I noticed that often when a scenic problem would worry me, it would exhilarate a cameraman.

All the cameramen I worked with were "great," a word that's been cheapened by overuse by show-business media people. If I were asked to choose one cameraman above the others, I'd refuse. But if a pistol were put to my head, I'd say Boris Kaufman. I remember that time after time I'd arrive on the location of the filmmaking with a very definite idea of how to approach that day's work and specifically how to shoot the basic first shot—that is, from where. I'd tell Boris what my conviction was, if I had a conviction. He'd walk with me to the position I was suggesting to launch the point of view for the day's work, he'd examine what I was offering him, listen to me, then say with crushing modesty, "Suppose we study it from another place—just to see." Then add, "For the challenge of it." Then, not at all bending to the producer's constant and inevitable prodding ("Get the first shot early in the can. If you do that, you'll have a good day's work"), I'd walk slowly to the position he suggested, and in a slow, that is, a civilized rhythm, we'd study the scene as it would be photographed from that point of view. Very often the pictorial approach he was suggesting was better than mine. But above all he taught me to stop and consider, to study all possibilities before plunging into an irrevocable decision. For Boris there was always the grace of patience and comradely consideration, weighing one attack against the other. He was a true artist, and I remember him with love.

The only cameraman I did not like personally was Haskell Wexler. But he was an excellent cameraman. He turned out to be further left politically than I believed when I engaged him, and I felt a certain resentment of me from him, of a kind with which I'd become familiar. We were in Turkey, so I could not replace him easily, but I didn't replace him for another reason: I saw that he would help me with my work. I respected him as a craftsman, but I disliked him as a man, thought him typical of many left-wing intellectuals. I also didn't like the crew he'd assembled. A cameraman's crew tells who he is. Perhaps too I couldn't take his insulting manner with me, a kind of left-wing snobbery, I believed it to be. He said to me one day, "You know you don't have a good eye." I resented that remark for years, but I resented even more what he said when the film was done: "I think I can see what you were getting at now," this after weeks and weeks together. About twenty years after *America America* was released, he wrote me that he'd seen the film at a film festival and thought it a "great, enduring movie." He thanked me for giving him the chance to be part of it. By then I didn't care. It was too late.

With Haskell
Wexler (*left*)
on the set of
*America
America*

The thing I like most about cameramen is a human quality: They actually enjoy the job of making a film, the work itself. Producers worry and wait for the end of shooting, sometimes to see if they can take the editing process away from the director. So they reveal themselves to be the director's enemy. Actors worry about their performance, whether it's a step forward or backward in the agent-market. Screenwriters sweat with fear, often believing that a director is lousing up their script. But the cameramen I've known and their crews come to work with joy; they come to "play." They're the men for me. Where a producer resents rain and smoke and snow and the movement of the clouds over the sun because they delay production, cameramen love these events of nature. Extreme cold or a burning sun makes an actor look less like an actor and more like an ordinary human being.

The cameraman I had the most fun with was Harry Stradling; he was a fearless person and could do anything and do it fast, give you two close-ups at the end of the afternoon as the light was going in fifteen minutes. Nothing fazed him, and he could move the lights himself if he had to. He also always had a congenial bottle handy, and at the end of the day's work we'd enjoy drinking and laughing together. The niftiest and gutsiest of them all was Joe MacDonald and perhaps the most beloved by his crew. He brightened each day we worked. The most dignified of them all and a man I liked very much was Ellsworth Fredericks. He always wore a city hat even when we worked in the deep countryside of the state of Tennessee.

"Be bold!" I used to cry out to them all; that was all the encouragement they needed to take a new tack, a fresh approach, and to respond with the unexpected. I never said, "Be careful."

Costumes

Anything one wears is a costume.

Who is it I am going to meet? Who do I want to impress? Who do I have to win over? What image of myself am I promoting? What a man or a woman finally decides to put on is a costume.

A danger for film and stage costuming is not that what's chosen won't be impressive or revealing but that it will tell too much, that it will give away what should be discovered during the course of the performance.

The first step in costuming is analysis of character and, even before that, defining the central motivation of the script and determining the style of the production to convey the intent of the work. Costuming must be a function of the whole, it must work in tandem with all the other visual elements.

There are very few productions, as I see it, that should be realistic. And I doubt there is any such thing as "realistic." The instant a choice is made, it is subjective; the costume reflects the director's analysis of the character, which will be a personal, unique, and idiosyncratic view.

Start at the bottom. Study what people wear on the street. Remind yourself that they are "costumed"; their clothes were chosen to make a certain impression. Think of no apparel as casually chosen, as "innocent." Think of it as functioning in a situation, one that you can only guess, or imagine, or make up. Think of it as worn for a purpose. This may be as simple as keeping out the cold or the rain. But within the practicality there is choice.

Now consider the top. Here is where the director needs to have studied history, to have an understanding of what was worn at a particular time, what was the temper of those times, and how it was reflected in what people wore. Again no accidents. The choices came from the basic values of the society, who its heroes were, what its aspirations, what role religion played, what was esteemed, what hoped for. What was worn to frighten the enemy, what to seek favor from the gods of the time. What were men trying to say with what they wore? What parts of their bodies did women feature?

Then there is class, which has historical relevance of its own. Aristocracy was more special once, poverty meaner. Photographic journalism, travel, television, the Internet have made us more alike in what we want to wear. But not very long ago only the few wore the glamorous uniforms of the armies, and in every country the poor dressed as they had to because of climate and environment; they had little choice. Now the people of the world are more in touch with each other, imitate each other. Russian statesmen wear the same clothes, down to particular neckties, that ours do.

Knowledge of class, geography, history, religion, and sexual modes is part of a director's equipment, not only for giving him a range of choice but also in underlining the dramatic expression. All that information is modulated and molded to the individual character. The swing has to be from the most general to the most individual and particular, so that the costume will appear to be an expression of the character's soul.

Before we started making the film of *A Streetcar Named Desire,* Vivien Leigh sent me photos of herself as Blanche DuBois on stage in London. She looked like a dowdy English matron—worn-out classy, and certainly not a tattered Southern belle—ready for a walk in the English rain but not for Southern heat. The costumes were wrong for the character and wrong for the geography. I packed off my designer Lucinda Ballard to England to get her measurements and to brave Vivien's powerful will. That was merely the beginning of my struggle to get Vivien's Blanche out of the Midlands and into New Orleans. I got what I wanted where it counted, and she got an Oscar.

Expect the first question from the costume designer to be, What is it you want? The director makes very clear what the play or film needs, what the impression and execution should be. The director is the one to make the basic choice, and he or she can't do it intelligently unless he is informed, as if he was the character looking in the closet or drawer at the start of the day.

The Actors

They say I'm an acting director, which I don't take as a compliment. I don't really agree, but I do deal with actors a lot. I love actors. I was an actor for eight years, so I do appreciate their job. One of the most important things in an acting scene, especially a short acting scene, is not to talk about the scene that precedes but to play out the scene that precedes. You play out where the actors have come from psychologically so their ride into a scene is a correct one. . . .

Once you've done that, you divide the scene—or I tend to—into sections, into movements. Stanislavsky called them "beats." The point is that there are sections in life. Sometimes even a short scene has a three-act structure. You lay bare the actor, you make him understand and appreciate the structure beneath the lines. That's what's called the subtext, and dealing with the subtext is one of the critical elements in directing actors. In other words, not what is said, but what happens.

In general, actors or actresses must have the art in the accumulation of their past. Their life's experience is the director's material. They can have all the training, all the techniques their teachers have taught them—private moments, improvisations, substitutions, associative memories, and so on—but if the precious material is not within them, the director cannot get it out. That is why it's so important for the director to have an intimate acquaintance with the people he casts in his plays. If it's "there," he has a chance of putting it on the screen or on the stage. If not, not.

That is why the practice of making an actor read the lines of a part has no value for me and can even be misleading. The best line readers, I've learned, are not the best actors for my films, which is why I take actors for a walk or for dinner and probe into their lives. That is especially easy to do with actresses. Women are easily led to reveal to anyone who seems to be a friend the secrets of their intimate lives; it is their most essential drama.

Before I directed my first film, I believed that a good actor was a good actor in either medium. A stage actor has to maintain a performance night after night, so a technique is necessary. He has to be both believable and highly visible, has to have a good voice and a way with words. Some intelligence helps. But I saw that these requirements were not essential for the screen actor. What is required, I learned, besides an essential "animal" magnetism, is whatever's necessary to provide for the camera a true piece of experience. Whereas you can—and many effective actors do—get away with faking, posturing, and indicating emotions on stage, it's difficult if not impossible to get away with anything false before the camera. A close-up demands absolute truth; it's a severe and awesome trial. Acting for the screen is a more honest trade.

. . .

Everybody's problem is his talent, not his faults. My problem is that I can always make things forceful. I used to make every scene GO GO GO! Mounting to a climax, and if I had sixty minutes in a picture there were sixty climaxes. Ready? Climax! All right, rest a minute—CLIMAX! That was what I used to do. And it's easy to do, you know, make somebody shout, or grab somebody by the neck or throw somebody out, or slam a door, or open a window, or hit somebody with a hammer, or eat something quick in disgust—it's easy to do. It's bullshit! Bullshit! So you see what I mean, the problem of a man is his virtues, not his faults. It was my facility, my experience, my knowledge I had to watch for.

In my first twenty years of moviemaking, I chose more flamboyant actors. They were the engines of the film, and the film was the vehicle of their expression; it was always a question of expressing, of exteriorizing what there was "in" them, and the free course that I left to this flamboyance made me tend sometimes almost toward opera. But little by little I lost interest in this expression as such, and in fact I almost turned against it. I began, too, to restrain my actors, in proportion as I saw things in a truer, calmer fashion.

I took something from the theatre, and that something is still there. But regarding that, let me be more specific about some points. The essence of the Stanislavsky method, and the fundamental interest that it had for us, in the way in which we learned it as students and used it later, dwelt in the action. That is to say, when someone felt or experienced something, our feeling—and our theory—was that this emotion would never become "of" the theatre unless it were expressed as a need, a hunger. And it is of this need, of this hunger, that such-and-such a precise action sprang incarnated as expression of this hunger. The play became a series of progressions, each of which consisted of the fact that a person did a certain thing that responded to a certain want. We stressed the word "want," and we did our best to emerge on the word "do." In short: To do. To want. To do.

The result was that our performances in the theatre, especially in the form in which I expressed myself at the start, were extremely violent, violent and amusing. But today, when I observe life, I see it takes much less direct paths, circuitous paths, subtle and subterranean. Moreover, when the actor is aware of this aim—because the director has pointed it out to him or he has analyzed it himself—he cannot but distance himself from life to the extent to which, in life, people are

Clockwise from top left:
With Richard Boone in *The Arrangement;* Eli Wallach and Carroll Baker in *Baby Doll;* Stathis Giallelis in *America America;* Julie Harris in *East of Eden.*

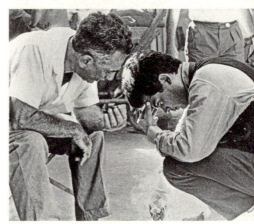

uncertain ultimately as to what they want. They oscillate, wander, drift, in relation to their aim—or they change their aim. In short, they want this, then that, but . . . but *that* is life, and it is there that the poetry of life dwells, in these contradictions, these sudden defections, these aspirations that spring up and disconcert. In short, while I once had a unilinear approach to life, I now interest myself more and more in the complexity of things.

I put terrific stress on what the person wants and why he wants it. What makes it meaningful for him. I don't start on how he goes about getting it until I get him wanting it. And then I make clear the circumstances under which he behaves; what happens before, and so on. Then I try to find the physical behavior, without preconception on my part if possible, but from what the actor does to achieve his objective under the circumstances.

It's also important for a director to know a lot about his actors as people. Not that you talk about their lives, but you begin to find out what affects them, what they love and hate, what's meaningful to them, how they react, how they do things.

It is very difficult to work with actors. Because the life that most of them live is a life of cafés. There is the school, the café, the stage, the studios. . . . Life cannot leave its marks on their faces. They do not live the despairing life that human beings live. They are for the most part childish, spoiled, plump, their faces have not been distorted or illuminated . . . in short, they do not bear on them the marks of life lived. It is very rare to find an actor who has that, and still more rare to find one who can play that.

I've generally liked actors I've worked with. But in the few exceptions, I believe the very things that annoyed me—their extra spirit, their pride, even their arrogance—turned out to be the most useful, admirable, thrilling, the things I needed most. Above all, in the case of the arrogant ones, I needed their energy and their passion to be good.

After all, I can be pretty damned proud and arrogant myself.

What I have to discover is whether what nettles me contains a bond with elements of my own character. Is there a bond between them and the part they are going to play and, even more important, with the theme of the film you are going to make? Just getting a "good actor," an able technician of the stage or screen, is not enough. You will end up with a British film. Find brothers and sisters who've been through a bit of what you've been through.

Everybody makes fun of the "method." Strasberg made it devious, deep, tricky, special. But it's the simplest thing—and especially obvious when it comes to casting. I have an idea for an actor to play a role. I don't know why. It's a hunch. But I have responded to something in that actor. So I say, "Let's take a walk."

And as we walk, I bring up various subjects, and we talk. I act innocent. But as we talk, I find out why I responded to the actor so strongly. That gossipy walk about love and marriage and nationality and parents is the essence of the job of casting.

The director finds out with minimal cleverness what his material is.

The material is this actor. What does he feel, what are the hidden elements of his personality, what life has he? Who is he?

If you find you don't like them as people, don't employ them. Make this decision, as it has to be made, early.

It is not essential that you should want to fuck the leading lady, but it is essential that you should feel emotions well past those of ordinary friendship and respect. Something about each actor, male or female, should delight and surprise you and even be capable of upsetting you. They should stir you, one way or another, as you hope the characters in the script will stir the audience.

There is no reason, I suppose, why the actors in the main roles should like you—but they should. This is important to investigate as early and as deeply as possible.

The production of a play or a film is deeper than a professional bond. It's deeper than a marriage because it is more fundamental. A marriage can be successful despite the fact that the pair have certain intellectual or temperamental disagreements. But if you find you have those disagreements with an actor you're proposing to put in an important part, beware!

So investigate. See if your ideas for the production or for the role arouse him or her. If not, stop! You can't like or agree with everyone.

But it's deeper than that. See if your very closeness, your presence, arouses him or her. You're going to be working with this person day and night for a very long time and in very difficult circumstances. And by contrast to a marriage, you have to get along.

You will probably find, since you're probably a son-of-a-bitch yourself, that you will get along better with a difficult actor than with a tame one.

But your connection with the actor should be stronger than cordiality of any kind. The play and the role should become a cause, something you and the actor are doing for a deep reason. That is part of getting close. The friendship you should develop with the actor playing your leading role should be more intense than the simple buddy-buddy relationship. Cordiality is not enough.

Respect is not enough. In fact it is dangerous. I respected Helen Hayes. I found I did not like her, and I distrusted her influence on the cast. She divided the cast into those who were her partisans and those who were mine. It had a bad result. I began to dislike going to the theatre. Helen needed buttering up.

If the relationship is a true and deep one, there is a danger—things are liable to get mixed up—but it is one you can risk because the rewards exceed the danger.

Final Cut

Why do many filmmakers consider France the most civilized country to work in? One reason is that you can schedule your workday from noon to seven. A light lunch is served during the shooting. The French and other Europeans prefer to eat dinner at nine or ten. They are thus assured a period of nocturnal play and a good sleep into the morning hours.

But that is only a casual reason. The real reason is that in France total artistic control belongs to the director by law. This is not challenged. In America the right to edit your film and be assured it will remain as you want it is a matter of contract negotiation, and this battle of words and clauses is won by a director only after he has had a run of financially successful films. In the years when my films made money, I had the contractual right of "final cut." When my films were no less worthy but did not make as much money, I was unable to secure this right.

This is absurd, of course, because how the bits of film that you photographed are chosen and arranged is as much a part of the creative process as any other part of filmmaking. An anxious producer, who has power derived from paying the film editor his salary every week, can be a terror, ruining the work of the director, actors, and everyone else. It is difficult for a director to police the cutting room when he has left the lot. Just before it opened and without my participation, snips and bits were taken out of my film of *A Streetcar Named Desire*, altering the scenes' intent to satisfy the censors. I made a public stink, but it had no effect.

All kinds of brilliant ideas, not those of the person who made the film, sprout in executive offices. Discussions are held between the producer and his agent, his wife, the money men, and sometimes even the stars, all in an effort to "save" the film, which means having the film make as much money as possible. These spurts of wisdom are the result of anxiety and nerves and have little to do with the filmmaker's original intentions. Everybody has good ideas in this anxious, dangerous time, a time when good ideas are not the point. The point is to realize the original intention of the filmmaker.

A great film cannot be made by consensus. In the late 1920s and 1930s—the first great period of American films—it was the unquestioned right of the major directors to cut their own films. They developed the shooting script with the writers. But by the time I got to Hollywood in the mid-1940s, the power was shifting. The industry was increasingly dominated by producers. Everyone at MGM served the wishes of the elite producers, and these producers did everything upside down as far as I was concerned—they bought the novels and plays, commissioned original screenplays, oversaw the writers, and when they had what would pass for a shooting script, they found the director. The director of course should have come first, for he is the one to enforce unity of intention. For David O. Selznick, producing was not enough: No matter what the credit lines read, in the end he directed and edited the movie and wrote the screenplay—if the photographer or director didn't do as he dictated, he fired them.

Today it is the people who put up the money who decide its use. They have turned an art into an industry, and the director into merely one of many functionaries. That is how these men will it, because in that contest they can rule everyone working on the film and they can supervise every choice. They select the film editor who, in most cases, becomes their servant. If they don't like what the film editor does, they replace him with another who is more pliable. They select the cameraman, and often they demand that he make the film as "pretty" as possible, with candy colors and clear definitions of all events no matter what the director was trying to create. Mood is a curse word to them.

Maybe the title "director" should be struck from the language since it implies one function among many. The correct word is "filmmaker," which implies a total process, one person responsible for everything, all decisions coming from the center.

Management

It's a question of power. Nothing less. Don't give anyone the power to distort what you're making. If it's a choice of control or money, take less money. You're better off. "Produced and Directed" is what you want. It's the only correct principle. Of course, a director needs staff help: set, office, financial assistants, and managers. And someone has to raise the money, enough money so that you can make the movie you want, but it's better to slim the budget than to concede power to a producer. You must be the boss, however quietly you speak, however gentle your smile, however agreeable your manners.

I've had all types of producers. When asked to direct a completed script by a producer, I had to remind myself (and once stifled the thought with tragic consequences) that the producer will own the film you make and do what he wants with your work. At the start, he will be a gracious host (his specialty, often), promising to give you a free hand. (No matter what he says, get an astute lawyer to read the contract.) But in the end, when a serious difference arises (and all differences as the work nears the end are serious), he will win. You are just an employee. You both talked a good game, but the fact remains that he owns the negative, and he'll do what he thinks necessary. He'll have good reasons and bring in respected witnesses (who agree with him, of course) to back him, and you will find yourself powerless. So when you're looking for money, if a producer shows up promising what you need in exchange for ultimate control, cut your needs, find another way, reduce the budget. Generally, the more money you take for your services, the less power you'll have. Take less than what you deserve; make the film on a smaller budget. Gamble on profit. The job itself is a gamble. If the film makes money, you will be well compensated; if not, you won't be living with the shame of having sold yourself to someone who doesn't share your aims.

I don't much like the alternative of a partnership with a producer who comes on with the argument that we are old friends, trusted allies, men who "think alike," and so on. Get the words "final cut" in the contract! I know money is a great seducer, and what's wrong with a friendship between producer and director? Nothing. It's great as long as you don't have to work together. No one, you'll find, thinks the same way you do. And you'll also find that in the interest of maintaining that old friendship, you'll make those little gentle compromises—compromises that will destroy your work. The friendship will finally be put at risk. And the producer-pal, who hasn't spent twenty-four hours a day on the set, isn't as tired as you are, is still thinking clearly, is not emotionally involved with the cast, and will make "very good sense" when you can't. And he'll bring in the witnesses and the jury, because he'll be dealing with the marketing of your film, and you'll discover that's where he's been looking, and is still looking, more ardently than ever.

In the theatre, if you and the playwright have, from the beginning, been consulting, the producer will be up against it to fight with that twosome. The best experiences I've had came when the playwright and I were as one. It is inevitable that the producer will try to slip in between you. The day will come when he inquires of you if he can speak to the playwright without you there. *Say no.* Remind the playwright to say no. And stick to it. You know the playwright's intentions, and he knows yours. That's your safeguard. But in film, it's more difficult. The end product is in pieces. The producer has easy contact with the cutter. He owns the film. The show (as a whole) is not running before the eyes of everyone concerned. There are often dangerous lapses when you, exhausted by a long shooting schedule, return to your home or go for a rest and are off the scene. Then, since he owns the film, he can experiment with different arrangements. And he will. "Just let me show it to you," he will say. Answer with one word: "No." "Let's get a reading from an audience," he'll say. Say "No." Do it your way. Making a film is, as you've seen, a supreme act of ego. It's your film, or should be, and the contract, when you have finally won power, should protect you. See to it, when your lawyer meets with his lawyer, that the contract does protect you in all imaginable circumstances.

The danger may come when the producer succeeds in partly winning over a star performer, by making him or her uneasy about what will happen to their careers if things remain as you have them. The simplest thing to say is that no one knows how the film should be except you and "Read the contract!" and stick to it, unreasonable as that sounds to everyone who has gathered around to watch the fun.

There isn't much you can do about the astonishing and desperate marketing ideas that come up when the fear grows that the finished work might not be commercial enough, especially if you've taken a lot of up-front money. Money makes its own terms. Even walking away doesn't help. So don't threaten that. You will have made an orphan of your film and left it in the hands of someone you've learned sees it differently. So stay close, fight, however uselessly, and join in the promotion and the advertising. There are directors who consider themselves above such crass concerns. That is absurd. You've made the film and by doing that hoped that people will come and see it, respond to it, be affected by it. Your job isn't finished until they do. Fight to the end. The film is your film. Besides, it's fun. Think of quarrels and fights over keeping the integrity of your work as fun, a pleasure. Make sure to keep a diary, day to day, of who says what, who does what. You'll have a record of extraordinary events, especially if you don't worry about sparing anyone's feelings.

Is all this unadulterated arrogance (supposedly a bad word)? If so, so be it. Will I never be engaged again to produce and direct another movie? So what. I'm through making movies, and I can say what I want now. Arrogance, however disguised, is the essence of every artist. What could be more arrogant than saying, "Pay attention to what I've done, it's of great worth and importance." The energy to paint, compose, sculpt, be an architect, comes from a belief that is without qualification at least during the hour of creation. When someone calls you arrogant, don't deny it. Smile and gently say, "Yes, I suppose I am."

A Director and His Energy

They've all said it. "Directing is a young man's game." And time passing proves them right.

What goes first? With an athlete, the legs go first. A director stands all day, even when he's provided with chairs, jeeps, and limos. He walks over to an actor, stands alongside and talks to him; with a star he may kneel at the side of the chair where his treasure sits. The legs do get weary. Mine have. I didn't think it would happen because I've taken care of my body, always exercised. But I suddenly found I don't want to play singles. Doubles, okay. I stand at the net when my partner serves, and I don't have to cover as much ground. But even at that . . .

I notice also that I want a shorter game—that is to say also, shorter workdays, which is the point. In conventional directing, the time of day when the director has to be most able, most prepared to push the actors hard and get what he needs, usually the close-ups of the so-called "master scene," is in the afternoon. A director can't afford to be tired in the late afternoon. That is also the time—after the thoughtful quiet of lunch—when he must correct what has not gone well in the morning. He better be prepared, he better be good.

The crew takes its tone, its spirit from the director. When he drives himself, they drive themselves to match. At the least sign of weariness, they go slack. Often the director wants to drive them—and himself too—to one final burst of work in the late afternoon. He needs all the energy he ever had to do that, and all that is now a memory. So the days grow shorter.

Even when the director is able to pump up his energy, at least his show of the old-time energy, it is often energy without passion. Everybody has that. That doesn't do the job. For one thing, there is a diminution of the arrogance that a director needs. You don't like the word arrogance? Call it pride. He's got to be sure that what he's asking for is right and that therefore he can overcome all obstacles of indifference and doubt and all other viewpoints except his own, especially the self-ish views of actors who don't like the scene "for themselves."

I've noticed this loss of energy in myself. And something more disheartening. I have been finding that I can't concentrate on my reading. I've depended on reading all my life. It has been my most precious way of participating in the world of others and understanding my own world. Now I start a page of a book I like, and barely halfway down, I find that my mind has wandered. It's gone elsewhere. So I go back and pick up somewhere in that page, now very aware that my mind won't stay fastened to what I'm reading, try to keep it going where I want it to be. That effort of itself is a diffusion of attention. And before I know why or where it's gone, my mind has wandered again. It takes me two or three times as long now to read any book.

Here's something worse. I keep falling asleep. I go along reading or watching TV or just listening to others, and before I know it, I'm about to fall asleep. Or have. I wake myself and force myself to attention. But suddenly I'm keeling over again and am sleeping.

I can get through with that problem, but there is a more terrible development. I've lost my empathy. I don't emotionally and personally connect. I'm in danger of becoming an automaton. There was a time when I used my anger. I was dependent on my sexual interest in a scene, call it empathy, to transmit some of that to the actors. I no longer have that kind of sexual feeling. Sex has become sympathetic companionship, not desire. I don't really need fucking anymore. Why can't I get along perfectly well without it? I ask myself. The answer to that question is: "You can." I can. And I do.

My humor is gentler. It's old man's humor. It used to have an element of scorn. It was a guffaw, not a chuckle. It's gentler now, the laughter. It goes with a shrug. It was once the humor of outrage. That's gone. It's "pleasant" now.

Of course, the daring is not there. I don't look for outrageous subjects that will get a lot of people angry. I couldn't do *On the Waterfront* now. I don't look for dangerous locations. *Baby Doll*. Or even uncomfortable ones to "try" myself. *Wild River*, for instance. I don't look forward now to going to Turkey and shooting the continuation of *America America*. I'm a little afraid. When I do, I wish I could live in the luxury and ease and comfort of the Istanbul Hilton with my wife while I am shooting. But it would be destructive. In the old days, I searched for locations with something of the primitive about them. It was an artistic tenet of mine that to be uncomfortable was necessary; if we were comfortable, the film would stink. I used to like to shoot in the rain. Now I protect myself. I appreciate comfort. I'm fragile.

Or am I? The fact is that I am planning to go to Turkey and Lesvos, an island without a halfway decent hotel, and shoot the toughest picture of my life.* An impossible film in an impossible location, with armies tossed between victory and defeat, and a city destroyed by flames. Why? That is the arrogance I am talking about. I don't want to be a lesser man, and being what I want to be or used to be involves

---

* The film, *Beyond the Aegean*, with a screeenplay by Kazan's son Chris, was part of Kazan's immigrant odyssey, taking Stavros Topouzoglou back to Anatolia years after the escape described in *America America*. (*The Anatolian* and *The Arrangement* are also parts of the odyssey.) Kazan was casting, choosing locations, and doing research for the film between his seventy-ninth year and his early eighties. But because financing fell through, it was never made, and Kazan reworked the material for the novel, published in 1994.

energy, fearlessness, and an insatiable taste for difficulties. Arrogance is a necessity!

So I'm preparing and casting, and another unfortunate development has become revealed to me. I don't know actors anymore. I have to use a casting director, a functionary I used to scorn. I usually had the screenplay cast before I finished writing or preparing it. I knew, always knew, what actors I wanted. And they were always "my kind of actor or actress." Now I flounder, thinking of this one and that, but always unsure. I don't have that absolute conviction about acting talent I used to have. And I don't take the chances that I used to take with unknowns. Well, I do, but I worry like hell about it. I keep asking myself, "Are you sure she's right for it?" I'm not.

I know when all this uncertainty started. At seventy-six, I'd plunged deep into an autobiography and felt proud of it, believed there wasn't a man living who could write about himself as boldly as I did. But as soon as I got through, I was seventy-eight and I said to myself, "It's good you started when you did. A year later would have been too late." I know damned well that I couldn't write that autobiography now. I don't have what it takes anymore.

García Márquez says that senility has come when you experience your first fall. The next fall, he says, kills you. My time is growing near. I wobble on my feet now, and my children have noticed it. My wife too. I've almost fallen several times, well, hell, I have fallen but caught myself against a wall just in time. The first one who noticed it was my son Nick. He said, "You look at the ground all the time when you walk now." So I'm aware of it, and I've tried to keep my head up. Even when I sit in a chair and have my breakfast, my head juts forward like an old man's, or it droops. It's begun to happen, senility. Foolishness!

Old age is a crime to nature, I know, but I don't wish I was dead or that I'd died last night in my sleep. Of course, I can't avoid the most incriminating evidence of all. I don't raise a hard-on like I used to. I bless my fidelity for this unhappy development, for marital fidelity disobliges me from having affairs. At the same time, I don't dare to now. I wouldn't do well, I'd be embarrassed.

Well, here's the truth. I'm about to embark, like a damned fool, on the most difficult and most trying film of my life. What makes me do it? It's to save my life. That's the simplest way to say it. What the hell am I when I'm not an artist of some kind, and specifically what am I when I'm not directing? "It will get you going again," my wife tells me. She urges me on. The only fear she has is that I might meet some young actress who will go for me. And not take no for an answer. I have already encountered such a lady or two, but I don't feel I have to prove some goddamn point about myself, and I remain quiet and kindly and sympathetic, and listen well.

The live part of me is still that need to be daring and take the risk and prove myself a man. And that means activating myself. I could relax like Joe Mankiewicz and enjoy my savings (modest indeed) and watch other directors come up and excel and go to the Actors Studio and be the grand old man. But that would sicken me, and I'd die for sure. Why go on? What's the choice? Death. I've seen people die, and I've often noticed a willingness to give up, to surrender it all.

An old friend, a veteran director and one of the best [in the margin is the name Billy Wilder], said, "Directing is a young man's game." To prove it, he made, toward the end of his life and out of habit, several indifferent films and spent most of his time doing what he preferred, enjoying his seaside home, football, his excellent wife, and his companions at cards. He was, it seemed, proving his point.

There is another, deeper cause for his spiritual shrinking and surrender to comfort. When the director is young and contemplates the intensely competitive industry where he hopes to make his mark, he sets himself the most absolute standards. He will outdo the great directors whom he adulated when he was beginning, or at least share their company in world esteem. He will make the most ambitious and original films—he will climb to the top. And there will be no limit to what he will ask of himself artistically.

As the years go by, he moderates his goals. He becomes sensible, knows he will never make it that far up the side of the cliff. He is more realistic about what he can and cannot do. When it comes to perhaps being a member of the elite of his profession, he has already made a number of films that, while they are worthy and even pride-provoking (*his* pride), nevertheless cannot be considered among the best films made. He has already done his best work, they are on record. There are very few men over sixty-five who can still be aroused by the prospect of goals beyond those they have already reached, or who still yearn with the degree of desperation necessary to compete with the great artists they admire.

What's happened? "He's lost it," people say. But what's the "it"? Energy? A very simple word for a complex phenomenon. But consider when an artist is young, he gets out of bed with a hard-on, is mean as spit in the morning and ready to chew up the world. When he's sixty-five, he wakes up relaxed, warm, and thoughtful, as well as wise—which usually means gentler, agreeable, and better tempered—and is given to lingering in bed. He rarely wants more than he has out of life, and he doesn't know what that more might be. Nor does he want what is unique and extraordinary, and often that is because it will cost him more energy and devotion than he has to spend.

He wishes to remain calm no matter what the circumstances. So that the prospect of dealing with a difficult and temperamental actress, whom he believes is the only one able to bring the script alive, suddenly seems to be more than he need put up with. He doesn't have the patience—or energy—to deal with her. "I'm too old for that shit."

One of the first things to go with the diminution of energy is a sense of humor. An actor who is always cutting up and whom he once would have valued for lowering the tension on the set now seems to be frivolous or silly and a distraction. The director can no longer tolerate this kind of fun, and he doesn't know why. It's generally nothing more than half-baked jokes, the actor's cover-up for anxiety, the director knows that, but it seems he has lost patience with it or with anything else except the steady progress of the work. "What am I when I'm not working?" he asks himself. Still deep down, he wants the film over and done with.

Surprises and sudden revelations from his collaborators no longer come as gifts that he's grateful for and embraces. They try his patience. Something has happened to the director's soul. He has become a professional director and notices that, after a few weeks halfway through the schedule, he may consider it a noose and secretly wish to get out of the job. He wants to go back to his quiet life, read a few books and scripts from writer friends, take the trip to the Serengeti with his children that he's been promising them for twenty years, then return to his old sidekicks beachside, men who don't challenge him.

The sudden appearance of a surprising event in his personal life that might once have stirred dormant emotions no longer has its rebellious effect. These are of course new love interests. He has cautioned himself, lying in bed in the morning, or on his ottoman, fresh coffee at his side, surrounded by order and affection, that he has what he wants and he must not chance losing it. He doesn't want to be bothered with a young stranger, a ravishing girl offering herself to be ravished. He doesn't really want the order he has to be disturbed. When emotional adventures are presented to him, he quickly finds he doesn't have the energy to embark on them—even though it occurs to him that such adventure might be the fountain of youth and restore him to what he once was.

Then something terrible happens at the end of a day's work, at the very hour of the day when all the most important psychological scenes are to be shot, that time of the afternoon when the director used to desperately hope for, and was sometimes awarded, inspiration. What occurs now? Nothing. Precisely that. He doesn't have the energy at four-thirty to get up out of his chair and arouse his actors to their task. "We'll do it first thing in the morning," the director says to artists and crew, perhaps hoping that rest will revive his emotional interest in what he's doing. Of course sleep has the opposite effect. "Perhaps I don't need that scene in the film after all," he tells himself. And goes home.

But the worst of all happens on the day when he accidentally uncovers notes he made twenty years before for "his favorite project, his supremely personal film," notes that he has been accumulating for years. He reads these notes and recalls how passionately aroused he was by the ideas they contained when he wrote them. When he thinks about it, he finds he still believes he has the makings, at least the kernel, of a great final film for himself, perhaps his "masterpiece." But something happened along the way. What was once alive in those notes is still a valid and valuable idea, but he doesn't care enough about this material, his "final" statement, and is unable or simply unwilling to make his old dream come true. He lingers over this depressing acknowledgment—this inner event; for a few days it depresses him. He may eventually conclude that he perhaps hasn't paid enough in the way of personal, painful experiences, hasn't risked enough in his life's course, to be able to make the film he dreamed of. But even if that is true, he doesn't care.

Why not leave his life where it is? He's had an acceptable career, earned general esteem, and has many good memories. Why spoil it all by an effort that is bound to fail to bring him what he once had and to put in question what he once achieved?

He settles for being a good soul. He contributes to charities, attends conferences on the art of film as a distinguished panel member, and helps young people getting started. He accepts a seat on the national board of the Directors Guild of America, an institution he respects, and there he is awarded the special distinction of Life Member. He's certainly earned it.

The director must recognize that it is very difficult to fight one's way back to the vanished self; it's painful. But one day, in the spring or fall, those unstable months, suppose he surprises himself and wants it all back, whatever it was he once had. Suppose he is eccentric enough to want to test himself again. Suppose he merely wants to prevent the death he feels coming on him. He wants the old fire back, burning where it was in his good days. It's a question of a rebirth. What he's lost, he now recognizes, is the very source of what artistic inspiration he once had and enjoyed.

He looks at his last films and finds them disappointing, lesser stuff, in fact, failures. They seem to lack some essential emotion he once had that supplied the fuel that drove him. What was it? Anger, desire, competition? "Why," he asks himself, "do I no longer feel what I once felt?" He knows the answer. He no longer really believes in himself, is no longer certain that he has that final energy—or that he can bring it back. Perhaps it's gone for good. Which only makes him want it more.

Is it a question of isolating what he once had, reawakening it, and so perhaps coming to believe again that he has something special to say? He's not sure he has. But he wants to give it a try, wants to make one final fundamental effort.

He finds that he has only one source for this intimate energy: his own life. He must make a film, however disguised, about a problem that is alive and kicking for him, that occupies every moment of his existence. His own feelings, however negative or devalued, are the most genuine he has: his anger and self-disgust, his essential unrest, his doubt about his own worth. He must put himself in danger, on the mortal block, and there, sacrificing all vanity, pride, until the life blood runs, there find rebirth through pain.

Then to his surprise he finds that those feelings of disappointment, fear, infinite sadness, all those black emotions are the realest he's felt for a long time. His negativism is more worthy of respect than his old ebullient optimism. It is in his despair that he is in touch with truer emotions—and the most universal. They will, once expressed, affect all men because the theme of decline and failure that I have attributed to an aging director applies to us all. And the yearning for a reawakening, a leap back, is also universal.

When one's belief in his or her own life fails, it can only be revived by delving deep into the subject, fearlessly, mercilessly. "Who the hell am I after all? Am I truly a successful artist? Who will in the end respect and remember me?" The answers are not flattering, but the very questions arouse the only true emotion he's felt for a long time.

Such crises—"I have not lived up to my hopes for myself. I am not what I should be. I am worthless. I don't know who I am anymore"— take place in the lives of all sensitive souls. Self-doubt is the curse of an artist's life. Also his blessing. Often it is the key to his talent and so to his reawakening. His pain is the real thing—it is not just drama—and he should hold on to that emotion. And give it full dramatic play. Within his own darkness is the only place where the essential energy he now lacks can be found. That painful and shameful thing, that discouraging echo he hears bouncing off the cavern walls of his soul, is the essential energy he needs. He must put himself and his talent and his career in mortal danger, and he will live again only as he emerges from it.

The Fountain of Youth is in yourself.

Afterword
Robert Cornfield

The first and indelibly defining productions of Arthur Miller's *Death of a Salesman* and Tennessee Williams's *A Streetcar Named Desire*—along with Eugene O'Neill's late plays, the most significant American dramas of the twentieth century—were directed by Elia Kazan. As Kazan would have been the first to protest, "directed by" is a meanly limited, misleading term for his contribution to the plays and movies he commanded. Early on in his Broadway career he required the credit "The Elia Kazan Production of . . ." His films, after the first ones, would be entitled "An Elia Kazan Production," with variants such as "Elia Kazan's Production of *Splendor in the Grass,*" "Elia Kazan's Production of John Steinbeck's *East of Eden,*" and the let's-not-beat-around-the-bush "Elia Kazan's *America America.*" The name above the title, as it was with Cecil B. DeMille, Alfred Hitchcock, and Frank Capra. After his grounding stint with Twentieth Century–Fox, Kazan refused to be a studio-contract pushover; instead, he was an *auteur*—molding and reworking and writing his scripts, overseeing casting, costuming, the music—he was the producer as well as the director, and more. He finagled with the censors, wrote the ads, quarreled over distribution. A mighty constituent of the demand for control is distrust—which he sometimes defined as his arrogance—and like the heroes of his best films, *On the Waterfront* and *America America,* he battled the brutish forces ranged to quash his freedom, his right to work, and his integrity. The engines of his most personal work are not the losers Blanche DuBois and Willy Loman but the defiant battlers Zapata, *East of Eden*'s Cal Trask, *On the Waterfront*'s Terry Malloy, *Baby Doll*'s Silva Vacarro, *America America*'s Stavros Topouzoglou, *The Arrangement*'s Eddie Anderson. All of them liberate themselves from a stultifying misconception of who they are. All of them ask and answer the first questions of existence: Where do I come from? Who am I? What do I want?

Kazan, born in Istanbul of Anatolian Greek Orthodox descent, immigrated to the United States from Turkey when he was four. He disappointed his father by not following him into the family rug-import business; instead, setting an example for his younger brothers, he attended a good college and planned for a life not delimited by the Old Country. His father's disapproval motored his intuitional rebelliousness, and his feelings of exclusion from indigenous American society were not assuaged as he busboyed his way through Williams College. In the early years of the Depression, happenstance brought him to the theatre, for which he had shown no youthful inclination. After graduating from Williams, he followed a friend to Yale Drama School because he had nothing else in mind; the theatre's very improbability as a profession was perhaps its most attractive appeal. The other surprise was his aptitude for all of it. He was a smart self-educated technician and stage manager; he had a quick sense of play construction; and as a dynamic performer, he had an almost instinctive grasp of acting technique. (From the 1940 movie *City for Conquest* we can gauge his triumphant stage performances in the Clifford Odets plays *Waiting for Lefty* and *Golden Boy*.) But he wanted the Big Job; he wanted to be a Director. Less than ten years after being allowed into the renegade Group Theatre as an unpaid apprentice, he was directing Broadway shows with stars like Tallulah Bankhead and Helen Hayes (never forgiving either of them for their temperamental grandstanding) and Mary Martin (suggesting her for the role of Blanche DuBois).

The Group's ambition to revolutionize American theatre was also a revolt against the genteel bigotry of commercial Broadway, which—except for producers, musical composers, and performers—was mainly off limits to Jews. Original members Luther and Stella Adler were the children of the Yiddish theatre giant Jacob Adler, and Morris Carnovsky was already a Yiddish theatre star; Harold Clurman and Lee Strasberg, the Group's guiding forces with Cheryl Crawford, had exchanged religious orthodoxy for fervid theatrical radicalism. The rebelliousness of the outsiders suited Kazan perfectly, since he was acutely sensitive to his status as an emigrant, but the Group's relationship to the Jewish heritage of most of its members had a peculiar air of, if not denial, then cloudiness: Its first major production was Paul Green's *The House of Connelly*, set on a fallen Southern plantation, and it took the company some years to make their grandest effect with a Jewish-themed play, Odets's *Awake and Sing!* Something of the Group's indirection infiltrates Arthur Miller's 1949 *Death of a Salesman,* which avoids specifying the Lomans' religion, as some contemporary critics noted. If Miller was generalizing the tragedy, whose idea was it that a Jewish family's saga could not be universal? Two years before *Salesman,* Kazan had directed the film *Gentleman's Agreement,* a notable "exposé of anti-Semitism" that had only one Jew in a leading role, John Garfield. A Group Theatre alumnus, Garfield made a token appearance as a character not intrinsic to the plot. Was Kazan chosen as director because he was thought Jewish by association? Themes of assimilation into American society by radicalism and social criticism underlie much of Kazan's work.

Before he met up with Arthur Miller and Tennessee Williams, boy-wonder Kazan was a 1940s hit-maker, with forgotten or slightly recalled plays such as *Harriet, Jacobowsky and the Colonel, One Touch of Venus, The Skin of Our Teeth,* and *Deep Are the Roots.* But this was not good enough, not the kind of success he really aimed at. His 1930s tutelage under stringent artistic moralists Clurman and Strasberg and a brush with moviemaking (both radical and as an assistant to Hollywood director Lewis Milestone) had cultivated in him grand aspirations. Later *Death of a Salesman,* Miller's attack on the American bitch goddess success (to whose wiles Kazan sensibly succumbed), offered Kazan, as director, a palliative bit of self-flagellation.

Kazan had three sequential and overlapping careers, as stage director, filmmaker, and writer. He was passionately committed to all three. Fervor, alertness, rigorous candor, emotional truth, energy, zest, and ethical and psychological ambiguities are the marks he stamps on his work. His novels, a retreat from a faltered film career, are not very good, but they gave him the full independence he always struggled for, and he was more joyful at the typewriter than he had been providing other writers with a platform. In the mid-1980s he wrote a lacerating, indiscreet, and exuberant autobiography that was as contentious and challenging as the best of his film and theatre work. But in the end, film was the form that meant the most to him.

Before the advent of D. W. Griffith, film technique—framing, movement, acting in a style fit for the camera, editing—was still finding its way; Griffith (along with John Ford, one of Kazan's masters), by development and extension and scale, elevated film into an art. Similarly, Kazan reformed American film acting—he codified and deepened a movement toward complex characterization and a more vivid filmic sense of reality. His semidocumentary manner, with a penchant for violence, joined to intense and emotionally fraught acting, determined the course of American film from the 1950s on. His first film, the 1945 *A Tree Grows in Brooklyn,* may seem unremarkable now, both stagy and sentimental, but its ensemble performances were tellingly different from what had previously been accepted as naturalistic acting. New styles in acting are not necessarily better than older ones, and American movies of the 1910s through the 1950s had burst with great performances, from Lillian Gish and Walter Huston, Bette Davis and Greta Garbo, John Barrymore and Charlie Chaplin and Buster Keaton. But Kazan's direction of *Tree* encouraged a unified approach from the cast and intimate playing by James Dunn and Peggy Ann Garner (both won Academy Awards): The camera seemed to capture a new refinement of emotional detail, a legible display of vulnerability and thought. This wasn't the moviemaking that Kazan most admired—he directed it as if it were a stage piece, he later said. But the acting is not stage acting—it is acting set before a camera, not a live audience. It was playing of a sort one found in French movies of the 1930s, in the films, for instance, of Jean Renoir and Marcel Pagnol, but for American film it was an innovation. James Agee, in his contemporary review in *The Nation,* registered that Kazan's direction of Peggy Ann Garner brought out her personal qualities in service of the character, handling "what I take to be her rigidity as an actress, turning it into a part of her personal visual charm, and of the role she is in those respects so well suited for."

Agee was less happy with the meticulous set re-creation of the turn-of-the-century Brooklyn streets and apartment. No matter how worthy the detail, "the best you can do in that way is as dead as an inch-by-inch description of a perfectly naturalistic painting, compared with accepting instead the still scarcely imagined difficulties and the enormous advantages of submerging your actors in the real thing."

Kazan felt the same way, more so after the arid, big-studio soundstages and grooved, implacable machinery of Metro-Goldwyn-Mayer defeated his second film, the dismal *Sea of Grass.* No matter how demoralized he was by the circumstances, Kazan had to accept responsibility for its sloggy pace and erratic playing. Things improved mightily with his third film, *Boomerang!,* produced for Twentieth Century–Fox by Louis de Rochemont, who had two years before supervised the trendsetting docudrama *The House on 92nd Street,* also based on an actual case. *Boomerang!* was a hit—and this time James Agee had praise: "Elia Kazan's *Boomerang!* is a work of journalistic art, which isn't necessarily a paradox, and of that kind is perfect." Filmed on location in Stamford, Connecticut, *Boomerang!* was cast with New York actors, among them Kazan "regulars" Lee J. Cobb, Arthur Kennedy, and Ed Begley, and as "extras" his uncle Joe Kazan (whose story he would tell in *America America*) and Arthur Miller, the author of his next Broadway production, *All My Sons.* The film proved a breakthrough for Kazan. He had learned through frustrating experience that Hollywood studio methods were not for him, that he preferred actors trained in emotional and psychological rigor, that he needed real streets and broad vistas, that his interest was contemporary social issues, and that he would not find his unique contribution, his "voice," unless the film had reverberant personal significance.

His next works for producer Darryl Zanuck, *Gentleman's Agreement* (winning the Academy Award for Best Director) and *Pinky,* substantiated his reputation as something more than a dependable team player. At the same time he set high the standard for Broadway achievement with his productions of *A Streetcar Named Desire* and *Death of a Salesman;* without drawing a breath, he also established the supreme institute for advanced professional theatrical training, the Actors Studio. Without the imprimatur of Studio membership (you had to be invited in), one simply did not qualify as a method actor. The near-legend grew that being directed by Kazan would make you a star, that his guidance of a playwright would grant genius, and that his knapsack held success for any movie or play he touched.

That was the 1940s. The 1950s would be different.

Real and fake New Orleans figured heavily in Kazan's two films of 1950. Its docks, streets, and bars were the locations for another "true to life" story, *Panic in the Streets.* In the cast was Barbara Bel Geddes, who had starred in his 1945 stage hit *Deep Are the Roots,* and stalwart performances came from Richard Widmark and Paul Douglas. But best were an implacable and bloodless Jack Palance as the villain and Zero Mostel as a panicked and sweating underling. The new element for Kazan was active influence over the camerawork; only visual control would allow him to believe himself a true moviemaker. Without the streetwise basic training of *Panic* and *Boomerang!,* Kazan would not have had the cojones for the Hoboken docks of his greatest film triumph, *On the Waterfront.* In the later years of his film career he relaxed his molding of the performances. In the 1970s, he admitted,

"I'm not as interested in the minutiae, in the small psychological turns, as I used to be—I'm interested in broader strokes now. I don't explain everything as I used to; I'm not psychologizing so much."

From the real New Orleans he moved to a Warner Bros. set for the film of *A Streetcar Named Desire,* its New York cast intact but for Jessica Tandy, who was replaced by Vivien Leigh as Blanche, hinting that Blanche might have been a blanched great-grandniece of Scarlett O'Hara. Kazan battled Leigh out of her stereotypical Southern-lady London stage interpretation and won by provoking a glorious performance from her. Though she got the Oscar, it was Brando who made history. Brando was repeating his stage Stanley, a notorious performance, imitated and copied and mocked especially by people who hadn't seen it. It was thought to be prototypical method acting (detractors found it incoherent and self-absorbed). For a time, Kazan and Brando were as much a coupled collaboration as Kazan and Tennessee Williams. Like Fellini and Mastroianni, or Martin Scorsese and Robert De Niro, or François Truffaut and Jean-Pierre Léaud, actor Brando and director Kazan had a symbiotic relationship, mutual vehicles for self- and wish-fulfillment, for insight and for the exploration of artistic possibility. For the remainder of his career Kazan thought of Brando first—he got him for *Viva Zapata!* and *On the Waterfront,* but not for *Baby Doll* or *The Arrangement* or *Wild River.* Kazan's films are virtually male-dominated because he never stopped surreptitiously rehearsing his own character and story.

A contributing factor to the Brando breakup and to Kazan's alienation from much of the New York theatre community was Kazan's appearances as a friendly witness before the House Un-American Activities Committee in 1952. He named names, those of his fellow members of his mid-1930s Communist cell and party functionaries, seventeen in all. Why did he do it? His ostensible reasons are easy to list: his revulsion at the massacres of Stalin; Communist perversion of the civil rights and other social movements; spy infiltration of American institutions; the naïveté and denial of certain liberals—and it would have been a criminal act if he hadn't. And he didn't entertain the option of taking refuge outside the country like Jules Dassin and Joseph Losey. Was the Red-scare paranoia fed exclusively by bigotry and xenophobia? The facts of Soviet interference in American institutions were known then and have been substantiated over and over again. Nevertheless, the xenophobic government response of self-righteousness and grandstanding, of vilification and professional destruction of well-intentioned "fellow travelers" was abhorrent, a shaming episode in American history. But there was a contemporaneous reality; as A. O. Scott, reviewing a documentary film of the life of folksinger Pete Seeger, remarked, "I wish [Mr. Seeger's detractors] or someone had pushed a little harder into the reality that lay beneath the beautiful abstractions of peace, justice and democracy that American Communists claimed to embrace. Yes, they were idealists, but most were damnably slow to acknowledge the monstrous truth about the Soviet paradise they defended. And while many of them, including Mr. Seeger, suffered banishment and harassment as a result of their political affiliations, the crimes of Joseph R. McCarthy and his allies come nowhere near those of Stalin."

The House investigation of Communist influence in the entertainment industry had begun in the late 1930s, a reaction to Franklin Roosevelt's federal arts funding, but had been put on hold during the Second World War, when the Soviet Union was an ally. It regained impetus at the war's end, when the Cold War emerged. The privately funded conservative journal *Counterattack* mounted a direct bombardment on specific actors, writers, and directors, and their unofficial listing of fellow travelers, "Red Channels," was first issued in 1950. Many of Kazan's Group Theatre colleagues were cited: Luther and Stella Adler, J. Edward Bromberg, Lee J. Cobb, John Garfield, Tony Kraber, Morris Carnovsky, and Phoebe Brand, as well as actors he had worked with and continued to work with: Zero Mostel, Burl Ives, Barbara Bel Geddes, Arthur Miller. The names Kazan gave to the committee two years later, his Group Theatre cell, had already appeared in "Red Channels"—he provided verification but no revelations.

Why was Kazan reviled more than others who succumbed? Because he was more famous. The true sin Kazan was accused of by the theatre and, later, movie communities was not ratting on others but careerism. Studio chief Spyros Skouras, it was gossiped, threatened him with cancellation of his Fox contract if he didn't testify; as false and malicious rumor went, Skouras rewarded him with a super-bonus. Kazan's crime was achieving success. The argument went that since he was so eminent, he should have set an example for civil disobedience: His error was one of complicity, of validation of the committee's right to investigate. According to this view, he should have been a "conscientious objector."

Richard Schickel believes that Kazan fueled the enmity against him by sending a gratuitous and grandiose letter of explanation to the *New*

York Times two days after his testimony: "But Kazan's advertisement for himself made him a permanent target. By this one act he became the celebrity informer—the namer of names nearly everyone could name, the great symbolic stooge, rat fink of the era." None of the at least seventy-three others who testified similarly became the monster of perfidy that Kazan was called. The punishment continued for the rest of his life, up to the nationally televised Oscar ceremony of 1999, almost a half-century after his testimony, when he was honored with an Academy Award for lifetime achievement. Those whose careers would not have been possible without Kazan's accomplishments sat on their hands and smirked. Hollywood's crass hypocrisy and ingratitude were a gesture as benighted as removing the name of D. W. Griffith from the Directors Guild of America awards in the late 1980s because of the dopey stereotypes and Old South prejudices of the 1916 *Birth of a Nation* (white actors in blackface; glorification of the Ku Klux Klan).

The paradox was that this persistent personal humiliation improved the belligerent, defiant Kazan as an artist. The mighty *On the Waterfront* (1954) is what its detractors say it is, a self-exculpation and accusation, and a gladiatorial display of Kazan skills and themes. Brando is here the super Kazan surrogate, undervalued by society, his conscience awakened, fighting against corruption, brutalized but not defeated. And what a collection of performances, from Karl Malden, Rod Steiger, Lee J. Cobb (these three knocking one another out of a win when they were all nominated for Best Supporting Actor) and from Eva Marie Saint (Academy Award for Best Supporting Actress). But there is more to *Waterfront*: a driving tempo, solid story construction (scriptwriter Budd Schulberg had also testified), locale authenticity, unremitting violence, and the powerful theme of redemption: Steiger is strung on a meat hook, Brando and Saint are chased by a car down dark alleys, Brando is beaten to a pulp, Saint's brother is thrown off a rooftop, pigeons are slaughtered, and dockworkers are beaten with clubs. And, beneath it all, an undercurrent of despair. Brando says famously to Steiger, "But I could have been a contender." A similar but more intimate mix of melancholy and fury would power Kazan's next film, *East of Eden,* this time in Cinemascope and color.

The circumstance of *On the Waterfront* had a backstory. Kazan had first planned a film of union corruption on Brooklyn's Red Hook docks initiated by Arthur Miller, but Miller withdrew from the project after Columbia Pictures chief Harry Cohn made strenuous suggestions for changes. Cohn had had the script vetted by the FBI and the union leader Roy Brewer, of the International Alliance of Theatrical and Stage Employees, and wasn't prepared to rile Hollywood unions with a tale of corruption; he wanted Miller to imply that the corrupted waterfront union was being infiltrated not by the mob but by Communists.

Contributing to Miller's exit might have been Miller's distrust of Kazan's political loyalties and, according to Miller (but not to Kazan), Kazan's willingness to consider Cohn's demand.[*] In his 1952 play, *The Crucible,* about badgered testimony, Miller found an analogy between the contemporary hounding of present and former Communists and the Salem witch trials. Some judged it a blast at Kazan, and Eric Bentley, with great presumption and insight, found more drama in the circumstances of production than in the play:

> Elia Kazan made a public confession of having been a communist and, while doing so, mentioned the name of several of his former comrades. Mr. Miller then brought out a play about an accused man who refuses to name comrades (who indeed dies rather than make a confession at all), and of course, decided to end his collaboration with the director who did so much to make him famous. The play has been directed by Jed Harris.
>
> I think there is as much drama in this bit of history as in any Salem witch hunt. The "guilty" director was rejected. An "innocent" one was chosen in his place. There are two stories in this. The first derives from the fact that the better fellow (assuming, for the purpose of argument, that Mr. Harris is this better fellow) is not always the better worker. The awkwardness I find in Mr. Miller's script is duplicated in Mr. Harris's directing. Mr. Kazan would have taken this script up like clay and re-molded it. He would have struck fire from the individual actor, and he would have brought one actor into much livelier relationship with another. . . . The second story is that of the interpenetration of good and evil. I am afraid that Mr. Miller needs a Kazan but also—his sense of guilt. Innocence is, for a mere human being, and especially for an artist, insufficient baggage. . . . The pressure of guilt.

[*] The Kazan-Miller relationship of this period was tellingly examined in the 2003 PBS American Masters series production *None Without Sin: Arthur Miller, Elia Kazan, and the Blacklist.*

The Crucible is about guilt yet nowhere in it is there any sense of guilt because the actor and director have joined forces to dissociate themselves and their hero from evil. This is the theatre of two Dr. Jekylls. Mr. Miller and Mr. Kazan were Dr. Jekyll and Mr. Hyde.

Waterfront was a rejoinder to *The Crucible,* and Miller took it as a challenge. His next play, *A View from the Bridge,* was about informing on an illegal alien, on the turf of the original Kazan-Miller project, Brooklyn's Red Hook. But this play featured no trial, just ostracism and murder, and the compassionate judgment that the informer had lost all conscious control of his motives.

An extraordinary rapprochement was attempted in the 1964 production of the meandering Miller play *After the Fall,* a self-exoneration of Miller's feelings of guilt toward his friends, his mother, brother, and father, his first wife, and for half the play, Marilyn Monroe. In the first act the Kazan-based character (a lawyer named Mickey) tells Miller (called Quentin): "I'm . . . going to name names. . . . I'll be voted out of the firm if I don't testify." While Miller is examining his implication in the guilt of others, he also trashes a deranged sex-crazed pill-popping castrating Marilyn, who had committed suicide two years before. The actress Lee Grant called the play "informing on Marilyn." Miller's spew of voyeurism under the guise of compassion and truthfulness give the play's second act vital and obscene interest. The big cast, picked out when needed by spotlights, wandered up and down sparsely furnished open playing space of various levels, while the audience was seated around and above in an auditorium inspired by a Greek amphitheatre, designed in a fit of grandiosity matching the play by Jo Mielziner, Kazan's great collaborator on *Streetcar, Salesman,* and *Cat on a Hot Tin Roof.* This shameless farrago (it all takes place in the protagonist's mind) was directed by Elia Kazan as the initial production of the Lincoln Center Repertory Theatre. Jason Robards played Quentin (he disappeared from rehearsals for a week) and Kazan's future second wife, Barbara Loden (who at the time of casting was pregnant with his son), enacted the surrogate Marilyn. The critics were justifiably brutal, and Miller went into a funk. This parody of Miller's, Mielziner's, Williams's theatrical achievements and his own transformation of the American theatre in the late 1940s was Kazan's virtual farewell to theatre. The play's title couldn't have been more apt.

Before *After the Fall* went into rehearsal, Kazan had been in Turkey and Greece filming the true culmination of his past (and future) career, the Homeric saga *America America*.

That film's faults are as much in evidence now as they were when it opened—a lengthy, unsure narrative focus, a sometimes-muddy soundtrack, and excess emoting. In greater evidence now than at the time of the film's opening are its distinctions: its grand scale and ambition, the rigor of its unsentimental vision, its iconoclastic storytelling, the way in which it implicates its determined and disturbing amoral protagonist in the grand and ambiguous destiny of American civilization. Though he hated Kazan personally, and the feeling was mutual, Haskell Wexler realized Kazan's distinction with breathtaking accuracy: The film is intense, without fakery, and aware of its environment. (The film falters only in the domestic scenes of the second part.) The first half is perfect, the second part spotty, great and weak; but it is as uniquely Kazan as *Citizen Kane* is Welles. *America America* is a work of supreme individuality that has the character of its maker: combative, unapologetic, ravenously alert. At all times you feel Kazan's presence, values, distinction, and sensibility. Its dispassion and its episodic structure, like *The Arabian Nights,* give it the feel of myth. It is an epic odyssey, a journey both in time and space, from a mountain village that trafficks ice down to lower regions, on to a Manhattan shoeshine parlor. Yet at each moment you know that something momentous is taking place. The film takes its breadth from the puzzlement of attempting a meaningful existence.

It does not fall easily into a categorical listing of American movies, and I am not sure of its influence, or if influence is a mark of achievement. But it is in the same list as King Vidor's *The Crowd,* Ford's *The Grapes of Wrath,* Von Stroheim's *Greed,* John Huston's *The Treasure of the Sierra Madre,* and Welles's *Citizen Kane*—films that upend expectations, that have a bracing ambiguity, that "go for broke"; films that are impertinent and unanswerable, that offer no easy precedents.

Kazan made a great film that owed nothing to anyone else. And he had answered the questions that had plagued and inspired him: Where do I come from? What do I know of what I want? Who am I?

Chronology

"I can get along all right with you liking me or disliking me, I'm O.K. I do my work, and that's what I feel is important for an artist—that he does his work in his way with his vision and he doesn't pay a lot of attention to the reaction. And I don't. I never did. . . . On my worst day, when I was being attacked by all sides, I didn't care, I didn't live by what people are saying about me. The only way we're ever going to be known is by our work, not by somebody boasting about us."

BIOGRAPHY

1909. Born September 7 Elia Kazanjioglou in Constantinople (Istanbul), Turkey, to George and Athena Kazanjioglou.

1913. September. Family moves to New York.

1920–26. Attends Mayfair School and New Rochelle High School. Enters Williams College, fall 1926.

1930. Receives B.A. cum laude in English from Williams. Group Theatre is founded by Harold Clurman, Cheryl Crawford, and Lee Strasberg. The first meeting occurs in November. Among the original members are Franchot Tone, Morris Carnovsky, Sanford Meisner, J. Edward Bromberg, Ruth Nelson, Margaret Barker, and Stella Adler.

1932. Marries Molly Day Thacher. Receives M.F.A. from Yale School of Drama. Attends Group Theatre second-year summer camp at Sterling Farms, Dover Falls, New York, as an apprentice, and is accepted as a full member in the fall. Theatrical debut as stage manager and understudy for the Theatre Guild production *The Pure in Heart* in Baltimore.

1933. Broadway acting debut in Sidney Kingsley's *Men in White* for the Group Theatre.

1934–36. Member of the Communist Party. Active in workers' theatres: Theatre Collective, Theatre Union, and Theatre of Action. Teaches acting and directing at the New Theatre League.

1935. Appears in Clifford Odets's *Waiting for Lefty*.

1936. Daughter Judy born.

1937. Lee Strasberg and Cheryl Crawford resign from the Group Theatre, leaving Harold Clurman as sole director, with an advisory council consisting of Kazan, Roman Bohnen, and Luther Adler. Appears in Clifford Odets's *Golden Boy*. Assistant director on the documentary film *People of the Cumberland*. Spends some months in Hollywood, assisting director Lewis Milestone.

1938. Son Chris born. Broadway directing debut, *Casey Jones*, for the Group Theatre.

1939. Directs plays: *Quiet City* and *Thunder Rock*.

1940. Appears in the film *City for Conquest*, starring James Cagney.

1941. Appears in the film *Blues in the Night*. The Group Theatre dissolves.

1942. Directs plays: *The Strings, My Lord, Are False; Café Crown;* and *The Skin of Our Teeth*, for which he receives New York Drama Critics' Circle Award for Best Director.

1943. Directs plays: *Harriet* and *One Touch of Venus* (musical).

1944. Directs plays: *Jacobowsky and the Colonel* and *Sing Out, Sweet Land* (musical).

1945. Son Nick born. Directs film: *A Tree Grows in Brooklyn*. Directs plays: *Dunnigan's Daughter* and *Deep Are the Roots*.

1947. Films: *Sea of Grass, Boomerang!, Gentleman's Agreement*. Plays: *All My Sons, A Streetcar Named Desire*. Wins Tony Award for direction of *All My Sons*. Receives Oscar and New York Film Critics awards for his direction of *Gentleman's Agreement*. Receives National Board of Review award for his direction of *Gentleman's Agreement* and *Boomerang!* Receives Golden Globe for direction of *Gentleman's Agreement*. Receives New York Drama Critics and Donaldson awards for direction of *Streetcar*. Co-founds the Actors Studio with Robert Lewis and Cheryl Crawford. There were to be two classes, an advanced one for professionals (to be conducted by Lewis) and one for young actors (to be taught by Kazan). Lewis leaves after the first year. Three years later Kazan invites Lee Strasberg to direct the Studio's acting program.

1948. Daughter, Katie, born. Play: *Love Life* (musical). Film: *Pinky*.

1949. Play: *Death of a Salesman*. Receives Tony Award for direction.

1950. Forms the motion picture company Newtown Productions. Film: *Panic in the Streets*.

1951. Film: *A Streetcar Named Desire*, for which he receives an Oscar nomination and receives New York Film Critics Circle Award for direction.

1952. Appears before an executive session of a subcommittee of the House Un-American Activities Committee, January 14. Admits to his former membership in the Communist Party but refuses to give the names of his associates. Some time later (April 10) he appears voluntarily and gives names of former fellow Communist Party members, including eight members of his Group Theatre unit, among them Clifford Odets, Morris Carnovsky, Tony Kraber, Art Smith, and Paula Strasberg. Offers a lengthy self-exculpatory notice in the *New York Times,* explaining the reasons for his testimony. Film: *Viva Zapata!* Play: *Flight into Egypt.*

1953. Film: *Man on a Tightrope.* Plays: *Camino Real* and *Tea and Sympathy,* for which he won a Donaldson Award as Best Director.

1954. Forms a second motion-picture producing company, Athena Enterprises. Film: *On the Waterfront.* Receives honorary doctorate from Wesleyan University for which he received for his direction an Academy Award, the New York Film Critics Circle Award, and a Golden Globe.

1955. Play: *Cat on a Hot Tin Roof,* for which he won a Donaldson Award for Best Director. Film: *East of Eden.*

1956. Film: *Baby Doll.*

1957. Play: *The Dark at the Top of the Stairs.* Film: *A Face in the Crowd.*

1958. Play: *J.B.* Receives Tony Award for direction.

1959. Receives honorary Master of Arts degree from Yale University. Play: *Sweet Bird of Youth.*

1960. Appointed co-director with Robert Whitehead of the Repertory Theatre of Lincoln Center. Film: *Wild River.*

1961. Film: *Splendor in the Grass.*

1962. Alters status at Actors Studio from active to inactive member. Book: *America America.* Receives honorary doctorate from Carnegie Institute of Technology. Son Leo born to Barbara Loden.

1963. Molly Day Thacher Kazan dies. Film: *America America,* for which he receives a Golden Globe for his direction.

1964. Stages for the Repertory Theatre of Lincoln Center: *After the Fall, But for Whom Charlie,* and *The Changeling.* Receives honorary doctorate from Williams College. Resigns from the Repertory Theatre of Lincoln Center.

1966. Discusses with Oscar Lewis a film of Lewis's *La Vida.*

1967. Marries second wife, Barbara Loden. Meets with James Baldwin and Alex Haley to discuss a film about Malcolm X. Book: *The Arrangement.*

1969. Film: *The Arrangement.*

1972. Receives New York City's Handel Medallion. Book: *The Assassins.* Film: *The Visitors.*

1975. Book: *The Understudy.*

1976. Film: *The Last Tycoon.*

1978. Discusses with Richard Burton a production of *King Lear.* Book: *Acts of Love.* Receives honorary doctorate from Katholieke Universiteit, Leuven, Belgium.

1980. Second wife, Barbara Loden, dies.

1982. Marries third wife, Frances Rudge. Book: *The Anatolian.*

1983. Receives Kennedy Center Honors Lifetime Award. Becomes Special Honorary Life Member of Directors Guild of America. Play: *The Chain.*

1986. Receives D. W. Griffith Special Lifetime Achievement Award from Directors Guild of America.

1987. Honoree, American Museum of the Living Image.

1988. Autobiography: *Elia Kazan: A Life.*

1989. American Film Institute refuses to honor Kazan: "He named names and we just can't honor someone who did that."

1991. Son Chris dies.

1994. Book: *Beyond the Aegean.*

1996. Receives Honorary Golden Bear Award from Berlin Film Festival.

1999. Receives Lifetime Achievement Award from Motion Picture Academy of Arts and Sciences.

2003. Dies September 28, aged ninety-four.

DIRECTING FOR THE STAGE

1931. *The Second Man* by S. N. Behrman. Toy Theatre, Atlantic City.

1934. *Dimitroff, a Play of Mass Pressure,* by Elia Kazan and Art Smith, co-directed with Art Smith for the Group Theatre.

1935. *The Young Go First* by Arthur Vogel, Peter Martin, Charles Scudder, and Charles Friedman. Co-directed with Alfred Saxe for the Theatre of Action.

1936. *The Crime* by Michael Blankfort. Co-directed with Alfred Saxe for the Theatre of Action. Cast: Martin Ritt, Nicholas Ray, Norman Lloyd.

1938. *Casey Jones,* by Robert Ardrey. Set design, Mordecai Gorelik. Cast: Van Heflin, Charles Bickford, Peggy Conklin. Kazan's Broadway debut. Group Theatre.

1939. *Quiet City* by Irwin Shaw. Score, Aaron Copland. Set design, Mordecai Gorelik. Cast: Morris Carnovsky, Luther Adler, Frances Farmer. Two private performances only. Group Theatre.

    Thunder Rock by Robert Ardrey. Set design, Mordecai Gorelik. Cast: Luther Adler, Morris Carnovsky, and Frances Farmer. Group Theatre.

1941. *It's Up to You* by Arthur Arent. Department of Agriculture.

1942. *Café Crown* by H. S. Kraft. Produced by Carly Wharton and Martin Gabel. Set design, Boris Aronson. Cast: Sam Jaffe, Morris Carnovsky.

    The Strings My Lord, Are False, by Paul Vincent Carroll. Cast: Art Smith, Walter Hampden, Constance Dowling, Will Lee, Ruth Gordon, Hurd Hatfield. Theatre Guild. Set in Scotland in 1941. In his biography of Kazan, Richard Schickel writes that Ruth Gordon recalled that Kazan, after a preview, declared that he loved most of what he had seen and that he could fix what had to be fixed. Nevertheless, he was fired before the opening but remained the director of record.

    The Skin of Our Teeth by Thornton Wilder. Produced by Michael Myerberg. Set design, Albert Johnson. Costumes, Mary Percy Schenck. Cast: Tallulah Bankhead (Sabina), Fredric March (Mr. Antrobus), Florence Eldridge (Mrs. Antrobus), Montgomery Clift (Henry), E. G. Marshall (Mr. Fitzpatrick), Florence Reed (Fortune Teller), Dick Van Patten (Telegraph Boy), Morton da Costa (Announcer). Plymouth Theatre, New York premiere, November 18, 1942. New York Drama Critics' Circle Award: Best Director. Pulitzer Prize for Drama.

[Also on Broadway that year: *Angel Street* (filmed in Hollywood as *Gaslight*), with Vincent Price and Judith Evelyn; Noel Coward's *Blithe Spirit,* with Clifton Webb, Peggy Wood, and Mildred Natwick; Rodgers and Hart's *By Jupiter,* with Ray Bolger; a revival of Elmer Rice's *Counsellor at Law,* with Paul Muni; Danny Kaye in Cole Porter's *Let's Face It;* Canada Lee in Orson Welles' production of Richard Wright's *Native Son;* and Philip Barry's *Without Love,* with Katharine Hepburn and Elliott Nugent.]

1943. *Harriet* by Florence Ryerson and Colin Clements. Produced by Gilbert Miller. Set design, Lemuel Ayres. Costumes, Aline Bernstein. Cast: Helen Hayes, Rhys Williams, Joan Tetzel.

One Touch of Venus by S. J. Perelman and Ogden Nash. Music by Kurt Weill. Lyrics by Ogden Nash. Produced by Cheryl Crawford. Choreography, Agnes De Mille. Set design, Howard Bay. Cast: Mary Martin, John Boles, Kenny Baker, Sono Osato, Pearl Lang.

1944. *Jacobowsky and the Colonel* by S. N. Behrman, adapted from a play by Franz Werfel. Produced by the Theatre Guild. Music, Paul Bowles. Set design, Stewart Chaney. Cast: Oscar Karlweis, Annabella, Louis Calhern. New York Drama Critics' Award: Best Foreign Play.

Sing Out, Sweet Land! Uncredited. A salute to American folk and popular music. Conceived and written by Walter Kerr. Staging attributed to Leon Leonidoff and Walter Kerr. Produced by the Theatre Guild. Cast: Alfred Drake, Burl Ives.

1945. *Deep Are the Roots* by Arnaud d'Usseau and James Gow. Produced by Kermit Bloomgarden and George Heller. Cast: Barbara Bel Geddes, Gordon Heath.

Dunnigan's Daughter by S. N. Behrman. Produced by the Theatre Guild. Set design, Stewart Chaney. Costumes, Mainbocher. Cast: Dennis King, June Havoc, Luther Adler, Richard Widmark, Jan Sterling. John Golden Theatre, December 26, 1945–January 26, 1946.

[Also on Broadway that year: Rodgers and Hammerstein's *Carousel;* Gertrude Lawrence and Raymond Massey in Shaw's *Pygmalion;* the musical *Song of Norway; The Magnificent Yankee;* Bobby Clark in Molière's *The Would-be Gentleman;* Shakespeare's *The Winter's Tale,* with Jessie Royce Landis and Henry Daniell; Tennessee Williams's *The Glass Menagerie,* with Laurette Taylor and Eddie Dowling.]

1946. *Truckline Café* by Maxwell Anderson. Directed by Harold Clurman. Co-produced by Elia Kazan in association with Harold Clurman and the Playwrights' Company (Maxwell Anderson, S. N. Behrman, Elmer Rice, Robert E. Sherwood, Sidney Howard). Set design, Boris Aronson. Costumes, Millia Davenport. Cast: Kevin McCarthy, June Walker, Virginia Gilmore, Karl Malden, Marlon Brando, Lou Gilbert, Richard Waring. Belasco Theatre, February 27, 1946–March 9, 1946.

[Also on Broadway that year: *Anna Lucasta; Billion Dollar Baby; Born Yesterday; Dear Ruth; Harvey,* with Frank Fay; Lunt and Fontanne in *O Mistress Mine; State of the Union; The Iceman Cometh.*]

1947. *All My Sons* by Arthur Miller. Produced by Elia Kazan, Harold Clurman, and Walter Fried, in association with Herbert H. Harris. Set design, Mordecai Gorelik. Cast: Arthur Kennedy (Chris Keller), Karl Malden (George Deever), Beth Merrill (Kate Keller), Ed Begley (Joe Keller), Lois Wheeler (Ann Deever). New York premiere, Coronet Theatre, January 29, 1947. Tony Awards: Best Author, Best Director. New York Drama Critics' Circle Award: Best American Play. Donaldson Award: Best Play.

A *Streetcar Named Desire* by Tennessee Williams. Produced by Irene Mayer Selznick. Scenery and lighting, Jo Mielziner. Costumes, Lucinda Ballard. Cast: Jessica Tandy (Blanche DuBois), Marlon Brando (Stanley Kowalski), Kim Hunter (Stella Kowalski), Karl Malden (Harold Mitchell, "Mitch"). New York premiere, Ethel Barrymore Theatre, December 3, 1947. Pulitzer Prize for Drama. New York Drama Critics' Circle Award: Best American Play. New York Drama Critics' Circle Award: Best Director. Donaldson Award: Best Director. Tony Award: Best Actress, Jessica Tandy.

[Also on Broadway that year: Rodgers and Hammerstein's *Allegro; Finian's Rainbow; The Heiress,* with Wendy Hiller and Basil Rathbone; Katharine Cornell in *Antony and Cleopatra;* Judith Anderson and John Gielgud in Euripides' *Medea;* Thomas Heggen and Joshua Logan's *Mr. Roberts,* with Henry Fonda.]

1948. *Sundown Beach* by Bessie Breuer. An Actors Studio Production. Set design, Ben Edwards. Cast: Phyllis Thaxter, Julie Harris, Cloris Leachman.

Love Life, a musical by Alan Jay Lerner and Kurt Weill. Produced by Cheryl Crawford. Choreography, Michael Kidd. Set design, Boris Aronson. Cast: Nanette Fabray, Ray Middleton.

1949. *Death of a Salesman* by Arthur Miller. Produced by Kermit Bloomgarten and Walter Fried. Sets, Jo Mielziner. Costumes, Julia Sze. Incidental music, Alex North. Cast: Lee J. Cobb (Willy Loman), Mildred Dunnock (Linda), Arthur Kennedy (Biff), Cameron Mitchell (Happy), Tom Pedi (Stanley), Howard Smith (Charley). New York premiere, Morosco Theatre, February 10, 1949. New York Drama Critics' Circle Award: Best American Play. Tony Award: Best Play, Best Director. Donaldson Award: Best Play. Pulitzer Prize for Drama.

1952. *Flight into Egypt* by George Tabori. Produced by Irene Mayer Selznick. Set design, Jo Mielziner. Costumes, Anna Hill Johnstone. Cast: Paul Lukas, Gusti Huber, Zero Mostel, Joseph Anthony, Jo Van Fleet.

1953. *Camino Real* by Tennessee Williams. Directed with the assistance of Anna Sokolow. Produced by Cheryl Crawford and Ethel Reiner, in association with Walter Chrysler, Jr. Sets and costumes, Lemuel Ayres. Cast: Eli Wallach (Kilroy), Frank Silvera (Gutman), Jo Van Fleet (Marguerite Gautier), Joseph Anthony (Casanova), Hurd Hatfield (Lord Byron), Jennie

Goldstein (The Gypsy), Barbara Baxley (Esmeralda), Salem Ludwig (Loan shark, Nursie), Martin Balsam, Gluck Sandor, Michael Gazzo. New York premiere, March 17, 1953, National Theatre.

Tea and Sympathy by Robert Anderson. Produced by the Playwrights' Company with Mary K. Frank. Set design, Jo Mielziner. Costumes, Anna Hill Johnstone. Cast: Deborah Kerr, John Kerr, Leif Erickson. Donaldson Award: Best Director, Best First Play.

1955. *Cat on a Hot Tin Roof* by Tennessee Williams. Produced by the Playwrights' Company. Set design, Jo Mielziner. Costumes, Lucinda Ballard. Cast: Barbara Bel Geddes (Margaret, "Maggie the Cat"), Ben Gazzara (Brick), Burl Ives (Big Daddy Pollitt), Mildred Dunnock (Big Mama), Pat Hingle (Gooper), Madeleine Sherwood (Mae). New York premiere, Morosco Theatre, March 24, 1955. Pulitzer Prize for Drama. New York Drama Critics' Circle Award: Best American Play.

1957. *The Dark at the Top of the Stairs* by William Inge. Produced by Arnold Saint-Subber and Elia Kazan. Set design, Ben Edwards. Costumes, Lucinda Ballard. Cast: Teresa Wright, Pat Hingle, Eileen Heckart, Evans Evans, Timmy Everett.

1958. *J.B.* by Archibald MacLeish. Produced by Alfred de Liagre, Jr. Set design, Boris Aronson. Costumes, Lucinda Ballard. Cast: Pat Hingle (J.B.), Raymond Massey (Mr. Zuss), Christopher Plummer (Nickles), Nan Martin (Sarah), and Bert Conway, Ivor Francis, Andreas Voutsinas (The Comforters). New York premiere, December 11, 1958, ANTA Theatre. Tony Award: Best Director, Best Play. Pulitzer Prize for Drama.

1959. *Sweet Bird of Youth* by Tennessee Williams. Produced by Cheryl Crawford. Sets and lighting, Jo Mielziner. Costumes, Anna Hill Johnstone. Cast: Paul Newman (Chance Wayne), Geraldine Page (Alexandra Del Lago, the Princess Kosmonopolis), Sidney Blackmer (Boss Finley), Rip Torn (Tom Junior), Diana Hyland (Heavenly Finley), Bruce Dern (Stuff), Madeleine Sherwood (Miss Lucy), Martine Bartlett (Aunt Nonnie). New York premiere, Martin Beck Theatre, March 10, 1959.

1964. *After the Fall* by Arthur Miller. Produced by the Repertory Theatre of Lincoln Center. Set design, Jo Mielziner. Costumes, Anna Hill Johnstone. Cast: Jason Robards, Zohra Lampert, Faye Dunaway, Barbara Loden, Salome Jens, Ralph Meeker, David Wayne, Hal Holbrook.

But for Whom Charlie by S. N. Behrman. Produced by the Repertory Theatre of Lincoln Center. Set design, Jo Mielziner. Costumes, Theoni V. Aldredge. Cast: Jason Robards, Faye Dunaway, David Wayne, Salome Jens.

The Changeling by Thomas Middleton and William Rowley. Produced by the Repertory Theatre of Lincoln Center. Set design, David Hays. Costumes, Ben Edwards. Cast: Barbara Loden, Faye Dunaway, John Phillip Law, Clinton Kimbrough.

1983. *The Chain* by Elia Kazan. An adaptation of Aeschylus' *Oresteia*. Cast: Joseph Ragno, Salem Ludwig, Corinne Neuchateu. Stamford, Conn.

DIRECTING FILMS

1935. *Pie in the Sky*. Co-directed with Ralph Steiner and Molly Thacher Kazan, for Nykino, a branch of Theatre of Action/Shocked Troupe, an agit-prop theatre group. A satire on organized religion.

1937. *People of the Cumberland*. Assistant Director. Directed by Sidney Meyers (Robert Stebbins) and Jay Leyda (Eugene Hill). Cinematography, Ralph Steiner. Frontier Films, a progressive film cooperative.

1941. *It's Up to You*. Screenplay, Arthur Arent. Music, Earl Robinson. Cast: Helen Tamiris. Department of Agriculture. A stage play with film material.

1945. *A Tree Grows in Brooklyn*. Producer, Louis D. Lighton. Screenplay, Tess Slesinger and Frank Davis, with additional dialogue by Anita Loos. Adapted from the novel by Betty Smith. Cinematography, Leon Shamroy. Editor, Dorothy Spencer. Art decoration, Lyle Wheeler. Cast: Dorothy McGuire (Katie Nolan), Joan Blondell (Aunt Sissy), James Dunn (Johnny Nolan), Peggy Ann Garner (Francie Nolan), Lloyd Nolan (Officer McShane), Ted Donaldson (Neely Nolan), James Gleason (McGarrity). Twentieth Century–Fox. Academy Awards: Best Supporting Actor, James Dunn; Special Award to Peggy Ann Garner as Outstanding Child Performer.

1947. *Sea of Grass*. Producer, Pandro S. Berman. Screenplay, Marguerite Roberts and Vincent Lawrence, based on the novel by Conrad Richter. Cinematography, Harry Stradling. Editor, Robert J. Kern. Cast: Spencer Tracy, Katharine Hepburn, Robert Walker, Melvyn Douglas. Metro-Goldwyn-Mayer.

   Boomerang! Producer, Louis de Rochemont, for Darryl F. Zanuck. Screenplay, Richard Murphy, from the article "The Perfect Case" by Anthony Abbot (Fulton Oursler). Cinematography, Norbert Brodine. Cast: Dana Andrews (Henry Harvey), Jane Wyatt (Madge Harvey), Arthur Kennedy (John Waldron), Lee J. Cobb (Chief Harold Robinson), Sam Levene (Dave Woods), Karl Malden (Lieutenant White), Ed Begley (Paul Harris), Joe Kazan. Twentieth Century–Fox. National Board of Review Award, Best Director (also for *Gentleman's Agreement*). New York Film Critics Circle Award, Best Director (also for *Gentleman's Agreement*).

   Gentleman's Agreement. Producer, Darryl F. Zanuck. Screenplay, Moss Hart, from the novel by Laura Z. Hobson. Cinematography, Arthur Miller. Editor, Harmon Jones. Cast: Gregory Peck (Philip Green), Dorothy McGuire (Kathy Lacy), John Garfield (Dave Goldman), Celeste Holm (Anne Dettrey), Anne Revere (Mrs. Green), June Havoc (Ethel Wales), Dean Stockwell (Tommy Green). Twentieth Century–Fox. Academy Awards: Best Supporting Actress, Celeste Holm; Best Director, Elia Kazan; Best Picture. National Board of Review Award: Best Director. New York Film Critics Circle Award: Best Film; Best Director, Elia Kazan. Golden Globes: Best Director.

1949. *Pinky*. Producer, Darryl F. Zanuck. Screenplay, Philip Dunne and Dud-

His first movie, *People of the Cumberland.* "I've always known since then that I could go into any environment and not only find interesting faces and people, but the drama and poetry the simplest people have."

ley Nichols, from the novel *Quality* by Cid Ricketts Sumner. Cinematography, Joe MacDonald. Editor, Harmon Jones. Cast: Jeanne Crain, Ethel Barrymore, Ethel Waters.

1950. *Panic in the Streets.* Producer, Sol C. Siegel. Screenplay, Richard Murphy, with contributions from Daniel Fuchs, based on a story by Edward and Edna Anhalt. Cinematography, Joe MacDonald. Editor, Harmon Jones. Cast: Richard Widmark (Dr. Clinton Reed), Paul Douglas (Police Captain Tom Warren), Barbara Bel Geddes (Nancy Reed), Walter Jack Palance (Blackie), Zero Mostel (Raymond Fitch). Twentieth Century–Fox. Academy Award, Best Screenplay. Venice Film Festival: International Prize.

1951. *A Streetcar Named Desire.* Producer, Charles K. Feldman. Screenplay, Tennessee Williams, adapted by Oscar Saul. Cinematography, Harry Stradling. Editor, David Weisbert. Cast: Vivien Leigh (Blanche DuBois), Marlon Brando (Stanley Kowalski), Kim Hunter (Stella Kowalski), Karl Malden (Mitch). Warner Bros. Academy Awards: Best Actress, Vivien Leigh; Best Supporting Actress, Kim Hunter; Best Supporting Actor, Karl Malden; Best Art Direction, Richard Day and George James Hopkins. New York Film Critics' Circle Awards: Best Film; Best Director, Elia Kazan. Venice Film Festival: Special Prize, Elia Kazan.

1952. *Viva Zapata!* Producer, Darryl F. Zanuck. Screenplay, John Steinbeck. Cinematographer, Joe MacDonald. Editor, Barbara McLean. Cast: Marlon Brando (Zapata), Jean Peters (Josefa), Anthony Quinn (Eufemio Zapata),

Joseph Wiseman (Fernando Aguirre), Margo (Soldadera), Mildred Dunnock (Señora Espejo), Arnold Moss (Don Nacio). Twentieth Century–Fox. Academy Award: Best Supporting Actor, Anthony Quinn.

1953. *Man on a Tightrope*. Producer, Robert L. Jacks. Screenplay, Robert Sherwood, based on the story "International Incident" by Neil Paterson. Cinematography, Georg Krause. Cast: Fredric March, Gloria Grahame, Terry Moore, Adolphe Menjou. Twentieth Century–Fox. Berlin Film Festival International Delegate: Jury Prize of the Berlin Senate.

1954. *On the Waterfront*. Produced by Sam Spiegel for Horizon-American Pictures. Screenplay, Budd Schulberg, based on articles by Malcolm Johnson. Cinematography, Boris Kaufman. Editor, Gene Milford. Score, Leonard Bernstein. Cast: Marlon Brando (Terry Malloy), Karl Malden (Father Barry), Lee J. Cobb (Johnny Friendly), Rod Steiger (Charley Malloy), Eva Marie Saint (Edie Doyle). Columbia. Academy Awards: Best Picture; Best Director, Elia Kazan. Best Actor, Marlon Brando; Best Supporting Actress, Eva Marie Saint; Best Writing, Budd Schulberg; Best Art Direction, Richard Day; Best Cinematography, Boris Kaufman; Best Film Editing, Gene Milford. New York Film Critics Circle Awards: Best Film; Best Director; Best Actor (Marlon Brando). Golden Globe, Best Director. Venice Film Festival: International Prize, Elia Kazan.

1955. *East of Eden*. Producer, Elia Kazan. Screenplay, Paul Osborn, from the novel by John Steinbeck. Cinematography, Ted D. McCord. Editor, Owen Marks. Art direction, James Basevi. Cast: James Dean (Cal Trask), Julie Harris (Abra), Raymond Massey (Adam Trask), Jo Van Fleet (Kate), Lois Smith (Anne), Burl Ives (Sam the sheriff), Richard Davalos (Aron Trask). Warner Bros. Academy Award (1955): Best Supporting Actress, Jo Van Fleet. Golden Globe Award: Best Motion Picture (Drama). Cannes Film Festival: Best Dramatic Film Award.

1956. *Baby Doll*. Producer, Elia Kazan. Screenplay, Tennessee Williams, based on his one-act plays "27 Wagons Full of Cotton" and "The Unsatisfactory Supper." Cinematography, Boris Kaufman. Editing, Gene Milford. Cast: Karl Malden (Archie Lee Meighan), Carroll Baker (Baby Doll Meighan), Eli Wallach (Silva Vacarro), Mildred Dunnock (Aunt Rose Comfort), Madeleine Sherwood, Rip Torn. Newtown Productions for Warner Bros.

1957. *A Face in the Crowd*. Producer, Elia Kazan. Screenplay and story, Budd Schulberg, from his book *Some Faces in the Crowd*. Cinematography, Harry Stradling, Gayne Rescher. Editor, Gene Milford. Cast: Andy Griffith (Larry "Lonesome" Rhodes), Patricia Neal (Marcia Jeffries), Anthony Franciosa (Joey DePalma), Walter Matthau (Mel Miller), Lee Remick (Betty Lou Fleckham). Newtown Productions–Warner Bros.

1960. *Wild River*. Producer, Elia Kazan. Screenplay, Paul Osborn, based on the novels *Mud on the Stars* by William Bradford Huie and *Dunbar's Cove* by Borden Deal. Cinematography, Ellsworth Fredricks. Editor, William Reynolds. Cast: Montgomery Clift (Chuck Glover), Lee Remick (Carol

Baldwin), Jo Van Fleet (Ella Garth), Albert Salmi (Hank Bailey), Barbara Loden (Betty Jackson), Bruce Dern (Jack Roper), Pat Hingle (Narrator). Twentieth Century–Fox.

1961. *Splendor in the Grass.* Producer, Elia Kazan. Screenplay, William Inge. Cinematography, Boris Kaufman. Editor, Gene Milford. Costumes, Anna Hill Johnstone. Sets, Gene Callahan. Production design, Richard Sylbert. Cast: Natalie Wood (Deanie Loomis), Audrey Christie (Freda Loomis), Warren Beatty (Bud Stamper), Pat Hingle (Ace Stamper), Barbara Loden (Ginny Stamper), Zohra Lampert (Angelina), Fred Stewart (Del Loomis), Sandy Dennis (Kay), Phyllis Diller (Texas Guinan), William Inge (Reverend Whitman). Warner Bros. Academy Award: Best Screenplay, William Inge.

1963. *America America.* Producer, Elia Kazan. Screenplay, Elia Kazan, based on his novel of the same name. Cinematography, Haskell Wexler. Editor: Dede Allen. Score, Manos Hadjidakis. Production design, Gene Callahan. Costume design, Anna Hill Johnstone. Cast: Stathis Giallelis (Stavros Topouzoglou), Frank Wolff (Vartan Damadian), Elena Karam (Vasso Topouzoglou), John Marley (Garabet), Katharine Balfour (Sophia Kebabian), Paul Mann (Aleko Sinnikoglou). Athena Enterprises–Warner Bros. Golden Globe: Best Director.

1969. *The Arrangement.* Producer, Elia Kazan. Screenplay, Elia Kazan, adapted from his novel. Cinematography, Robert Surtees. Editor, Stephan Amsten. Production design, Gene Callahan. Cast: Kirk Douglas (Eddie Anderson), Faye Dunaway (Gwen), Deborah Kerr (Florence Anderson), Richard Boone (Sam), Hume Cronyn (Arthur). Athena Enterprises Warner Bros.–Seven Arts Production.

1972. *The Visitors.* Producers, Chris Kazan and Nick Proferes. Screenplay, Chris Kazan. Cinematography, Nick Proferes. Cast: Patrick McVey, Patricia Joyce, James Woods, Steve Railsback, Chico Martinez. United Artists.

1976. *The Last Tycoon.* Producer, Sam Spiegel. Screenplay, Harold Pinter, based on the novel by F. Scott Fitzgerald. Cinematographer, Victor Kemper. Cast: Robert De Niro (Monroe Stahr), Tony Curtis (Rodriguez), Robert Mitchum (Pat Brady), Jeanne Moreau (Didi), Jack Nicholson (Brimmer), Ingrid Boulting (Kathleen Moore), Dana Andrews (Red Ridingwood), Theresa Russell (Cecilia Brady). A Sam Spiegel–Elia Kazan Film. Paramount.

ACTOR

"I was an actor for eight years. My last part was in Five Alarm Waltz; *it was inspired by the American writer William Saroyan, a great talent, so pretty eccentric, but no more than I can be when I get going. I decided to play one scene wearing only the bottom half of my underwear, for which I was mocked by the most important New York drama critic of the day, Brooks Atkinson. He wrote a teasing*

*paragraph about me which I took as derogatory and insulting. I
decided never again to give a critic the opportunity of making fun of
me. And I stood by that decision.*

*"The few successes I managed to have as an actor were in "tough
guy" and gangster parts. This is ironic—because I'm a gentle, rather
timid man who, when possible, avoids physical confrontation. But
they told me that I was very menacing in* Golden Boy. *I don't know
how that could have happened."*

Acting Onstage

1932. "Louis, a bartender," in *Chrysalis*, by Rose Albert Porter; also stage
manager. Directed by Theresa Helburn. Theatre Guild.

1933. "An orderly," in *Men in White*, by Sidney Kingsley. Directed by Lee
Strasberg. Stage manager for *Gentlewoman*, by John Howard Lawson.
Group Theatre.

1934. "Polyziodes," in *Gold Eagle Guy*, by Melvin Levy; also stage manager.
Directed by Lee Strasberg. Stage manager for *Awake and Sing!*, by Clifford Odets. Group Theatre.

1935. "Agate Keller" ("my first real part") and "Clancy," in *Waiting for Lefty*,
by Clifford Odets. Directed by Clifford Odets and Sanford Meisner.
"Baum," in *Till the Day I Die*, by Clifford Odets. Directed by Cheryl Crawford. Group Theatre.

"Kewpie," in *Paradise Lost*, by Clifford Odets. Directed by Harold
Clurman. Group Theatre.

1936. "Private Kearns," in *Johnny Johnson*, by Paul Green and Kurt Weill.
Directed by Lee Strasberg. Group Theatre.

1937. "Eddie Fuselli," in *Golden Boy*, by Clifford Odets. Directed by Harold
Clurman. Group Theatre. Brooks Atkinson of the *New York Times* called
Kazan "one of the most exciting actors in America." Drama critic Walter
Kerr remembered: "I saw Kazan play Eddie Fuselli, the gangster in
Golden Boy, when I was still in college in Chicago, and I was stunned. I
mean, I was so startled by this performance: highly stylized—way beyond
anything else in the show. Mesmerizing—you couldn't take your eyes off of
him. Damn good."

1938–39. "Joe Bonaparte," the lead role, tour of *Golden Boy*. Group Theatre.

1939. "Eli Lieber," in *The Gentle People*, by Irwin Shaw. Directed by Harold
Clurman. Group Theatre.

1940. "Ficzur, the Sparrow," in *Liliom*, by Ferenc Molnár. Directed by Benno
Schneider. This production starred Burgess Meredith and Ingrid
Bergman. Produced by Vinton Freedley.

"Steve Takis," in *Night Music*, by Clifford Odets. Directed by Harold
Clurman. Group Theatre.

1941. "Adam Boguris," in *Five Alarm Waltz*, by Lucille S. Prumbs. Directed
by Robert Lewis. Produced by Everett Wile. Character based on writer
William Saroyan.

Acting in Films

1934. In short films *Café Universal* and *Pie in the Sky,* both directed by Ralph Steiner.

1940. "Googi Zucco," in *City for Conquest,* directed by Anatole Litvak. Warner Bros.

1941. "Nickie Haroyen, a clarinet player," in *Blues in the Night,* directed by Anatole Litvak. Warner Bros. Also, uncredited contribution to the script.

1950. "Mortuary Assistant" (uncredited), in *Panic in the Streets.*

1988. "Old man in coffee shop," in *Le Brouillard,* directed by Omer Zulfi Livanelli.

PLAYWRIGHT

1934. *Dmitroff: A Play of Mass Pressure,* one-act play by Kazan and Art Smith, as benefit for *New Theatre* magazine. League of Workers Theatre.

1983. *The Chain.*

NOVELIST

1961. *America America.* New York: Stein & Day.

1967. *The Arrangement.* New York: Stein & Day.

1972. *The Assassins.* New York: Stein & Day.

1975. *The Understudy.* New York: Stein & Day.

1978. *Acts of Love.* New York: Alfred A. Knopf.

1982. *The Anatolian.* New York: Alfred A. Knopf.

1994. *Beyond the Aegean.* New York: Alfred A. Knopf.

AUTOBIOGRAPHY

1988. *An American Odyssey.* Edited by Michel Ciment. London: Bloomsbury.

Elia Kazan: A Life. New York: Alfred A. Knopf.

Bibliography

BOOKS AND PERIODICALS

Agee, James. *Agee on Film.* New York: McDowell Obolensky, 1958.

Baer, William, ed. *Elia Kazan Interviews.* Jackson: University Press of Mississippi, 2000.

Behlmer, Rudy, ed. *Memo from Darryl F. Zanuck.* New York: Grove Press, 1993.

Bentley, Eric. *In Search of Theatre.* New York: Alfred A. Knopf, 1983.

———. *What Is Theatre? 1944–1967.* New York: Hill and Wang, 2000.

Bigsby, Christopher. *The Cambridge Companion to Arthur Miller.* Cambridge, U.K.: Cambridge University Press, 1997.

Bosworth, Patricia. *Marlon Brando.* New York: Viking, 2001.

———. "Kazan's Choice." *Vanity Fair.* September 1999.

Braudy, Leo. *On the Waterfront.* London: BFI Publishing, 2005.

Byron, Stuart, and Martin L. Rubin. "Elia Kazan Interview." *Movie,* Winter 1971–72.

Callow, Simon. *Orson Welles: The Road to Xanadu.* New York: Viking, 1995.

Ciment, Michel. *Kazan on Kazan.* New York: Viking Press, 1974.

Clurman, Harold. *Lies Like Truth.* New York: Macmillan, 1958.

———. *On Directing.* New York: Simon & Schuster, 1972.

———. *The Fervent Years,* New York: Alfred A. Knopf, 1973.

———. *The Divine Pastime.* New York: Macmillan, 1974.

Delahaye, Michael. "Interview with Elia Kazan." *Cahiers du Cinéma in English,* March 1967.

Finstad, Suzanne. *Warren Beatty: A Private Man.* New York: Harmony, 2005.

Garfield, David. *A Player's Place: The Story of the Actors Studio.* New York: Macmillan, 1980.

Hirsch, Foster. *A Method to Their Madness: The History of the Actors Studio.* New York: W. W. Norton, 1984.

Hurrell, John D. *Two Modern American Tragedies.* New York: Charles Scribner's, 1961.

Jones, David Richard. *Great Directors at Work.* Berkeley: University of California Press, 1986.

Kael, Pauline. *Kiss Kiss Bang Bang.* Boston: Little, Brown, 1965.

Kazan, Elia. *A Life.* New York: Alfred A. Knopf, 1988.

———. *An American Odyssey.* Edited by Michel Ciment. London: Bloomsbury, 1988.

Kazan, Elia, J. E. Bromberg, and Lee Strasberg. "Outline for an Elementary Course in Acting (1935)." *Drama Review* 28, no. 4 (Winter 1984).

Kazan, Elia, and Archibald MacLeish. "The Staging of a Play." *Esquire,* May 1959, 144–57.

Lambert, Gavin. *Natalie Wood: A Life.* New York: Alfred A. Knopf, 2004.

Leitner, Samuel L. *The Great Stage Directors: 100 Distinguished Careers of the Theater.* New York: Facts on File, 1994.

Lumet, Sidney. *Making Movies.* New York: Alfred A. Knopf, 1995.

Miller, Arthur. *Death of a Salesman.* New York: Viking, 1949.

———. *After the Fall.* New York: Viking, 1964.

———. *Timebends.* New York: Penguin, 1995.

———. *A Streetcar Named Desire.* Introduction by Arthur Miller. New York: New Directions, 2004.

———. *Collected Plays, 1944–1961.* New York: The Library of America, 2006.

Morton, Frederic. "Gadg." *Esquire,* February 1957.

Murphy, Brenda. *Tennessee Williams and Elia Kazan: A Collaboration in the Theatre.* Cambridge, U.K.: Cambridge University Press, 2003.

Navasky, Victor S. *Naming Names.* New York: Penguin, 1980.

Neal, Patricia. "What Kazan Did for Me." *Films and Filming,* October 1957.

Schechner, Richard, and Theodore Hoffman. "Look, There's the American Theatre." *Tulane Drama Review,* Winter 1964.

Schickel, Richard. *Brando.* New York: Thunder's Mouth Press, 1999.

———. *Elia Kazan.* New York: HarperCollins, 2005.

Shelton, Lewis. "Elia Kazan and the American Tradition of Direction." *A&S: The Magazine of the College of Arts and Sciences* [Kansas State University], Spring 1983.

Smith, Wendy. *Real Life Drama: The Group Theatre and America, 1931–1940.* New York: Alfred A. Knopf, 1990.

Spoto, Donald. *The Kindness of Strangers: The Life of Tennessee Williams.* Boston: Little, Brown, 1985.

Staggs, Sam. *When Blanche Met Brando: The Scandalous Story of "A Streetcar Named Desire."* New York: St. Martin's Press, 2005.

Steinbeck, John. *Zapata.* New York: Penguin, 1993.

Stevens, George, Jr., ed. *Conversations with the Great Moviemakers of Hollywood's Golden Age.* New York: Alfred A. Knopf, 2006.

Stott, William, with Jane Stott. *On Broadway: Performance Photographs by Fred Fehl.* Austin: University of Texas Press, 1978.

Thomson, David. *Marlon Brando.* New York: DK, 2003.

Wallach, Eli. *The Good, the Bad, and Me.* New York: Harcourt, 2005.

Williams, Jay. *Stage Left.* New York: Charles Scribner's Sons, 1974.

Williams, Tennessee. *Memoirs*. New York: Doubleday, 1975.

———. *Letters to Donald Windham, 1940–1965*. New York: Holt, 1976.

———. *Where I Live: Selected Essays by Tennessee Williams*. Edited by Christine R. Day and Bob Woods. New York: New Directions, 1977.

———. *Conversations*. Edited by Albert J. Devlin. Jackson: University of Mississippi Press, 1986.

———. *Plays, 1937–1955*. New York: Library of America, 2000.

———. *Selected Letters*. Vol. 2, *1945–1957*. Edited by Albert J. Devlin and Nancy Tischler. New York: New Directions, 2004.

———. *A Streetcar Named Desire*. New York: New Directions, 2004.

———. *Notebooks*. Edited by Margaret Bradham Thornton. New Haven, Conn.: Yale University Press, 2006.

Young, Jeff. *Kazan: The Master Director Discusses His Films*. New York: Newmarket, 1999.

Zanuck, Darryl. *Memo from Darryl Zanuck*. Edited by Rudy Behlmer. New York: Grove, 1993.

DATABASES

AFI (American Film Institute)
DGA (Directors Guild of America)
Frontier Films
IBDB (Internet Broadway Database)
IMDB (Internet Movie Database)
MPAA (Motion Picture Association of America Archives)
TCMDB (Turner Classic Movies Database)

The Elia Kazan papers are located at the Wesleyan University Cinema Archives

Notes

INTRODUCTION

xix "How is the world better . . . not then, not now." Kazan, *A Life,* 685.

xx "You have to start . . . his emotional resources." Ciment, 36.

xxi "There's a conversation . . . in film for me." Young, 107.

xxii "[Kazan] does not direct . . . move toward it." Miller, *Timebends,* 83.

xxii "All my actors . . . no matter how quiet." Kazan, *A Life,* 150.

QUIET CITY

11 "was inwardly uncertain . . . to his authority." Smith, 357.

THE SKIN OF OUR TEETH

17 "This was the first play . . . and finally stuffy." Kazan, *A Life,* 206.

20 *The Skin of Our Teeth* . . . in our theatre. Kazan, *An American Odyssey,*
160–61.

DUNNIGAN'S DAUGHTER

21 "high comedy . . . in my hands." Kazan, *A Life,* 297–98.

ALL MY SONS

38 "We were both . . . business worlds antihuman." Kazan, *A Life,* 319.

38 "Clurman kept saying . . . it annoyed me." Ibid., 320.

38 "Like other plays . . . a social statement." Ibid., 319.

40 "He had cast . . . to its demands." Miller, *Timebends,* 132–33.

40 "Life in a Kazan production . . . in the world." Ibid., 272–73.

A STREETCAR NAMED DESIRE

44 "Sometimes . . . so quickly!" Miller, *Streetcar,* 116.

44 "Come to think . . . from the beginning!" Ibid., 161–62.

44 "Whoever you are . . . kindness of strangers." Ibid., 178.

49 "I never was hard . . . someone's protection." Ibid., 92.

49 "I want to rest! . . . anyone's problem." Ibid., 95.

50 "There has been . . . with the brutes!" Ibid., 83.

52 "slap me if I go too far." Ibid.

59 "Gadg. I am a bit concerned . . . of an effort." Williams, *Notebooks,* 506.

61 "I wasn't sure . . . theatre animal." Kazan, *A Life,* 246.

62 "I will try to clarify . . . the naked bulb!" Williams, *Letters,* 95–96.

63 "Here she was . . . and gratitude." Kazan, *A Life,* 340.

63 "I can't tell you . . . among young veterans." Williams, *Letters,* 95–96.

64 "adjusting rhythm . . . and opening night." Jones, 183.

64 "in either blue . . . or candlelight." Murphy, 28.

65 "Now, the first week . . . giving me a tip." Morton, 24.

65 "It took only . . . language free play." Miller, *Streetcar,* ix–xiv.

66 "If art . . . attempts at decoration." Mary McCarthy, *Partisan Review,* 131–35.

66 "quite wrong for the part . . . sexiness of the play." Bentley, *Search,* 83.

67 "In *Streetcar* all . . . irredeemably coarse." Clurman, *Divine,* 11–23.

67 "Tennessee in this version . . . struggle to reach." Kazan, *A Life,* 352–53.

DEATH OF A SALESMAN

69 "Of all the plays . . . is my favorite." Kazan, *A Life,* 355.

69 "Willy Loman . . . such a person." Miller, *Death of a Salesman,* 38–39.

82 "Studying the play . . . and didn't get?" Kazan, *A Life,* 357.

83 "What did you do in Boston, Willy?" Miller, *Death of a Salesman.*

83 "I came to believe . . . taking his woman!" Kazan, *A Life,* 358–59.

84 "The concept of a house . . . Jo had conceived." Ibid., 361.

84 "syncopating the speech . . . speeded or slowed." Miller, *Timebends,* 188–89.

85 "He took an old broomstick . . . she never exists in herself." Stott, 132–33.

85 "By common consent . . . in the performing." *New York Times,* February 20, 1949, sec. 2, p. 1.

86 "Elia Kazan's production . . . or for beautiful decoration." Clurman, *Lies,* 68–72.

CAMINO REAL

88 "As I said . . . logically in advance." Williams to Kazan, November 11, 1949, Wesleyan Archives.

90 "Yesterday eve . . . I'll go cruising now." Williams, *Notebooks,* 557.

90 "Dear Lem . . . theatricality." Kazan to Ayres, December 1952, Wesleyan Archives.

92 "I wrote the designer . . . was a friend." Kazan, *A Life,* 497.

94   "I wanted a production . . . cost to the Williams play." Ibid., 494–97.

95   "Unfortunately the play . . . best plays." Kazan, *An American Odyssey*, 167.

96   "Williams is our greatest playwright, and this is his worst play." Walter Kerr, *New York Herald Tribune*, March 18, 1953.

96   "To me the evening . . . wicked fascination of Elia Kazan." Bentley, *What Is*, 74–78.

CAT ON A HOT TIN ROOF

98   "No living playwright . . . as Elia Kazan." Williams, afterword to published script, *Plays*.

98   "the play was . . . that makes them survive." Williams, *Notebooks*, 658.

99   "In *Cat* . . . emotion of that moment." Schechner, 67.

99   "Jo Mielziner and I . . . as I preferred." Kazan, *A Life*, 542–43.

101   "Some mystery . . . to himself in life." Williams, *Plays*, 945.

101   "Got a 5 page letter . . . compromise with him." Williams, *Notebooks*, 663.

101   I "buy" a lot of your letter . . . something like liquor." Williams, *Letters*, 554–55.

102   "I didn't want Big Daddy . . . state of spiritual disrepair." Williams, *Plays*, 978.

103   "I especially resented . . . the Dramatists Guild." Kazan, *A Life*, 544.

103   "Significantly, the reading version . . . audience would tolerate." Murphy, 106.

103   "The general scheme . . . always manages to give." Bentley, *What Is*, 224–31.

J.B.

105   "The best work . . . was never heard." Kazan, *A Life*, 592.

105   "*J.B.* ranks with the finest work in American drama." Review of the Yale production, *New York Times*, April 24, 1959.

105   "In general . . . be able to take it?' " Kazan and MacLeish.

110   "Lil [Lillian Hellman] thought the play . . . after the bombing." Ibid.

111   "The primary trouble . . . feeling of let-down." On the Washington opening, *Variety*, November 1955.

111   "A wave of depression . . . in his own manliness." Kazan and MacLeish.

111   "I must confess . . . not my ear." Kazan, *A Life*, 582.

SWEET BIRD OF YOUTH

113   "It necessitated . . . between us." Kazan, *A Life*, 545.

114   "First I want to say . . . Love, Gadg." Kazan to Williams, May 20, 1958, Wesleyan Archives.

119 "Dear Tenn . . . Chance has done." Kazan to Williams, September 2, 1958, Wesleyan Archives.

123 "Dear Jo . . . talk this thing out." Kazan to Mielziner, September 9, 1958, Wesleyan Archives.

131 "The next day . . . back for good." Ibid.

132 "in a symbolic manner . . . until the end." Williams, *Conversations,* 45.

133 "And so I am trying . . . in us all." Mielziner Archives.

133 "a lack of cohesion . . . a wonderful production." Murphy, 140.

133 "If there is any truth . . . if only approximately, nearly." *New York Times,* March 8, 1959.

133 "close to parody . . . at imitating himself." *Time,* March 3, 1959.

134 "Right now I have put aside . . . to be explicit." Williams, *Letters to Windham,* April 4, 1960.

134 "Dear Tenn . . . I love you." Kazan to Williams, April 22, 1960, Wesleyan Archives.

SHORT TAKES

138 This was a play . . . the days! Kazan, *An American Odyssey,* 159.

139 *Casey Jones* . . . not a backdrop. Ibid.

139 During the Second . . . enjoyed myself. Ibid.

140 I had three . . . best field. Ibid, 161.

140 This was . . . its merits too. Ibid., 163.

140 *Deep Are* . . . never to surpass it. Ibid.

141 *Tea and Sympathy* . . . one false step. Ibid., 197.

141 *The Dark at the Top of the Stairs* . . . what's on TV. Ibid., 167–69.

142 *After the Fall* . . . murderous feelings. Ibid., 169.

143 *The Changeling* . . . my failing. Ibid.

143 I finally . . . failed. Ibid.

A TREE GROWS IN BROOKLYN

147 "Bud" Lighton surrounded me . . . in her values. Ciment, 49–52.

BOOMERANG!

149 We shot that entirely . . . would I do now. Byron, in Baer, 129.

149 I cast the movie . . . of making films. Kazan, *A Life,* 316–18.

150 On *Boomerang!* I learned . . . "This is life." Young, 43.

151 "You have performed . . . finding them out." Zanuck, 115–16.

GENTLEMAN'S AGREEMENT

152 No matter what I think . . . when it got over. Baer, 130.

155 Well, by the time . . . That changed everything. Baer, 132–34.

159 "*Streetcar* is a beautiful theatre piece . . . his force was healthier." Baer,
      134–35.
161 "Dear Joe . . . discuss it too." Wesleyan Archives.
162 "Mr. Kazan has just informed me . . . for taste and propriety." Williams,
      Letters, 355–56.
163 "Dear Gadg . . . never back again." Wesleyan Archives.
163 "Vivien Leigh gives . . . just about perfection." Kael, 352.

165 Marlon delighted me . . . it often happened. Kazan, *A Life,* 428–29.
167 The competition between . . . the same praise. Young, 106.
167 My favorite scene . . . become a filmmaker. Kazan, *A Life,* 431.
167 Even in a film . . . "two weeks ago!" Baer, 152.
168 The first thing . . . and progressive. Young, 93.
168 In the scene . . . start giving directions. Ibid., 99–100.
168 Well, everybody influences everybody . . . down to the casting. Byron, in
      Baer, 136.
169 "Is this the right time . . . in making it?'" Zanuck, 175–76.
169 "*Sunset Boulevard* . . . actors in English." Ibid. 177.
170 "Dear Darryl . . . nor ever will." Kazan to Zanuck, January 29, 1952,
      Wesleyan Archives.
171 "a sort of Mexican Robin Hood . . . colorful Mexican bandit." Zanuck,
      214.

172 "*On the Waterfront* . . . and fuck themselves." Kazan, *A Life,* 529.
173 "Dear Marlon . . . beyond challenge." Kazan to Brando, November 2,
      1983, Wesleyan Archives.
176n "He named names . . . work with actors." Kazan, *A Life,* 499–500.
177 "Strange . . . Miller pulls out." Navasky, 213.
178 "I believe . . . to become interested." Zanuck, 224–53.
178 "Schulberg's story . . . fighting for." Braudy, 68.
180 "We shot . . . it shows, doesn't it?" Baer, 140.
180 "No, I didn't . . . kind of osmosis." *New York Post,* August 30, 1954.
181 "Maybe I did wrong, probably did." Young, 175.
181 "The whole story . . . by all sides." Ibid., 160.
181 "Kazan said . . . wouldn't have worked." Stevens, 136.

EAST OF EDEN

182 *"East of Eden . . .* are no longer afraid." Baer, 95–96.

183 Jack Warner hadn't . . . backing at all. Kazan, *A Life,* 534.

183 "Dear John . . . We'd be outside." Kazan to Steinbeck, May 18, 1953, Wesleyan Archives.

185 "said he sure as hell was, and that was it." Kazan, *A Life,* 534.

185 "Jimmy would either . . . get it at all." Ibid., 538.

185 Ray Massey . . . to the end.: Ibid., 535.

185 I felt . . . "being lost here!" Baer, 142.

186 Dean had the most natural talent . . . they were ample. Kazan, *Odyssey,* 217–18.

187 There is no real . . . theatre emotions—awe! Ibid., 40.

BABY DOLL

190 "It is the best film . . . from Williams." Baer, 143.

190 A penny-ante entrepreneur . . . his revenge. Kazan, *A Life,* 561–62.

191 "The first of these . . . seemed to indicate." Letter, October 24, 1955, MPAA Archives.

191 "Dear Jack . . . homes to see." Letter, November 14, 1955, MPAA Archives.

194 "Carroll stretched herself . . . Print 3 and 4. Lunch!" Morton, in Baer, 23–24.

196 "You say . . . goes before it." Williams, *Letters,* 597.

196 "He sent me . . . taste and convictions." Ibid., 586.

197 "The subject matter . . . morality and decency." MPAA Archives.

197 "Those who do . . . sinned in viewing it." *Los Angeles Times,* December 24, 1956.

A FACE IN THE CROWD

198 "The film has . . . women as conscience." Kazan, *A Life,* 568.

201 "Again as with the *Waterfront* . . . you can get it." From *Working with Kazan* (tribute book, Wesleyan, 1973).

202 "When I first . . . wanted it." Neal, "Working with Kazan."

WILD RIVER

203 "I love . . . I've made." Baer, 147.

206 "engaged in the difficult task . . . obstructing progress." Kazan, *A Life,* 596–97.

206 "The Jew was all right . . . bullshit!" Ciment, 131.

SPLENDOR IN THE GRASS

208 The basic story . . . pretty good job. Ciment, 139.
217 "Warren—it was obvious . . . even by hints." Kazan, *A Life,* 603.
217 "All of a sudden . . . love scenes." Ibid.
217 "I think the best thing . . . and refusing change." Delahaye, in Baer, 96.

AMERICA AMERICA

218 "It's my favorite . . . entirely mine." Young, 288.
219 I asked my father . . . "Take my son!" *New York Times,* December 15, 1963.
220 I tried to make the film . . . on that track. Young, 273.
220 Everything this boy . . . those questions? Baer, 77.
220 The prime relationship . . . "for my career." Kazan, *A Life,* 640.
221 I think that *America* . . . with an amateur. Baer, 86.
222 "I don't think . . . not always good." Henry Miller, note, April 16, 1965, Wesleyan Archives.

THE ARRANGEMENT

223 "I feel certain . . . activity gripped me." Kazan, *A Life,* 752.
223 I've never been attacked . . . turn away if you can! Kazan, *Odyssey,* 126–31.

THE LAST TYCOON

228 "The ending I devised . . . I knew it." Kazan, *A Life,* 781.

SHORT TAKES

232 So now I had some . . . a very bad reception. Kazan, *An American Odyssey,* 65.
232 Don't blame . . . was a filmmaker. Kazan, *An American Odyssey,* 70.
233 I thought that with *Panic* . . . help on that. Kazan, *An American Odyssey,* 79.
233 *The Arrangement* . . . recommend it to you. Kazan, *An American Odyssey,* 94.

THE PLEASURES OF DIRECTING

250 The films that I don't like . . . than the successes. Baer, 45.
253 I am a mediocre . . . life's experience. Kazan, *A Life,* 363.
253 I don't move . . . my hopes. Stevens, 407.
258 A filmscript is more . . . a new art. Kazan, *A Life,* 380.

261 There's no such thing . . . you can't duck it. Schechner, 67.
261 Stage operates through . . . helps the story get there. Baer, 12.
266 In my film work . . . "Be careful." Kazan, *Odyssey,* 52–57.
271 They say I'm an acting . . . but what happens. Stevens, 396.
272 In general, actors . . . If not, not. Kazan, *A Life,* 541.
272 That is why the . . . a more honest trade. Ibid., 256.
273 Everybody's problem . . . to watch for. Ciment, 47–48.
273 In my first twenty years . . . complexity of things. Delahaye, in Baer, 74.
275 I put terrific stress . . . how they do things. Baer, 62.
275 It is very difficult . . . who can play that. Ibid., 85–86.

AFTERWORD

294 "the best you can do . . . in the real thing." Agee, 141–43.
295 "Elia Kazan's *Boomerang!* . . . is perfect." Ibid., 245.
296 "I'm not as interested . . . psychologizing so much." Ciment, 43.
297 "I wish . . . those of Stalin." *New York Times,* October 26, 2007.
298 "But Kazan's advertisement . . . rat fink of the era." Schickel, *Elia Kazan,* 272.
299 "Elia Kazan made a public . . . Jekyll and Mr. Hyde." Bentley, *What Is?,* 173.
300 "I'm . . . going to name . . . don't testify." Miller, *After.*

Acknowledgments

My first thanks go to Katherine Hourigan of Alfred A. Knopf and Frances Kazan for granting me the privilege of the company of the extraordinary and courageous Elia Kazan. Reading and wondering over his work meant spending time with an unguarded, generous, and rare intelligence, a genius of a unique kind.

The acumen, readiness, and guidance of the staffs of a number of institutions made the search for Kazan material a pleasure. I am particularly grateful to Joan Miller and Leith Johnson of the Wesleyan University Film Archives, the repository of the Elia Kazan papers. They knew where everything was, and they guard it well.

My gratitude goes also to Barbara Hall of the Margaret Herrick Library of the American Academy of Motion Picture Arts and Sciences; Noelle Carter of the Warner Bros. Archives; Ned Comstock of the Library of the University of Southern California; Lauren Buisson of the Library at the University of California, Los Angeles; and to Joan Cohen, liaison of my California research.

Immensely helpful was the full staff at the Library of the Performing Arts at Lincoln Center, New York, with special thanks to Louise Martzinek and Bob Taylor. Every day there I found someone else to admire, and not one of them was ever stumped.

For encouragement and direction I am grateful to Clive Miller, Austin Pendleton, Maria Tucci, Eileen Shanahan, Robert Gottlieb, Patricia Bosworth, and Sidney Lumet. Two preeminent scholars of American drama, Brenda Murphy and Albert J. Devlin, provided me with invaluable insights: Without their superior knowledge this task would have been impossible. A special thanks to Wendy Smith, whose scrupulous book on the Group Theatre gave me crucial perspective.

To Margaret Davison, who gave my life direction, I dedicate the portion of this book that is mine. A first love is sometimes the best.

—Robert Cornfield

Index

Page numbers in *italics* refer to illustrations.

A NOTE ON THE TYPE

This book was set in Caledonia, a Linotype face designed by W. A. Dwiggins (1880–1956). It belongs to the family of printing types called "modern face" by printers—a term used to mark the change in style of the type letters that occurred around 1800. Caledonia borders on the general design of Scotch Roman but it is more freely drawn than that letter.

COMPOSED BY
North Market Street Graphics, Lancaster, Pennsylvania

PRINTED AND BOUND BY
Berryville Graphics, Berryville, Virginia

DESIGNED BY
Iris Weinstein